Let's go to The Grand!

100 YEARS OF ENTERTAINMENT AT LONDON'S GRAND THEATRE

Sheila M.F. Johnston

NATURAL HERITAGE BOOKS

Let's Go To The Grand!
100 Years of Entertainment at London's Grand Theatre
Sheila M.F. Johnston

Natural Heritage/Natural History Inc.

Published by Natural Heritage/Natural History Inc.
(P.O. Box 95, Station O, Toronto, Ontario, M4A 2M8)

Cover and text design: Sari Naworynski
Editor: Jane Gibson
Printed and bound in Canada by Hignell Printing Limited, Winnipeg, Manitoba

National Library of Canada Cataloguing in Publication Data

Johnston, Sheila M.F.
    Let's go to the grand! : 100 years of entertainment at London's Grand Theatre

Includes bibliographical references and index.
ISBN 1-896219-75-6

1. Grand Theatre (London, Ont.) — History. 2. Theatre — Ontario. I. Title.

FC3099.L65Z57 2001   971.3'26   C2001-902762-1
                                              F1059.5.L6J64 2001

Natural Heritage/Natural History Inc. acknowledges the support received for its publishing program from the Canada Council Block Grant Program and the assistance of the Association for the Export of Canadian Books, Ottawa. Natural Heritage also acknowledges the support of The Ontario Council for the Arts for its publishing program

ILLUSTRATION CREDITS

I wish to identify and acknowledge the various sources of the illustrations in this book and to thank the many individuals and public institutions who gave me permission to use them.

While every effort has been made to locate and contact copyright holders, some errors and omissions may have occurred. Any such oversights are regretted and the author would appreciate having them brought to her attention.

Front cover: Interior of The Grand, courtesy of The Grand Theatre.

Back cover: Top photo; Exterior of The Grand, courtesy of LRAHM, London, ON. Bottom photo; Hume Cronyn and Jessica Tandy, courtesy of The Grand Theatre.

COPYRIGHT PERMISSIONS

Excerpts from the *London Free Press* newspaper, *The Stratford Beacon Herald*, *The Toronto Star*, *Canadian Press*, *Scene Magazine*, *The Gazette* and *The Globe & Mail* and selected books are reprinted by permission.

EQUITY PERMISSIONS

Photographs of actors who are members of the Canadian Actors' Equity Association (CAEA) are reprinted by permission from CAEA.

A NOTE FROM THE AUTHOR

I do not claim to have listed every production produced by the Grand Theatre, nor every production presented at the Grand Theatre. The lists of productions which follow each chapter/season are only meant to be representative of that season.

Any inadvertent oversights on the part of the author, with regard to permissions, will be rectified in future editions.

DEDICATION

I dedicate this book to my grandparents:

On my mother's side
LILY GARDNER and GEORGE ROY GARDNER,
who, as young parents in the 1920s, went to
the Grand Theatre to enjoy the Dumbells.

On my father's side
JESSIE FERGUSON,
who, in 1937, experienced both her debut and retirement from
a brief stage career at the Grand Theatre,
and
DUNCAN FERGUSON.

With Love

TABLE OF CONTENTS

ACKNOWLEDGMENTS

The preparation of a book of this scope is an impossible task for a single person. I have sought the help of many people, and my requests for assistance have been met with enthusiasm. Four people who make it their business to preserve the history of the London and Middlesex area have been especially helpful. Thank you: Mike Baker, Curator of Regional History, London Regional Art and Historical Museums; Christopher Doty, documentary filmmaker; Anita McCallum, Librarian, *London Free Press*; Theresa Regnier, Library Assistant, J.J. Talman Regional Collection, The University of Western Ontario.

I was fortunate in having three people on my team throughout the preparation of this book. It is my pleasure to say a heartfelt thank you to: Michele Ebel; Sonia Halpern; William Johnston.

Thank you to everyone who took an interest in this project, and who assisted me: Phyllis Anderson; Don Allan; Jean Back, interview; Ashleigh Barney; *The Stratford Beacon Herald*, permission; Jack Beattie, anecdote; Rod Beattie, interview, use of photograph; Sonia Bilyea; Geoff Bingle, interview; Peggy Bingle, interview; Patricia Black, anecdotes; Craig Blackley; Laurie Blackley; Maggie Blake, use of photograph; Heather Brandt, interviews; Jay Brazeau, use of photograph; Charles Brown, interview; Chris Britton; CBC Radio, permission Douglas Campbell, interview; Canadian Actors' Equity Association; Canadian Press, permission; David Caron; Pat Carson; Garrison Chrisjohn, use of photograph; Diana Coatsworth, use of photograph; Rob Cole; Peter Colley, anecdotes; John Cooper, interview; Sandra Coulson; Jonathan Crombie, use of photograph; Hume Cronyn, use of photographs; Corus Entertainment, permission; Dicky Dean; Robin Dearing, interview, use of photograph; Aiden de Salaiz, anecdote, use of photograph; Hazel Desbarats, anecdotes, use of photograph; Noreen de Shane, interview; Caroline Dolney-Guerin, anecdote; Peter Donaldson, use of photograph; Doubleday, a division of Random House, Inc., permission; John Douglas; Wally Duffield, interview; Russ Dufton (deceased); Jennifer Duncan; Barbara Dunlop; James W. Dunlop; ; Paul Eck, interview; Jane Edmonds; Art Ender, interview, use of photograph; Eleanor Ender, interview; Eddie Escaf, interview, use of photographs; Pam Evans; Louise Fagan; Geoffrey Farrow, interviews, use of photographs; Eric D. Ferguson, my father, love and support; E. Madeline Ferguson, my mother, love and support; Emmett Ferguson; David Ferry, anecdotes; Elisabeth Feryn, use of photographs; Art Fidler, anecdotes; Marilyn (Min) Fidler, anecdotes; Don Fleckser, interviews, use of photographs; Debbie Fox; Celia Franca, use of photograph; Irene Fretz; Patricia Gage, use of photograph; Victor Garber, use of photograph; Rita Gardiner; The Gazette, student newspaper, UWO, permission; John Gerry; Alice Gibb, permission; Mary Ann Gibbons, interview; Michael Gibbons, interview; Jane Gibson, publishing; *The Globe & Mail*, permission; Maurice Godin,; anecdotes, use of photograph; Maxine Graham, anecdotes; The Grand Theatre; M. Lucille "Sam" Grant, anecdotes; Al Green, anecdotes, use of photograph; Deb Greenfield; Dorinda Greenway, interview, use of photographs; Monda Halpern, anecdote; Kelly Handerek, use of photograph; Tom Hammond; Stephen Harding V. Tony Hauser, use of photograph; Martha Henry, interview, use of photographs; Bernard Hopkins, interview, use of photograph; Lesley Humphrey; Janelle Hutchison, use of photograph; William Hutt, interview, use of photographs; Frances Hyland, use of photograph; Young In Turner, anecdote; Barbara Ivey, interview; Beryl Ivey, interview; J.J. Talman Regional Collection, The D.B. Weldon Library, The University of Western Ontario, permission; Eric James, use of photograph; Col. Greg Johnson; Jackie Johnston; Simon Johnston,; my husband, love and support; D. Jones, anecdote; John Judson; Cliff Kearns, use of drawing; Frank Kerner; Martin Kinch, use of photograph; David Allan King; Inez King; Robert King, use of photograph; David Kirby, anecdotes; Christine Kopal; Hilda Larke; Elizabeth Lawson, interview, use of photograph; Patricia Leavens, anecdotes; Diana Leblanc, use of photograph; Loreta LeBlanc; Andrew Lewis, use of drawing; Brock Liscumb; *London Free Press*, permission; London Room; Kip Longstaff, anecdotes; Grace Lydiatt Shaw, interview; Michelle Lundgren, use of photograph; John Lutman; Peter Lynch, interview, use of programs; Flora MacKenzie, interview; Ann MacMillan, anecdotes; Martha Mann, anecdotes; Sheila Martindale, anecdotes; Walter Massey, anecdotes, use of photograph; Brenda May, interview; Tom McCamus, anecdote, use of photograph; Sheila McCarthy, anecdote, use of photograph; Arthur McClelland; Doug McCullough, interview; John F. McGarry, interview; Don McKellar, interview; Ted Minhinnick; Mark Mooney, anecdote; Stephanie Morgenstern, use of photograph; Chris Mounteer, anecdote; Elizabeth Murray, interview; Martha Murray, anecdote; Judy Nancekivell, interview; National Archives of Canada; John Neville, use of photograph; Miriam Newhouse; Ron Nichol; B. O'Donnell; Christine Overvelde, anecdote; Nancy Palk, use of photograph; Mari Parks; Kathleen Pasquini; Arthur Patterson, use of photograph; Dorothy Pearce; Barry Penhale, publishing; Jane Penistan, interview; Shelley Peterson, use of photograph; Andrew Petrasiunas, use of photograph; Edward C.H. Phelps; Heinar Piller, interview, use of photographs; Melodie Pinches; Edwin Pincombe Muriel Podmore; Nancy Poole; Edwin R. Procunier, anecdote; Linda Rae; Robert Ragsdale, use of photographs; Dr. James Reaney, interview; Dr. Peter Rechnitzer, interview; Ric Reid, anecdote, use of photograph; Anni Rendl; Liisa Repo-Martell, use of photograph; Alec Richmond, interviews, use of photograph; Harry Ronson, interview; David Rottman, interview (deceased); Ruth Rottman, interview; A. Frank Ruffo, anecdote; Shelley Rutherford, interview; *Scene Magazine*, permission; Jane Schmuck, use of house programs; Dave Semple, use of photograph; Jim Shaefer, anecdotes; Joan Sherrin; Daryl Shuttleworth, use of photograph; Ruth Slater; Mary Slemin; Florence Smith, interview (deceased); Peter Smith, interview, use of drawing; Nora Snelgrove, interview, use of photographs; Jim Soper, anecdote; Lynda Spence, interview; *The Toronto Star*, permission; John Stephenson; David Storch, use of photograph; Diana Stott, interviews; Southpaw Design (William Johnson), design concept; Wendy Subity;

Colleen Thibideau, interview; Anne Tillman; Kate Trotter, anecdotes, use of photograph; Jean Trudell; William Trudell, interviews; University of Guelph, Theatre Archives; University of Toronto Press, permission; Tony Van Bridge, use of photograph ; Mary Velaitis; Sheila Walker, anecdote; Lisa Walterson; Julia Watts, interview, use of photograph; O. B. Watts, interview, use of photograph; Rob Wellan, interview; Ric Wellwood, anecdotes; Dorothy Westhead, interviews; Les Wheable; Pat Wheeler; Rick Whelan, anecdotes; Ron White, use of photograph; Lascelle Wingate; Marion Woodman, anecdotes; Eric Woolfe, use of photograph; Janet Wright, use of photograph; Louise Wyatt, interview (deceased); Leslie Yeo, permission; William Ziegler, interviews, use of photographs; Janice Zolf, anecdotes

If I have been remiss in neglecting to mention and to thank anyone who assisted me in this project please accept my sincere apology.

AUTHOR'S INTRODUCTION

There are two kinds of theatre people: those who are stage-struck and those who are audience-struck. I belong in the latter category. For me, nothing equals the experience of being in the audience and watching a theatre performance.

My introduction to London's Grand Theatre came in November of 1978. The theatre's house manager, John Gerry, hired me as an usher for the 1978/79 season. I was studying at the University of Western Ontario that year, but I still had time to catch the bus and travel to The Grand Theatre, don my beige-and-burgundy uniform, and usher patrons to their plush red seats. What I didn't realize was that The Grand Theatre had just undergone a multimillion dollar reconstruction. While the rest of London was celebrating the rebirth of its beloved Grand Old Lady of Richmond Street, I took it for granted that the theatre had always been as beautiful as this, with its 1901 interior and its glass, brick and polished brass lobbies. What did I know then? Much less than I know now.

The Grand Theatre's magic became crystal clear when the orchestra launched into the opening musical number for *Kiss Me Kate* and when the boundlessly energetic and high-kicking A. Frank Ruffo burst from stage right and led the dancing chorus in a joyful "Another Opening, Another Show." I thought "Wow!" then, and I still think "Wow!" when I remember that theatre moment. By the end of the production's run, I was in love with London's Grand Theatre. I still am.

My introduction to theatre happened ten years earlier, when my parents, Eric and Madeline Ferguson, took me to see a performance of Shakespeare's *Romeo and Juliet* at the Stratford Festival Theatre in the summer of 1968. I was 11 years old. The stunningly beautiful Louise Marleau was Juliet, and the strikingly handsome Christopher Walken was Romeo. On stage that day I also saw Anne Anglin, Mervyn Blake, Joyce Campion, Leo Ciceri, Patrick Crean, Neil Dainard, Amelia Hall, Max Helpmann, Neil Munro, Christopher Newton, Kenneth Pogue, Leon Pownall and Powys Thomas, all under the direction of Douglas Campbell. Is it any surprise I was bewitched by the spell woven by theatre and by theatre people? My long-term love affair with theatre sprang to life that day as I watched from my seat in that wonderful theatre in my hometown of Stratford.

I am grateful to Tom Patterson, founder of the Stratford Festival, and to all of those who helped him achieve his dream of a theatre on the banks of Ontario's Avon River.

This book gives me the opportunity to share with readers my passion for theatre, my love for London's Grand Theatre, my respect for theatre people, and my interest in the history of 20th century entertainment. I hope that in its pages you will find pleasure.

I wish you many magical moments at the theatre.

Sheila M. F. Johnston, Richmond, B. C.

AMBROSE J. SMALL ERA

1901-1919

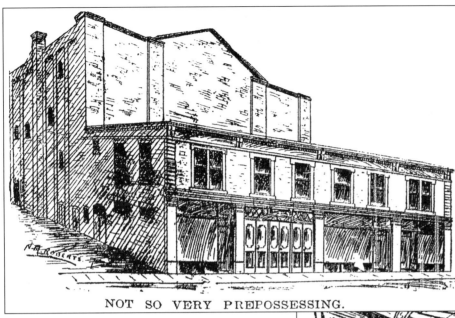

NOT SO VERY PREPOSSESSING.

BUT THE PLAYHOUSE HAS A MAGNIFICENT INTERIOR.

A hand-drawn sketch of the exterior of the just con-structed New Grand Opera House, and a sketch of the interior of the theatre, published in the September 4, 1901, edition of the London Free Press. (Courtesy of the London Free Press)

1901/02

AMBROSE J. SMALL ERA

THE THEATRE OPENS

The story of London's Grand Theatre starts on the fine, warm evening of September 9, 1901. It was the week of the annual fall fair in the bustling Southwestern Ontario city, and while many people flocked to the fairgrounds, others crowded around 471 Richmond Street to get into the sparkling New Grand Opera House. After months of construction the theatre was open for business, ready to welcome 1,850 patrons for each performance. What of the old Grand Opera House? We must pause for a moment, and learn the story of London's former Grand Opera House.

In 1880/81, at the northwest corner of Richmond and King Streets in downtown London, the Masonic Temple building was erected. Incorporated into its plan was the Grand Opera House, covering the rear section of the imposing building. The lessee of the theatre was Colonel C. J. Whitney, a Detroit man whose business was show business.

After 20 years of operation, the Grand Opera House ceased to be. On February 23, 1900, the Masonic Temple building burned, damaging the interior of the Grand Opera House so badly that no more shows could be mounted in the space. Almost as soon as the smoke cleared and the dust settled, Londoners heard about plans for a new Grand Opera House. The Grand Opera House Company Limited, created by a group of Londoners, was going to erect a new building, dedicated to entertainment. The company was owned by Londoners Colonel Leys, Police Magistrate Love, John Ferguson, A.S. Leys and Alfred Robinson. The location they chose was on Richmond Street, opposite St. Paul's Cathedral, where the stables adjoining the Western Hotel used to stand.

The architect was Mr. J.M. Wood of Detroit. The contractors were the London firm of Messrs. Burnett and Son and John Purdom. The lessee/managers of the new Grand Opera House were Colonel Whitney and his partner, Ambrose Joseph Small, of Toronto.

The modern theatre had its own telephone, something of a novelty where theatres were concerned. Also, the New Grand Opera House included the most modern stage equipment available. The theatre was big enough to accommodate the largest road show that passed through London, either coming from or heading to Detroit. The new theatre did not include any rehearsal halls, workshops or large storage areas because London's New Grand Opera House was not meant to accommodate a producing theatre company. Its sole purpose was to showcase prepackaged shows that originated elsewhere and were out on the road.

Arching above the large stage was a proscenium featuring the original artwork of celebrated muralist Frederick S. Challener. He had travelled to England and Italy in 1898/99 and had been excited by the wealth of murals he saw. He returned to Canada just when new theatres were under construction and in need of murals. Challener executed murals in Ottawa, Winnipeg, Toronto and in London, where his large mural spanned the full expanse of the proscenium arch at the New Grand Opera House. With its beautiful female figures, its bucolic setting and its ravishing colours, Challener's incredible mural, high above the heads of the first audience, must have caused these theatre patrons to gasp in awe.

On Monday, September 9, 1901, the curtain of the New Grand

Opera House parted to reveal the setting for *Way Down East*, the popular melodrama by Lottie Blair Parker. A new era in theatrical entertainment in London began.

J.F. CAIRNS

To maximize ticket sales, the New Grand Opera House advertised its telephone number 176, and opened its box office at 9 a.m.. It remained open until 10 p.m. on show days, and until 6 p.m. on dark days. On hand to manage the day-to-day business was local manager J.F. Cairns. He oversaw a staff of nine people. Together they welcomed the steady stream of players sent their way by Whitney and Small.

W.C. FIELDS

Shea's High-Class Vaudeville company played the New Grand Opera House early in October of 1901. This was a variety show, and the bill of fare included Elizabeth Murray in "Songs and Stories." Poor Miss Murray, already fourth on the bill, had to follow a young man advertised as "W.C. Fields, Eccentric." Twenty-two years old at the time, Fields already had eight years in the business under his belt. He was a skilled juggler who pretended to drop the items he was juggling, only to catch them at the last possible moment, thereby assuring himself huge applause.

YEAR-END ENTERTAINMENT

Not everyone stayed home on Christmas Day. Some people were at the theatre enjoying a performance of *A Cavalier of France*. Open for business on New Year's Eve, the New Grand Opera House hosted a road company of 40 performers who presented *The Flaming Arrow*. Patrons could enjoy this year-end entertainment for only 25 cents, 35 cents or 50 cents.

GENE LOCKHART

As a budding professional I used to impose the prerogatives of my calling by presenting myself at matinees at The Grand Opera House and asking the manager if he 'recognized the profession.' The Grand Opera manager at the time would invariably respond, as would Tom Marks of the Marks Brothers Company, when they presented their 'one week only of great dramatic successes, where virtue is triumphant and villainy is foiled, wholesome and educational; bring the kiddies; 10-20-30 cents; complete change of program tomorrow night.'
– Gene Lockhart, London-born actor, playwright, musician, quoted in the *London Free Press*, October 6, 1934

CHARLES A. TAYLOR

The King of the Opium Ring was onstage in January of 1902. The play was set in San Francisco, in the year 1890. The promotional material promised: "The Human Tower of Chinks; Native Chinese Actors and Children; The Chinese Theatre on a New Year's Night;" and the climax…"The Police Raid on an Opium Joint." This melodrama was penned by Charles A. Taylor, known at the turn of the century as the 'Master of Melodrama.' He was prolific, if nothing else. As a top playwright of the day, he earned $1,250 per week in royalties. This particular play was billed as the inside story of life in San Francisco's Chinatown. Claptrap by today's standards, in 1902 it was what the audience loved. The scene featuring the rescue of the heroine, included a trio of Chinese acrobats standing on each other's shoulders while they fetched the young woman from a second-story window. As the audience held its breath, the top man received the unconscious heroine in his arms, and then the bottom man moved the column-of-three across the stage. When they reached the opposite side of the stage, the actress was literally flung through another second-story window, into the safe arms of her friends. What a thrill to see!

JAMES O'NEILL

On March 21 of 1902, James O'Neill was at the New Grand Opera House in his popular play *The Count of Monte Cristo*. The story concerns a young sailor, Edmond Dantes, who is inconveniently arrested on his wedding day. He is falsely accused of political involvement and confined to a dungeon. Eighteen years pass until the day an imprisoned abbé, who is making an escape attempt, tunnels into Edmond's cell. As the abbé falls ill, he tells the hero of a fortune hidden on the island of Monte Cristo. Edmond places the body of the dead abbé in his own bed, then gets into the sack that is intended for the corpse. Guards throw the sack into the sea, thus helping the prisoner escape. The Act II curtain comes down after Edmond (James O'Neill) shouts the famous line: "Saved! Mine, the treasures of Monte Cristo! The world is mine!"

Because the play is really a celebration of revenge, Act III concerns Edmond's successful attempts to ruin the three men who did him wrong. The play's final line was familiar to playgoers everywhere: "The world is mine! …One! …Two! …Three!" Back in 1882, sensing that the play spelled his fortune, O'Neill purchased the dramatization rights and later purchased the entire production. He toured with it for years, enjoying great popularity and prosperity. At the height of his career, O'Neill was earning $50,000 each theatre season, tax free. Accompanying him on his gruelling annual tours was his wife, Ella O'Neill. The couple had two sons, James O'Neill Jr. and Eugene O'Neill, the future Pulitzer Prize-winning playwright who wrote *Long Days Journey Into Night*, which gives insight into the O'Neill family dynamic. Eugene O'Neill was in his early teens when his celebrated father was on stage in 1902.

Audiences throughout North American never tired of seeing James O'Neill in this vehicle. They would burst into thunderous applause each time he vanquished his enemies. O'Neill retired the role in 1914.

PROGRAMME

NEW GRAND OPERA HOUSE
LONDON, ONT.

C. J. WHITNEY & A. J. SMALL, Lessees and Managers. A. H. O'NEIL, Local Manager.

Road Shows included:
Way Down East, by Lottie Blair Parker
Uncle Tom's Cabin, from Harriet Beecher Stowe
The Girl from Paris, "pretty music…pretty girls"
San Toy, "a Chinese-English musical comedy, dainty, delightful, delicious, chorus of 75"
The Fast Mail, "scenic melodrama with full sized practical locomotive and 14 freight cars"
The Telephone Girl, "a merry jingle, the frothy musical delight with 13 telephone girls"
The Hottest Coon in Dixie, "new musical comedy travesty"
Romeo and Juliet and *Hamlet*, by William Shakespeare
The House That Jack Built, "built for laughter only, if you want to cry don't come"
The Princess Chic, "comprising 60 carefully selected artists of rare talent"
The Little Minister, by J.M. Barrie, "as the ending of the play is peculiar, the audience is requested to remain seated until the curtain falls"

In A Woman's Power, "new melo-dramatic success with a multitude of startling scenic efffects"
Floradora, "the English musical comedy, set on the Island of Floradora, Philippines"
Sweet Clover, "a story thoroughly clean in its moral"
David Harum, "the greatest comedy success"

Vaudeville:
Shea's High-Class Vaudeville

Minstrels:
Guy Bros. Minstrels
Primrose and Dockstader's Great American Minstrels

Stock Company:
Marks Bros. No. 1 Company, starring Tom Marks

Magician:
The Great and Only Herrmann in a Unique Entertainment of Magic, Mirth and Mystery

Music:
John Philip Sousa, conducted his band

1902/03

AMBROSE J. SMALL ERA

Emma Albani, the French-Canadian soprano, was an opera diva. She performed at The New Grand Opera House on February 4, 1903. Box seats were $2 each. Albani had been an opera star since her debut at England's Covent Garden in 1872. She had started her training in Montreal and continued her voice studies in Paris and Milan. After enjoying an international career, she retired from the opera stage in 1896, but she toured Canada giving concerts. Before her death in 1930, she had become Dame Emma Albani. (National Archives of Canada, C - 49491)

THE SYNDICATE

New York City had 41 theatres in 1903. On his annual autumn scouting trips, Ambrose J. Small would visit as many of these theatres as possible to ascertain what shows would appeal to his audience. He had a good eye for popular shows. If Small wanted the top shows to be routed through his theatre towns, he had to deal directly with the Syndicate. Since 1895, a handful of men had controlled theatres across the United States. The group included Charles Frohman, his brother Daniel Frohman, and Mark Klaw, as well as the loathed and feared Abraham Erlanger. The Syndicate had resolved confusion in the theatre business by signing up theatre owners across the United States and assuring them that the Syndicate would exclusively book their theatre and send them a steady stream of first-class productions. The formula was simple and appealing – stage stars in pleasing plays. As a Canadian impresario, it was likely that Ambrose J. Small could pick and choose productions handled by the Syndicate, as well as productions offered by independent, hold-out producers, something his American counterparts could not do for fear of reprisals from the mighty – and organized – New York producers.

As the legend about Ambrose J. Small has grown, he is often described as tough, or as someone difficult to deal with and easy to dislike. If this is true, he was not unlike the other men operating in the high-stakes, high-finance world of theatre in the first two decades of the 20th century. Placing Ambrose J. Small in this context, he was exactly like the men with whom he had to deal – shrewd, ruthless, tough, aggressive, litigious and money-mad. These men just happened to be in the business of making theatre-goers happy.

DUSKY MAIDENS

A Trip to Coontown, In a Day and a Night was on tour in October of 1902. Promising "new songs, new dances, new costumes, new scenery and clever comedians," the show was augmented by a "Chorus of Colored Beauties." Listed in the program as Dusky Maidens were women whose stage names were limited to first names: Salina, Florinda, Clotinda and Aminda, while the Coontown Belles were listed as: Lucinda, Clorinda, Clarissa and Glendina. The real names of these talented young women, whose life on the road must have been as exhilarating as it was exhausting, are forever lost.

TOURING MAGIC SHOWS

In April, Londoners who loved magic could get their fill from a trio of touring magic shows – The Great Herrmann, the Great Kellar and Le Roy-Talma-Bosco.

"The Great and Only Herrmann" was Leon Herrmann. He was

the nephew of the late Alexander Herrmann, the original "Great" Herrmann. Billed as a unique entertainment of magic, mirth, mystery and music, an intriguing program note read: "During the progress of the entertainment it will be necessary to borrow from the audience such articles as watches, rings, hats, etc. The audience is requested, therefore, to comply with the request cheerfully, as the program is so long it will not permit of tedious waits for articles and if not forthcoming, it will be necessary to dispense with that number and go on with the next one, as Mr. Herrmann cannot use his own articles for these tricks." One can only guess what kind of trouble the magician had encountered in some town, somewhere, when a less than cheerful audience member had struggled to keep his watch from being used as part of a magic trick. Mr. Herrmann did not want that fiasco repeated – ever!

Harry Kellar was popular with audiences because of his elegance on stage, his brilliant display of skill, and the mysteries he brought back to North America from his extensive travels to exotic places like China, Hong Kong, India, Indonesia and Japan.

The celebrated team of Le Roy, Talma and Bosco was unusual in that it featured Mercedes Talma, a female performer who was not used as a backup to male magicians, but was in her own right a skilled coin manipulator. She performed as the Queen of Coins, producing a rain of silver coins from her fingertips. Audiences loved to watch her perform, wearing a black full-length gown in front of a bright red background. A single red rose in her hair completed the picture. Servais Le Roy wowed audiences with his Decapitation Mystery routine. Married since 1890, Le Roy and Talma brought their show to the Grand Opera House, along with Bosco, whose job was to add slapstick humour to the magic show.

WESTERN THEMES
Arizona was on tour this season, billed as the play that pleases

everyone. It had debuted on Broadway during the previous season, and was such a hit that it sparked a vogue for westerns in drama. Theatregoers' passionate interest in seeing the wild west was fed by such plays as *The Squaw Man* and *The Virginian*. When it came time to put stage plays in front of motion picture cameras, early movie makers had no trouble stealing western stage plays for their screenplays. Audiences loved anything with a western theme.

PROGRAMME
Grand Opera House
LONDON, ONTARIO.
C. J. WHITNEY & A. J. SMALL, Lessees & Mgrs.   A. H. O'NEIL, Local Manager.

Road Shows included:
When Knighthood Was in Flower, by Paul Kester
Way Down East, by Lottie Blair Parker
Sherlock Holmes, by Sir A. Conan Doyle, "a play of infinite zest and startling incidents"
Floradora, Floradorean girls: Monta, Inez, Jose, Junita, Violante, Calista
Le Voyage en Suisse, "goes beyond anything yet presented to the public"
Alaska, "a realistic story of the Far North, see the great volcano"
The Convict's Daughter, by J.A. Fraser, "the most powerful melodrama of the day"
A Trip to Coontown, in A Day and A Night, "augmented chorus of coloured beauties"
Rice's Show Girls, "just a jolly bit of tomfoolery, a host of pretty girls"
The Wizard of Oz, by L. Frank Baum, "the gorgeous new spectacular extravaganza"
The Two Schools, "Charles Frohman presents his greatest laughing

success"
A Montana Outlaw, "a flawless play founded on facts"
Arizona, by Augustus Thomas, "the play that pleases everyone"
Macbeth, by William Shakespeare
The School for Scandal, the Restoration classic by Richard Brinsley Sheridan,
Carmen, by Bizet

Minstrels:
The McKinney Bros. Minstrels
The Al. G. Field Greater Minstrels
The Quinlan and Wall Imperial Minstrels

Stock Companies:
The Famous Aubrey Stock Co.
Holden Bros. Dramatic Co.
R.W. Marks' Big Dramatic and Vaudeville Co.
The Famous King Dramatic Co.

Magicians:
The Great and Only Herrmann
The Great Kellar, The Astounder of All Nations
Le Roy – Talma – Bosco, The World's Monarchs of Magic

1903/04

AMBROSE J. SMALL ERA

F.X. KORMANN

Colonel Whitney died early in 1903, leaving Ambrose J. Small as the sole lessee of London's Grand Opera House. It would be a few more years before Small would own this popular Grand Opera House outright. Small managed the theatre from his headquarters in Toronto, while he supervised F.X. Kormann, the theatre's local manager. Mr. Kormann was the third local manager in as many years, testifying, perhaps, to the difficulty in pleasing Mr. Small.

HENRIK IBSEN

On September 3, 1903, Henrik Ibsen's drama, *Ghosts,* was on stage, starring Edith Ellis Baker as Mrs. Alving. Ibsen is considered an inventor of the New Drama (along with August Strindberg, Anton Chekhov and George Bernard Shaw) that took theatre away from melodrama and toward realism.

In *Ghosts*, written in 1881, Ibsen wrote of hereditary syphilis, the horror of its effects, and the hypocrisy that surrounded it. This subject differed completely from the steady diet of melodramatic plays promoting virtue over vice that audiences of the day enjoyed. Ibsen tackled serious, unspeakable social problems. Brave was the actress and the acting company that staged and toured them. Ibsen's plays shocked their viewers. Theatregoers who loathed Ibsen twisted his name so that it was sneeringly pronounced 'Ibscene'. They thought his work very unhealthy and

Celebrated Canadian actress Margaret Anglin played the title role in Cynthia *opposite her leading man Henry Miller, on December 7, 1903. In this giddy romantic comedy, Cynthia was the effervescent wife to Henry Miller's exasperated but adoring husband. The acting team of Anglin and Miller achieved great popularity and success. Critics especially applauded Anglin's glowing, penetrating portrayals of her many characters. Born in Ottawa in 1876, Anglin made her professional stage debut in New York City in 1894. She enjoyed a 50 year career on the stage, and died in Toronto in 1958. (Courtesy of National Archives of Canada C - 22761)*

injurious. Rejecting all the devices of melodrama, his plays began just before the crisis of the action, then moved on to expose the past lives of his not always likable characters. Finally, he expanded on the complications that led to the climax and the conclusion. The impact of Ibsen's work reverberated through the theatre in the 1880s, the 1890s and into the first decade of the 20th century. While serious actresses were thrilled at the opportunity to portray Ibsen's heroines, the majority of audience members wanted lighter fare. This season offered a double dose of Ibsen – shortly after the *Ghosts* company left town, American stage star Minnie Maddern Fiske arrived on October 31, 1903, to perform the lead role in Ibesn's play *Hedda Gabler*.

LILLIE LANGTRY

Lillie Langtry appeared on the Grand Opera House stage on October 14, 1903, in *Mrs. Deering's Divorce*. Her fame began when she was celebrated as a society beauty in London, England. She was soon on stage, acting in benefit performances for various charitable causes. She became a successful actress-manager, and performed in both Great Britain and North America. Her fame as an actress was eclipsed by her notoriety as the first publicly avowed mistress of England's King Edward VII. It was because of this naughty reputation that she was a major draw at every theatre she played.

MOVING PICTURES

There was something new and thrilling to experience at The Grand Opera House on December 30 and 31, 1903: moving pictures. Tickets were just 10 cents, 20 cents or 30 cents, and the entertainment value was high. Audiences sat back and watched the screen as sledding in the Alps was projected, or as up-to-date surgery appeared, or as a visit to Coney Island flickered in front of them. The finale was a daring daylight robbery. Astounding new technology meant a great advance in entertainment, and it came at bargain prices. The novelty years of motion pictures, 1894 through 1902, came to an end when movie makers started to apply story-telling techniques to what they filmed. As soon as an 11-minute film, entitled *The Great Train Robbery*, hit the screen in 1903, audiences sat up and took notice of a motion picture with a story. New life was pumped into the fledging motion picture industry. Unlike other, more skeptical theatre managers, Ambrose J. Small did not want to be left behind. He wanted in on the trend. Besides, if Londoners paid a dime or two to sit in his seats to watch flickering images on a wavy screen, then he was pleased to accommodate them and their developing tastes in a new entertainment medium.

UNCLE TOM'S CABIN

A mammoth production of *Uncle Tom's Cabin* moved into The Grand Opera house in March, 1904. So familiar was this show (it had enjoyed success since its debut in 1852), theatregoers everywhere knew the show by its initials – *UTC*. It was responsible for bringing more people into North American theatres than any

A poster advertising the popular hit **When Knighthood Was In Flower.** *Starring Effie Ellsler, this romance of chivalry of 16th century England was a hit everywhere. Miss Ellsler as Mary Tudor was supported by 26 actors with speaking roles, plus countless guards, pages and ladies of the court. There was a lot of theatre work for walk-ons. (Courtesy of The Grand Theatre)*

other show. Advertised as the immortal American drama, adapted from the late Harriet Beecher Stowe's novel, this production boasted "a carefully selected cast of white actors of talent and reputation." Besides the 35 white actors, there were "25 colored men and women" in the company, along with 10 Cuban and Russian bloodhounds, to be deployed on stage to pursue the fleeing Eliza across the ice-filled Ohio River, with her infant in her arms. There were also 20 ponies, donkeys and horses to thrill the audience. No wonder the show required an entire train of special cars to haul it from place to place. *UTC* was a good, long evening of entertainment: eight scenes in Act I, eight scenes in Act II and seven scenes in Act III, all for tickets no more expensive than 50 cents. Audiences loved precocious Little Eva, they adored old

Tom, they laughed with giggley Topsy, and they hated the evil Simon Legree. Not all productions of *UTC* were as respectable as this one, as noted in the December 6, 1902, edition of *Billboard Magazine*: "The wonderful popularity of Harriet Beecher Stowe's masterpiece has led to its production by all kinds of managers with all kinds of actors – good, bad and indifferent. There is magic in the name of Uncle Tom and its capacity to draw the public to see it. This, as pretty much all theatre patrons are aware, has been fully taken advantage of by hordes of irresponsibles and a production by them at once wild and wooly has been too often the result. When produced with a proper dramatic cast, coupled with proper scenic and mechanical equipment no such story of American life prior to the great crisis in our national affairs has ever been penned." In 1903, *UTC* was made into a movie, and Londoners could see it at the Grand Opera House, thanks to savvy programming by Ambrose J. Small. Despite audiences' enjoyment of the play's excessive pathos, lush sentimentality and dollop of low comedy, the depression of the 1930s finished off the few companies still touring *UTC*. It enjoyed one last gasp, in 1933, when a revival was produced on Broadway. After that, *UTC* was mothballed, its pre-eminence but a memory.

I've seen the Tom shows come in with as many as eight freight cars of sets. The parades through the streets prior to the shows were spectacles of an era... I can remember seeing 'Tom' in the parade of the company being chased along the street at the same time he's being flogged.
– Alexander Knox, Strathroy-born actor/writer quoted in a *London Free Press* interview, 1981

WAR PICTURES
The heat of June didn't prevent Ambrose J. Small from pro-

gramming entertainment at the Grand Opera House. Using "the finest picture machine on the American continent," theatregoers watched "100,000 scenes of the sights and progress of the world" featuring Russo-Japanese war pictures. The action on the screen must have seemed remote from quiet and peaceful London, Ontario.

PROGRAMME
Grand Opera House
LONDON, ONTARIO.   SEASON 1903-1904.
A. J. SMALL, Lessee and Manager.
F. X. KORMANN, Local Manager.   J. R. STEWART, Treasurer.

Road Shows included:
When Knighthood Was in Flower, by Paul Kester, "a romance of chivalry"
Ghosts and *Hedda Gabler*, by Henrik Ibsen
Imprudence, by H.V. Esmond
Too Proud to Beg, "irradiated by a magnificent cast, a revelation in the melodramatic field"
Mrs. Deering's Divorce, by Percy Fendall
The Sign of the Cross, "original London production of Wilson Barrett's religious drama"
The Second Mrs. Tanqueray, by Sir Arthur Wing Pinero
Over Niagara Falls, "an imperious, rushing, roaring, resistless torrent of sights and sensations"
Lover's Lane, by Clyde Fitch
Cynthia, by H. H. Davies
The Real Widow Brown, "the funniest show that's on the road, all laughs"
Hoity-Toity, "the original $25,000 production direct from New York, 50 people"
Under Southern Skies, "the most

original, unhackneyed and diverting play of Southern life"
Uncle Tom's Cabin, from Harriet Beecher Stowe

Minstrels:
Culhane, Chace and Weston's Minstrels and Vaudeville
The Wm. H. West Big Minstrel Jubilee
Lew Dockstader and His Ministrel Co.

Stock Companies:
Tom Marks and His Big New Dramatic and Vaudeville Co.
The Famous Aubrey Stock Co.
Geo. H. Summers, Belle Stevenson and the Summers Stock Co.
Chester De Vonde Stock Co.

Magicians:
The Great Magician Powell in a unique series of amusing developments in necromancy

Movies:
Uncle Tom's Cabin, from Harriet Beecher Stowe
Living Canada, and *Russo-Jap War Pictures*

1904/05

AMBROSE J. SMALL ERA

FEATURES AND DIMENSIONS

In the literature promoting London's Grand Opera House as a destination for road show companies, Ambrose J. Small advertised the following features and dimensions: electrical illumination; proscenium width opening 42 feet, height 34 feet; distance from the curtain line to the footlights 3 feet; distance between the side walls 80 feet; distance between fly girders 55 feet; height to rigging loft 70 feet; depth under the stage 12 feet; usual number of traps, in the usual places; height to the fly gallery 24 feet, 2 bridges. He was also sure to mention that Jas. Cresswell was the orchestra leader, and that the Grand Opera House orchestra boasted no less than nine musicians.

EAST LYNNE

East Lynne had been around since 1863. A soap opera if ever there was one, *East Lynne* was a hit when it opened and it became a staple of the theatre for decades. In a nutshell, the heroine, Isabel, marries Archibald, who takes her to live at East Lynne, and they have two children. But then Isabel suspects that Archibald is in love with Barbara, the neighbour. At this point Isabel divorces Archibald and goes off and marries the oily rogue Levison. Soon Levison is berating her, telling her that "you must be aware that it is an awful sacrifice for a man in my position to marry a divorced woman." So, with that, Isabel goes away. She dons a disguise, that of a governess, and presents herself at East Lynne, where she undertakes to teach her own children, who are living with their father and his wife Barbara, the former neighbour. As the play reaches its climax Willie (Isabel's child by Archibald) is dying, and expresses a wish to see his mother in heaven, not knowing that his mother is the governess, in disguise, at his bedside. Just before final curtain Isabel, who has thrown off her governess disguise, also dies – in the arms of Archibald. Of course there was never a dry eye in the house, and that was the point; if the players could ensure a good weep at the end of the evening, playgoers were grateful, and would a return visit to the Grand Opera House whenever *East Lynne* posters appeared around town.

GENTLEMAN JIM CORBETT

Pals was a light and fluffy piece of entertainment with a special drawing card – Gentleman Jim Corbett, the famed boxer who had defeated John L. Sullivan in 1892, earning the world heavyweight championship. On stage November 1 and 2 of 1904, Corbett flexed his acting muscles at the Grand Opera House. People were more accustomed to seeing his name on the sports pages, not the entertainment section of the newspaper. Corbett was trying his hand at acting, and enjoyed being touted as "the talented actor and world famous athlete."

BELASCO AND DEMILLE

Successful and powerful Broadway producer David Belasco (known as the Bishop of Broadway because of his habit of wearing a clerical collar as part of his everyday wardrobe even though he was not ordained) and playwright Henry DeMille had collaborated on the script of *Lord Chumley*. The play had premiered in 1888 and was such a success it was still touring in the first decade of the 20th century. A Belasco production promised exciting staging and big stars. Henry's son, Cecil B. DeMille,

A production shot from the hit play Way Down East *which was on stage in November, 1904. Promotional material stated: "Endorsed by press, public and pulpit; a play of universal sympathy, containing honest, homely, health humour, evoking alternate tears and laughter." (Author's collection)*

headlined the company of 11 actors. Before his career as one of Hollywood's most successful directors, a very young Cecil was on stage at London's Grand Opera House on March 20, 1905.

MINSTREL SHOWS

Minstrel shows were enormously popular and always drew people to the Grand Opera House. In this season alone, the Dan Quinlan Imperial Minstrels played in October, the Guy Brothers Minstrels played in November, and the Famous Georgia Minstrels played in May. Minstrel shows presented cork-faced entertainment. Both white and black entertainers applied burnt cork to their faces for this form of mass entertainment. The performers then applied white makeup to exaggerate their mouths. The traditional minstrel costume included striped trousers, swallow-tailed coats, oversize collars and white gloves. Having mined the music, humour and dance of the black community in the United States, minstrels made fortunes touring for several decades. If you paid 30 cents and attended a minstrel show at the Grand Opera House, what would you see? If it was a truly traditional minstrel show, the curtain would part to reveal a semi-circle of men in blackface. In the centre would be the dignified interlocutor. At one end of the line was the banjo player, Mr. Tambo, and at the opposite end was Mr. Bones. The interlocutor was the straight man and would address questions to Tambo or Bones. Their funny answers made audiences roar with laughter. This, the first half of the program, would be followed by the second act, or "the olio," which was really a vaudeville show consisting of a quartet of singers, a monologue by the chief comedian, maybe a humorous sketch or a miniature review.

Then the afterpiece would begin. This third act of the evening was an opportunity for the minstrel company to lampoon or satirize everything they had done during the show so far. A witty and romping afterpiece would send you home with a smile on your face, a song on your lips, repeating the punch line to the show's funniest joke. The peak years for minstrel shows were between 1840 and 1880, after which they went into a decline in the early years of the 1900s, although a tenacious minstrel company played London's Grand Theatre during the 1920/21 season. The song and dance men simply could no longer entice large audiences, despite their exaggerated painted faces, over-the-top costumes and jaunty songs. Tastes and moves were changing.

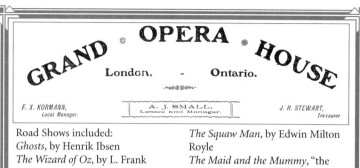

GRAND · OPERA · HOUSE

London, - Ontario.

F. X. KORMANN,
Local Manager.

A. J. SMALL,
Lessee and Manager.

J. R. STEWART,
Treasurer.

Road Shows included:
Ghosts, by Henrik Ibsen
The Wizard of Oz, by L. Frank Baum
Hamlet, *As You Like It*, by William Shakespeare
Twelfth Night, *Macbeth*, by William Shakespeare
Way Down East, by Lottie Blair Parker
Candida, by George Bernard Shaw, "the great London writer and wit"
East Lynne, "a team of horses and carriage used in this production, with 12 actors"
Uncle Tom's Cabin, from Harriett Beecher Stowe
Jewel of Asia, "gorgeous oriental musical comedy success"
The Princess Chic, "the elaborate opera comique, electrical effects"
The Smart Set, "the most colossal show of its kind in the world, 50 people and all colored"
The Factory Girl, "a great labour play, a thousand heart throbs and a smile for every tear"
On the Bridge at Mid-Night, "pathos and comedy delicately intermingled"
Lord Chumley, by Henry C. DeMille and David Belasco, "an original comedy"

The Squaw Man, by Edwin Milton Royle
The Maid and the Mummy, "the ringing, swinging, musical melange"

Vaudeville:
The Jessie Millward Vaudeville Co., on the bill was the Projectoscope, presenting the latest in moving pictures
Miss May Yohe and her Own Company Presenting Fashionable Vaudeville

Minstrels:
The Dan Quinlan Imperial Minstrels
Guy Bros. Minstrels
Richard and Pringle's Famous Georgia Minstrels

Stock Companies:
Marks Bros., No A 1 Dramatic and Vaudeville Co.
Irene Jeavons Dramatic and Vaudeville Co.
Vernon Stock Co.

Movies:
The Great American Vitagraph, presenting all the latest attractions in moving pictures
Biograph, "moving life-like pictures"

1905/06

AMBROSE J. SMALL ERA

THEATRE AS BUSINESS

Theatre in North America was big business. From his Empire Theatre office in New York, producer Charles Frohman oversaw an annual payroll of $35 million, paid to ten thousand employees who wrote, designed and performed in his shows. In New York City a total of 311 shows opened this season. Of these 111 were going out on the road. In Chicago, 150 more were produced and also sent on the road. There were over 3,000 theatres in the United States to absorb this amount of activity, plus theatres in Canada, like Ambrose J. Small's Grand Opera House. It was a very good time for Small to be in the theatre business.

SUGGESTIONS TO PATRONS

With 1,850 seats to fill, and with competition from the rival London Opera House (capacity 850 seats), Ambrose J. Small kept his box office open 13 hours a day – 9:00 a.m. to 10:00 p.m. Seats went on sale a full three days in advance of performances. Helpfully the management included the following "Suggestions to Patrons" in the programme:

1. Ladies who remove their hats will favour the management and add greatly to the comfort of those sitting behind. Old ladies in danger of catching cold need not conform to this request.

2. This theatre has no rules except those which are invariably observed by Ladies and Gentlemen.

3. Attaches– Every Attache (usher) of this theatre is eager to lend every possible attention and courtesy to its patrons. Any information required will be cheerfully given, and it is unnecessary to tender gratuities, as this practice is not permitted by the management and renders the recipient subject to dismissal.

FLORADORA SEXTET

Yet another touring production of the hit *Floradora* stopped over at London's Grand Opera House, for a one night stand in September of 1905. This musical had transferred to New York City from England in 1900, and had enjoyed a run of over 550 performances. The storyline involved a beautiful young heiress and the scheme to prevent her from acquiring the rights to a perfume. The main attraction was the famous Floradora sextet. Everyone in the audience could hum to the hit tune "Tell Me, Pretty Maiden, Are There Any More at Home Like You?" The Floradora Girls were known for their prettiness and perkiness.

HIS LAST DOLLAR

In November, 1905, the play *His Last Dollar* was on stage. The lively plot pulled audiences into the Grand Opera House: "Joe Braxton (the hero), started in life as a jockey for Colonel Downs of Kentucky, but at the opening of the play we see him a millionaire in New York. Tom Linson is Braxton's broker and most trusted friend, but, betraying his friend and employer, he conspires with a designing woman, who has entrapped Braxton into a proposal of marriage, to rob Braxton of everything, after which the guilty ones will elope. But Eleanor Downs comes East with her race horse, and a woman's intuition sees through the plot. Joe is warned – Eleanor's jockey is disabled – Joe rides her horse to victory, outwits the plotters and marries Eleanor. Incidentally to the above, there is an abundance of clean, bright comedy." And , if that wasn't enough entertainment, a review in the *Chicago Daily News* (May 21, 1904)

In 1905, Ambrose J. Small achieved his goal of owning, not leasing, London's Grand Theatre. For the first and last time his photograph was featured on program covers this season. Equal billing was given to his newest manager, J.E. Turton. (Courtesy of J.J. Talman Regional Collection, The D.B. Weldon Library, The University of Western Ontario, London, ON)

stated: "The race track scene is one that is always good for at least half a dozen calls."

TRILBY

Trilby was on stage in February of 1906. Novelist George du Maurier had created the story of Trilby, a girl who possessed the vocal cords of a singer, but was totally unmusical and unable to sing in tune. Musician and hypnotist Svengali takes her under his wing, and she becomes a world famous singer. The novel was a best seller, and in the 1890s it was adapted for the stage. By 1906 *Trilby* was familiar to every theatregoer. Year after year audiences came back to see the famous story reenacted.

DUSTIN FARNUM

On March 28,1906, stage star Dustin Farnum was on stage at the Grand Opera House in the huge hit *The Virginian*. The 1905/06 season represented for him, and the supporting cast thirty-eight, weeks of good wages. Not too many years after this tour, Dustin Farnum would be lured to perform this play in front of the movie camera. The Jesse L. Lasky Feature Play Company persuaded the star to put his performance on film. Of course acting in movies was beneath a stage star of this magnitude, but the money was

extremely good, and Farnum didn't have to endure a gruelling tour, he just had to show up at the New York studio. Slowly but surely new technology was invading the entertainment industry, turning the life of touring players upside down.

GEORGE PRIMROSE

"The Greatest Constellation of Burnt Cork Celebrities Ever Assembled Together", was how Primrose and Dockstader and their 20th Century Minstrels were advertised in the Grand Opera House program. Audiences also knew they were "Canada's Contribution to the Amusement Lovers of the World." George Primrose was born in St. Catharines in 1852, and grew up in London, Ontario. He worked as a bell-boy at a hotel, and in his spare time he practised dancing. While still in his teens he broke into show business as a clog dancer, and toured with small minstrel groups. George Primrose teamed with William West and they enjoyed tremendous success as a song-and-dance team. They were a major attraction for a number of minstrel troops they joined. The partnership broke up because Primrose held onto black-face traditions while West embraced new ideas in entertainment. Primrose then created a partnership with Dockstader and together they enjoyed success. Known as the Millionaire

100 Years of Entertainment at London's Grand Theatre

Minstrel, George Primrose was the Fred Astaire of his day. He was a master of both clog and soft-shoe dancing. He inspired a generation of young dancers. George Primrose remained active as an entertainer until his death in 1919.

When this photograph was taken in September of 1905, the road work being done on Talbot Street, near Carling, was of interest. Today it is the huge poster advertising the smash hit Floradora that catches the eye. Audiences couldn't get enough of the Floradora Girls, and the production toured relentlessly during the first decade of the 20th century. The producers had to keep auditioning and recasting Floradora Girls as the original ones succumbed to the charms of Stage Door Johnnys. (Courtesy of LRAHM)

FRISCO-EARTHQUAKE AND FIRE

1906 was the year of San Francisco's great earthquake. In mid-May Londoners could pay between 15 cents and 50 cents to sit safely in the Grand Opera House seats to watch "6000 feet of film – every detail from the first shock to the complete destruction – most awe inspiring scenes since the Fall of Pompeii." While presented as a documentary of the event, much of the film included special effects. Put another way, many scenes were faked.

Road Shows included:
When Knighthood Was In Flower
Uncle Tom's Cabin, from Harriet Beecher Stowe
Way Down East, by Lottie Blair Parker
Faust
Floradora
The Girl from Kay's, "a farcical comedy with music"
Little Johnny Jones, by George M. Cohan
The Genius and the Model, by Wm. C. deMille and Cecil B. DeMille
The Woman in the Cast, by Clyde Fitch
Girls Will be Girls, "just nonsense, that's all, in three acts"
Serio-Comic Governess, "the mirthful melodious hit of the season
Her First False Step, "a play depicting the suffering of a wayward girl"
Black Patti Show, "fine and dandy, new and swell, with 40 Gay Troubadours"
The Wayward Son, "startling, sensational situations; marvellous, mechanical masterpieces"
A Desperate Chance, "a plausible melodrama with a thrilling story and sensational climaxes"

Trilby, from du Maurier's novel
The Merchant of Venice, Macbeth, King Lear, by William Shakespeare

Minstrels:
George Primrose and His Big Minstrel Co.
Guy Bros. Minstrels
Famous Georgia Minstrels

Stock Companies:
The Miller-Kilpatrick Co.
Chicago Stock Co.
Pollard Juvenile Opera Co. (artists 8 to 15 years of age)
Stoddart Stock Co.
Bijou Comedy Co. with Vaudeville between acts
Summers Stock Co, with High-Class Vaudeville between acts

Magicians:
Svengola, Hypnotism up-to-Date

Movies:
The American Vitagraph, "the Daddy of them all when it is a question of animated photography"
Frisco – Earthquake and Fire, "moving pictures, 6000 feet of film"
Kelley's Moving Pictures
Bioscope
The Ouimetoscope

1906/07

AMBROSE J. SMALL ERA

MYSTERY SEASON

A mystery surrounds the 1906/07 season. Sole Proprietor A.J. Small leased his London Grand Opera House to a pair of gentlemen identified in the house programs as Fitzpatrick and Stewart, Lessees and Managers. They touted the "Big Shubert and Independent Shows That Will be Seen At The Grand During the Season," and listed in the program household name stars and popular plays that London theatregoers could anticipate seeing throughout the season.

STOCK SHOWS

The Livingstone Stock Company moved into the Grand Opera House for a few days' run in late November. They offered four shows from their stock: *Fortune's Fool, The Man from the West, A Southern Romance* and *Are You Crazy?* Not exactly the highbrow entertainment Messrs. Fitzpatrick and Stewart promoted at the beginning of the season. These no-name shows were followed on December 10 and 11th by *The Earl and the Girl* starring Eddie Foy, produced by the successful brother team of Sam S. Shubert and Lee Shubert.

DANIEL RYAN

An actor named Daniel Ryan moved into the theatre in late December, and besides presenting Shakespeare's *Richard III*, *Macbeth* and *Othello*, he also starred as Mathias in melodrama

The Bells. Anyone who had been to church on Christmas Day, 1907, but who had some leisure time in the afternoon, could enjoy a matinee of *A Royal Lover* (starring Daniel Ryan), or an evening performance of *The Three Musketeers* (starring Daniel Ryan). *The Merchant of Venice* (starring Daniel Ryan) and *Dr. Jekyll and Mr. Hyde* (starring Daniel Ryan) were presented late in the month. By December 30th Londoners were probably wondering – would Daniel Ryan and Company ever vacate their Grand Opera House?

A.J. SMALL RETURNS

It remains unclear whether the stars that Fitzpatrick and Stewart so proudly proclaimed in October of 1906 materialized during this mystery season. Certainly one or two stars trouped through the city, but there was an emphasis on obscure stock companies, such as the Dora Mystic Lindley Stock Co., the White Stock Co., and the Livingstone Stock Co. What is clear is that as soon as the 1907/08 season began A.J. Small's name was again featured on programmes as "Sole Proprietor" and the names of Fitzpatrick and Stewart had vanished. Presumably the experiment of leasing his London theatre to others had not worked in Small's favour. Perhaps there was a dip in revenue, a dip he wished to reverse. Maybe he heard from London's theatre-goers that they were displeased with the standard of theatre offered to them. Whatever the real story of the 1906/07 season, Small was back in charge and things were looking up.

1907/08

Road Shows included:
The Greater Love, founded upon episodes of Mozart's life
The Earl and the Girl, "Eddie Foy in the merry English musical whirl"
The Three Musketeers
The Stolen Story, "a comedy drama of American political, social and newspaper life"
The Count of Monte Cristo
Will-o'-the-Wisp, "a new musical comedy" by Emlyn Williams
The Merchant of Venice, by William Shakespeare
Dr. Jekyll and Mr. Hyde
Widowers' Houses, by George Bernard Shaw, "a clean social study"
When Women Love, "the greatest love and labour drama ever produced"
Uncle Dudley from Missouri

Minstrels:
Lew Dockstader and His Minstrel Company

Vaudeville:
Big New York Vaudeville Bill, including New Moving Pictures High Class Vaudeville

Stock Companies:
Dora Mystic Lindley Stock Company
The White Stock Company
The Livingstone Stock Company
Mr. Daniel Ryan and Company

Magicians:
Shungopavi "the Weird Wonder Worker and his Company"
Durne "The Mysterious" and Company

Movies:
Vitagraph Films; *Child's Revenge* (extremely interesting); *Female Spy* (very sensational);
Bill Goes to a Party (comedy); *How Office Boy Saw the Ball Game* (a scream).

Animal Act:
The Bostock Arena, "the greatest exhibition of trained wild animals; don't fail to see
Consul, the educated chimpanzee"

ALLA NAZIMOVA

Nazimova was one of those famous stars whom playgoers knew by only one name. She appeared at The Grand in September of 1907 in the comedy *The Marionettes*. Russian-born Alla Nazimova came to New York with a company of Russian players. Audiences were captivated by her blue-black hair, her large black eyes, her white skin and soft voice. While her acting skills were good, her wardrobe was better. People went to her plays to see what she would be wearing. In this play Nazimova portrayed the Marquise Fernande de Monclars, and the house program noted that Nazimova's gowns were "by the Maison Jacqueline."

SYBIL THORNDIKE

The Ben Greet Players of England came to London to play at the Grand Opera House on October 22 and 23rd. *The Merchant of Venice* and *Macbeth* were presented. In the company was a young actress by the name of Sybil Thorndike.

> *Ben Greet simply lives for the theatre – they say about him that if we had 20 minutes' wait at a station he'd be off to see if there were a theatre of any sort. – Sybil Thorndike*

Years later Sybil Thorndike's contribution to theatre would be rewarded with her being appointed Dame Sybil Thorndike. She and her husband, Lewis Casson, were the parents of the late

A poster advertising the play **The Fatal Flower.** *The program carried a curious note: "The management earnestly and seriously requests that any patron of the Grand Opera House who, after having witnessed a performance of* **The Fatal Flower,** *can suggest a title or name for this play to replace the present one, which will adequately realize its purpose and atmosphere, and which will briefly convey and more fully proclaim to the public the play's real intrinsic worth, will kindly submit a name or title which they deem more appropriate, by letter to Mr. A.E. Root, Manager of the Company, care of this theatre." (Courtesy of The Grand Theatre)*

actress Ann Casson. Ann Casson married actor Douglas Campbell and the theatre dynasty continued. Both Douglas Campbell and his son, actor Benedict Campbell, have performed many times at London's Grand Theatre.

MRS. PATRICK CAMPBELL

On December 10, 1907, London theatregoers were able to see *The Notorious Mrs. Ebbsmith* by Sir Arthur Wing Pinero, starring the notorious Mrs. Patrick Campbell. Mrs. Campbell was known for the havoc she caused, for her capriciousness and moodiness, for her practical joking and for her sharp tongue. Her fellow actors found her quarrelsome, demanding and badly behaved. Despite driving her fellow actors to distraction, audiences flocked to see the star. Her career was a long and colourful one. This would not be her last appearance at London's Grand Opera House.

GRAND OPERA HOUSE

AMBROSE J. SMALL
Sole Proprietor

LOUIS H. BOWERS
Resident Manager

Road Shows included:
Faust
Way Down East, by Lottie Blair Parker, "the success of the century"
My Wife's Family, "merry musical farce comedy"
Sis in New York, "comedy of Indiana rural life"
The Girl Who Has Everything, by Clyde Fitch
Side Tracked, "illustrating the comic side of life on the rail"
The Great Divide, "romantic drama of the Western country"
The Rosary, "a play of human interest founded upon an emblem of purity"
Bunty Pulls the Strings, "a Scottish comedy"
The Merry Widow, by Franz Lehar, "a new and lavish production of the world's most famous operetta"
The Merchant of Venice, Macbeth, by William Shakespeare
A Social Whirl, "presenting a real casino beauty chorus"
The Wizard of Oz, by L. Frank Baum
Uncle Tom's Cabin, from Harriet Beecher Stowe
The Time, the Place and the Girl, "a company of nearly 100 people"
The Notorious Mrs. Ebbsmith, by Sir Arthur Wing Pinero
The Fatal Flower, "a powerful drama in four acts, 15 actors"
Three Twins, "see the giant electric swing and marvellous faceograph"
The Shoo-Fly Regiment, "clever colored comedians"
His Last Dollar, "five thoroughbred running horses in a dash for victory, professional jockeys"

Minstrels:
Guy Brothers' Minstrels, "10 Vaudeville acts, 10 solo vocalists, 30 expert dancers"

Animal Act:
Prof. E.K. Crocker's Educated Horses, Ponies, Donkeys and Mules

---

1908/09

AMBROSE J. SMALL ERA

THE WITCHING HOUR

The Witching Hour was a hit play by American writer Augustus Thomas. The playwright was deeply interested in telepathy, and had given the subject months of study before he wrote about it in this play. Thomas offered it first to the great producer, Charles Frohman. At first greatly enthusiastic about the play's potential, Frohman cooled on the idea after he showed it to his brother, producer Daniel Frohman, who had no faith it would be a hit. After Charles Frohman passed on the script, the playwright took it down the street to the Shubert brothers who accepted it. *The Witching Hour* became a huge hit on Broadway or on the road. It was estimated that Frohman lost $250,000 by passing on the script.

J. STANLEY MEREDITH

A farce called Night Out *was played by a local cast which included Patty and Marian McLaren, Frank Reid and Mary Love. The outstanding moment in my recollection was when Frank Reid fell flat on his back and Mary Love sat on his stomach while she declaimed in true tragedian style: 'Dead, dead, dead old man…why do you lie there?', to which Frank replied: 'Because I can't get up.'*

– J. Stanley Meredith, who in 1916, formed his own theatrical company, and remained active in London theatre circles throughout the 1920s and 1930s

The front cover of an 1908/09 program. No space was wasted, and audiences were encouraged to keep coming back to The Grand to see the exciting fare programmed for the coming weeks. (Courtesy of William K. Trudell)

MELODRAMA

Melodrama ruled the stage in the first decade of the 20th century. Audiences knew exactly what they were in for when they put their money down and bought a ticket for the latest "melo." Stereotyped plot, characterization and dialogue were used to reinforce that villainy is punished, virtue triumphs, and love wins the day. The typical melodrama included five principal characters: the stalwart hero, the trembling heroine, the light-comedy boy, the soubrette and the villainous heavy. These stock characters behaved true to type. The strict code of morality of the day was safe in the melo-dramatist's hands. Audiences didn't mind wooden dialogue, over-the-top sentimentality or even predictability as long as writers could invent new plot devices and create new climaxes. Hence the reliance on "effects" that would heighten the excitement. A thundering train bearing down on a helpless heroine, perhaps, or the hero up to his neck in water in an airtight dungeon. Just as the movies of today promote the special effects viewers can thrill to, so the melodramas came to rely more and more on "mechanical" or "electrical" effects to lure audiences. The public seemed to have an insatiable appetite for the melo. Playgoers came to the opera house to watch as the hero saved the heroine, or, on a rare occasion, the heroine rescue the hero, so he could, just before the final curtain, rescue her. Satisfied audience members spilled out into the night, feeling that all was right with the world.

1909/10

AMBROSE J. SMALL ERA

THE TIME, THE PLACE AND THE GIRL
"It's seldom, if ever
You find them together,
The Time, the Place, and the Girl."

The plot of *The Time, the Place and the Girl* was wafer thin, but that didn't stop it from touring for several years and reaping massive profits. The play's heroes were forced to hide in a sanatorium, after participating in an unfortunate brawl. There, one of the men reignites an old romance with his childhood sweetheart. The other young man falls in love with a nurse. Fortunately, a quarantine allows the couples to pursue their courtships. Contemporary slang included in the script greatly appealed to the audiences of the day, as did the play's senti-mentality.

JOHN R. MINHINNICK

After hiring a series of managers who never seemed to stay long, Ambrose J. Small finally found one who would stay in his employ. Londoner John R. Minhinnick resigned from his position as chief accountant for Carling Brewing and Malting Company and became, during the 1909/10 season, manager of the Grand Opera House. He applied all of his accounting skills to keeping the theatre's books, and he quickly learned the theatre business from Ambrose J. Small.

Road Shows included:
Cavalleria Rusticana, by Mascagni
Carmen, by Bizet
I Pagliacci, by Leoncavello
The Witching Hour, by Augustus Thomas, "the dramatic sensation with a cast of incomparable actors and actresses and scenic investiture of wondrous realism and beauty"

For Her Children's Sake, "gigantic scenic production of the new melo-dramatic success, a pathetic story intermingled with bright and sparkling comedy"
The Devil, "an adaptation of the sensational continental play "Der Teufel"

NEIL BURGESS

Ben-Hur was on tour this season and filled the Grand Opera House for three days in March, 1910. Klaw and Erlanger's production of General Lew Wallace's famous story was big, big, BIG! Richard Buhler played the hero Ben-Hur, while Mitchell Harris played his friend, and nemesis Messala. For Act II the stage was turned into the Roman galley Astrea. Of course *Ben-Hur* would not be *Ben-Hur* if the galley's slave hold was not shown, and if there was not the breathless rescue at sea. And what would *Ben-Hur* be without the chariot race scene? It just would not be *Ben-Hur*! The effect of chariots, drawn by real horses, racing around the coliseum was realized with the help of a treadmill mechanism. The device had been invented by one Neil Burgess, an actor who also had a talent for designing stage machinery. Smart enough to patent his invention in the 1880s, Mr. Burgess earned hundreds of thousands of dollars from producers who used his treadmill invention in their productions of *Ben-Hur*, and countless other stage plays that called for nothing short of thrilling climaxes.

Road Shows included:
Trilby, from du Maurier's novel, "opening of the regular season, special fair week attraction"
The Rosary, by Edward Rose, "the play everyone is talking about and the one they want to see"
Ghosts, by Henrik Ibsen
The White Sister, by F. Marion Crawford
The Red Moon, "Cole and Johnson in an American musical comedy in red and black"
Ben Hur, from Gen. Lew Wallace's novel, "Klaw and Erlanger's production"

The Time, the Place and the Girl, "that favourite musical triumph"
The Merry Widow, "a Viennese operetta in three acts, new costumes, brilliant cast"
Fluffy Ruffles, "a riot of fun and music, girls you'll look again at, songs you'll whistle"
The Servant in the House, "the most remarkable play in the English language"

Minstrels:
Cohan & Harris' Minstrels with George Evans and his 100 Honey Boys

1910/11

AMBROSE J. SMALL ERA

SARAH BERNHART

When Sarah Bernhardt came to London in 1910, she was 67 years old. She had enjoyed super stardom for many decades, not just in her native France, but around the world. Her program for the 1910/11 tour included Edmond Rostand's *L'Aiglon* (*The Eaglet*, the story of the son of Napoleon), *La Dame Aux Camelias* from Alexandr Dumas, and Emile Moreau's historical drama *La Process de Jeanne d'Arc*. "In a special train of five cars, Madame Sarah Bernhardt, the world's most famous actress, came into London at about half past eleven this morning. A fast run had been made from Grand Rapids, Michigan, where the actress played last night. 'The madame will not be up till some time after one o'clock,' was the announcement of manager E. J. Sullivan. 'We were late in leaving Grand Rapids, and it is a rather long run. But it is wonderful how well she stands the continuous journeying, on the go everyday, with rehearsals every afternoon.' This is not Sarah Bernhardt's first visit to London. Her last previous appearance here was on April 8, 1896, when she played in the old Grand Opera House in the Masonic Temple. There will be many Londoners hearing Bernhardt tonight who heard her on that occasion, and will remember the ovation which she won. The gallery at the Grand Opera House for the Sarah Bernhardt performance will be open to-night at seven o'clock to allow all to get their seats as the curtain is set for 7:45 sharp." (– *London Free Press*, November 24, 1910)

Reviewing Bernhardt's performance in *L'Aiglon* during this tour, a Boston reviewer noted: "Once she acted in the theatre, for the theatre, by the ways of the theatre…Now she acts out of insight, to beauty. The spirit, not the substance of her personages concerns her; the sublimation and not the shows of acting stimulates her. She began in sophisticated theatrical power; and she is ending in spiritualized simplicity." (– H.T. Parker, *Boston Transcript*, 1910)

KLEEN THE HYPNOTIST

For a complete change of pace Kleen, "the World's Famous Hypnotist, Master of the Human Mind" took over the stage during the week of December 19. He was assisted by Lillian Lynbrook, proclaimed to be a natural born clairvoyant. "Kleen hangs a man on the open stage every night," according to the

Sarah Bernhardt graced the stage on November 24, 1910. She presented an evening of entertainment, spoken entirely in French. "From the spectator's standpoint there can be no question that Bernhardt knows how to die well." (– London Free Press, 1910; Courtesy of Jane Schmuck)

program. Ambrose J. Small either carried a lot of insurance, or he had an agreement that he was not liable if Kleen's hanging act misfired and dispatched one of Small's patrons to the next world, before their time.

1911/12

MODERN MYSTERY PLAY

The Passing of the Third Floor Back, by Jerome K. Jerome, was billed as a modern mystery play. Appearing in the role of "The Passer By" was Ian Robertson. "*The Passing of the Third Floor Back* needs no recommendation to London playgoers," as the house program boldly stated. "The run of twelve months in London, England, seven months in New York, and the three visits to Toronto within the year, will be within memory. Mr. Ian Robertson is brother to Forbes Robertson, and for years has been his leading man and producer. He is a fine actor, and is on this occasion supported by an entirely English company, all of whom are leading people over the other side. The company for its delicate representation of this beautiful work has gained the admiration of critics all through America."

AMBROSE J. SMALL ERA

On November 2, 1911 Scottish sensation Harry Lauder came to town. Billed as the star's "only appearance in this city for three years", audiences packed the Grand Opera House for an evening of solid entertainment from one of the world's biggest stage stars. They were not disappointed as Lauder launched into his biggest hits one after the other: "I Love a Lassie", "She's Ma Daisy", "Stop You're Ticklin' Jock," "Keep Right on to the End of the Road" and, of course, "Roamin' in the Gloamin." Knighted in 1919, Sir Harry Lauder retired from the stage in 1935. He was without question one of vaudeville's greatest box office attractions, and while he toured it was true that "The whole world laughed with Lauder."
(Courtesy of Jane Schmuck)

Road Shows included:
Le Process de Jeanne d'Arc, La Dame aux Camelias, L'Aiglon, starring Sarah Bernhardt
The Fortune Teller, starring Elsie Janis "the world's greatest imitator"
What Every Woman Knows, by J.M. Barrie
Call of the Wild, "the most notable dramatic event of the season"
The Thief, "a powerfully gripping drama of a woman who steals to make herself attractive"
The Happiest Night of His Life, "chockablock with bright situations and smart dialogue"

The Passing of the Third Floor Back, by Jerome K. Jerome, "the modern mystery play"
The Jolly Bachelors, "100 people, big musical show"
Raffles, "the famous detective play"
The Man of the Hour, "a stirring love story"
Magician:
Kleen "The World's Famous Hypnotist, Master of the Human Mind"

Dance:
Mlle. Anna Pavlova, "in her famous *Swan Dance*"

BILLIE BURKE

The Runaway starred Miss Billie Burke. The star was type-cast as a mad-cap, charming and innocently provocative heroine. Also in the cast was venerable actor C. Aubrey Smith. Producer Charles Frohman had taken Billie Burke under his wing and made her into a huge stage star. She worked for Frohman between 1907 and 1914, right up until her marriage to another powerful producer, Florenz Ziegfeld, Jr.. There was great animosity between the two maverick theatre mavens. Frohman felt betrayed by Billie Burke's decision to marry Ziegfeld, and Frohman never spoke to Burke after 1914. Today, Billie Burke is remembered by fans of the 1939 movie *The Wizard of Oz*. She played Glenda, the good witch in that classic film.

MANTELL'S *MACBETH*

The stage version of *Macbeth*, with the lead role ably played by Robert B. Mantell on October 17, 1911, entertained the evening's audience, although it is questionable whether today's audiences would recognize Shakespeare's classic tale as it appeared on stage that evening. The disclaimer in the house program read: "The stage version used was prepared from Edwin Booth's prompt-book and is marked by the usual omission of both text and character. The cuts include the scenes laid in England, while the English characters taking part in these scenes are also dropped. None of the passages is dramatically essential in forwarding the tragedy." What was left of the text?! Shakespearean purists were probably shocked by what they saw…and by what they did not see.

ETHEL BARRYMORE

Ethel Barrymore was on tour in November playing the meaty role of Stella Ballantyne in the Charles Frohman production of *Witness for the Defence*. Ethel Barrymore was pregnant at the time, but kept trouping across North America despite her condition. This was her first appearance at London's Grand Opera House, but would not be her last. Her uncle, the hugely popular matinee idol, John Drew, also toured through London, from time to time, in hits from the Broadway stage. In the December 7, 1901 edition of *Billboard Magazine*, Ethel Barrymore's deep roots in the theatre were explained: "Her mother was the talented Georgia Drew, whose untimely death bereaved the stage of one of its most brilliant

daughters. Her father, Maurice Barrymore, was long an actor of prominence. Her grandmother, Mrs. John Drew, was a favourite with three generations of theatre-goers. Her uncle, John Drew, of our day, has long been regarded as one of our leading actors." Ethel's two siblings, John and Lionel, also went into the family business.

GRAND OPERA HOUSE

A. J. SMALL, Sole Proprietor.

J. R. MINHINNICK, Manager.

SEASON 1911-12.

PHONE 188

Road Shows included:
The Runaway
The Little French Maid, "the Parisian musical melange in two acts"
Baby Mine, "the funniest play ever written, a scream from start to finish"
Macbeth, by William Shakespeare
The Mummy and the Hummingbird, "that society production"
The Squaw Man, "the great play of Western ranch life, a pretentious production"
Chantecler, by Edmond Rostand
The Rosary
The White Squaw, "romantic drama"
The Witness for the Defence, by A.E.W. Mason
The Gamblers, "a conspiracy of Wall Street"
H.M.S. Pinafore, "notable all-star revival of Gilbert and Sullivan's masterpiece"

Movies:
Dante's Inferno

Entertainer:
Harry Lauder and a Large Company of International Stars, "the fourth American tour of the comprehensible - vital - interesting comedian, the world's greatest entertainer"

1912/13

AMBROSE J. SMALL ERA

MARIE DRESSLER

Star Marie Dressler headlined Dressler's Players in her *All Star Gambol*, on stage in April, 1913. According to the house program, "gambol" meant "a somewhat new style of entertainment. It consists of a combination of drama, comedy, music, dancing and burlesque, all held together by a slightly connected libretto, in which the four muses represented by pretty girls, describe what each of her favourite players will offer." While this may not clarify anything, the audiences of the day eagerly greeted Dressler's *Gambol* wherever it played, and made it a huge success for the star. Marie Dressler was in her early 40s at this time, and still had Hollywood to conquer. Who can forget her as Tugboat Annie or as the society matron in the Jean Harlow movie *Dinner at Eight*? Dressler earned a best actress

In the play Everywoman *there was an elaborate banquet scene. "Everywoman, Walter Browne's inspiring and beautiful modern morality play, one of the noblest theatrical ventures of the season, has been received with almost universal critical acclaim. Seldom since the early days of the 19th century has rhetoric so decorative and cadences so spacious fallen from a dramatist's pen. Everywoman is just a young girl when the play begins. She has three friends, Youth, Beauty and Modesty, and a handmaiden, Conscience, although she does not have Conscience until the second act." (Stage Magazine, New York, August 1936) (Author's collection)*

Academy Award in 1930 for *Min and Bill*. Born in Cobourg, Ontario, in 1869, Miss Dressler was never described as pretty. Her act included a burlesque of *Camille* in which she impersonated the frail and delicate heroine of the tale. The comedy was in the fact that Miss Dressler was anything but frail and delicate. Her comedic abilities won over audiences, first on the stage and later on the screen. Fans mourned Miss Dressler's passing in 1934

THE CANADIAN KINGS OF REPERTOIRE

Canada's Marks Bros. Company, this one headed by Joe Marks and starring Gracie Marks, was at the Grand Opera House presenting *Virgie's Sweetheart* and *The Girl from Sunny Alberta,* among other titles from their stock. This was one of three successful Marks Bros. stock companies touring Canada. Known as The Canadian Kings of Repertoire, the family business had been started by Robert William Marks, the eldest of seven Marks brothers, based in Christie Lake, Ontario. In the 1870s, Robert had hired actors, developed a repertoire, organized a theatrical touring company, and took to the road, trouping as far west as Winnipeg by 1879. By the 1890s, three separate Marks Bros. companies had been established, each headed by a separate Marks brother. The companies toured for 42 weeks each year. Each company took care to be playing different towns some distance from one another, and to present different plays from their vast stock of titles.

"We'd rehearse in Perth, Ontario, and our rehearsal would be for two weeks. I used to have gowns made according to the parts I played. We were always very well-dressed. Our shows were respectable shows; melodrama, dramatic shows. My husband, Ernie Marks, never directed. We'd have one of our actors direct. Do you know how long it took me to walk on the stage properly? To know what to do with my hands? It took me 10 years to walk on the stage

properly. You've got to work at that. And you've got to know what people like and what they don't like. Our audiences were always very loyal." – Kitty Marks, star of the Ernie Marks Company, in a 1962 CBC Radio interview, conducted by Grace Lydiatt Shaw

Road Shows included:
The Taming of the Shrew, Henry IV, Twelfth Night, Hamlet, by William Shakespeare
Dressler's Players in an *All Star Gambol*
Everywoman, "be merciful, be just, be fair, to every woman, everwhere, her faults are many"
Ben-Hur
The Trail of the Lonesome Pine, "the most pronounced dramatic success of the season"
Little Miss Fix-It, "a revival of the nation's light opera"
Uncle Tom's Cabin, from Harriet Beecher Stowe
Passers By, "a fantastic conceit and full of human touches and is sincere in its appeal"

Bought and Paid For, "the biggest play in the history of our stage"
The Quaker Girl, "the musical hit of three continents"
Alice in Wonderland, "glittering spectacular extravaganza, 350 people, 35 musical numbers"
She Stoops to Conquer, by Oliver Goldsmith

Stock Companies:
The Ernie Marks Stock Company
May A. Bell Marks and the Marks Bros. Company
Marks Bros. Dramatic and Vaudeville Co., with Gracie Marks
Stanley Stock Company

Movies:
Edison's Talking Pictures

1913/14

AMBROSE J. SMALL ERA

MRS. FISKE – ACTRESS, DIRECTOR, MANAGER

Minnie Maddern Fiske played London's Grand in September, 1913, in the Edward Sheldon play *The High Road*. Fiske was a star who shunned the established star system in the United States, and tried to develop a company of players in which the ensemble, not the individual, was important. She was a triple threat, working as an actress on stage, a director off stage, and as manager of her own company. Fiske had an independent spirit and refused to submit to the control of the Syndicate. She sustained a long career between 1882 and 1832, despite bucking the system of her time. Unlike many of the other actresses of her day, Fiske embraced the naturalist style that playwrights, such as Ibsen, demanded of actors. Naturalism to Mrs. Fiske included speaking with rapid diction, sometimes speaking indistinctly, and with her back turned to the audience. This of course was very distracting and irritating to audiences and fellow actors. Once when the actor George Arliss was sharing the stage with Mrs. Fiske, he encountered the following situation:

"She was so interested in getting the best out of everybody else that she always seemed to regard herself as negligible in the play. I remember saying to her, 'Are you going to speak all that with your back to the audience?' 'Yes,' she said, 'I want them to see your face.' 'But,' I remonstrated, 'it's a very long speech for you to deliver in that position.' 'Yes, I know,' she sighed. 'It's such a long speech, I want to get through with it as quickly as I can.' – George Arliss, actor

MAUDE ADAMS

Broadway superstar Maude Adams was on tour in *Peter Pan* in September. American actress Ruth Gordon gives some insight into Miss Adams' star power, and her mystery. "She was the prettiest person I had ever seen, and in all my life I had never heard a lovelier voice. She never came on the stage until just before her entrance. She remained in her dressing room, and the stage manager tapped on her door to let her know that the overture had begun. He returned a few minutes later and let her know that the curtain was rising. Several minutes after that he tapped on the door again and told her a line that had just been spoken on the stage. And then some minutes later he tapped again and told her another line. Then she came out of her dressing-room, preceded by one stage manager and followed by another. Nobody ever thought of speaking to her on her way to the stage or between her scenes. She was not haughty or stand-offish, but nobody ever thought of saying 'how-do-you-do'. She was like royalty…The Maude Adams Company was one of the last to travel in the grand manner. She always had a private car, and the ladies of the company were invited to live in the car and to breakfast there. Cabs were provided to take them from the station to their hotels; Miss Adams thought it was not dignified for the ladies of her company to go scrambling about in street cars. In fact, the dignity of Miss Adams affected the lives of every company member every minute of the day. No actor in her company ever dared to be seen in any unsuitable place or costume. While on tour we did not leave the train to walk on the station platforms." (– Ruth Gordon, "A Great Lady in the Grand Manner," *Stage Magazine*, January, 1937, NY).

No actor wants to teach people to laugh at those things that should not be laughed at, to interest them in things that should

Peter Pan, *the hit play by J.M. Barrie featured stage star Maude Adams (second from left) and was on stage at the Grand Opera House on September 20, 1913. Though almost forgotten today, Maude Adams was one of the biggest stage stars of her era. Respected by her peers and adored by her public, she enjoyed success in* Peter Pan, *and in roles in other plays by J.M. Barrie. The play endures to this day. Many other actresses have played Peter, but the role was Barrie's gift to Maude Adams. (Author's collection)*

not be seen on the stage, or to deride the values that he himself holds dear.
– Maude Adams, actress

Maude Adams was Charles Frohmans' greatest star. He excelled as a star maker. But his career was coming to an end as Miss Adams toured North America in *Peter Pan*. Returning from a scouting trip to London's West End theatres, Frohman was on board the *Lusitania* when it was torpedoed and sank off the coast of Ireland in May of 1915. His death made his family of stage stars bereft. It probably left a huge financial mess as well, as it was rumored that Frohman relied on verbal, not written contracts for his players and productions.

PEG O' MY HEART

Peg O' My Heart played The Grand in October, 1913. This play made a fortune for its playwright, J. Hartley Manners, and brought fame to its star Laurette Taylor (also known as Mrs. Hartley Manners.) The play follows the adventures of a warm-hearted Irish colleen who, by the terms of an uncle's will, is sent to live in the unfriendly household of her aristocratic English relatives. Peg brings her little dog Michael. It was a wonderful formula for laughter and tears. *Peg O' My Heart* opened in May of 1912, not on Broadway, but in Burbank, California, at the Morosco Theatre. It played to standing-room-only houses, and smashed all records for stock runs in the Los Angeles area. Soon it transferred to New York City. Laurette Taylor as Peg was big business. Audiences just couldn't get enough of the winsome Irish lass. Four road companies were sent out across North America. Then to meet the growing demand, four more were assembled, rehearsed and sent on their way. Audiences everywhere thought they were witnessing Broadway star Laurette Taylor in the lead role, because each road

company poster carried her name above the name of the company's female lead, pronouncing Laurette Taylor as "the creator of Peg." The play proved to be J. Hartley Manners' ticket to fortune. The weekly royalties sent to the playwright totalled $10,000. By 1919 the play had earned the playwright and the actress over $1 million dollars. In 1921 it enjoyed a revival. It was so enduring that during the summer of 1952, London audiences could see the Shelton-Amos Players' production of the play, and during the 1955/1956 London Little Theatre season Martin O'Meara directed a production of the play. *Peg O' My Heart* had legs.

KINETOPHONE

For five days in early October, matinee and evening shows of Thomas A. Edison's Kinetophone were screened. Billed as "not simply moving pictures, but laughing, singing, talking pictures, with the voices of the actors and every sound faithfully reproduced true to life, the sensation of the century, the greatest amusement novelty every shown," the Edison apparatus was set up at the Grand Opera House. Amplification of the sound would have been extremely limited, leaving some of the paying customers happy to experience the talking pictures, but the majority of them frustrated by the bad sound.

THE BENSON COMPANY

Frank Benson and his wife Constance Benson were the nucleus of The Benson Company of The Shakespeare Memorial Theatre, Stratford-Upon-Avon, England. In October of 1913 they were on their first American tour, and it brought them to London's Grand Theatre. The Bensons had acted in Shakespeare's classics since 1886 and would do so until 1916. In 1913 London audiences enjoyed the company in: *The Taming of the Shrew, King Henry the Fourth, Twelfth Night* and *Hamlet*. The Benson Company provided superb

The cover of a souvenir program featuring actress Minnie Maddern Fiske in a play produced by her husband, Harrison Grey Fiske. Mrs. Fiske was known as The First Lady of the Stage. She toured North America relentlessly, playing all the theatres not controlled by New York City's powerful Syndicate. Her defiance kept Mrs. Fiske playing in drafty, dusty theatres on the edge of towns across the land. (Courtesy of Jane Schmuck)

training for the generation of Shakespearean actors who followed in their footsteps.

JOHN DREW

On February 6, 1914, elegant matinee idol John Drew graced London's Grand Opera House stage in two shows: *The Will* and *The Tyranny of Tears*. John Drew was described as "a man of grace and humour, a polished, expert comedian who contributed mightily to the dignity and the stability of the American stage for a full half century. He set the style for the playing of drawing-room comedy; he had a great influence in forming the taste of the play going public, in improving the manners of the American actor on stage and off." (– Ward Morehouse, *Matinee Tomorrow*)

ILLUSTRATED LECTURE – 1914

I remember being taken to the Grand Opera House to attend the illustrated lecture about Captain Scott's doomed Antarctic Expedition. It was in April of 1914 that Commander Evans, second in command of the infamous expedition came to London. I listened intently, and I watched as the moving and coloured pictures were projected. The footage had been shot by Herbert Ponting, and by Dr. Wilson who, I later learned, had died, attempting to return from the Antarctic.

– Miss Louise Wyatt, retired teacher

HOWARD THURSTON

Howard Thurston billed himself as the World's Greatest Magician and, during the 1913/14 season, he was touring with The Wonder Show of the Universe: "Presenting new and bewildering mysteries that dazzle the eye, astound the mind, exhaust the vocabulary, and surpass anything previously attempted by the master minds in the history of magic," as the program copy read. As a young magician Thurston had mastered the trick that was his own speciality: The Rising Cards. The audience watched as cards, called for by the audience, rose from the deck and floated up to the fingertips of Thurston. How was it done? His magic went beyond card tricks to include such things as The Levitation of Princess Karnac, among other show-stopping illusions. Thurston would tour for nine months of the year then rest up, while his props were repaired and repainted, then it was back on the road, to bewitch audiences who came to see his shows right up until his retirement from the stage in 1931.

Road Shows included:
The Lady of Ostend, "famous farcical comedy"
Way Down East, "the big city company with horses, cows, sheep, calves, etc."
Peter Pan, or, The Boy Who Wouldn't Grow Up, by J.M. Barrie
The High Road, by Edward Shelton
The Pink Lady, "a company of 90 people"
Peg O' My Heart, "J. Hartley Manners' perpetual success"
The Quaker Girl, "the daintiest and most delightful of all musical plays"
Fanny's First Play, by G. B. Shaw
Romeo and Juliet, The Merry Wives of Windsor, by William Shakespeare
In Old Kentucky, "concert given in front of the theatre by the Picaninny Band"
A Christmas Carol, Nicholas Nickelby, A Tale of Two Cities, from Charles Dickens
Anthony and Cleopatra, As You Like It, Twelfth Night, by William Shakespeare
A Butterfly on the Wheel, "the great English divorce play"
The Only Way, from Dickens' *A Tale of Two Cities*
A Cigarette Maker's Romance, "setting – a cigarette shop in Munich"
The Importance of Being Earnest, by Oscar Wilde, "a trivial comedy for serious people"

Minstrels:
Primrose and Dockstader and Their 20th Century Minstrels; including Six Brown Brothers, the world's greatest musical act, Canada's contribution to the amusement lovers of the world

Stock Companies:
The Ernie Marks Stock Company, starring Miss Kitty Marks
R.W. Marks presents the Marks Bros. Co and May A. Bell Marks
Perry's Peerless Players
Tom Terriss and His Charles Dickens English Players
The Gilbert and Sullivan Festival Company
The Boyer Stock Company, "in all high class plays"

Magician:
Thurston, The World's Greatest Magician, "the wonder show of the universe"

Movies:
Thos. A. Edison's Kinetophone
The Cines Photo Drama Glorious *Anthony and Cleopatra*, "do not miss this great picture – they do not play the regular picture theatres, only the large theatres"
East Lynne, "see the great picture, 117 gorgeous scenes, 7000 feet of perfect photography"

Dance:
Mlle. Anna Pavlova "and a great company of matchless dancers and a complete symphony orchestra"

Lecture:
Commander Evans' lecture on Captain Scott's Last Expedition

1914/15

AMBROSE J. SMALL ERA

KISMET

To start this season with a bang Ambrose J. Small programmed the spectacle *Kismet*. The hapless actor playing the evil Wazir Mansur was thrown into a large pool of water every performance during the final act. Evil Wazir would drown, much to the delight and relief of the audience. The stage manager attempted to keep the water warmer than 60 degrees F, and no hotter than 75 degrees F, but it was difficult to maintain the temperature. It seems that the girls who were immersed in the tank at the beginning of the final act, and the Evil Wazir, often emerged from the water blue with cold.

DISRAELI

For one evening only, George Arliss the "distinguished actor" was in London to perform in *Disraeli*. A hit on Broadway in 1911, the play was still doing gangbuster business in 1914. "It all began with a talk between George Arliss and George C. Tyler over in England a couple of years ago. Mr. Arliss was complaining that he could not find a suitable vehicle, and Mr. Tyler suggested that a play written about the great statesman Disraeli, might be just the thing. So they called in playwright Louis N. Parker and the piece took shape as a dramatization of the historic incident of the purchase of the Suez Canal. It opened in Montreal with Mr. Arliss in the title role. The play, however, lacked that spark needed to capture the imaginations of its audience. Mr. Parker, Mr. Tyler

COMING!

All Next Week

MAT. WED. AND SAT.

Farewell Engagement

MAY BELL MARKS

Marks Bros. No. 1 Coy.

In All New Plays And Vaudeville

Evg. 10c., 15c., 25c.

Mat. 10c., 20c.

May Bell Marks

Actress May A. Bell Marks was featured in the house program during December 1914. She starred in seven plays in five days. "May Bell was so clever. She was very well-known in Canada." – Kitty Marks, in a 1962 interview, conducted by Grace Lydiatt Shaw (Courtesy of Jane Schmuck)

and Hugh Ford, who staged it, were about to give the whole thing up, when Mr. Parker decided to have one more try at it. He merely re-wrote one of the curtain lines and *Disraeli* immediately became, instead of a meritorious failure, a tremendous hit." (– *Stage Magazine*, August 1936, NY) George Arliss played The Right Honourable Benjamin Disraeli, and Mrs. Arliss played Lady Beaconsfield. When the play was filmed, George Arliss received a best actor Academy Award in 1928/29.

WORLD WAR I

World War I had started in August of 1914. The world did not know at that time that it would become known as "the war to end all wars." Everyone thought the conflict would be over by Christmas of 1914. By February of 1915, a play entitled *It's A Long Way To Tipperary* was on stage at London's Grand Opera House. A program ad encouraged patriotism by advertising: "Be Loyal Smoke The Allied Armies Cigar, 5 cents straight; The Triple Entente Cigar 10 cents; 3 for 25 cents."

Road Shows included:
Kismet, "the tremendous triumph that has sent playhouse thrills around the world"
Disraeli, by Louis N. Parker
Othello, by William Shakespeare
Prince of To-Night, "the tuneful musical fantasy"
The Beauty Shop, "a new musical comedy"
Martha by Day, "a new comedy"
Mutt and Jeff in Mexico, "see the big chorus of Mexican beauties, 50 people"
A Prince of Tatters, "the song-bedecked play"

It's A Long Way To Tipperary, "a play of the hour"

Stock Company:
May A. Bells Marks and the Marks Bros. No. 1 Company, "in all new plays and vaudeville"

Minstrels:
George Evans Honey Boy Minstrels

Moving Pictures:
Thirty Leagues Under the Sea, "the first and only submarine motion picture"
Martha of the Lowlands, "five reels of motion pictures"

1915/16

AMBROSE J. SMALL ERA

IT PAYS TO ADVERTISE

On November 6, 1915, *It Pays to Advertise* was on stage at London's Grand Opera House. There was a matinee and an evening performance of this sprightly farce comedy. The racy plot involved two young men with very little capital who create a demand for a brand of soap. Of course, they possessed the only recipe for the product. The play delivered lots of laughs as the pair eventually sell the trademark for $500,000 and a 51% interest in the profits of a factory for the manufacture of the soap. Besides making millions of dollars, one of the young heroes also gets the girl. The play made audiences laugh. If any Londoners missed it during this season they could catch it another season. It was still on tour in 1918.

MRS. PATRICK CAMPBELL AND *PYGMALION*

On February 5, 1916, the mercurial star Mrs. Patrick Campbell was back in London, this time as Eliza Doolittle in George Bernard Shaw's play *Pygmalion*. Mrs. Pat gave a spirited and amusing performance as the flower girl who is schooled in society's ways by Professor Higgins. Critics thought privately that as a mature woman of 50 years, Mrs. Pat was a little too old to portray the innocent flower girl, but audiences flocked to see the prima donna in the role. The play was a consistent success since its debut in 1913. It caused a sensation in London, England, because it introduced the word 'bloody' to the stage. George Bernard Shaw, writing to the New York producer, George C. Tyler, in October of

1914, gives some insight into what it was like working with Mrs. Pat: "You will find that Mrs. Patrick Campbell's changes of dress will take longer than the change of scenery. The play is very hard work for her in this way; and you must arrange her dressing accommodation in such a position as to avoid running up and down stairs. If you cannot give her a room on the stage level she will agitate for a tent; and when *she* starts agitating, don't argue but surrender at once, even if it involves rebuilding the theatre; you will find it cheaper in the long run. When you have fixed her up comfortably in this respect you can then press her if necessary to keep pace with the stage staff. If she does that, the play can be got through between 8 and 11 p.m. Mrs. Campbell wants to cut the play, partly because its length hurries her dressing and interferes

"She's superstitious all right."

*It Pays to Advertise **came complete with its own souvenir package of postcards. A production shot from this modern comedy shows that the women on stage are dressed in the height of 1915 fashion, while the men all looked dapper. (Courtesy of M. Torrance)***

with the delightful levees she holds in her dressing-room, and partly because she thinks that Mrs. Pearce and Doolittle are insufferable boors and should be cut down to two or three lines apiece." (– *Theatrical Companion to Shaw*, Pitman Publishing Co., New York, 1955)

ROBIN HOOD

The deKoven Opera Company presented the comic opera *Robin Hood* in June, 1916.

> *I went to see* Robin Hood *at the Grand Opera House and it was a hit with the audience. The score included the song 'O Promise Me', which was very popular at the time. In fact many brides chose it as their wedding song, I remember that.*
> – Miss Louise Wyatt, teacher

1916/17

AMBROSE J. SMALL ERA

THE LUCK OF THE NAVY

"I don't remember the year but I do know that during the war years I was taken to the Grand Opera House to see a wartime play called *The Luck of the Navy*. The prologue and the epilogue were done to great effect. At the top of the show, the curtains opened slowly to reveal the sea. There was a hospital ship sailing on the sea, and underneath was a submarine. The ship was blown up, and it appeared that the play's hero was also blown up. But no! The hero survived the blast. It was very exciting." – Florence Smith, former LLT board member, backstage volunteer

---

THE GRAND OPERA HOUSE

The following excerpts is taken from the 1914 London Business Association brochure. The information still applied in 1916:

> *Citizens of London have in the Grand Opera House one of the leading playhouses of Canada, and, under the ownership and control of Mr. Ambrose J. Small, it offers all of the big attractions of the road which come into the Dominion. The Grand is centrally located, being but a couple of blocks from the heart of the business district, on Richmond Street. It is operated by Mr. Small, in conjunction with his extensive chain of theatres, which is made up of all of the principal cities of Ontario, and, by reason of this fact, furnishes Londoners with a class of entertainment not surpassed anywhere.*

The main entrance of The Grand Opera House featuring the entrance doors leading into the auditorium.

The foyer of The Grand Theatre. Once theatregoers went through the first set of doors leading into the auditorium, they were in the foyer. The decorative border above the doors is visible. (Courtesy of LRAHM)

The theatre has a stage accommodation second to none on the continent, having capacity for the staging of the largest productions. Its appointments in front of the curtain line are also the equal of any house in the Dominion, and the seating accommodation is most extensive. The illumination of the theatre, its decorative effects and furnishings, are all worthy of commendation, while a staff of courteous attaches is at all times maintained.

The building is thoroughly protected against fire hazard with all appliances of the most modern kind, while the number of exits is far in excess of the requirements of the underwriters or municipal public-safety regulations. The orchestra (which is on ground level), balcony and gallery may all be speedily emptied.

The exterior of the building is of handsome design, the veneer being of a high class of red pressed brick. There is an elaborate canopy above the main entrance from Richmond

Street, affording protection to patrons of the house who come or leave by motor or other vehicle. Like all the houses of the big circuit under the guidance of Mr. Small, the local management is in the hands of a Canadian, Mr. John R. Minhinnick, a London boy, having supervision of the business of the theatre.

Mr. Small manifests a close personal interest in all of the houses of his circuit, but his especial attention is at all times very generously given to London. The Grand, therefore, secures the highest class of productions, and the newest plays on the road. The ventilation of the theatre has been very carefully arranged, and in consequence the place is always the coolest spot in summer and delightfully comfortable in the winter.

KITTY MARKS

We booked into London with Ambrose J. Small. It was a

beautiful theatre. It had a manager, a man named Minhinnick, a big man. We went over to rehearsal one morning and Minhinnick was there. He hated a stock company. He wanted a repertoire company to be in that beautiful theatre and he thought we wouldn't do any business. Ernie (Marks) couldn't bear him and I couldn't bear him, but we rehearsed. We were playing a play called The Third Degree. *We opened Monday night. The house was packed. Next day Ernie came home about noon and he was boiling mad at this Minhinnick. I guess they'd had words over our stock company playing the beautiful theatre in London. My husband wasn't in the play until the last act, Act III. Ernie was to play a stern judge and when the curtain went up on Act III he was to sit at this desk, and we were all to sit around him and he would give us our cues and we would answer him. He had a very important part. That evening he came to the dressing room and I looked around and I said: 'Ernie you've had a drink.' And he said: 'Yes, I had a drink; who wouldn't have a drink with that guy out there not wanting us to play.' We went on with* The Third Degree *and the curtain went up on the last act and Ernie sat at the desk. I looked at him, and he had one side of his face made up and not the other. Oh, I was raging. I was mad!*

– Kitty Marks, in a 1962 interview conducted by Grace Lydiatt Shaw

---

Road Shows included:	Music:
Faust, "a grand opera", The Boston English Opera Company	Andreeff's Imperial Russian Court Balalaika Orchestra
The Girl from Rector's	
Ben-Hur, "Klaw and Erlinger's stupendous international production"	Movies:
	Mothers of France, starring the divine Sarah Bernhardt

1917/18

AMBROSE J. SMALL ERA

MILITARY MELODRAMA

As World War I raged on and on, plays with a military theme were popular with the public. Many of them toured through London and played the Grand Opera House. One of these was *Seven Days' Leave*, billed as "a modern military melodrama in four acts."

VAUDEVILLE

Vaudeville was still thriving throughout the war years. Top vaudeville stars whose spots were established at the top of the bill, could earn a weekly salary of $2,500. Legitimate theatre, vaudeville and motion pictures competed furiously for the attention of theatre-goers. To keep his spirits up, one vaudevillian was moved to write the following: "The Vaudeville Artist's Creed: I believe in my profession, in my act, and in myself. I believe in sunshine and smiles, laughter and jest, beauty, grace and song. I believe that the chap who makes a nation forget its griefs is greater than he who leads it into battle. I believe that the Great Stage Manager is not without a sense of humour, himself, or he would not have bestowed it on so many of his own. I believe the best about my fellow players – the worst about those who run them down. I believe that when the last big bill is made up those who make good here needn't worry much about their "spot" up there."
– Herbert Moore, *Billboard Magazine*, October 9, 1915

The origin of the word vaudeville has been given as "voix de ville," or "songs of the city streets." The birth year of vaudeville,

An interior shot of The Grand Opera House showing the orchestra pit, the four boxes on house right, part of the first balcony and some of the gods. Footlights are clearly visible, ringing the front of the stage. The theatre is brightly lit by dozens of electric bulbs bordering the proscenium arch. (Courtesy of LRAHM)

the North American equivalent of England's Music Hall, is generally accepted as 1881, when Tony Pastor brought together the finer elements of the dime shows, burlesques (or caricatures) and beer hall acts. At his theatre in New York City, Pastor invented a variety show that was clean, or in other words, was suitable fare for the whole family, not just men. He lured female audience members with ladies' nights, and with gifts of flowers, dolls and even sewing machines. He featured 35 acts on an average bill, and made sure that each act succeeded the other without pause, thereby eliminating the opportunity for customers to wander out of the theatre. Pastor's innovations earned him the nickname "The King of Vaudeville." Pastor died in 1908. By that time, vaudeville had become big business, with lots of money at stake and voracious producers vying for the best acts and the most income at the box office. Partners Edward F. Albee and Benjamin F. Keith monopolized vaudeville in New York City and across North America in the early years of the 20th century. These powerful producers made sure that if there was money to be made from struggling performers, and from dedicated audiences, it flowed into their pockets.

Albee wrote about the constant need to introduce fresh new acts onto the vaudeville bills: "Of course the public thinks that we are cold to beginners. But that isn't the case. We must constantly have fresh people, new acts. If it were easy to obtain actors and actresses, we would not have to maintain a force of representatives, not unlike baseball scouts who tour the world over, and count themselves lucky if a trip of thousands of miles results in one really good act being added to our lists. There isn't a continent that our men don't visit in the search for talent. At times we find it in our very backyard. At others we have to reach out to the boundaries of civilization. In either case we welcome real talent with open arms. Of course we are besieged by aspirants who have no talent and never will have talent. But we cannot afford to turn down anybody without a hearing. The person to whom we might deny a chance to show his goods might be the greatest potential headliner of all time." (– *Collier's Weekly*, May 1, 1926)

Keith wrote about the type of entertainment he could comfortably promote: "Two things I determined would prevail. One was that my fixed policy of cleanliness and order should be continued, and the other that the stage show must be free from vulgarisms and coarseness of any kind, so that the house and entertainment would directly appeal to the support of ladies and children – in fact that my playhouse must be as homelike an entertainment resort as it was possible to make it. In the early days of my business career, many worthy but mistaken people ridiculed the idea of a clean and respectable house and entertainment being conducted at the price of admission (only 10 cents), but I successfully demonstrated that such a thing was possible."
– Benjamin Franklin Keith, *National Magazine*, November 1898

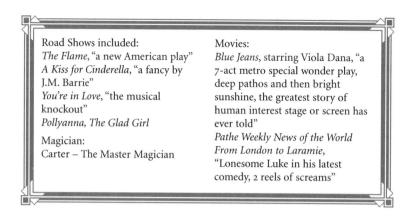

Road Shows included:
The Flame, "a new American play"
A Kiss for Cinderella, "a fancy by J.M. Barrie"
You're in Love, "the musical knockout"
Pollyanna, The Glad Girl

Magician:
Carter – The Master Magician

Movies:
Blue Jeans, starring Viola Dana, "a 7-act metro special wonder play, deep pathos and then bright sunshine, the greatest story of human interest stage or screen has ever told"
Pathe Weekly News of the World From London to Laramie, "Lonesome Luke in his latest comedy, 2 reels of screams"

JOHN SAUNDERS

So many people have no idea how much fun it is to be in a play. If it hadn't been for my dad, John Saunders, who was the stage manager at The Grand for over 50 years, I probably wouldn't have been so involved, but when a theatre company visiting from England, or any other touring group for that matter, came to town, and they needed a few extras for small parts, Dad would come home and say: 'Do you want to be in a play?' Well, of course I couldn't resist, and I have many wonderful memories of those companies. I started when I was only about eight years old. I have never lost my love for it all.
– Dorothy Westhead, London Little Theatre (LLT) actress

1918/19

AMBROSE J. SMALL ERA

ANNA PAVLOVA

Londoners flocked to see Anna Pavlova dance on the Grand Opera House stage this season. A woman of beauty and genius, Anna Pavlova developed a devoted legion of fans during her travels around the world. She was widely celebrated and deeply loved. Often her curtain calls took longer than the dance she had just performed because her audiences did not wish this enchanting and beautiful dancer to disappear into the wings. A few years earlier she had given some insight into her on-stage wardrobe:

The tutu? I like it and I don't. Certainly, the short skirt is the ideal one for a dancer. In the tutu one can best show off the technique and art of the dance. The legs are free; every movement can clearly be seen. Every muscle's movement must be correct. All the movements are exact, precise – it is impossible to give way to any sudden caprice. The pattern one established must remain as it is. In general the dress should suit the character of the dance. There are dances which can only be danced in the short skirt because in these, lightness and a freedom from gravity are shown off to their best advantage. The tutu is like a butterfly's wing. It flaps and flutters round the body and swings harmoniously with every movement. I try to individualize the dances as far as possible, as well as ensuring that the outer appurtenances are suited to the content. Today there are so many kinds of dance – Egyptian, Indian, peasant dances – whose full charm is expressed by the costume.
– Anna Pavlova, My Little Ballet Skirt, 1914

Born in St. Petersburg, Russia, in 1881, Pavlova's training took place at the Imperial Ballet School. She brought her famous *Swan Dance* to the Grand Opera House in January of 1911. With her was the Imperial Russian Ballet Orchestra. Bringing the glamour of Czarist Russia with her, the 1911 stop in London was part of the ballerina's first tour of North America. Pavlova left Russia permanently in 1914, to make her home in England. She toured the world constantly, wishing to carry her classical ballet to all corners of the world. She was still touring in 1930, but in January of 1931 at the age of 50 she died in France. Pavlova's dancing combined the spiritual and the dramatic, making it difficult, if not impossible, to forget her once you had seen her dance.

Pavlova, all Nations are Thine

Pavlova, all nations are thine,
No country thy country alone.
Terpsichore who shall confine?
Has genius a land or a zone?
You have danced at the foot of a throne;
Republics have worshiped your shrine –
Pavlova, all nations are thine,
No country thy country alone.

Pavlova, O dancer divine,
Thou art not one woman alone.
For though art all women – the wine

Two portraits of Anna Pavlova, "the consummate artist," taken from a souvenir booklet entitled Pictures and Paragraphs, *celebrating the international dance star. (Courtesy of Jane Schmuck)*

That all of life's lovers have known.
The love in thy eyes that has shone
Another has looked into mine –
Pavlova, O dancer divine,
Thou art not one woman alone.
(Source: booklet of poems published in 1913 by Douglas Malloch)

ESCAPIST FARE

A Daughter of the Sun was on stage on September 27 and 28, 1918. Escapist fare at its best, this play was set on the Hawaiian Islands. Playgoers were treated to a group of Hawaiian singers who accompanied themselves on ukeleles. The villain (a Jap, as described in the program) plans to seize the beautiful islands, but his plot is thwarted by Americans living on the island. Of course there is a love story. A young American doctor loves an island woman whom he refers to as an Hawaiian butterfly. The *London Free Press* reviewer pronounced "the scenic effects are most impressive, all the scenes being striking for their novelty." (– Fanfan, *London Free Press* September 27, 1918) Perhaps the scenery was more impressive than either the plot or the acting.

GRACE BLACKBURN

"Fanfan" was the pen name of Grace Blackburn, the *London Free Press* theatre reviewer. Miss Blackburn had joined the newspaper staff in 1900. One of nine Blackburn children, her brother, Walter Josiah Blackburn, was president of the London Free Press Publishing Company. Grace's keen love of drama developed during her childhood. In the Blackburn home on Albert Street, London, the young people of the household tested their dramatic ability in amateur theatricals. Later Grace Blackburn was one of the instigators of the London Drama League, a leading amateur company in the city. She produced some successful plays in London, and was also noted for her talent at building sets. Londoners were fortunate to have such an experienced, well travelled and insightful reviewer for so many years. Grace Blackburn died in March of 1928, the whimsical pen name "Fanfan" was retired.

WARTIME NOTATION

On October 10, 1918, a musical comedy romance entitled *The Kiss Burglar* was on stage, complete with its 16-girl chorus. This notation in the program was typical for wartime: "All male members of this organization have fulfilled their obligations to their respective governments." This assured all those mothers, sisters, wives and girlfriends in the audience that while their men were putting their lives at risk overseas, the actors on stage had done their duty. The war had gone on for too long. But Armistice was only a month away.

Road Shows included:
The Daughter of the Sun, "the story of a Hawaiian butterfly"
The Pierrot Players, "the all-English musical comedy revue, all music, songs and comedy"
The Kiss Burglar, "smacking musical comedy romance"
Daddy Long Legs, "the most fascinating comedy of the day"
Furs and Frills, "musical comedy success"

General Post, "the social event of the season, gala military night"
Chin-Chin, "greatest musical comedy, a musical fantasy"

Movies:
We Should Worry, "a sparkling impish comedy-drama"
Pathe Weekly News
A Pair of Cupids, starring Francis X. Bushman and Beverly Bayne, "delightful co-stars"

1919/20

END OF THE AMBROSE J. SMALL ERA
BEGINNING OF THE TRANS-CANADA THEATRE ERA

A.J. SMALL DISAPPEARS

In August of 1919 Ambrose J. Small was corresponding with a potential buyer for his chain of theatres. Trans-Canada Theatres Limited, headquartered in Montreal, was interested in buying them. In a letter dated September 5, 1919, Small mentioned to the recipient, George F. Driscoll of Montreal, that "the principal consideration for my retiring from present activities was to be relieved of all responsibility." Small wanted the transaction to take place as fast as possible, and had cited December 1 as his desired deadline. The buyer suggested December 15, but, in the end, the transaction was finalized on December 2. What was it that prompted Small to unload his theatre real estate? And was there any significance to Small's desire to finish the deal on December 1? Especially since we now know that he disappeared on December 2, never to be seen or heard from again? There are no answers to these intriguing questions. Some contributing factors to his desire to sell may have included the August/September 1919 strike by Actors' Equity members, which put producers and presenters like Small on tenterhooks, fearing that the 1919/20 season might be a financial nightmare. Or perhaps he was tired of surprises that cut into his bottom line, like the unexpected yet compulsory closure of theatres in October 1918, when the Spanish flu epidemic spread throughout the world. Perhaps the growing popularity of motion pictures was a threat to Small. Or, perhaps he had simply lost his appetite for the cutthroat business of presenting entertainment. Maybe Small wanted to retire to pursue his love of gambling, or take up golf. Or, and this is pure speculation, perhaps Small was in debt and this forced him to put his real estate on the market in order to get his hands on some money, fast. Whatever the reasons, he and his lawyer, Londoner E.W.M. Flock, spent August through November negotiating the sale of Small's theatres.

EUGENE LOCKHART

During the first week of September 1919, Eugene Lockhart, advertised as "pianolog and travesty," was on stage at the Grand Opera House. He grew up in the Clarence Street and Queens Avenue neighbourhood in London, Ontario. At the time of his 1919 appearance on The Grand's stage, he was well known as the lyricist of the song "The World is Waiting for the Sunrise." Later in his career, he went by the name of Gene Lockhart. Between the years 1935 and 1957, he found success in Hollywood. He appeared in such films as *Miracle on 34th Street*, *His Girl Friday* and in the film version of the hit musical *Carousel*. His daughter, actress June Lockhart, is best remembered for her role as the mother in the television series *Lassie*.

VAUDEVILLE

B.F. Keith's Big Time Acts were featured at The Grand in late September, 1919. Vaudeville was alive and well, and still under the control of the Keith and Albee Co., efficiently run by Edward F.

Albee, since the death in 1914 of B.F. Keith. There were five acts on the bill this month: Chas. and Sadie MacDonald & Co. (a comedy sketch); Swain's Cockatoos (a novelty from bird land); The Carr Trio (an offering of varieties); Fred S. Paine (King of the xylophone); and the headlining Sam Yee Troupe of Chinese Sensational and Novelty Artists.

The most famous vaudeville theatre was the Palace Theatre in New York City, opened by Keith in 1913. A vaudevillian who played The Palace had arrived. Vaudeville enjoyed popularity until the late 1920s. Radio was one contributing factor to vaudeville's decline and death in the early 1930s. "Radio offered a problem similar to nothing ever previously encountered. Material had to be changed with every performance. The good old days, when a standard act could play for years without altering a line or changing a gag, were gone. The small, and the big towns, which formerly it took two years to cover completely, now were covered in two minutes."
– George Jessel, writing in *Billboard Magazine*, 1932

THE DUMBELLS

With plush drops, costumes and special lighting equipment, the Dumbells had a grand opening at London's Grand Opera House, the site of their postwar premiere show entitled *Biff, Bing, Bang*. The historic night was September 29, 1919. The curtain went up at 8:15 p.m. and the audience was filled to capacity with war veterans and their young wives and sweethearts. The night was a triumphant success for the ex-servicemen of the Dumbell troop. The theatre's rafters echoed with thunderous applause. Ambrose J. Small was too impatient to wait for theatre manager John Minhinnick to send a show report to Toronto, so Small telephoned London's Grand before the first act was over. Mr. Small stayed glued to the telephone throughout the remainder of the evening, enjoying London's enthusiastic response to a risky show.

I am the sole remaining survivor of the Dumbells company that played London's Grand. We opened our North American tour there in September of 1919 and went on to play in many places across Canada. We also played in towns and cities throughout the United States, including a season on Broadway. I well remember how impressed we were with the huge stage area at The Grand. Also we found the manager, John R. Minhinnick, one of the best that we came in contact with on our tour. We were playing at the Grand Theatre in Toronto when Ambrose J. Small mysteriously disappeared.
– Jack McLaren of Goderich, in an August, 1978 letter to the editor, *London Free Press*

Ambrose J. Small saw potential in the Dumbells. Despite the risks of producing the show, he promised to give them a tryout at one of his theatres if the director, Merton Plunkett, could enlarge the cast and put in more musical numbers. Plunkett raised an additional $12,000 from his uncles, and the show premiered in London, Ontario. Small's gamble paid off. Dumbell cast members included Jack McLaren, Ross Hamilton, Alan Murray, Bill Tennant, Bert Langley, Jerry Brayford, Leonard Young, Jack Ayre and Ted Charters. Just one of the many highlights of the show was Red Newman's performance of the song "Oh, It's a Lovely War." Newman appeared in a bedraggled Private's uniform, topped off with a red wig. At one point in the song, he started tearing at his clothes, searching for imaginary cooties. The veterans in the audience instantly recognized themselves in this scene. They roared with laughter as they recognized themselves in Red Newman's character. Only now, in peacetime, could they take their bad memories of life in the trenches at the front, and turn them into good ones. The Dumbells went on to make $80,000 in the first few years on the road. Before disbanding in 1932, the

Dumbells played 12 cross-Canada tours, staging a new show every year. They had a good run. The Dumbells made Canadian theatre history.

KITTY MARKS DESCRIBES A.J. SMALL

"Small was a very good friend, if he liked you, but a very vindictive man if he didn't like you. Now, he didn't like it if you went over his head. Supposing that there was a time open in London that we'd want to fill in, and Ernie Marks would write [to] him for an engagement. If he didn't book us he could be very, very nasty. And we knew Mr. John Doughty (Small's long-serving secretary and booking manager) very well, although I never cared much for him, but he really had nothing to do with us. Only, he hated A.J. Small, hated him. He used to discuss him with Ernie. He hated A.J. Small. Hated the work he did for him. But Small wouldn't give us the stage time we wanted. When he wouldn't give us the time we wanted, after a while we saw his judgement in that, and Ernie would go to him and thank him. And Small would say: 'Well if I had let you go on then, you could have lost your accounts, but you see, I saved you, and you made money.'

I remember that I was shopping in Toronto and I had quite a few parcels and Ernie was going up to see Small, and he asked me if I'd like to go up to the office. I said no, I'd sit on the steps at the old Grand Opera House. I sat down and at once the door opened and this little fellow came in, Small. He wasn't a big man, and he had a moustache. He said: 'Who do we have here?' And I said: 'Don't you remember me, Mr. Small?' And he said: 'Oh my God, it's you Kitty Marks! What are you doing sitting down here in the dark?' 'Well, I was too tired to go upstairs, Mr. Small, and I thought I'd wait here for Ernie.' 'Well, I see you're spending Ernie's money,' he said. And he went off. Just shortly after that he was murdered. And to this day I still think he was murdered in that theatre right in Toronto. And I think the man that murdered him was the man who didn't like him. Ernie and I often discussed it; his body being put in the furnace and that's why they never found him. That's what we believe. But Small was awfully kind to Ernie and me." – Kitty Marks, star of the Ernie Marks Co., in a 1962 CBC Radio interview, conducted by Grace Lydiatt Shaw

THE DISAPPEARANCE OF AMBROSE J. SMALL

It is well documented that December 2, 1919, was the date that Ambrose J. Small disappeared. However, the general public learned about the disappearance only after the *Toronto Daily Star* newspaper ran this item in their January 3, 1920, edition: "The whereabouts of Mr. Ambrose J. Small, one of Canada's most prominent theatrical men, is causing gravest concern to his relatives and business associates. Mr. Small was last seen in Toronto on December 2, 1919, after he had closed the sale of his vast theatrical holdings to the Trans-Canada Theatres Limited, and had received a very large cheque as initial payment. The *Star* interviewed Mr. E.W.M. Flock of London, Mr. Small's attorney, by long distance telephone this morning who said: 'I left Mr. Small in his office about 5:30 p.m. on Tuesday, December 2 and further than that I know nothing about him. He had closed up the sale of his Grand Opera circuit, six houses in all, to the Trans-Canada Theatres Ltd. He closed with me, as his solicitor, later that day. He received the initial payment, which was a large sum of money and it was immediately deposited. I was with Mr. Small about an hour at his office and he was never more pleasant or genial and was full of pep and vim. I told him I might be down to see him the following week. I have been to Toronto two or three times since then, but have been told that he was not at the office. As in cases of this kind newspapers are invaluable in locating a man, I see no reason why I should not tell you what I have.'" The large sum of

The south wall of London's Grand Opera House, looking down the alley toward Richmond Street. The owner of a local fruit stand reported that he had noticed a man dragging a heavy sack down this alley shortly after Small's disappearance. As the fruit seller watched, the mystery man allegedly shoved the object in the sack through the window of the theatre's furnace room. A theatre stagehand later reported that on the evening following this alleged sighting of strange activities, The Grand's furnace belched out some unusually pungent smoke. The police, who searched London's Grand Theatre as part of their investigation into the mysterious disappearance of Ambrose J. Small, found no bones or other clues after sifting through the ashes in the theatre's furnace. It's a good story. (National Archives of Canada, Ottawa #203813)

money which Small received on December 2 from Trans-Canada Theatres Limited was $1 million. Furthermore, if Ambrose J. Small had not disappeared so inconveniently on December 2, the condition of sale also included $750,000 to be paid in equal, consecutive annual payments of $37,500 each (without interest) for 20 years. If Ambrose J. Small did stage his own, very successful, dis-

appearing act, he walked away from the $750,000 and he took none of the $1 million, which stayed safely in the bank.

My father was sent from his office in Calgary, Alberta, to Toronto, Ontario, to personally hand the $1 million cheque to Mr. Small. He did this, I believe, at the King Edward Hotel in downtown Toronto. As Vice-President of Trans-Canada Theatre Co., R. Jeffery Lydiatt was the appointed courier. The Trans-Canada Theatre Company was a booking agent and wanted to book road shows from England and Australia into Canadian theatres. By purchasing Mr. Small's chain of Ontario theatres, Trans-Canada purchased their first real estate holdings, and at the same time helped itself to complete the links in its cross-Canada theatre chain.
– Grace Lydiatt Shaw, writer, broadcaster

And what of Mrs. Theresa Small? It was not she who alerted the police, the press or the public to the fact that her husband was missing. When interviewed, she claimed that her husband "was in the arms of a designing woman."

Lack of evidence pointing to assault and murder, suicide, or a planned change of identity and disappearance by Small himself, has led to speculation about his disappearance that has continued. To this day his fate is unknown.

JOHN MINHINNICK

After the disappearance of Mr. Small, it fell to John Minhinnick to get on with business at London's Grand Opera House. It was a time of great uncertainty for Mr. Minhinnick, but he soldiered on and kept The Grand's doors open, despite the mysterious disappearance of the man who for so long had been his employer. Despite the fact that Trans-Canada Theatres Ltd. took ownership of London's

Grand Opera House on December 2, 1919, the April 1920 house program still displayed "A.J. Small Sole Proprietor" in print.

LONDON DRAMA LEAGUE

In early 1920, seeds were sown for what would soon become London Little Theatre. Members of London's Women's Press Club, including such theatre buffs as Frances Beatrice Taylor, Grace Blackburn and Winnifred Dance Hutchinson, sponsored a play. This sponsorship spawned the London Drama League (LDL), formed in 1921. For some 15 years, the LDL fostered amateur theatre in London.

MAXINE ELLIOTT

The play *Lord and Lady Algy* was on stage in April, 1920, starring William Faversham and Maxine Elliott. Miss Elliott was an incredibly beautiful woman who had enjoyed a successful stage career since the early days of the century. Besides beauty, she was said to have charm and warmth. She was not known for her brilliant talent, but she could out-sob any other actress of her day. This trick kept drawing in the customers, and sending them away satisfied, after they had had a good cry in their seats, watching their heroine triumph over tragedy.

Road Shows included:
Biff, Bing, Bang, the Dumbells "in their original overseas revue"
Seven Days' Leave
Lord and Lady Algy
The Better 'Ole, "a comedy with music, a fragment from France in two explosions, seven splinters, and a short gas attack"
P.B.I., or Mademoiselle of Bully Grenay, a four-act Canadian war play by W.L. McGeary,

M.C. Private P.P.C.L.I.
The Mikado, Gilbert and Sullivan

Vaudeville:
B.F. Keith's Big Time Acts

Movies:
Revue A La Carte, "6 classy artists in a miniature musical comedy feature
The Hoodlum, starring Mary Pickford, "the picture of 1,000 laughs"

TRANS-CANADA THEATRE LIMITED ERA

1920-1924

The Guy Lombardo band on stage at the Grand Theatre. At the far left is young Guy Lombardo with his violin. Harry Hadwin is at the piano, Lebert Lombardo is on drums, and Carmen Lombardo is on sax. Francis Henry holds the banjo. The other people were members of a vaudeville act which the Lombardo quintet accompanied on stage. In 1919, Guy, Carmen and Lebert had quit school to pursue careers as professional musicians. (Courtesy of The Guy Lombardo Music Centre, London)

1920/21

TRANS-CANADA THEATRE LIMITED ERA

HARRY BLACKSTONE

Blackstone the Magician was on stage in September of 1920. He remarked that Ambrose J. Small could not be dead because he had seen Small gambling in Mexico. Soon stories of Ambrose J. Small sightings would fade away, replaced by ghost stories of Ambrose J. Small haunting London's Grand Opera House.

Harry Blackstone's specialties were the Floating Light Bulb and the Dancing Handkerchief. Despite being short of stature, and having a minor speech impediment, Blackstone was a powerful performer. On stage he appeared to have great height and he was able to project his voice to the back of the second balcony. On this occasion Blackstone performed his popular number "Tanzar, The Girl of the Air." Using as many adjectives as possible this act was described thus: "The great hypnotic scene. The most daring and bewildering illusion. By far the most difficult achievement ever attempted. Absolutely new in principle. The dream in mid-air of the dainty Princess surpasses the fabled miraculous tales of levitation that come out of India. It is the profoundest achievement of either ancient or modern magic. Its perfection represents ten years of patient research and study and the expenditure of many thousands of dollars. The results of these labours is a masterpiece of magic." Somehow Blackstone had to top this with his Grand Finale, entitled "A Bachelor's Dream."

CHU CHIN CHOW

Chu Chin Chow, loosely based on "The Arabian Nights and The Forty Thieves" stories, was a smash hit in London, England, at the end of World War I. A touring production came to London's Grand Theatre in mid-September 1920, and the program boasted that it was "a musical extravaganza of the Orient, now in its fifth year at His Majesty's Theatre, London, and still playing there to capacity." The local audience was asked to duly note: "The panoramic curtain showing a view of ancient Bagdad was painted by the Harker Brothers of London and the screen is an exact copy of the famous Chinese screen presented to the late Lord Kitchener by the former Empress of China." The play was named for the main character "Abu Hasan, the robber sheyk, alias Chu Chin Chow." The company was huge. Besides 25 speaking parts, the program lists personnel of the ensemble: Javanese Fanners, Bermese Dancers, Desert Dancers, Jewel Dancers, Dervish Dancers, Nile Girls, Circassian slaves, Turkestan slaves, Indian slaves, Pot girls, Fruit girls, Mannequins in the Fashion Show, Carrier girls, robbers, peddlers, water carriers, and wedding guests. How they all fit backstage at The Grand, and how they all made their marks on the stage, is anyone's guess.

MOVIE TECHNOLOGY WITH STAGE CRAFT

Madonnas and Men burst onto The Grand's stage for the entire week of December 20th. "The most brilliant, stupendous, daring presentation ever attempted anywhere. A thrilling story of the orgies of Rome, to the present day nightlife in New York. The Barnum & Bailey of all picture presentations, combining for the first time on screen and stage." Movie technology was used in combination with stage craft. Horses on stage was nothing new to Grand Theatre patrons, but this event promised "4 Live Plunging

Snow White Arabian Horses" driven by "Live Dare-Devil Drivers at Breakneck Speed Right on the Grand Stage!!!" Surely something not to be missed.

Road Shows included:
Chu Chin Chow, by Oscar Asche
Twin Beds, by Margaret Mayo and Salisbury Field
The Law Divine, by H.V. Esmond
The Merchant of Venice, *Much Ado About Nothing*, by William Shakespeare
The School for Scandal, by Richard Brinsley Sheridan
The Prince and the Pauper, from Mark Twain
The Country Fair, "see live horses in big racing scene"

The Only Way, starring John Martin-Harvey

Magician:
Blackstone, the World's Master Magician

Minstrels:
Herbert's Greater Minstrels, the Peer of all Minstrel Shows

Movies:
High and Dizzy, starring Harold Lloyd
Pollyanna, starring Mary Pickford
The Round-Up, starring Fatty Arbuckle

1921/22

TRANS-CANADA THEATRE LIMITED ERA

FEDORA

Marie Lohr was on a tour in the play *Fedora*. When she played The Grand, Fanfan attempted to explain the plot to her readers: "The Russian Princess Fedora Romazova is betrothed to a society rake, Count Vladimir, and he is mysteriously murdered by Count Ipanoff, as Fedora thinks, for political reasons. She vows to track the murderer, give him up to justice, or if not, kill him with her own hands. How she tracks Ipanoff, how she finds him, how she loves him, how she betrays him, how revenge turns on her and rends her – it is the task of the dramatist to tell. Emotion is pressed down and running over. The denouement is as unexpected as it is fine…A large and enthusiastic audience, every member of whom listened to Marie Lohr and her company with delight…At the end Miss Lohr was presented with a splendid bunch of yellow mums by the London Drama League." – Fanfan, *London Free Press*, October 1921

HARRY TATE

Hullo, Canada arrived at the Grand Theatre for a two-day run in November, 1921. The revue travelled complete with the "Hullo, Canada Beauty Chorus." Its star, Harry Tate, was known as "Great Britain's funniest comedian," and in reviewing the performance Fanfan had this to say: "Tate's fun for the most part, is of the imperturbable order. Mockery, quiz, banter, buffoonery, tomfoolery, skip of the tongue, raillery, travesty - nothing disturbs

The Grand Theatre as it looked during the 1921/22 season. (Courtesy of: The J.J. Talman Regional Collection, the D.B. Weldon Library, The University of Western Ontario, London, ON)

the whimsically solemn face of Harry Tate. He says the funniest things and remains face blank in the saying of them. He performs prodgies of preposterousness and never winks an eyelash. Humour as dry as this is thirst-provoking." (– Fanfan, *London Free Press*, November 9, 1921)

WAITING IN LINE

It was always big news at Princess Avenue School when there was a new play on at The Grand, more so than a movie. We would take a second lunch with us, eat it in Victoria Park after classes, then hang out in front of St. Paul's Cathedral. When people started lining up in the alley, next to the theatre, we would join the line to purchase 25 cent tickets to the gods. We would be waiting for hours. I had some great times waiting in line, because all my classmates were with me.
– Edna French, Londoner

POST-WAR THEATRE

Memories of the Great War were still very fresh in the public's mind. Grand Theatre flyers told patrons they could enjoy motion pictures "at pre-war prices." In her review for the play, *Smilin' Through*, Fanfan ruminated about the effects of the war: "Of all the things that came out of the war none is so precious as the new light men got on death and on the closeness of the so-called spiritual and the so-called material world. In that sense, *Smilin' Through* cannot be called a war play, although one of the characters is a war hero and the denouement of the story turns upon the fact that he is wounded and shell shocked and too much battered about perhaps for any comfort save that of an old English country doctor and a very loving Irish girl. Jane Cowl is the personification of radiant girlhood, Irish girlhood, with the slip of the brogue and the tongue and a wit that draws one after her as

though the words she spoke were magic. No creature more adorable in her frankness and her fascination has moved across our stage this season. Miss Cowl won the admiration of her audience, and its sincere affection. Bravo!" (–Fanfan, *London Free Press*, March, 1922)

TRANS-CANADA THEATRES, LTD., Montreal, Canada.
Sole Owners and Managers.
J. R. MINHINNICK, Resident Manager.

Road Shows included:
Hullo, Canada, Albert De Courville's first Canadian Revue
Three Live Ghosts, by Frederic S. Isham
Hamlet, Romeo and Juliet, The Taming of the Shrew, The Merchant of Venice by William Shakespeare, starring Walter Hampden
Just Suppose, by A. E. Thomas
The Winnipeg Kiddies, "World's Greatest Juvenile Road Show" (all children are under 14)
The Title, by Arnold Bennett
Mutt & Jeff in Chinatown
The Marionettes, by Pierre Wolff
Bringing Up Father in Wall Street, by Nat LaRoy and Edward Hutchison
Dumbells' Revue of 1922

Entertainer:
Sir Harry Lauder

Local Production:
Billeted, a farce in three acts, produced by London's Western University

Movies:
Way Down East, "elaborated by Mr. D.W. Griffith from the stage play by Lottie Blair Parker" starring Lillian Gish
The Three Musketeers, starring Douglas Fairbanks, "his master picture"
The Four Horsemen of the Apocalypse

Music:
Ameltia Galli-Curci, the World's Greatest Singer

1922/23

TRANS-CANADA THEATRE LIMITED ERA

RUTH ST. DENIS

Under the leadership of dancers Ruth St. Denis and Ted Shawn, the Denishawn Dancers, based in the United States, toured the world in the 1920s. When The Grand hosted the Denishawn Dancers, the company included Martha Graham, a very young, very talented young dancer. In her autobiography Martha Graham writes about her mentor, Ruth St. Denis: "She was a goddess figure and a deeply religious being, but she was also a performer. Once, when we were watching her in an East Indian ballet, she dropped a rose. We thought it was an accident, but it was deliberate. The fact that she decided to drop the rose at that point…well, I was utterly beguiled by it. It was completely planned. I learned that it is the planning of those little things that sometimes makes the magic, the real magic. Miss Ruth had a great love of the body, of beauty, and a knowledge of things not generally known in the dance world." Martha Graham reveals the hazards of too many one-night stands, too much touring across North America: "Miss Ruth's mind was always on other things. Particularly (the) evening in Detroit, when in response to a standing ovation, she walked to the footlights, thanked the audience at great length and said, 'For the rest of my performing days I will always keep in my heart, in memory of this reception of me, a special place for the wonderful people of Chicago.'" (– Martha Graham, *Blood Memory, An Autobiography*)

Scenes from **Blossom Time** *as they appeared in the souvenir program for the play's run at the Grand Theatre, January, 1922. The story was a fabricated account of the life and work of Hungarian-born composer Franz Schubert (b. 1797 – d. 1828). The young musician is sponsored by wealthy arts patron Herr Krantz who happens to have three attractive daughters: Mitzi, Kitzi and Fritzi. Schubert falls for Mitzi. Audiences of the time knew how it all turned out because numerous touring companies took the production across North America. (Courtesy of Jane Schmuck)*

Another member of the Denishawn Dancers was Louise Brooks. Soon after her appearance at The Grand, Brooks went to Hollywood where she found fame in silent movies.

THE BAT

The Bat was a spine-tingling hit on Broadway when it opened in 1920, and was a popular attraction at The Grand when it arrived in March, 1923. The basic plot concerned a group of people in a spooky house. More specifically the story concerned an older single woman who rents an isolated home of a man who is dead, or is he? Stolen bank funds are hidden in the house. Frightening and unexplained occurrences take place. A masked figure is spotted in the shadows of the house. When the woman hires a detective to get to the bottom of the goings-on, other people arrive who want to get their hands on the money, and the fun continues.

ROBIN HOOD

The Grand was proud to announce that Douglas Fairbanks' motion picture *Robin Hood* was coming for the entire week of March 26, 1923. "Imagine all the big spectacles you have ever seen; all the great climaxes over which you have thrilled; the big moments of the best plays you have witnessed; the high spots of the world's greatest dramas, then you will have a faint idea of the sheer beauty and colossal magnitude of this production. It's Fairbanks as never before! And to think that Londoners are enabled to witness this cinema wonder of wonders. At popular prices. Cast of 3,000." The entire lower floor of The Grand was priced at 75 cents a seat.

Road Shows included:
Aida by Verdi, *Madame Butterfly,* by Puccini, *Carmen,* by Bizet, *Pagliacci,* by Leoncavallo, *Tosca,* by Puccini, all produced by the De Feo Grand Opera Company
The Intimate Strangers, by Booth Tarkington
Majorlaine, adapted from Louis N. Parker
The Bat, by Mary Roberts Reinhart and Avery Hopwood
The Dover Road, by A. A. Milne
Blossom Time, libretto by Dorothy Donnelly

Carry-On, the Dumbells
The Card, with Laddie Cliff, "the Idol of the London Music Hall"

Movies:
Dr. Jack, starring Harold Lloyd
Robin Hood, starring Douglas Fairbanks

Magician:
Thurston, the Great Magician in the Wonder Show of the Universe

Dance:
Ruth St. Denis and Ted Shawn with the Denishawn Dancers

1923/24

TRANS-CANADA THEATRE LIMITED ERA ENDS/ FAMOUS PLAYERS ERA BEGINS

PROGRAM NOTE

Management at The Grand felt compelled to run this program note: "Patrons are respectfully asked to keep their seats until the curtain drops on the last act. This courtesy is due those who want to see and enjoy the entire performance." It seems that early-leavers were more of a problem than latecomers.

GEORGE M. COHAN

Little Nellie Kelly, George M. Cohan's hit, played The Grand in February 1924. A huge hit on Broadway, Cohan's Nellie is the daughter of a policeman and she is courted by two men; one is a polished, wealthy playboy; the other a wisecracking boy from the Bronx who has, of course, no money but a heart of pure gold. Cohan acknowledged the formulaic and cliched plot himself. He also understood that audiences of the time were onto the formula. So he used a device whereby the characters talked to the audience about the plot just at the time it became predictable, and they promised to speed things up. Critics didn't know how to define the show; it wasn't a revue, nor was it a conventional musical comedy, it had a bit of drama, a bit of comic pertness, a bit of mystery, music ran through the whole show and characters burst into dance numbers frequently. All this was served up with a large dollop of love. It was great fun and audiences loved it. George M. Cohan, the ultimate song-and-dance man, died in 1942. In 1959 a bronze statue of Cohan was erected in Times Square in New York City, at Broadway at 46th Street.

AN APPEAL TO FEMININE PATRONS

Trans-Canada Theatres collapsed in 1924, still owing money to the estate of Ambrose J. Small. The Grand was purchased by Canadian Famous Players Theatre (the Canadian theatrical arm of Paramount Pictures in the United States). London's downtown movie theatre, the Capitol, was also owned by Famous Players. The Grand's new owners found it more profitable to accept a small fee from other London movie houses to keep The Grand dark, in order to limit competition for the movie-going dollar.

Long-serving Grand Theatre manager John R. Minhinnick had been in the business enough years to know that something had to change. He surveyed the house, did the math and realized that The Grand's seats were not filling up as it once had. Hoping to stem the red ink, he ran this letter in a January 1924 house program:

Dear Feminine Patrons: First off, accept my sincere thanks and keen appreciation of your highly esteemed patronage. I hope you enjoy the entertainment; it was created soley for that purpose. But, why shouldn't there be several hundred more of you in attendance each day? I'll tell you why there isn't; it's because you thoughtlessly kept it a secret from your lady friends that there is offered such a wonderful program at the bargain price you pay for your ticket. So now, here's what I beg of you to do: let each lady here today consider herself as a committee of one to inform one or more lady friends of the delightful afternoons you spend here in The Grand. Tell them of the gorgeous wardrobe, the clean fun, the pretentiously staged musical numbers and the fact that the shows appearing at The Grand are the very same companies that play in New York,

This photo was taken in May of 1924 and shows Richmond Street as it curved north from Dundas Street. At the upper left-hand corner of the picture is the large vertical keyhole marquee indicating the Grand Theatre. (Courtesy of The J.J. Talman Regional Collection, D.B. Weldon Library, The University of Western Ontario, London, ON)

Chicago, Philadelphia, Cleveland, Baltimore, Washington – in fact in all the really big cities of the U.S. and that by long odds the entertainment you buy here at a bargain price at matinees is far and above in quality and quantity than that which is offered by any other theatre. Now, dear lady, you knew all these things before I called your attention to them – the thing is, tell your own lady friends so that they, too, may enjoy the biggest amusement value at the same bargain price offered you. P.S. You will understand of course and can explain it to your lady friends that the companies playing here are always composed of from 45 to 60 people and that the entire two and one-half hours are consumed by the musical and comedy program offered – there are not time-killing movies to annoy you or to make you think you've had an afternoon's entertainment – it's just real enjoyment all the time, and because of the volume of business done, is offered at the lowest price in London. To satisfy yourself of this, just enquire around. Result: you'll be stronger than ever for The Grand.

Very sincerely,
John R. Minhinnick

What did the future hold for The Grand? And what of the loyal Mr. Minhinnick? Would the new owners of The Grand keep him on as theatre manager?

TRANS-CANADA THEATRES, LIMITED, MONTREAL
SOLE OWNERS AND MANAGERS.

J. R. MINHINNICK   :-:   :-:   RESIDENT MANAGER

Road Shows included:
Little Nellie Kelly, by George M. Cohan
The Heart of Cellini, by Anthony Wharton
Brevities of 1923
Good Morning Dearie, music by Jerome Kern
Dancing Around, a revue with "Buck & Bubbles, Highest Salaried Colored Performers
    in the U.S."
He Who Gets Slapped, by Leonid Andreyev, starring Basil Sydney
The Devil's Disciple, by G.B. Shaw
Peer Gynt, by Henrik Ibsen
The Whirl of Girls, a revue with "Ten Musical Spillers and Feminine Charm a Plenty"
The Queens of Paris, "The Snappiest Show on Earth! Another Knock-Out Bill!"
A Cigarette Maker's Romance,
starring Sir John Martin-Harvey
Hamlet, by William Shakespeare, starring Sir John Martin-Harvey
Wine, Woman and Song, with "the unsurpassed Flapper Chorus"
Jig Time, "the Burlesque Sensation of the Century; Columbia Burlesque is presented in this theatre by original companies – intact and direct – from Columbia Theatre, New York City
Sweet Lavender, by Sir Arthur Wing Pinero
Thieves in Clover, by Eugene Walter
Too Many Husbands, by Somerset Maugham
Let 'Er Go, with the Dumbells

Summer Stock:
The Garry McGarry Players

Dance:
Ruth St. Denis and Ted Shawn and the Denishawn Dancers

FAMOUS PLAYERS THEATRE ERA

1925-1933

"THE DUMBELLS" [Coliseum London]

HANA PHOTO

The Dumbells were back. Throughout the 1920s, audiences didn't tire of the group's impudent, sentimental and irreverent humour. They also loved the Canadian patriotism demonstrated in such songs as "Canada for Canadians" and "Good-Bye Broadway, Hello Montreal." The troop had taken its name from the dumbells that served as the divisional insignia for the Canadian Army Third Division. Audiences always went crazy when the two female impersonators came on stage. Honorary Captain Merton Plunkett, the man who had first organized a rough and ready variety show while the war raged around him in France, was enjoying peacetime success with his theatrical career. Ross Hamilton, as Marjorie, is third from the left, seated in the centre row, while Al Murray, as Marie, is seated second from the right. Seated between the men in drag is Captain M.W. Plunkett. His brother, ballad singer Al Plunkett, stands on the far left in the back row. Seated front, centre is Sergeant Charter, and E. Redpath is on the far right, centre row. (Photo taken in October, 1918; Courtesy of The National Archives PA - 5734)

1924/25

FAMOUS PLAYERS THEATRE ERA

JOHN R. MINHINNICK

The Grand Theatre kept John R. Minhinnick working as the manager under the new regime of Famous Players. It was beginning to look as if nothing could deter Mr. Minhinnick from running the theatre, not the sudden and unexplained disappearance of the man who had hired him in 1911, nor the subsequent change of ownership. In fact, Mr. Minhinnick would be a fixture at the Grand Theatre in London until his retirement from the job in May 1937.

COMPETITION

Theatre managers faced duel threats this season – more sophisticated silent films and radio. Each medium was taking a big bite out of playhouse revenues. Radio stations started broadcasting operas and plays over the airwaves. In London, CJGC, the predecessor of CFPL Radio, had been broadcasting since 1922. Londoners could also listen to radio shows from Detroit, Michigan. Grand Theatre house programs continued to make direct appeals to women to continue to support live shows: "Every Day Is Ladies' Day…Every Night Is Ladies' Night; Ladies' Special Matinee Ticket 25 Cents; More Amusement For Your Money Than Is Possible In Any Other London Theatre." And management invoked the group bookings stand-by strategy when single tickets sales slump: "Get Up A Party."

Road Shows included:
Ace High, with the Dumbells (September 1924)
Oh, Yes!, with the Dumbells (May, 1925)
Discarded Wives, "a startling drama of loveless marriage, tensely appealing!"

Local Production
The Cameo Girl, presented by the IODE, proceeds for War Memorial Educational Fund

1925/26

FAMOUS PLAYERS THEATRE ERA

ABIE'S IRISH ROSE

In October of 1925, *Abie's Irish Rose* was staged at the Grand Theatre, starring Warren Ashe as Abraham Levy (Abie) and Grace Stafford as Rosemary Murphy, (his Irish Rose). *Abie's Irish Rose*, written by Anne Nichols, was a phenomenon of the Broadway stage. The playwright had had an affection for "her Abbie" ever since the evening in Buffalo when she was sitting in a restaurant with her husband. A Jewish boy named Berg entered. He was in tears – positively frantic. As he sobbed, he told Miss Nichols of his plight. He had just become a bridegroom, but he had lied to his stern father, telling him the girl was Jewish, when his bride was, in fact, Irish. "There is a situation for a wonderful farce comedy. I shall write it," said Miss Nichols. It was finished three months later, and then she began trying to sell it in New York. It was rejected by every New York manager to whom it was shown; one told her that it would bring forth protests from both Jews and Catholics. Miss Nichols ignored this warning, went west and got a production in Los Angeles. When it opened there, it achieved a remarkable run of 30 weeks. Miss Nichols, determined to have a New York showing, took the production there. And on the evening of May 23, 1922, the comedy that cost $5,000 and that earned $6 million, had its historic premiere. The majority of the reviews were gentle. *Abie's Irish Rose*, owned outright by Anne Nichols, had a struggle to survive during its early weeks. There was not a winning week from May until October – and then the landslide. Miss Nichols became desperate

Backstage at The Grand, high above the stage on the fly floor, this photograph shows the profusion of ropes used to fly sets, props and, at times, actors, in and out of the scene. Pasted on the wall are large posters from plays that toured through in the first two decades of the theatre's life. (Photo: Ian Besch; Courtesy of The Grand Theatre)

early in the run; more money was needed to keep *Abie* alive. She went boldly one afternoon to the gambler Arnold Rothstein, and asked for a loan of $30,000. "Do you believe in this play" he asked quietly. "Completely," said Miss Nichols. Miss Nichols walked out with Rothstein's cheque for $30,000. *Abie's Irish Rose* fought its way through and became the sensation of show business; it became America's favourite play. Ten companies, five years in New York, 2,327 Broadway performances, selling out night after night, month after month, year after year." (– Ward Stonehouse, *Matinee Tomorrow*)

CAUSES OF DECLINE

Billboard Magazine ran this piece in its August 14, 1926, issue: "Causes of Decline of Legitimate Stage – More than 70 per cent of the returns in the theatre census give the movies as the cause of the decline of the legitimate stage. Other causes named are as follows: (1) high cost of production making ventures unprofitable; (2) high cost of admissions; (3) legitimate theatres not as attractive as movie and vaudeville houses; (4) high transportation costs; (5) change in public amusement taste; (6) radio; (7) inadequate publicity; (8) vaudeville; (9) decline in quality of plays; (10) poor casting; (11) hostility of church; (12) hostility of other local organizations; (13) decline of art of acting; (14) hostility of press."(– *Billboard Magazine*, August 14, 1926) It is no wonder theatre managers were feeling assaulted on all sides.

Road Shows included:
Abie's Irish Rose, by Anne Nichols
Lucky 7, with the Dumbells
No, No, Nanette

Burlesque:
"every Thursday, Friday, Saturday, twice daily 2:15 and 8:15"
Margie Pennetti and Her Famous Stolen Sweets

1926/27

FAMOUS PLAYERS THEATRE ERA

SONG OF THE STAGE HAND
BY SIR ALAN PATRICK HERBERT (1948)

We work in the wings
At various things
That nobody sees from the stalls:
You don't think of us
Unless there's a fuss
And bits of the scenery falls.
But what would be seen of the old Fairy Queen
If the palace came down on her head?
The actors may bark: but if they're in the dark
It don't matter what Shakespeare said.
It's the same thing wherever you go:
The bloke in the front gets the show.
But where would he be
If it wasn't for we –
Working away in the wings?

It looks all serene:
You see a new scene –
From the bed-chamber, so, to the yacht.
But you'd change your mind
If you came 'round behind
And saw what a job we have got.
We lower the mast but the damn thing sticks fast:

The rigging is foul of the punt.
We push houses round, but we mayn't make a sound,
For the hero's proposing in front.
And then, when we change to the wood,
With the moon coming out as it should,
Well, give us a hand,
The invisible band,
Working away in the wings.

But still we're all proud
We're one of the crowd
That's pulling the jolly old strings:
For, bless you, we know
We're as much in the show
As the fellow who dances or sings.
We've got no bouquets, and they don't wait for days
To see us come out of the door.
We can't write a play, but if we go away
There won't be no plays any more.

But there – though we bark we don't bite:
It'll all be right on the night.
Enjoy yourselves, do:
For we'll see you through,
Working away in the wings.

MEMORIES OF THE GRAND

"My memories of the Grand Theatre began in the 1920s, when we walked three miles or so along Wonderland Road on Friday evenings to board the Springbank streetcar to attend The Grand. When we arrived we had to sit up in the gods, a second balcony entered only by an outside fire escape. Some of the shows I remember seeing were *Mutt and Jeff*, *Bringing Up Father* and the Al Plunkett in the Dumbells. One of my favourites was *Uncle Tom's Cabin*, where Uncle Tom, Little Eva and the slaves tried to escape across the ice floes (wooden blocks) on the river, while the slave owners, including Simon Legree, with their barking hound dogs stood on the riverbanks shooting with their guns at the escapees. One of the greatest shows to play in The Grand was *Ben Hur*. Real horses and chariots with Roman soldiers fighting were on a round turntable to which the chariots were fastened, slowly revolving until the end of the show when the chariots were released and the horses raced off the stage, pulling the chariots behind them. In those days the stage was larger than the body of the theatre. After the show was over we boarded the streetcar, and then walked the rest of the way home in the dark after midnight along the gravel road. There were very few cars in those days so we didn't have to worry about traffic." – Edwin Pincombe, Toronto

GRAND THEATRE STOCK COMPANY

A stock company was created at London's Grand Theatre. Road shows had fallen off and Minhinnick had to keep the lights on and the crowds coming. As a seasoned theatre manager, he was all too aware of the statistics:

Companies on Tour:	Year:
339	1900
311	1905
236	1910
124	1915
39	1920

What better way to keep audiences coming to The Grand than to hire eager actors and cast them in a series of plays from stock? The General Manager of the Grand Theatre Stock Company was none other than John R. Minhinnick himself. He assumed the role of

A rare backstage photograph featuring the stage crew at The Grand proudly posing in front of some of the backstage equipment. From left to right are: Jack Saunders, unknown, John Saunders (father of young Jack), and Harry Drennan. John Saunders was crew chief and was a fixture at The Grand for five decades. The men were forewarned about the photograph and dressed up in suits, vests, cardigans and ties. (Courtesy Dorothy Westhead, daughter of John Saunders, sister of Jack Saunders)

producer. It was not an easy transition from presenter to producer. A future Grand Theatre manager, Ken Baskette, reminisced in the mid-1950s, that as a boy he remembers three actors going on stage "on book"; carrying copies of the script during a Grand Theatre Stock Company production of *The Goose Hangs High*. The story goes that three actors in the company had argued with Mr. Minhinnick, had walked out of the show, and three other actors had picked up the scripts and the play went on.

Grand Theatre Stock Company
Sis Hopkins, by Rose Melville, directed by Norman Wendell
Grounds for Divorce, directed by Norman Wendell
The Patsy, by Barry Conners
Why Men Leave Home, by Avery Hopwood, directed by Norman Wendell
Beware of Widows, by Owen Davis, directed by Norman Wendell
Three Live Ghosts, by Frederic S. Isham, and Max Macin, directed by Norman Wendell

Getting Gertie's Garter, directed by Norman Wendell
Cat and the Canary, by John Willard, directed by Norman Wendell
Uncle Tom's Cabin, from Harriet Beecher Stowe, directed by Norman Wendell
The Kiss in a Taxi, by A.H. Woods

Entertainer:
Beatrice Lillie

1927/28

FAMOUS PLAYERS THEATRE ERA

SIR JOHN MARTIN-HARVEY

"In the 1920s I was in my mid-teens when Sir John Martin-Harvey came to the Grand Opera House to play in *The Only Way* (Dickens' *A Tale of Two Cities*). We were just a few years out from England and my mother had seen Sir John in London, England. We were rather short of money but this was special; for 50 cents we went up in the gods and it was all very thrilling but one thing has particularly stayed in my memory. When Sir John stood on the platform that contained the guillotine and said that famous last line: "It is a far, far better thing that I do, than I have ever done; it is a far, far better rest that I go to than I have ever known," we could see him only from the waist down, we being so high up. It was wonderful anyway and started my lifelong love of theatre." – Mrs. Muriel Podmore, London

Sir John Martin-Harvey was onstage in England as early as 1899 as Sydney Carton in this adaptation of Dickens' tale. The play was a hit with the public on both sides of the Atlantic. The actor continued in the role almost up to his death, in 1944. During the memorable scene when Sydney Carton mounts the stairs to the guillotine. London playgoer, Miss Louise Wyatt, remembers sitting literally at the edge of her seat, peering intently over the railing in the gods as the great actor slowly climbed the stairs to his death. "I wept and wept and wept as the hero met his death on the Grand Theatre's stage," remembered Miss Wyatt.

ASSISTANT TO SCENE PAINTER

"I went to work as assistant to the scene painter at the Grand Theatre just after Labour Day, 1927. I lived in St. Thomas and was determined to get into the theatre in any way possible. The stage manager, Mr. Saunders, offered me the job of apprentice to the scene painter, a man named William Drake. I think that the salary was something like $10 a week, and I didn't have much left after paying my fare on the LPS railway every day. The theatre had a resident stock company that did a new show every week. Drake came down from Toronto every Monday evening or early Tuesday morning, and we did the sets for the next week, having them finished by late Friday evening when he went back to Toronto. I went in on Mondays, when they would be setting up for the new show, to touch up any edges or new pieces that had been overlooked. At that time the manager of The Grand was Mr. Minhinnick." – John S. Corbett, Morrisburg, writing to the *London Free Press* editor, February 1979

SILENCE

What of the quality of the Stock Company's productions? The *London Free Press* reviewer had this to say about a performance of *Silence*: "Enthralling a capacity house throughout two hours of almost continuous performance, the famous crook drama, hailed as one of the greatest of the present-day melodramas, presented by The Grand Stock Company players, was undoubtedly one of the most successful productions which the company has yet attempted. It offers a type of tragedy/drama which is unusual in many aspects, always entertaining and of such quality that it holds its audience spellbound at all times." (– *London Free Press*, January 17, 1928)

ZIEGFELD FOLLIES

The *Ziegfeld Follies* finally came to the Grand Theatre in April 1928. The first *Follies*, named for its flamboyant producer, Florenz Ziegfeld Jr., had debuted in New York City in 1907. The truly great *Follies* were produced between 1918 and 1922. Stage star Anna Held, Ziegfeld's first wife, proposed the title *Follies* to her husband, based on a New York newspaper column entitled "Follies of the Day." Originally, the shows were framed around a serious of humorous comments on the events of the year, but soon beautiful girls and spectacle took over and comedians were sidelined. The *Follies* became an annual event, much anticipated by theatre-goers, and Ziegfeld's investment of many hundreds of thousands of dollars guaranteed that each one would be more elaborate than the one before. Londoners paid $3 for good seats in the evening, and between 50 cents and $2 for "bargain" Tuesday matinee tickets. With the stock market crash in October 1929, Florenz Ziegfeld lost everything. Despite this he kept working and produced his final *Follies* in 1931. The Great Showman died one year later – broke.

END OF THE SILENT FILM ERA

Moviemakers, by now concern about talking films having given way to panic in March 1928, saw the writing on the wall for the future of silent films. Until that time, talking films were considered gimmicky, a fad that would fade. Hundreds of other sound experiments throughout the first 30 years of movie history had come and gone. As far back as 1898 Thomas Edison had been the first to have a "talking" picture, but he had dropped the idea when silent movies proved so profitable. In 1921, innovative film director D.W. Griffith had used recorded dialogue in a film

entitled *Dream Street*. Although synchronizing of sound and picture had been achieved well before 1928, the one major obstacle to the commercial success of talkies had been the inability to make the sound loud enough for everyone in the theatre to hear it. But as the 1920s came to an end, strides in technology solved all the problems of recording, synchronizing and amplifying dialogue. These major developments spelled the end of the silent film era.

Road Shows included:
Bubbling Over, with the Dumbells
Ziegfeld Follies, "brilliant Broadway cast of 100 including 50 'Glorified' Girls"
Some Baby, "not maybe, not perhaps, but, the funniest farce comedy of the season"
Scaramouche, by Rafael Sabatina
Abie's Irish Rose, by Anne Nichols

Journey's End, by R.C. Sherriff
Aladdin, a pantomime

Grand Theatre Stock Company:
My Son, by Martha Stanley
The Gossipy Sex, by Lawrence Grattan
Madame X, adapted from Alexandr Bisson
The Servant in the House
Silence, by Max Marcin

1928/29

FAMOUS PLAYERS THEATRE ERA

GILBERT AND SULLIVAN

Londoners who loved Gilbert and Sullivan operettas could indulge their tastes at The Grand this season. The partnership of W.S. Gilbert (writer), Arthur Sullivan (composer), and Richard D'Oyly Carte (impresario/producer) invented a new kind of entertainment. It combined wit, musicianship, satire and high production standards. This type of theatre was a unique combination when it exploded onto the theatre scene in Victorian England in the 1880s. Until the G & S operettas came along there was a reluctance on the part of the British middle class to view musical theatre. Mostly, it was thought of as tawdry, even vulgar. Gilbert met Sullivan in 1869 and, in 1875, with Richard D'Oyly Carte backing them, they produced *Trial by Jury*. This is the only G & S work with no spoken dialogue, and it runs less than 40 minutes in length. Gilbert & Sullivan's work enjoyed worldwide success since 1878, when their smash hit *H.M.S. Pinafore* was produced in the United States, after its successful debut in England.

Fifty years later, audiences were still responding to the comic operas penned during the heyday of Queen Victoria: *The Pirates of Penzance* (1880); *Patience* (1881); *Iolanthe* (1882); *The Mikado* (1885); *Ruddigore* (1886/87). After Gilbert's death in 1910, and throughout the First World War, no company took the beloved G & S operas overseas on tour. Under the supervision of Rupert D'Oyly Carte (son of Richard D'Oyly Carte), the operas were refurbished and enjoyed a rebirth in 1919 during a season in London's West End. When D'Oyly Carte broached the idea of an American tour, to start in 1927, American businessmen advised against it, arguing that there were well-established G & S companies in America. So young D'Oyle Carte decided that his English company would tour Canada instead. After enjoying success during the 1927/28 season, he put London's Grand Theatre on the 1928/29 itinerary, much to the delight of local theatre-goers. What was, in the 1880s, a revolution, by the 1920s had become an institution.

ENEMIES OF THE THEATRE

The following passage appeared in the December 5, 1928, edition of the popular British magazine *Punch*. While it applies to West End theatres in the other London, it might just as well have been written for any theatre, anywhere, including London, Ontario's, Grand Theatre: "The difficulties of theatrical management are notorious. It has constantly been proved that there is no season of the year which is favourable for the production of a play. In the long winter months people do not want to leave their cosy homes; when spring comes, with Daylight Saving, the people are busy in their gardens; in the hot summer they do not want to be cooped up in a stuffy theatre; in the treacherous autumn months, when the first colds begin, they are afraid of draughts, and then too, having just finished their holiday, are hard up and are settling down to work; just before a holiday season they are saving up their money, and just after a holiday season they have no money left. During the week they are too tired or busy to go to the theatre, and over the weekend they are out of town…" Forty-five different enemies of the theatre were listed, including these six: (1) very good weather (2) very bad weather (3) films (4) monday (5) friday (6) the critics.

This 1929 interior shot of the Grand Opera House (GOH) is so well-lit that details of the decorative curtain and of Challener's arch mural are clearly seen. Note the valances suspended over the boxes with the letters GOH entwined. The boxes are illuminated by their own chandeliers. Taken from the back of the first balcony, the backs of the unpadded theatre seats gleam in the light. (Photo: Art Gleason)

PROGRAM NOTES

Typical house program notes from this season included: "Ladies are requested to remove their hats during the performance." The following note was directed to those in the medical profession: "Physicians and others who anticipate being summoned during the performance they may attend, are requested to acquaint the box office with the number of their seats or boxes, in order that they can be promptly notified should any message be received for them." Manager Minhinnick ran a tight ship, and holding a regular place in the program was this note: "It is desired that the comfort of visitors to this theatre should be studied in every detail. Complaints of incivility or inattention on the part of any official or employee should be at once reported to the management." (– January 1929 program)

For two nights in January 1929, Gene and Kathleen Lockhart appeared on stage in their *Intimate Recital Revue*. Two of the many numbers that evening were: "I Do Love To Sing In My Bath" – Mr. Lockhart reveals how he first discovered he had what he is pleased to call a voice. This music confession will appeal to anyone who has ever had a bath; and "Criminal Tendencies of Concert Artists" – impressed with the idea that there are too many sad songs and too many stout prima donnas, Mr. Lockhart outlines his method of disposing of both.

Road Shows included:
Here 'Tis, with the Dumbells
The Desert Song, "a new operetta"
Oddities of 1929, "the revue of revues"
Blossom Time, libretto by Dorothy Donnelly
You Never Can Tell, by G. B. Shaw, starring Baliol Holloway

Iolanthe, Patience, Ruddigore, The Mikado, Trial by Jury and *The Pirates of Penzance*, by Gilbert and Sullivan, presented by The D'Oyle Carte Opera Company

Music
The Westminster Glee Singers, "famous English choir on world tour"

1929/30

FAMOUS PLAYERS THEATRE ERA

WIRED FOR TALKIES

The 1929/30 season was a short one, running from September 1929 to January 25, 1930, only. The Grand Opera House was closed and under construction, or more accurately, deconstruction, for the remainder of the season. The job at hand was to pull out the second balcony, fondly referred to by everyone as the gods. The men in charge of the job picked dayworkers from the local soup lineup. It was early in the Depression, but not too early for able-bodied London men to be out of work and looking for anything. The removal of the second balcony was overdue, as it was pulling away from the wall. It had not been safe for quite some time. The removal of this upper balcony freed enough space for Famous Players to install a projection booth for talking movies. The Grand was the last London theatre to be wired for talkies, but it was up to speed in 1930. Before this time projection equipment had been set up in one of the two balconies, with the surrounding patrons putting up with the racket of film being fed through the projectors.

JOURNEY'S END

Journey's End, an anti-war play with an all-male cast, was written by Robert Cedric Sherriff. Producers had warned the playwright that no play could succeed without a woman in the cast. Despite this drawback, *Journey's End* created a sensation when it premiered in London's West End in 1929. It eventually played around the world. This play is one of the most significant plays

'She's frightened of something." "Perhaps I was responsible'

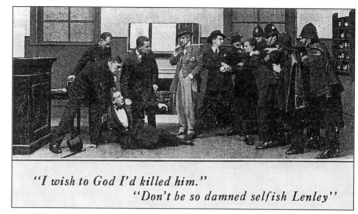

"I wish to God I'd killed him."
"Don't be so damned selfish Lenley"

The Ringer by Edgar Wallace, was on stage at the Grand Theatre for three days commencing October 31, 1929. "It's all about London (England) and its crimes and criminals. The humours of Cockney life are depicted with a knowledge few writers possess. Mr. Wallace's secret is preserved to the last and preserved with such good use of humour and mystification that a delighted audience was always laughing when not under an obligation to hold its breath. No one could guess the enthralling curtain." – house program notes, Grand Opera House, October, 1929. (Courtesy of The J.J. Talman Collection, D.B. Weldon Library, The University of Western Ontario, London, ON)

dealing with 20th century warfare. London, Ontario audiences were able to see it not too long after its world premiere.

"*Journey's End* has been called the play that should end war. This may seem like an impossible task, which it undoubtedly is, but nevertheless the fact remains that having seen it, few people will leave the theatre with any conception of modern warfare other than that of futility. It is three solid hours of sheer entertainment, depicting more magnificently than any story yet told of what it was like out there. For all its stalwart and monumental drama, it is more amusing than any play in town. It is full of the humour of simplicity which is life." (– house program, October 1929)

The story opens on a March evening, 1918, when Second Lieutenant James Raleigh, only 18 years of age, reports for his first active duty to a British dug-out in France. He schemed to join this particular unit, so that he could serve with Captain Stanhope, who was his hero at school. But after three years of active service, Stanhope has taken to alcohol to deal with the pressures of command. The unit's Colonel orders a day-light raid to take German prisoners. The Colonel rejects Captain Stanhope's requests to lead the party, and instead assigns the young Raleigh and a young Lieutenant. The play ends with Stanhope having to face the outcome of the raid alone.

Road Shows included
Rosemary, *The Only Way*, *The Lowland Wolf*, starring Sir John Martin-Harvey
Blossom Time, libretto by Dorothy Donnelly
Miss Elizabeth's Prisoner, "a romantic comedy"
Mother Goose and *Humpty Dumpty*, pantomimes, with Dan Leno, Jr. in the cast
Journey's End, by R. C. Sherriff, directed by James Whale
The Ringer, by Edgar Wallace, "it is impossible not to be thrilled by Edgar Wallace"
Romeo and Juliet, *Much Ado About Nothing*, *Macbeth*, *Twelfth Night*, by William Shakespeare, presented by The Stratford-Upon-Avon Festival Company, under the management of the Board of Governors of the Shakespeare Memorial Theatre, Stratford-Upon-Avon, Patron: His Majesty the King
The Vagabond King, "the celebrated French musical comedy, with a brilliant cast of 100, and with a superb touring orchestra"
Arms and the Man, *The Philanderer*, by G.B. Shaw, presented by Maurice Colbourne and Barry Jones

1930/31

FAMOUS PLAYERS THEATRE ERA

ALL QUIET ON THE WESTERN FRONT

"Dedicated to the new medium of drama, tragedy and comedy – the talking picture – the Grand Theatre opened last night with the presentation of the greatest of all war pictures *All Quiet on the Western Front*. Opening ceremonies with short addresses by civic representatives and theatre officials marked the performance, attended by a capacity audience. Long before the show opened, hundreds were turned away from the box office, unable to obtain seats. Clarence Robson, eastern division supervisor of Famous Players Canadian Corporation, gave all of the credit for the reopening of The Grand to John R. Minhinnick, who has been manager of the Grand Opera House for 22 years. Minhinnick announced that the theatre would present worthwhile road shows and the better class of moving pictures in the future. Minhinnick was given a great ovation when he spoke a few words to the large audience." (– *London Free Press*, Friday, September 5, 1930)

EDITORIAL ON THE REOPENED GRAND

The September 6 edition of the *London Free Press* dedicated an editorial to the newly-reopened Grand Theatre: "Locally, and indeed throughout Canada, much has been said in regard to the

The Grand's second balcony was gone and, as this 1977 photograph shows, a projection booth had been installed. It appears that the ceiling had been dropped during the renovations. (Photo: Ian Besch; Courtesy of The Grand Theatre)

gradual disappearance of the stage production from the country's former road show theatres. Much, in fact most of it, has been wild supposition. The road shows will play the leading cities, London included, if they can be secured. The trouble really is in the fast-waning taste of the public for this special type of entertainment. The talking pictures have made it possible to present in the smallest town, gorgeous musical spectacles, great stars and sensational dramatic hits in much better shape, with so much more attention to detail, and with such a wider scope in scenic effects, that the public will no longer be content with the limitations or the old-time stage. Whereas it cost from $1 to $4 to see a truly good stage production, that same attraction now may be seen in such greater beauty on the talking screen, at from 25 cents to 50 cents, that the public will no longer spend the extra money. Believe it or not, if the public would support the road show then they would get their fill of them – the best of them at that. But the policy of the Grand Theatre is to be made elastic enough to take care of any road attraction that the public desires and the management can induce to come to London." (– *London Free Press*, September 6, 1930)

SURVIVAL

Despite the policy set out by Famous Players for London's Grand Theatre to schedule the better talking films being made, it became apparent throughout the course of this season that The Grand could not survive on just these better films. By May of 1931 the theatre was screening studio quickies, B movies, and double bills.

JOHN R. MINHINNICK

By 1931, Grand Theatre manager John R. Minhinnick was fondly known as the dean of Canada's showmen. He had learned his craft well under the tutelage of the missing Ambrose J. Small. For many years the Grand Theatre *was* John R. Minhinnick. In August of 1931

he had just celebrated his 23rd anniversary in the theatre business, and the *London Advertiser* ran this approving and complementary article: "Twenty-three crowded, active years dedicated to a ceaseless quest for entertainment for his master, the public. Good shows that have been superlatively good, and shows not so good and not so bad. From whatever direction they came, and in whatever guise, John R. had them, and still has them, "spotted" for what they are. If there is one thing that John R. abominates and detests it is an attempt to short-change the theatre-going public. A high-placed official of the Famous Players Corporation once said: 'Minhinnick knows shows.' And that's a fact. He has an uncanny knack of sizing up box office values, and can estimate almost to a fraction from the script-book and a cast, just how many shekels any given show is good for. He says he has a lot of smart pictures coming. They most certainly will be, for the Famous Players Corporation knows that this interpreter of the public's fancy in pictures insists always on a good product, and when he is happy, look out for some worthwhile entertainment in his bailiwick."

Road Shows included:
Passion Play, "the world's oldest and biggest stage production, the original German company, first American tour, featuring Adolf Fassnacht, the world's greatest Christus portrayer, not a motion picture"
Happy Days Are Here Again, with the Dumbells' 12th annual show
Good Gracious Annabelle!

Movies:
All Quiet on the Western Front
Dixiana, "all talking, all singing, all dancing musical movie" (and…partly filmed in colour)
Tom Sawyer
Big Boy, starring Al Jolson
Along Came Youth
Resurrection
Bad Sister, "she took what she wanted and made them like it! smashing story of the girl who couldn't be good", starring Humphrey Bogart and Bette Davis
Not Exactly Gentlemen, "three bold, bad hombres who said nix on dames until …" starring Victor McLaglen and Fay Wray

---

1931/32

FAMOUS PLAYERS THEATRE ERA

THE REVUE

Paris, France was the birthplace of the revue, an entertainment once described as "tall girls and low comedy." The main ingredient has always been girls, girls, girls. What started in Paris shifted to New York City's Broadway, after Florenz Ziegfeld Jr. exploited the genre and glorified the most beautiful girls in the United States. By the early 1930s the revue hit the Grand Theatre in London, Ontario. But, by the time the *Kiwanis Follies* turned the stage of The Grand into a showcase for local beauty and talent, the success of the revue had peaked, and was beginning to subside. But that didn't stop young London women like Dorothy Saunders from rehearsing for hours, donning costumes and stage make-up, and waiting in The Grand's wings for their cue to hit the stage, kick their legs high, and smile, smile, smile!

BRITISH PLAYERS

Sir Barry Jackson was on the road with his company of British Players: "The present tour is Sir Barry Jackson's first Canadian venture, and he hopes to make it an annual event. He has chosen what he considers to be five worthwhile plays with which to introduce to Canadian audiences his company of British Players, and he personally supervised all productions so as to insure Canadians of witnessing these plays exactly as they are staged in London. His three days' engagement begins at the Grand Theatre on November 23 with Rudolf Besier's dramatization of the romance of the Brownings *The Barretts of Wimpole Street.*" (– *London Free Press*, November 13, 1931.) Playing Robert Browning was a young actor named Donald Wolfit. He would return to The Grand in the 1940s as the actor-manager of his own company.

THE GRAND BECOMES A MOVIE HOUSE

"By the time I got to my teens the Depression had caught up with live theatre and The Grand became a movie house. Its programs consisted of second run or "B" movies. I was a horror-movie fan at the time and I remember seeing films at The Grand like *Dracula* and *Frankenstein* (as a double bill), *Murder in the Rue Morgue,*

A chorus of sixteen London beauties pose backstage at The Grand. The hats are worn at a jaunty angle, the shirts are a shimmering satin, and the shorts are short. In stage makeup and ready to go on, these young women were part of the popular **Kiwanis Follies.** *If the* **Ziegfeld Follies** *were good enough for New York City, than this* **Follies** *would do London proud. In the back row, fourth from the right, is Dorothy Saunders (later Westhead), who gave permission to use this photograph.*

Mystery of the Wax Museum and other gems. At that time The Grand rivalled the Patricia, and later the Centre as a downtown, second class theatre, behind the Capitol and Loew's." – Les Wheable of Aurora, Ontario

Road Shows included:
The Barretts of Wimpole Street, *Yellow Sands*, *Dear Brutus*, *Quality Street*, *She Stoops to Conquer*, Sir Barry Jackson's touring company presented:
The King's Messenger, starring Sir John Martin-Harvey

Movies:
Secret Service, starring Richard Dix

Mickey Steps Out, a Mickey Mouse cartoon, "plus news and scenic and Vaudeville"
Under Eighteen, starring Marian Marsh
Skip the Maloo, starring Charley Chase, plus "news – cartoon"
Grand Hotel, starring John Barrymore, Greta Garbo and Joan Crawford

1932/33

FAMOUS PLAYERS THEATRE ERA

DOMINION DRAMA FESTIVAL

When Lord Bessborough became Canada's Governor-General and learned that many of the country's Opera Houses were now movie houses, and that there was an appalling lack of live theatre activity, he decided to do something about it. In October of 1932 the Dominion Drama Festival (DDF) was inaugurated. This was done at a meeting called by His Excellency, and convened at Government House in Ottawa. The Governor-General summoned approximately 60 men and women from across the country. Criteria for an invitation to such an auspicious meeting was an interest in drama. London, Ontario was represented by Catharine McCormick Brickenden, who had amply demonstrated her commitment to theatre endeavours in her home town by directing and producing amateur productions. It was decided that the first DDF would be held in Ottawa in April 1933. The competitors were to be amateur groups, regional competitions as representative of the best dramatic work being done across Canada. In future years London's Grand Theatre would be the site of both regional (Western Ontario Drama League) and national (Dominion Drama Festival) competitions. Londoners would travel across Canada showcasing their theatrical talents to the best advantage in front of a national audience.

THE MERRY WIDOW

Hungarian composer Franz Lehar premiered his gladsome

What appears to be a cast of thousands is in fact a cast of 92 people assembled on stage at the Grand Theatre for the Kiwanis Follies. Pat Carson of London remembers that her father, Gordon Thompson, undertook the Master of Ceremonies duties for these vast Follies. This edition had a nautical theme, including Britannia who stands at the centre back surrounded by a drum corp. Young men in sailor suits and young women in pseudo-sailor suits kneel in the foreground, just behind six small children who are either from London's black community, or who are white in complexion but made up in black-face. (Courtesy of Dorothy Westhead)

operetta *The Merry Widow* in Vienna in 1905. It opened on Broadway in October of 1907, and became a classic of the musical theatre. It was still being revived and sent on tour in the early years of the Great Depression, as just the tonic the Depression-weary public needed. "The revival of *The Merry Widow*, one of the most tuneful and best-loved operettas ever staged with Donald Brian again playing Prince Danilo, was greeted by a crowded house at the Grand Theatre last evening. Because Donald Brian played the same role 25 years ago by no means brands him as passe. His voice is certainly not heavy, but it is true, which is more than can be said for one of the other male members of the company who has a prominent role. Virginia O'Brien, as Sonia, is the typical Merry Widow blond, who plays and sings the part with suitable lightness. It is a role familiar to most theatre-goers of few or many seasons, the part of a lovely young widow whose hand – and money – is greatly in demand. Prince Danilo had once, years ago, been her lover, until she married wealth, after he had spurned her because of her humble birth. Now they meet again at a time when, for diplomatic reasons, it is most advisable that her wealth be kept within the Marsovian domain." (– *London Free Press*, 1932)

The Merry Widow was but one of 30 operettas Lehar wrote between 1902 and 1932. Its worldwide popularity was such that at one time it was playing simultaneously in Buenos Aires, in five languages, at five separate theatres.

MEMORIES OF THE GRAND

I was born in London and have attended The Grand off and on over the years. My one memory was the 1930s when The Grand became a movie theatre and we went Saturday afternoons. If I remember correctly they showed more British movies than the other theatres. I felt that when I went to The Grand it was a niche above the rest, partially because of its architecture. The Grand usually had a British serial, a detective type that brought you back the next week. I would argue with the other kids who went to theatres that had cowboy serials, that The Grand was much better. The cost for shows in the 1930s was about 10 cents.

– Tom Hammond, London

Road Shows included:
The Queen's Husband, by Robert E. Sherwood, starring Maurice Colbourne
The Merry Widow, starring Virginia O'Brien and Donald Brian

Movies:
Thirteen Women, starring Irene Dunn
Heroes of the West, a serial thriller shown in "chapters"

Horse Feathers, starring the Marx Brothers
Liberty Road starring Richard Dix
The Broadway Cheyenne starring Rex Bell

Entertainer:
Sir Harry Lauder

Local Production:
Lithuania, by Rupert Brooke, directed by John Burton, produced by the London Drama League

DOMINION DRAMA FESTIVAL

My first trip to Ottawa for the Dominion Drama Festival involved me as an actress, playing a murdering old wretch in a play by Rupert Brooke, Lithuania. I think I still hold the record as being the loudest screamer in the entire history of the DDF. No awards for screams!

– Catharine McCormick Brickenden

1933/34

FAMOUS PLAYERS THEATRE ERA

London Little Theatre's production of **Half an Hour** *was the winner of the Western Ontario Drama League (WODL) Festival of 1934. This production shot was taken in Ottawa by famed Canadian photographer Yousuf Karsh. It features four of the players: (left to right) Philip Morris, Lorraine M. Smith, Arthur Leggatt and William Bentley. (Courtesy of Dorinda Greenway)*

WESTERN ONTARIO DRAMA LEAGUE

The Western Ontario Drama League (WODL) Festival was at the Grand Theatre February 1 through 3, 1934. Curtain time was 8:15 p.m. The adjudicator, Mr. Rupert Harvey, had travelled from England to assess players from Guelph, Sarnia, London, Ridgetown and Hamilton. Entered in the competition was *The Dark Lady of the Sonnets* produced by London's Half-Way House Theatre. The London Drama League's piece was *Half an Hour* which came out a winner at the WODL. The executive of the DDF decided that Western Ontario would be one of Canada's twelve regions. A regional competition would provide the participants with the opportunity to observe each other's work and to discuss mutual activities and challenges. The Meredith Players, the Half-Way House Theatre and the London Drama League were three actively producing amateur groups in London at the time WODL was created.

Local Productions:
The Dark Lady of the Sonnets, by G.B. Shaw, directed by Hilda Smith
Half an Hour, by J.M. Barrie, directed by Catharine McCormick Brickenden and Philip Morris

Movies:
Damaged Lives, a film about venereal disease partially funded by the Canadian Social Hygiene Council, and shown to audiences of adults (over the age of 16) segregated into women-only and men-only
Be Mine Tonight, a minor musical, which marked the end of an era, The Grand ceased operation as a regular movie theatre early in September of 1933

Festival:
Western Ontario Drama League (WODL), February, 1934

1934/35

FAMOUS PLAYERS THEATRE ERA

RICHARD BERRY HARRISON

The Green Pastures was a religious fable that retold Old Testament stories in African-American dialect and settings. Covering everything from the Garden of Eden, to the passion of Christ, the play's point of view was that of a Southern backwoods preacher, explaining Bible stories to his Sunday-school students. Casting for *The Green Pastures* was done in a Negro actors' agency in Harlem, New York City. More than a thousand people auditioned. A week of casting sessions was held by playwright/director Marc Connelly, but he could not find someone to play De Lawd. One day, in walked 65-year-old actor Richard B. Harrison, and Connelly's search was over. Harrison had toured the country giving readings from the Bible and from Shakespeare. He had a calm authority that suited him for the role of De Lawd. Although Harrison wanted to play the part, he first consulted Bishop Herbert Shipman, the bishop of the Episcopal Diocese of New

A portrait of the actor Richard Berry Harrison. Born in London, Ontario, in 1864, Richard Harrison was the son of former slaves who had come to Canada by way of the Underground Railroad. Intent on a career in drama, Harrison had attended the Detroit Training School of Dramatic Art after leaving London in the 1870s. He achieved widespread fame in the 1930s after being cast as De Lawd in Marc Connelly's play The Green Pastures. *The touring production of the play was at the Grand Theatre in October 1934, starring Richard B. Harrison. (Courtesy* **London Free Press***)*

York, to relieve his misgivings about taking the part of God. The bishop approved of the play, of the role of De Lawd and of the casting of Harrison in that role. The play premiered in New York in February 1930 and played there for 640 performances. It then made five tours of North America before returning to Broadway in 1935.

If I thought there was a trace of satire in the play I could not appear in it at all. I studied the spirit of the piece for weeks before I began learning the lines. All the time I kept thinking of old man Blunt back in (London) Ontario and the way he felt about the God I was going to represent. The part I play is that of the kind of God in which Blunt believed. He had escaped from slavery. He knew about a jealous God who punished his children and then he knew about a generous and forgiving God who let members of the coloured race find peace and happiness in Canada. When I had that thought in mind I was able to go ahead and memorize Marc Connelly's lines.
– Richard B. Harrison (*London Free Press*, October 25, 1934)

The train carrying the huge acting company and the weighty production elements of *The Green Pastures* rolled into London's CN Railway Station in October of 1934. There to greet Richard B. Harrison was Mayor George Wenige. Back in New York City in 1935, while preparing for his 1,659 performance, Harrison collapsed in his dressing room from a stroke. At 70 years of age, Richard B. Harrison passed away after playing the role of a lifetime.

LORD BESSBOROUGH
It was a big night for the Grand Theatre when it hosted Canada's governor general: "It is our privilege and honour this evening to welcome Lord and Lady Bessborough and we extend our sincere and grateful appreciation for the honour they have conferred upon us in coming to London. May we also take this opportunity of extending our 'thank yous' to Lord Bessborough for the impetus he has given the Little Theatre movement in Canada, through his inauguration of the annual Dominion Drama Festival." (– November 23, 1934, London Drama League program)

LONDON LITTLE THEATRE
The Depression had eaten into ticket sales for London's amateur dramatic companies. Members of the London Drama League, led by President Harry C. Lecky, spoke with representatives of the city's other dramatic clubs. It was agreed that they shared similar interests and goals. If they worked together and combined their efforts under one executive they could achieve those goals. John Stevens headed the new combined executive and was the first president of London Little Theatre (LLT). The three original companies that formed LLT were The London Drama League (founded in 1922), The Half-Way House Players (founded in 1929) and The Meredith Players (founded in 1932). Shortly after the December 1934 amalgamation, a fourth dramatic company came on side, The Community Drama Guild (founded in 1932). With pooled financial resources, LLT rented the Grand Theatre for $2,100 per year. Tickets to LLT plays were 50 cents each. The three objectives of LLT were: (i) service to the community, (ii) development of the highest standard of amateur theatre, and (iii) the highest standard of amateur theatre and the promotion and encouragement of professional theatre, particularly in Canada. A new era in London's theatre history began with this amalgamation.

"The House of Amusement"

Grand THEATRE

LONDON CANADA

J. R. MINHINNICK, Resident Manager   PHONE MET. 188

London Little Theatre Season (#1):
A Murder Has Been Arranged, by Emlyn Williams, directed by John Burton
The Ivory Door, by A.A. Milne, directed by Hilda Smith
Dangerous Corner, by J.B. Priestley, directed by John Burton
Glamour, by Jacques Bernard, directed by J. Stanley Meredith
The Wind and the Rain, by Merton Hodge, directed by John Burton
Mrs. Moonlight, by Benn W. Levy, directed by Hilda Smith
Whistling in the Dark, by Lawrence Gross and Edward Childs Carpenter, directed by Shirley White

Road Shows:
The Green Pastures, by Marc Connelly, starring Richard B. Harrison
Juno and the Paycock, by Sean O'Casey, produced by the Abbey Theatre Players
The New Gossoon, by George Shiels, produced by the Abbey Theatre Players
San Carlo Grand Opera Company
A Bill of Divorcement, by Clemence Dane, starring Gordon McLeod

Magician:
Blackstone, the World's Super Magician and His Show of 1001 Wonders, on his 32nd Anniversary Tour

Festival:
WODL, February/March, 1935

100 Years of Entertainment at London's Grand Theatre

81

LONDON LITTLE THEATRE ERA

1934-1971

Twenty-Five Cents was written by Eric Harris of Sarnia, Ontario, and directed by Catharine McCormick Brickenden. It created a stir in London when it was mounted. It was a gritty, shockingly realistic, daring drama, focussing on the life of a Canadian family trying to survive the Depression. Despite opposition within the LLT, Brickenden championed the play and finally got the green light to produce it. It was sent to Ottawa for the DDF, where festival adjudicator Harley Granville-Barker awarded it the festival's top prize, The Bessborough Trophy, thus recognizing it as Canada's best amateur production of the season. It was also the first time in the history of the DDF that a play written by a Canadian won the coveted trophy. Victory was sweet for Catharine McCormick Brickenden personally. It also brought a great deal of attention to LLT. Pictured (left to right) Marvyn Kenyon, Kitty Bletz Walker, Jack Glennie and Margaret Glass. (Courtesy of the J.J. Talman Regional Collection, D.B. Weldon Library, University of Western Ontario, London, ON)

1935/36

LONDON LITTLE THEATRE ERA

LADIES OF THE JURY

"Launched most auspiciously into its second season, the London Little Theatre scored a triumph at The Grand last night in the presentation of *Ladies of the Jury*, as the first show of the autumn. Almost a full house greeted the capable cast of 21 talented London players. The play deals with a murder trial. The first act is in the courtroom; the two remaining acts in the jury room, where the oddly polyglot jury is seeking a verdict. If the play proved a triumph for London Little Theatre, it was decidedly a personal triumph for Ruth White who played the lead, a long and most exacting part. Miss White, always an entirely dependable player, has many good parts to her credit on the London amateur stage, and has played tragedy and comedy with equal ability."
(– F.B. Taylor, *London Free Press*, October 22, 1935)

JOHN BURTON

It was fitting that Ivor Novello's play *The Truth Game* be directed by John Burton. "John Burton was the most dignified gentleman I ever met," recalled London actor/director Don Fleckser. "In his youth he had been Ivor Novello's understudy. He knew a great deal about directing and acting." As a very young actor John Burton had toured his native England and had come to North America as a member of Sir John Martin-Harvey's company. For some reason John Burton decided to settle down and make London, Ontario, his home.

LONDON LITTLE THEATRE

On May 21 of 1936 London Little Theatre changed from being an "amalgamated" group of four separate dramatic entities, to being "incorporated." The newly incorporated entity was now formally and legally known as the London Little Theatre, or LLT for short. It would exist, through ups and downs, until the end of the 1970/71 season. Its 37 theatre seasons demonstrate an astounding record for a community amateur theatre company.

A RISKY SCHEME

This was LLT's last season of selling 50 cent tickets per show. The need to raise money to rent the Grand Theatre precipitated a move away from an "open box office" to a "closed box office," or a subscription scheme for ticket sales. Heading into the 1936/37 LLT season, theatre-goers were asked to purchase all plays on the playbill ahead of time. This risky scheme met with success. LLT was free of the pressure of accumulating their rent money over many months. Instead, they could bank it before the season began.

London Little Theatre Season #2:
Ladies of the Jury, by Fred Ballard, directed by Vincent G. Perry
She Stoops to Conquer, by Oliver Goldsmith, directed by Hilda Smith
Laburnum Grove, by J. B. Priestley, directed by John Burton
Three one-act plays: *Candle-Light*, by Siegfried Geyer, directed by Llewellyn Graham and Hilda Smith, *Twenty-Five Cents*, by Eric Harris, directed by Catharine McCormick Brickenden, *Noah*, by Andre Obey, directed by Vincent G. Perry and Ena L. Thirsk
Double Door, by Elizabeth McFadden, directed by Shirley White
The Truth Game, by Ivor Novello, directed by John Burton

Road Show:
Ten Minute Alibi, by Anthony Armstrong

Movies:
The Great Ziegfeld
A Midsummer Night's Dream

Entertainer:
Ruth Draper in her Character Sketches

Festival:
WODL, March 1936

1936/37

LONDON LITTLE THEATRE ERA

TOUR TO GODERICH

LLT's production of *Front Page* was performed over two nights at The Grand, then it toured to Goderich. By touring its productions to Goderich this season, LLT hoped to increase its scope and its impact on the region surrounding London. The Board of Directors hoped that other centres would follow suit and invite the theatre company to play out of town in the future. The *Front Page* company of 23 departed for Goderich at 6:00 p.m. on a chartered bus. Stage manager Ward Cornell travelled to Goderich during the day to set the stage for the actors. The company arrived with just 10 minutes to warm up. The curtain went up; the Goderich audience enjoyed the show, and the Goderich chapter of the I.O.D.E. hosted a post-show reception for the LLT troupers.

MRS. DUNCAN FERGUSON

In February the psychological crime drama *Crime at Blossoms* was on stage. The story was about a married couple who rent out their home, Blossoms, then depart for a holiday. During their absence a murder is committed in the house. The play's action begins after the couple returns to Blossoms. The audience was rivetted, as it witnessed the actors portray the couples' emotional and psychological reactions to the crime committed in their home. With a dramatic, unexpected, denouement, the play was a hit with London audiences. Listed as a member of the cast of 22 was Mrs. Duncan Ferguson, as "an old lady." This was my grandmother

Jessie Ferguson. I discovered this secret detail of her life when I came across a brittle, yellowed clipping from the *London Free Press*. The kind reviewer had this to say about Mrs. Ferguson's stage debut (and her retirement from the stage, as it turned out): "Mrs. Duncan Ferguson in a small part revealed a lovely speaking voice and a charming diction." I can only assume that the play's director, Shirley White, desperately needed to cast a woman with good diction for this small role, and turned to her friend Jessie. For a bit of fun, my Grandmother Ferguson agreed to indulge in the fame that only the theatre can bring, for two nights of her life.
– Sheila (Ferguson) Johnston, Author

London Little Theatre Season #3:
Front Page, by Ben Hecht and Charles McArthur, produced by Vincent Perry
Squaring the Circle, by Valentine Kataez, produced by Hilda M. Smith
Mary Rose, by J.M. Barrie, produced by John Burton

Crime at Blossoms, by Mordaunt Sharp, produced by Shirley E. White
Bird in Hand, by John Drinkwater, produced by John Burton

Dance
Uday Shan-Kar and his Hindu Ballet, "Barbaric Splendors of Authentic Hindu Ballet"

1937/38

LONDON LITTLE THEATRE ERA

THE PRODUCTION COMES FIRST

In 1938, Harding Greenwood joined LLT. A teacher by profession, he spent summers acting with professional stock companies. "London Little Theatre was social, but that came second or third. I've never been in a theatre like that where the production came first over anything else and nobody was cast because of his social position unless that person was the right person. The theatre was open to anybody – talent was the only thing that mattered." – Harding Greenwood (*London Free Press*, November 11, 1984)

SEASONAL PROMOTION

To promote its season LLT ran wordy ads in the local newspaper: "The Little Theatre movement is sweeping to success because it is a necessity. It provides flesh-and-blood presentations to audiences otherwise restricted to two-dimensional portrayals. It aims at the founding of a national Canadian theatre. It offers encouragement to Canadian playwrights. It provides a means for the recognition of many talented Canadian men and women. Five good full-length plays, well presented, furnishing five nights of most delightful entertainment at an average cost of 60 cents per evening. An assured seat at meritorious productions of master plays of today and former days. A rounding out of your cultural program as patron of an art that was old when the Greeks were young. The membership of LLT now stands at 1,300. Due to theatre seating capacity, the list must be closed at 1,500. If you plan to become associated with this worth-while Canadian movement, please phone headquarters (Fairmont 3285) and a representative will wait upon you with full information." (– *London Free Press*, September 18, 1937)

SEATING REQUIREMENTS

Buried deep in the London Little Theatre files at Canada's National Archives are these two notes from the 1937/38 subscription campaign: "Very deaf. Would like five rows from front. Orchestra. Every Monday"; and: "Stiff leg. Must sit on aisle. Two seats, five or six rows back. Orchestra. Monday evening each time." Seating requirements never change, no matter what the decade.

London Little Theatre Season #4:
The Mask and the Face, by C.B. Fernald, directed by Catharine McCormick Brickenden
Escape, by John Galsworthy, directed by Blanch Tancock
The Late Christopher Bean, by Sidney Howard, directed by Vincent Perry
Michael and Mary, by A.A. Milne, directed by Hilda Smith
First Lady, by Katharine Dayton and George S. Kaufman, directed by Ruth White

Road Show:
Whiteoaks, from Mazo de la Roch

Movies:
Three Women, Russian dialogue-English titles, "Soviet Russia's stirring tribute to her women"
Snow White and the Seven Dwarfs, "Walt Disney's full length picture in multiplane Technicolor"
Second Honeymoon, starring Tyrone Power and Loretta Young
Ebb Tide, starring Ray Milland, "a tidal wave of entertainment in colour"

1938/39

LONDON LITTLE THEATRE ERA

HERE I WILL NEST

"An important milestone in the progress of London Little Theatre was passed last night when the first full-length play by a London author was presented by LLT. *Here Will I Nest*, Hilda Smith's three-act drama, has the life of Colonel Thomas Talbot as its theme." (– *London Free Press*, November 15, 1938) Hilda Smith's research for the play had given her an intimate knowledge of Colonel Thomas Talbot, the pioneer settler and creator of the famous Talbot Settlement on Lake Erie, in the 19th century. She entitled her play after a quote from Colonel Talbot himself. She cast her husband, Richard Smith, in the lead role. On opening night she responded to the audience's calls for "Author! Author!", and gave a gracious curtain speech. Smith's play was adapted into Canada's first feature-length colour film. In April of 1942 the movie *Here Will I Nest* previewed at the Elsie Perrin Williams Memorial Library on Queens Avenue in London. It was directed by pioneer filmmaker Mel Turner, and starred John Burton in the role of Colonel Talbot. It is the earliest filmed record of a London Little Theatre production.

HOSTING THE DOMINION DRAMA FESTIVAL

The Grand Theatre hosted the Dominion Drama Festival which ran from April 10 to 15, 1939. On April 14 the Festival was graced with the presence of His Excellency, the Right Honourable Lord Tweedsmuir, Governor General of Canada (1935-40), and Lady Tweedsmuir. The adjudicator for this festival was S.R. Littlewood, Esq., who was described in the DDF brochure as "dean of London (England) dramatic critics." In London at the time, but not on stage, was actor Hume Cronyn, who participated in a discussion exploring the topic of a truly Canadian national theatre. The idea did not get past the discussion stage, despite Cronyn championing the idea of fostering such an entity.

On stage were players from Regina, Edmonton, Ottawa, Kingston, Charlottetown, Montreal, Nanaimo, Halifax, Toronto, Windsor and Winnipeg. The DDF was a big deal. It was, to use a sports comparison, the Olympics of Canadian theatre. And it was in London. And it was at The Grand!

TOO MUCH PROFANITY

Part of Dr. Alan Skinner's duties as LLT board president, was to make pre-curtain speeches to encourage playgoers to support LLT by subscribing annually. Fortunately, Dr. Skinner archived the correspondence that poured in. During this season one correspondent, a self-described "departing subscriber," wrote: "Having been a subscriber for many years I feel I would like to make a few kindly criticisms; the first one is that there is far too much profanity used in all the plays. The first play, when presented, some of the language used was lurid. I am speaking for a number of friends who are not joining this year on that account." – October 1938, letter to Dr. Skinner

A production shot of the mob scene from the play **John Ferguson.** *The lead role was taken by E.S. Detwiler. "In the presentation of* **John Ferguson** *at the Grand Theatre last night, LLT offered one of the few tragedies played in the history of amateur drama in this city. The story is not new. Playwright and poet have used again and again the theme of the Irish peasant, the stern landlord, the mortgage and the ultimate tragedy of murder. The use of an Irish accent was not quite satisfactory. The one set employed was excellent, though the lighting was not very satisfactory." (– F.B. Taylor,* **London Free Press,** *February 14, 1939) (Courtesy of Lynda Spence)*

London Little Theatre Season #5:
The Bishop Misbehaves, by Frederick Jackson, directed by Walter Dixon
Here Will I Nest, by Hilda Smith, directed by Hilda Smith
Baa, Baa Black Sheep, by P. G. Wodehouse and Ian Hay, directed by Cara Malcolm
John Ferguson, by St. John Ervine, directed by Blanch Tancock
To-Night at Eight-Thirty, by Noel Coward, directed by Walter Dixon

Road Shows:
The Flashing Stream, by Charles Morgan, starring Godfrey Tearle and Margaret Rawlings
I Have Been Here Before, by J. B. Priestley
Yes My Darling Daughter, by Mark Reed, "Jo Allison and her All American company"
San Carlo Opera Company presenting *Rigoletto* by Verdi
The Student Prince, by Sigmund Romberg

Dance:
The Ballet Russe de Monte Carlo

Movies:
Ignace Jan Paderewski in his first and only motion picture! "the world's greatest pianist"
The Mikado, "in Technicolor"

Festival:
The Dominion Drama Festival (DDF), April, 1939

1939/40

LONDON LITTLE THEATRE ERA

EXPANSION OF LLT

By August of 1939, LLT was finding that the Grand Theatre was too small for the expanding activities of the organization, so it took over several rooms in the Green-Swift Building, at the southeast corner of Queens Avenue and Talbot Street. They were used as storage space, rehearsal rooms and a prop room. Adjacent to the new prop room was an office that would serve as headquarters for the annual LLT subscription campaign. An LLT member gave a tour of the unequipped office to a reporter: "'You have a telephone," (the visiting reporter commented). "Well," the subscription committee member admitted: "The telephone is a prop, too, set up temporarily to give a business-like touch to the room." (– *London Free Press*, August 29, 1939)

WORLD WAR II

As LLT headed into its next season, World War II was heading into its first year. The decision was taken by the board of directors that LLT would adopt a "business as usual" attitude and forge ahead, despite the war. While other amateur theatre groups in other Ontario towns ceased operations, LLT defied the odds and continued its work. At the national level the Dominion Drama Festival was suspended for the duration of the war. Board president, Dr. Alan Skinner, believed that if the organization was to be of any help during this time of national crisis, it must continue as a unit "holding its membership and offering such

services as it has to the Red Cross and other patriotic organizations…Only with a strong membership can we give any valuable services, either financially or for purposes of entertainment," he was quoted as saying. (– *London Free Press*, September 18, 1939) Any surplus of funds from the 1939/40 LLT season would be given to the Red Cross or patriotic funds to provide entertainment for the men in training.

INSPECTION

Mr. Allen M. Taylor, an inspector of theatres, visited London's Grand Theatre and filed a comprehensive report on its interior and exterior condition. Dated November 17, 1939, it was noted that there were 1,208 seats in The Grand, that the theatre lacked an emergency lighting system, and that one was required. (– Ontario Archives)

CONTROVERSY

Maurice Colbourne and Barry Jones and their London (England) Company moved into the Grand Theatre in November of 1939 to present *Geneva* by George Bernard Shaw and *Charles the King* by Maurice Colbourne. Cast in the second play as Henrietta Maria, the Queen, was young actress Jessica Tandy. She would return to the Grand Theatre stage in the 1970s.

After completing his tour of Canada, Maurice Colbourne submitted an article to the *New York Times* in January 1940, and ignited a controversy. The incendiary comments to which amateur theatre practitioners in Canada took exception were: "Barry Jones and I took the Colbourne-Jones Company across Canada and back on a sort of voyage of discovery to see whether the theatre still existed in a territory that was a profitable and happy hunting ground ten years ago. Let me say at once that we found the theatre. But it was moribund. Frankly, I do not see how the patient is going to survive. It not only cannot afford the drastic new treatment which any sound doctor of the theatre would prescribe but it lacks at present even the will to live. The harm done to the theatre by the Little Theatre, though incalculable, is great. What is wanted from the Little Theatre if it is to justify its existence is a band of enthusiastic playgoers instead of groups of (in the main) astoundingly self-satisfied would-be play-performers. Too often self-expression is only a polite name for exhibitionism. Amateur means lover, and the least a lover of the theatre can do to show his or her love is to go to the theatre on the increasingly rare occasions when the real theatre comes along. But the amateurs are generally too busy amateuring."(– *New York Times*, January 28, 1940)

A firestorm erupted in the wake of this ungracious article. Trying to be kind, LLT board president, Dr. Alan Skinner, wrote: "Colbourne must have been misquoted. He knows as well as we do that the Little Theatre movement is doing its best to keep alive the interest of the public largely for the legitimate or professional theatre. We thoroughly enjoyed Mr. Colbourne when he played here recently." (– *London Free Press*, January 1940)

Others were not so forgiving. President of Toronto's Royal Alexandra Theatre, Gordon Perry, responded with: "Mr. Colbourne is simply trying to alibi the failure of his company on its Canadian tour. The facts are entirely contrary to that statement. The only shows we have lost money on here the last two seasons have been those produced by Colbourne and Jones. Their productions were completely unsuitable vehicles, performed by an unsuitable company."(– Toronto, February 1940)

And from across the Atlantic, S.R. Littlewood weighed into the debate. He had been in Canada a year earlier to adjudicate the DDF: "I read with amazement Maurice Colbourne's attack on the Canadian theatre and amateur players who are bringing to it a new, vigorous life all over the Dominion. Not all the acting I saw in Canada was great, but many performances were of the highest

William K. Trudell was manager of both the Grand Theatre and the Capitol Theatre, owned by Famous Players. He took over the management of the theatres in November 1939. When asked what he thought of Ambrose J. Small ghost stories, Mr. Trudell had a one word response: "Malarky!" (Photo Victor Aziz; Courtesy of William K. Trudell)

quality. The playing of Robert Haskins, from Alberta, in Chekhov's *The Bear*, was so far from being 'inexpert' that it showed powers quite beyond those revealed by Mr. Colbourne himself in any of the parts I have seen him essay upon the London stage." (– London, England, February 26, 1940)

Attempting, but failing, to be contrite, Mr. Colbourne submitted a letter to the editor of the *New York Times* in February, wherein he stated that he was delighted with the vitality of the Canadian Little Theatre, and had been trying to suggest merely that it should be "a play-going as well as play-acting body." As for the term "moribund" he said he applied it to the road in Canada. To illustrate just how "moribund" the road was, Mr. Colbourne said he had found that the "majority of stagehands in Canada were either so out of practice that they had lost their skill, or so new to their craft that they had not acquired skill." (– *New York Times*, February 12, 1940)

Was this an apology? I think not.

ELIZABETH MURRAY

The theatre loves plays about the theatre, and this season featured one of the best, *Stage Door*. The action takes place in the Footlights Club, a place for girls seeking fame and fortune in the glamorous world of show business. The cast included Libby Harvey (known in later seasons as Elizabeth Murray.) She was active in LLT productions, and on the board, for many years. "The first time I ever actually played The Grand was during the 1939/40 season. And that's really hysterical when I think about it, because I played the boarding house keeper and I was supposed to be 65 years old. I was probably 19 years old. I can remember I was terribly skinny and I was padded to play this role. It must have been quite ludicrous. But I did it." – Elizabeth Murray, actress, former LLT board president

LETTERS

Among the many letters sent to Dr. Alan Skinner this season was one dated October, 1939:

In your curtain talk you said the subscription base was much lower this year and you requested us to solicit our friends for subscription. I hope you will receive this letter in the kindly spirit in which I send it. I do not think the decrease in subscriptions is entirely due to the war. Is it necessary to play into the hands of the liquor interests by making it appear smart to give drinking such prominence? Surely it is deplorable that our young people are being ruined, without adding the glamour of

the stage to it. I have been a loyal subscriber for some years, and would like to continue to be. Each year I have hoped there would be an improvement but I regret to say this year has started out the same way. Please do not force those who feel as I do to still further reduce your subscriptions.
Sincerely yours, a loyal subscriber.

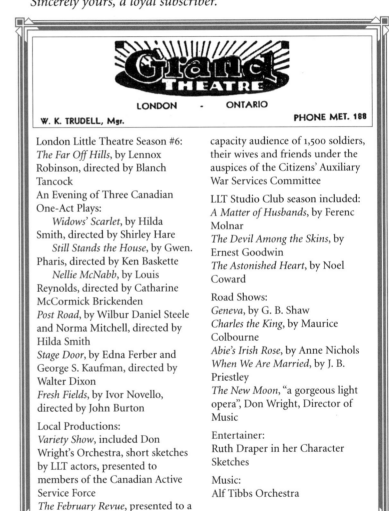

Grand THEATRE
LONDON - ONTARIO
W. K. TRUDELL, Mgr.   PHONE MET. 188

London Little Theatre Season #6:
The Far Off Hills, by Lennox Robinson, directed by Blanch Tancock
An Evening of Three Canadian One-Act Plays:
 Widows' Scarlet, by Hilda Smith, directed by Shirley Hare
 Still Stands the House, by Gwen. Pharis, directed by Ken Baskette
 Nellie McNabb, by Louis Reynolds, directed by Catharine McCormick Brickenden
Post Road, by Wilbur Daniel Steele and Norma Mitchell, directed by Hilda Smith
Stage Door, by Edna Ferber and George S. Kaufman, directed by Walter Dixon
Fresh Fields, by Ivor Novello, directed by John Burton

Local Productions:
Variety Show, included Don Wright's Orchestra, short sketches by LLT actors, presented to members of the Canadian Active Service Force
The February Revue, presented to a capacity audience of 1,500 soldiers, their wives and friends under the auspices of the Citizens' Auxiliary War Services Committee

LLT Studio Club season included:
A Matter of Husbands, by Ferenc Molnar
The Devil Among the Skins, by Ernest Goodwin
The Astonished Heart, by Noel Coward

Road Shows:
Geneva, by G. B. Shaw
Charles the King, by Maurice Colbourne
Abie's Irish Rose, by Anne Nichols
When We Are Married, by J. B. Priestley
The New Moon, "a gorgeous light opera", Don Wright, Director of Music

Entertainer:
Ruth Draper in her Character Sketches

Music:
Alf Tibbs Orchestra

1940/41

LONDON LITTLE THEATRE ERA

This photo was taken in May 1940 at the annual general meeting of London Little Theatre. Standing left is Mrs. W.J. Hogg (secretary), and standing right is Charles Ross. Seated is LLT president Dr. Alan Skinner. He was a Professor of Anatomy, and an Assistant Dean of the University of Western Ontario's Medical School. In his spare time he devoted many hours to board matters for LLT. A man of vision and of energy, Dr. Skinner guided the LLT through a period of great expansion. (Courtesy of the J.J. Talman Regional Collection, D.B. Weldon Library, University of Western Ontario, London, ON)

FOUND WANTING

LLT's season opened with the comedy *Springtime for Henry*, which the *London Free Press* reviewer found wanting: "One wonders why Mr. Levy should have taken the time to write the play and why LLT or any other group should go to the trouble of performing it. The play is by no means original. The lines skate over ice that was thin even before thousands of other playwrights skated over it, and the perennial zest with which playwrights revive these time-worn themes is always surprising. But anyway the playing of this bit of triviality was entirely commendable and the approach of the players was fresh…if the subject was not." (– F. B. Taylor, *London Free Press*, November, 1940) Many playgoers agreed: "Why waste so much time and talent on so poor a play? I consider the choice of such a one, a display of poor judgement and bad taste. It is not worthwhile and the lines are not clever or humorous enough to even partly excuse its suggestiveness. I am not alone in this opinion. You would be surprised to know how many people heartily agree that we do not want this sort of thing. What is the use of anyone working to put things on a higher moral and spiritual plane if a group of intelligent people, like members of LLT, who should be leaders in any such movement, are engaged in presenting plays which leave a bad taste in the mouth?"(– subscriber, November 1940)

STUDIO CLUB

LLT's quarters in the Greene-Swift Building accommodated a large room known as the Green Room. The organization installed a stage in the Green Room, as well as seating, so Studio Club plays could be mounted throughout the season. The Studio Club gave rookie actors and novice directors an opportunity to develop their talents. With experience gained in Studio Club productions, actors and directors moved on to bigger challengers in productions featured on The Grand's stage. "This, then, is one of the reasons why LLT productions have that professional quality which characterizes them. The director, cast and others taking part have all learned by doing." (– *London Free Press*, October 26, 1940)

THE SHOW MUST GO ON

Tension was high on opening night of the final play of the season, *George and Margaret*. Director John Burton, who was also cast in a leading part on stage, was taken ill just two days before opening night. His assistant director, Margaret Skinner, stepped in and took over full directing duties, while actor Harding Greenwood, after only two emergency rehearsals, took over John Burton's on-stage duties. As the age-old theatre saying goes…the show must go on.

MORE CONSTRUCTIVE CRITICISM

As this season came to a close, Dr. Alan Skinner again carefully stored the letters of support, and the letters of constructive criticism he had received. One of the latter had yet another bone to pick with LLT: "I did not renew my subscription in the LLT last season because of the coarse, vulgar and salacious character of some of the plays of season 1938/39. I am convinced that more patrons than you are aware of adversely criticised the plays of Noel Coward. Very numerous were the condemnatory comments of your patrons on leaving the theatre. I believe it is unnecessary to cater to the bestial in human frailty and by so doing, still further degrade. The theatre is regarded by many as an important vehicle in our education system, but it should be uplifting rather than degrading. We are seeing enough degradation in Hitlerism and we do not want to have other forms thrust upon us. In the hope that this season's offerings will be of a higher type, I have renewed my subscription for the current season. Incidentally, I heard that, last season, some parts of certain plays were omitted on the second evening, which is evidence of your desire to avoid offensive episodes. But why not on the first evening?" (– October, 1940)

GRAND THEATRE
LONDON

LLT Season #7:
Springtime for Henry, by Benn W. Levy, directed by Catharine McCormick Brickenden
Dear Octopus, by Dodie Smith, directed by Ken Baskette
The House Master, by Ian Hay, directed by Walter Dixon
Ten Minute Alibi, by Anthony Armstrong, directed by Ruth White
George and Margaret, by Gerald Savory, directed by John Burton

Revue:
Take It Or Leave It, LLT's show to entertain the troops

LLT Studio Club included:
To the Dead Man, by K.W. Edge
The End of the Beginning, by Sean O'Casey
Five at the George, by Stuart Ready

Road Shows:
Autumn Crocus, by C.L. Anthony
New Pins and Needles

Entertainer:
Ruth Draper

1941/42

LONDON LITTLE THEATRE ERA

GRACIE FIELDS

By the time comedienne and singer Gracie Fields played London's Grand Theatre in November of 1941, she was a 43-year-old star and had been in show business since the age of seven. Born in England, Fields had learned her craft in the music halls. Her comic singing made her reputation with her signature song being "Sally." Fields made her film debut in 1931, which led to a series of highly successful films shot in England and Hollywood. By 1938 Gracie Fields was ranked as the world's highest paid star. She moved to the United States in 1940, and toured extensively during the war, entertaining in practically every zone of the war between 1942 and 1945. She donated all of the proceeds to the British war relief effort. At the Grand Theatre in 1941, the audience sat through six bits (including a baritone solo, a violin solo and a dance routine) before Miss Fields hit the stage just before intermission. Audiences welcomed her Act II reappearance and by the end of the evening gave her a rousing ovation.

The Mad Hopes' *elaborate set with five cast members on stage: (l. to r.) Leon Bennett-Alder, unknown, Muriel Thompson (seated), Barbara Hunt (later Ivey), and Bob Colucci. "The director, Kizzie Brickenden, went to the University of Western Ontario and auditioned members of the university's Players' Guild. I was among one of the young students cast and that's how my London Little Theatre acting career started."*
– Alec Richmond, actor (Courtesy of Dorinda Greenway)

WALTER DIXON

LLT's production of *Three Live Ghosts* was directed by Walter Dixon. He was a loved and admired member of the LLT organization for many years. Born in London, England, he learned to dance from his father, a dance teacher. In 1909, at the age of 20, Dixon left England to be dance master in New York for the Broadway production of *The Pink Lady*. When he travelled to Canada for a vacation he found that he enjoyed this country better than either England or the United States, and he settled down first in Lindsay, Ontario, and later in London. In 1923, Dixon opened a photography studio and earned his living as a professional photographer. Before too long he was involved in amateur theatrics in the city. Dixon became active with LLT in 1933 and remained a member throughout the 1930s, 1940s and 1950s. Many LLT actors, dressed in character, sat for portraits by Walter Dixon. These portraits, as well as the numerous production shots he took over the years, captured the heyday of LLT. Dixon's photography studio became a place where members of London's arts scene met and exchanged news. Walter Dixon died in 1969, leaving his wife Mona, and many fond memories in the hearts of his friends.

Walter Dixon was a real gentleman. He was one of my mentors.
– Flora MacKenzie, LLT actress, singer

LLT Season #8:
Three Live Ghosts, by Frederick Isham and Max Marcin, directed by Walter Dixon
Another Language, by Rose Franken, directed by Ken Baskette
The Mad Hopes, by Romney Brent, directed by Catharine McCormick Brickenden
Lot's Wife, by Peter Blackmore, directed by Florence Phelps
Candida, by G.B. Shaw, directed by Margaret Glass

Revue:
Take It or Leave It, LLT troop show

LLT Studio Club season included:

For Better For Worse, by Lorraine Smith
Breathes There the Man, by John Charles Sullivan
The Plumbers, by Harry Gratton

Entertainer:
Gracie Fields, presented by The Navy League of Canada

Dance:
Ballet Theatre, America's Foremost Ballet Company

Music:
The Ten-Piano Ensemble, of the Musical Manifesto Group of Toronto

1942/43

LONDON LITTLE THEATRE ERA

ACTIVE SERVICE REVUE

LLT's Active Service Revue, *Take It Or Leave It*, entertained troops of training men in area camps. In November of 1942, LLT received this complimentary letter from the Chairman of the Citizens' Auxiliary War Services Committee: "I welcome this opportunity to express publicly the Committee's deep appreciation to the workers of our Entertainment Division for the great service which they have rendered to the troops in training since the outbreak of the war. It is to you 250 people who, since the outbreak of war, have given your time and talents to entertain the troops, that I wish to pay tribute. Your services have been given gratuitously – your contribution – magnificent! Last year you entertained 77,000 men in uniform. In addition to your many rehearsals you will, in

A singing duet with Wilma Fortner (left) and Nora Rooney (later Snelgrove) was a highlight of the LLT sponsored troop show Take It Or Leave It. *Many enlisted men were entertained throughout the war years by talented young people like Wilma and Nora in LLT's revue. (Courtesy Nora Snelgrove)*

this current season alone, present over 100 shows and will play before well over 100,000 persons in the twenty camps and air stations within a radius of 80 miles of London. You will leave your work at 5:00 o'clock to rush down to the YMCA to board a bus which will transport you to the scene of action. You will eat a cold box lunch on the way. Tired as you may be from your day's work, you will take your part in the performance with pep and a smile. You are never late for the bus. The shows always start on time. After the performance you will bump along home in a bus, arriving in the city somewhere between 1:00 and 2:00 a.m. and you will be up and at work on time the following morning. You have done these things for three seasons. This is a tribute to your ability and energy. It is for all these things that the Citizens' Committee and all the citizens of London whom we represent, owe to you, and express to you on behalf of the Members of the Armed Forces, a deep debt of gratitude for the splendid service which you have rendered and will continue to give as one of your contributions toward ultimate victory." – J.G. Thompson, Chairman.

ARSENIC AND OLD LACE

Arsenic and Old Lace was still enjoying a New York City run when the touring production, starring Walter Hampden, came to London. In a nutshell, the story is about two spinster sisters, Abby and Martha, who put lonely old gentlemen out of their misery by plying them with glasses of poisoned elderberry wine. "It kept a large crowd of Londoners at the Grand Theatre in a prolonged intoxication of laughter. For this play is super-burlesque, and in the hands of the gifted company who has Walter Hampden for its star, it proved entertainment of a quite original kind. This whole most competently performed and cleverly produced play is entirely original fare. It is tongue-in-the-cheek stuff but most judiciously and aptly designed and executed. If you have never

enjoyed a murder before you will enjoy these; if you have tears of laughter to shed, you shed them here." (– F.B. Taylor, *London Free Press*, December 5, 1942)

LLT Season #9:
Hay Fever, by Noel Coward, directed by Catharine McCormick Brickenden
The Cradle Song, by Gregorio Martinez Sierra, directed by Blanch Tancock
Ladies in Retirement, by Edward Percy and Reginal Denham, directed by John Burton
Theatre, by Somerset Maugham and Guy Bolton, directed by Walter Dixon
Hobson's Choice, by Harold Brighouse, directed by Christine Thomas

Revue:
Take It Or Leave It, LLT troop show

LLT Studio Club season included:
According to the Prophet, dramatized and produced by Catharine McCormick Brickenden
The Lampshade, by W.S. Milne
Joint Owners in Spain, by Will Brown

Road Show:
Arsenic and Old Lace, by Joseph Kesselring, starring Walter Hampden

1943/44

LONDON LITTLE THEATRE ERA

CLAUDIA

"With the largest subscription in its history, necessitating three performances of each play, LLT embarked at the Grand Theatre on its ninth consecutive season. For this, the 41st performance, the currently popular play *Claudia* was chosen, and to this effective, though not altogether convincing comedy-drama, the cast gave a finished and satisfactory performance. Honors may be dropped lavishly at the feet of Patricia Robinson, this zestful ingenue who played a long and difficult role with undiminished sympathy, vivacity and charm, practically line perfect, and moving with control and emphasis from the gamin wit of the first two acts to the wistful gallantry with which she met the final curtain. Young Miss Robinson gave an excellent performance; her name twinkles brightly in the LLT galaxy."(– F.B. Taylor, *London Free Press*, October 26, 1943)

We did a show called Claudia. *I got called up by some irate female at the other end of the line and she was absolutely appalled at the idea of this play being put on. The idea of a high school girl being portrayed as a pregnant woman! Disgusting! Disgusting! 'Oh,' she said, 'I think young people today are just dreadful, don't you?' And I said, 'No I don't. I think young people today are wonderful and I think it's a crying shame that so many of them are overseas right now dying for fools like you.'*
– Catharine McCormick Brickenden
1962 CFPL interview, conducted by Paul Soles

Catharine (Kizzie) McCormick Brickenden was active in theatre in London from the 1920s, when she acted in London Drama League productions. As a member of London Little Theatre she directed many plays. McCormick Brickenden wrote many plays and enjoyed having them produced by various theatre companies. She championed the cause of Canadian playwrights and was passionate about presenting Canadian plays to Canadian audiences. In the mid-1940s, McCormick Brickenden worked effectively behind the scenes to enable LLT to purchase the Grand Theatre, and in the early 1970s she supported the idea of LLT turning into the professional company, Theatre London. (Courtesy of her daughter Dorinda Greenway)

GRAND THEATRE
LONDON

LLT Season #10:
Claudia, by Rose Franken, directed by Ken Baskette
Too Many Husbands, by Somerset Maugham, directed by Agnes Arnott
Watch on the Rhine, by Lillian Hellman, directed by Doris Isard
Papa Is All, by Patterson Greene, directed by Florence Smith
Quiet Wedding, by Esther McCracken, directed by Doris Isard

Revue:
Take It Or Leave It, LLT troop show

LLT Studio season included:
Thank You Doctor, by Gilbert Emory
The First Dress Suit, by Russell Metcalfe

Road Show:
Blossom Time, by Dorothy Donnelly

Music:
Don Cossack Chorus

BERNICE HARPER

LLT member Bernice Harper worked for hours on end, choreographing dance routines for the popular wartime revue *Take It Or Leave It*. Miss Harper came to London as part of a road show company. Legend has it that the play died on the road and stranded the young actress/dancer in London, Ontario. She found a secretarial job, but soon a London Little Theatre director talked her into going back on stage. The spell of the footlights encouraged her to give up the office job, dig her tights from her trunk and become a full-time dance instructor and a choreographer for many LLT productions. Scores of Londoners learned to dance from the tireless Bernice Harper.

PURCHASE OF THE GRAND

During this season, the executive of LLT made a bid to purchase the Grand Theatre from its owner, Famous Players. Although there were other interested parties who wished to purchase the building, to raze it and to replace it with either a bowling alley or a parking garage, LLT was ultimately the successful buyer. LLT achieved this because it could rely on three things: (i) the efforts of enthusiastic workers, (ii) interested public support and (iii) the backing of a small group of persuasive London businessmen and influential women.

On June 7 of 1945, LLT president, Dr. Alan Skinner, received this letter from J.J. Fitzgibbons of Famous Players Canadian Corporation, Toronto:

LLT's Studio Club was going strong throughout the war years, and in May of 1945 featured a production of Cry Havoc. *Pictured are (l. to r.): Dorothy Westhead, Mary Campbell, Wilma Crozier, Clair Foster, Robina Richardson, (sitting at table) Mary Ashwell, Bernice Harper, June Miller, Nora Snelgrove, Andre Pearce, Isabelle Shaw and Frieda Stephens. (Courtesy of Nora Snelgrove). In the cast, but not pictured, was Florence Smith who was also assistant director, and who assisted her husband, Laurie C. Smith, in designing and building the set. "Ken Baskette, in directing* Cry Havoc, *has done a controlled and sensitive piece of work, with sharp drama and excellent comedy. Pettiness and gallantry cross each other on the little stage." (–* London Free Press, *May, 1945)*

"Dear Dr. Skinner: Because we want to demonstrate our appreciation of the splendid work you and your associates have done in the development of the Little Theatre Group of London, and because we appreciate very much the contribution your organization makes to community life in London, and to the needed cultural development of our way of life, I am happy to inform you that at a meeting this morning, our directors elected to accept your offer, although it was considerably less than another offer pending. We wish you and your associates and all the members of the Little Theatre Group of London, continued success in your very worthy work." (– National Archives of Canada)

On June 11, Dr. Skinner responded to this welcome news: "Dear Mr. Fitzgibbons: Thank you very much for your letter of June 7. May I thank you specially for your appreciation of the achievements of London Little Theatre as expressed in your letter, and may I express the hope that we may continue to maintain cordial relationships in connection with the entertainment field in London. At our annual meeting, I referred particularly to your generous and sympathetic reception of our proposition, and to your friendly interest in the group. I can assure you that a hearty round of applause from the active members of LLT followed these remarks." (– National Archives of Canada)

Writing in a LLT house program during the 1965/66 season, Fred Phelps fills in some of the blanks in this happy story: "Catharine (Kizzie) McCormick Brickenden knew Mr. J. J. Fitzgibbons, president of Famous Players in the United States and Canada, and while they were both attending the Royal Horse Show in Toronto, Kizzie managed to persuade the president of the movie empire to make the very generous gesture of accepting LLT's offer of $35,000 for The Grand, providing it was made within a month. Committees sprang into action. Charles Isard with a team of volunteer canvassers appealed to the citizens of London who donated $17,000, the first contribution to this Citizens Fund coming from the *London Free Press*. Each board member of the theatre was asked to contribute $100 – they all did. However by the end, the campaign was still $12,000 short of the objective. An advisory board was formed and among its members were: Mr. Bev Hay, Ted Margrett, Mr. Hugh Labatt, Jack Stevens, Verse Cronyn, Charles Isard and Gordon Thompson. It was Mr. Gordon Thompson who eventually contributed $12,000 to push the campaign over the top. Dr. Alan Skinner was the originator, the creator and the driving force behind the plan. It is agreed that without his foresight and vision, plus guts and determination, The Grand would not be, and there would be a bowling alley on 471 Richmond Street."

By 1965 the theatre building was valued at $75,000, and by 1999 the building's estimated value was over $7 million.

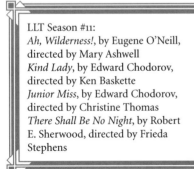

LLT Season #11:
Ah, Wilderness!, by Eugene O'Neill, directed by Mary Ashwell
Kind Lady, by Edward Chodorov, directed by Ken Baskette
Junior Miss, by Edward Chodorov, directed by Christine Thomas
There Shall Be No Night, by Robert E. Sherwood, directed by Frieda Stephens

Springtide, by J.B. Priestley and George Billam, directed by Walter Dixon

Revue:
Take It Or Leave It, the 12th edition of the troop show, directed by Ken Baskette

LLT Studio Club season included:
Cry Havoc, by Allan R. Kenward

1945/46

LONDON LITTLE THEATRE ERA

ITS OWN PLAYHOUSE

The 1945/46 season represented a break from the past for LLT. Before that time the group was a tenant in the theatre. Now the thriving organization had its own playhouse. Writing in 1962, in a dissertation for Ohio State University, Ian MacDonald observed that: "The acquisition of the Grand Theatre provided new avenues of development and opportunities for self-expression for the enterprising workers of LLT. It also enabled them to improve the calibre of their productions. The multiplicity of their activities and the high standard of their productions, attested to the exceptional size of the subscription membership, established the organization both locally and nationally, as an enterprising and highly successful institution."

LLT now had to budget for its season *and* budget for operating the theatre building. For the 1945/46 season it estimated that it could produce six plays for $2,000 each and, with other expenses, it would expend $18,000. Operating the theatre would cost LLT $14,150, but it estimated revenues on the building, earned from professional shows rentals and local organizations rentals, at $14,150, thereby breaking even.

KEN BASKETTE

As a proud theatre owner, LLT hired a theatre manager. At a board meeting in August of 1945, Ken Baskette was made business manager for the Grand Theatre. Before that time he had been business manager for LLT. London actor/director Don Fleckser says: "Ken Baskette could not recognize that there was a thing called amateur theatre. He brought to each production the standard and the expectations of professional theatre. He was a shy and different kind of person who quietly stood out of the limelight always. His right arm was a lady named Benva Menzies. Together they ran the box office and the theatre like it was sitting square on Broadway. During his years as manager some of the world's greatest performers appeared on The Grand's stage. One of my memories about Ken was his office, which was filled with autographed pictures of every star in the business. Everyone wanted to see those pictures."

One of Ken Baskette's jobs as business manager was to bring touring productions into the theatre. LLT made it a habit to support such professional touring companies by loaning them its subscription lists, by canvassing its subscribers, and by actively encouraging the LLT audience to support the visiting players by attending touring shows.

THE GREEN ROOM

The Grand Theatre and LLT drew the attention of Canada's national magazine, *Maclean's*, in April of 1946. Part of the magazine's story dealt with the theatre's Green Room: "Casting six full-length plays a season means that producers must have a wide choice of experienced players to draw from. London keeps a constant flow of new talent developing in its Green Room, the combination clubroom, junior theatre and experimental lab situated near The Grand. It is to the Green Room that some casual subscriber is invited for tea, and suddenly finds a typewritten script thrust into her trembling hand and a director coaxing, 'Now try that line again with more feeling!' Here tired businessmen arrive after work, shed their coats and go to it.

Directors compare marked scripts. In one corner a crew of young women in shorts and sunsuits doggedly punish their figures with back bends, pushups and basic ballet routines."

LLT Season #12:
Call It A Day, by Dodie Smith, directed by Catharine McCormick Brickenden
My Sister Eileen, by Edward Chodorov, directed by Mary Ashwell
Our Town, by Thornton Wilder, directed by Blanch Tancock
Blithe Spirit, by Noel Coward, directed by Christine Thomas
Uncle Harry, by Thomas Job, directed by Ken Baskette and Frieda Stephens
You Can't Take It With You, by Moss Hart and George S. Kaufman, directed by Walter Dixon

LLT Studio Club season included:
Twelfth Night, by William Shakespeare
People With Light Coming Out of Them, by William Saroyan
The Enchanted Cottage, by Sir Arthur Wing Pinero

Revues:
Kiwanis Follies, produced by LLT
Up On The Hill, UWO's First Annual Follies, "a musical hodgepodge"

Plays on Tour:
Life With Father
School for Brides
The Forgotten Factor, an industrial drama for national teamwork; produced by a joint Canadian-American cast who are giving their time to the work of Moral Re-Armament as a national service.

Festival:
WODL, May 10/11, 1946

1st Annual Summer School of Theatre:
The Changeling, by Thomas Middleton and William Rowley, directed by Norris Houghton, on stage at The Grand, August 1/2 1946, presented by the students enroled in the University of Western Ontario/ London Little Theatre Summer School

Music:
Witold Malcuzynski, world-famous pianist

Radio:
In January of 1946 LLT began production of radio drama for CFPL, which would continue on and off, until the early 1950s.

1946/47

LONDON LITTLE THEATRE ERA

JOHN GIELGUD

In early November 1946, Londoners learned from their newspaper that the city had been chosen for the opening of the first North American tour in ten years, of the John Gielgud Repertory Company from England. The renowned company would arrive in the city in mid-January. Toronto playwright Brian Doherty (known for his 1937 play *Father Malachy's Miracle*) had written to

A rare exterior shot showing the Grand Theatre at night, all lit up to attract the crowds. The marquee is promoting the LLT production of Pride and Prejudice. *In the newspaper review it was noted that actress Jean Back, playing Elizabeth Bennet, was "a British bride (who) has not played before. She has a charming voice and appearance and moves with grace." (—* **London Free Press,** *February 1947) (Courtesy of Jean Back)*

Gielgud and informed the star of London's great interest in theatre, about the progressiveness of LLT and about the Summer Theatre School. Upon hearing of this activity, Gielgud made up his mind to open his first post-war North American tour at London's Grand Theatre. True to the promotional hype, "The World's Greatest Actor in the World's Wittiest Play" was coming to town!

On January 19, 1947, John Gielgud and his company, which included Margaret Rutherford (the irresistible comedienne who specialized in delightful dowager roles) and Pamela Brown (who, at 23 years of age, was already a stage star) arrived at London's train station. After pausing briefly at Hotel London, the company made its way to the Grand Theatre. A few days of rehearsal followed. It was a historic night at the Grand Theatre when, on Thursday, January 23, the house lights went down and the stage lights came up on Gielgud's production of Oscar Wilde's comedy *The Importance of Being Earnest*. In what has been described as a high-comedy with a plot of monumental unimportance, Gielgud was the dandy Jack Worthin', with Robert Flemyng taking the role as Algernon. Miss Rutherford was Lady Bracknell, and Miss Brown played Gwendolyn. The opening night audience was thrilled. Londoners enjoyed a witty and engaging night of theatre in the cold, dark month of January. The day after the opening, Gielgud delivered a lecture to LLT members in the Green Room.

Appreciation of drama and good theatre is an acquired taste – and it may be compared with a taste for oysters and beer. You get to know the good things only if you persevere a bit.
– John Gielgud, Globe & Mail, *January 22, 1947*
(Reprinted with permission from the Globe & Mail.*)*

MARGARET RUTHERFORD

London actor/director Don Fleckser tells the story of Miss

Rutherford, Kingsmill's Department Store and the "Nylon Stockings": "The great actress was more interested in purchasing nylons, which she had been told she could acquire at Kingsmill's on Dundas Street, instead of Act III of *Earnest*. She had not been able to purchase nylon stockings in Britain during the war. After her exit in Act II she returned to her dressing room at The Grand, slipped out of her Edwardian costume and into her street clothes, and walked south on Richmond Street to the department store. Her absence was soon noticed. Theatre manager Ken Baskette was dispatched post-haste to retrieve Miss Rutherford so that she could deliver her lines in Act III. He raced down to Kingsmill's, found the actress seated comfortably at the nylon counter assisted by star-struck store staff. When Mr. Baskette reminded her that the matinee performance was not yet over and that she was needed on stage, they raced back to The Grand together, where Miss Rutherford enacted her scenes in Act III in her own clothes."

FROM LONDON TO LONDON

We opened our tour in London, Ontario. We had really wonderful audiences there. Packed houses at each performance, and most responsive they were, too. 'Twas absolutely thrilling. Just one week after we'd left London, England, we were in London, Canada, complete with a Canadian Thames River and everything. We felt at home right away.
– John Gielgud, speaking on CBC Radio, broadcast on January 28, 1947, interviewed by Rupert Caplan

Such a good time was had by John Gielgud and his company in London in January, that he promised to return in July with his production of William Congreve's *Love for Love*. Upon his return, critic F. B. Taylor wrote: "Gielgud's return to London last night drew a packed house to The Grand in midsummer. Gielgud has surrounded himself with an excellent company of players; the whole play is polished (and slightly pruned) to a perfection of diction and movement; it is superbly mounted; it glitters with style, and is as rowdy as a barn dance." (– *London Free Press*, July 26, 1947)

DONALD WOLFIT

The great actor-manager Donald Wolfit, and his Shakespeare Company, followed closely on Gielgud's heels. He came to London in February of 1947 to present *King Lear* and *The Merchant of Venice*. F.B. Taylor's diligence as a theatre critic turned up a small nugget of trivia when she interviewed the actor-manager – his mother was born in London, Ontario. "It was a family joke that it should have been London, Ontario instead of London, England" the great actor commented to London's theatre critic. (–*London Free Press*, February 2, 1947).

Wolfit's grandfather sailed to Canada and while on board fell in love with a young British woman. They settled in Canada and while living in London, Ontario, the couple had a baby daughter. Soon the young family sailed back to England and the girl born in London, Canada, later had a son who became actor Donald Wolfit.

"Donald Wolfit's curtain calls were always a show in themselves. He would come to centre stage and appear between the curtains. He clung to the curtains as he took his bow. Just to let the audience know how much the performance had exhausted him!"
– Florence Smith, former LLT board president

In summing up Wolfit's company's effect on London theatre-goers, F.B. Taylor wrote: "As exhilarating a draught of Shakespearean drama as London has quaffed in many a day." (– *London Free Press*, February 10, 1947) Donald Wolfit is best known today as the role model for the "Actor" in Ronald Harwood's hit play from 1980, *The Dresser*.

DOMINION DRAMA FESTIVAL

Just when it seemed that The Grand's 1946/47 season could not get any more exciting, LLT members prepared for the annual Dominion Drama Festival, "the high spot of the year for all patrons of Canadian amateur drama," which would be held at London's Grand Theatre. (LLT's *Call-Boy*, April 1947). While World War II raged on, the DDF was on hold, but in May of 1947 the DDF was back and bigger than ever, with all that pent up theatrical energy ready to burst forth. This DDF presented an opportunity for players from across the country to stage, and see, 13 plays, all for the price of $7.50. Players from Ottawa, Edmonton, Montreal, Vancouver, Simcoe (Ontario), Halifax, Toronto and Windsor descended upon the Grand Theatre, and stretched its dressing room capacity to the full. Thousands of theatre enthusiasts from coast to coast also headed for The Grand. The Right Honourable Governor General Vincent Massey, former High Commissioner to Great Britain and President of the DDF, came to London and sat in a Grand Theatre box with the Honourable Ray Lawrence, Lieutenant-Governor of Ontario, and Mrs. Lawrence. The adjudicator was Prof. Emrys M. Jones of the University of Saskatchewan.

It will not be all work for Canada's festival entries. There will be a round of teas, supper parties and balls to keep them busy. The first social event took place at the Green Room of the LLT, where east met west and, over a cup of tea, talked shop.
– Mary Ashwell, reporting for CFPL Radio, May 1947

Covering the DDF for Canadian Press was Fred Kerner. He filed this story from London, Ontario on May 10, 1947: "The Little Theatre movement across Canada consumes its own smoke. This is its chief difficulty in the opinion of Robertson Davies, editor of the *Peterborough Examiner*. Mr. Davies, graduate of the Old Vic Theatre in London, England, is here with his father, Senator Rupert Davies, publisher of the *Kingston Whig-Standard* and a member of the board of governors of the DDF. Admitting he wants 'to beat the drums as much as is possible for Canadians plays,' the actor-newspaperman has definite ideas on the Little Theatre movement, on plays and on criticism. 'The Little Theatre is inclined to be self-defeating in some ways unless something happens to give it new ideas,' he said. Little Theatre amateurs get little opportunity in the Dominion to see the professional theatre from which its inspiration might spring. 'The greatest duty of the press is to develop better criticism,' Mr. Davies said. 'This is not easy – we need the co-operation of the readers. They are usually most resentful of criticism. As long as criticism is regarded as a personal attack there will be no intelligent criticism. You can't have good art without good criticism.' Criticism now is on the level the public demands, Mr. Davies said. In reference to plays, Mr. Davies' particular interest, he felt that 'considering the lack of encouragement, I think it is surprising that we have any Canadian drama at all. But what there is of it is very good.'"

I think we always felt we had to live up to this building. And I can remember playing in Dominion Drama Festivals and some of the other groups would say: 'But you've got that theatre. It must make it so much easier for you because you're used to working in a really professional theatre.' On the other hand we had to live up to this theatre, and not only did we have to live up to it, we had to support it. We had to be good.
– Elizabeth Murray, former LLT board president, actress

IMPROVEMENTS TO THE BUILDING

LLT, the Grand Theatre's owner, set about making improvements to the building. The *London Free Press* reported on the latest change in the building: "A bit of the past is being taken from the Grand Theatre. Cubicles which gave privacy for the great and near great who over many years trod the boards of The Grand, while they dressed and applied their grease paint, are falling to the hammers of wreckers. In their place staunch and clean concrete brick partitions are being constructed. Directors of LLT see the passing of the old dressing rooms without a sigh of regret. At best they were dingy. Those longest associated with the building say both professional and amateur talent who used them were much less complimentary in their descriptions. And with reason. The rooms were dark and dank, inadequately lighted and unsuitable." (– April 12, 1947)

LLT Season #13:
While the Sun Shines, by Terence Rattigan, directed by Catharine McCormick Brickenden / Doris Isard
Ten Little Indians, by Agatha Christie, directed by Ken Baskette
The Corn is Green, by Emlyn Williams, directed by John Burton
Pride and Prejudice, by Helen Jerome, directed by Christine Thomas
Winterset, by Maxwell Anderson, directed by Blanch Tancock
Mr. Pim Passes By, by A.A. Milne, directed by Florence Phelps

LLT Studio Club season included:
Scapegoats, by Eric Harris
Banquo's Chair, by Rupert Croft-Cooke
Fumed Oak, by Noel Coward

LLT Children's Theatre:
The Frog Fairy, adapted from Grimm
Legend, by Hilda Hooke

Revue:
Flashbacks of '47, "a sparkling new dance revue" featuring Bernice Harper Dancers, and Johnny Downs and His Orchestra, and a cast of 80

2nd Annual Summer School of Theatre:
Stage Door, by Edna Ferber and George S. Kaufman
The Happy Journey, by Thornton Wilder

Festival:
Dominion Drama Festival, May 5 – 10, 1947

Roadshows:
The Importance of Being Earnest, by Oscar Wilde, starring John Gielgud
Love for Love, by William Congreve, starring John Gielgud
King Lear, The Merchant of Venice, As You Like It, starring Donald Wolfit

Entertainer:
Ruth Draper in Her Inimitable Character Sketches

Dance:
Jooss Ballet, the Contemporary Dance-Theatre

Music:
Thomas L. Thomas, baritone
Witold Malcuzynski, in an All Chopin Recital

1947/48

LONDON LITTLE THEATRE ERA

PROGRAM MESSAGES

LLT house programs carried the following friendly messages this season: "Once again, it seems, we must remind all and sundry that LLT productions start promptly at 8:30 and patrons who are not then in their seats will be obliged to wait in the lobby until the first intermission." And: "Ladies are asked to remove their hats at LLT performances if same are likely to hamper the view of folks seated behind. As far as we are concerned, ladies' hats have already taken enough of a kicking around at the hands – or feet – of humorists and comedians, so we attempt no facetious addenda to this notice." (– LLT *Call-Boy*, November, 1947)

PURPLE PATCHES

During the first week of December 1947, the musical revue *Purple Patches* was on The Grand's vast stage. Produced by Roger Shirley and Al Deadman, and directed by Ken Baskette, it featured dancing and choreography by Bernice Harper. A male choir and clever skits were the outstanding features. *Purple Patches* built on the success of the University's Medical School *Follies*, and the Arts and Science *Up on the Hill* productions. This production marked the beginning of a new venture, wherein students from the School of Nursing, the Faculty of Medicine and University College's Faculty of Arts and Science combined their efforts to produce *Purple Patches*, to emphasize the spirit of the University of Western Ontario.

SAINT JOAN

LLT's December play was an ambitious production of George Bernard Shaw's *Saint Joan*. The lead role was taken by Olga Landiak. By day she was a switchboard operator at the Bank of Montreal; by night she became France's heroine. She had come to London from her home near Fort William to attend the UWO/LLT summer theatre school. She stayed in London and Blanch Tancock cast her in this production. It went on to win the DDF's award for best play of 1948, and Olga Landiak's performance was recognized by the adjudicator as the best performance by a woman at that year's festival. LLT presented Olga Landiak with a $1000 scholarship, which she used to study for a year at the Royal Academy of Dramatic Arts in England.

Another member of the *Saint Joan* cast was Jack Hutt. Born in Ingersoll, Ontario, Jack first performed at UWO, where he studied in the late 1940s. After graduation he studied acting, directing and stage technique at Northwestern University in Chicago. He returned to London with an M.A. In a 1967 interview with the *London Free Press*, he recalled making a telephone call to director Blanch Tancock: "I'd heard they were doing *Saint Joan* and I was interested in doing a part. It took a great deal of nerve to make that call, but I did and asked her if she had anything. The part I wanted, Brother Martin, was already cast, but she told me to come down anyway. By chance, the actor dropped out and I got the part…I often think about that phone call. If I hadn't made it I'd probably be teaching now." (– August 18, 1967). The late Jack Hutt, cousin of actor William Hutt, later became production manager at the Stratford Festival. By the 1970s he was the genial and much-loved Front of House Manager for the Stratford Festival.

Blanch Tancock, director, is pictured with Governor General Vincent Massey, who presented her with the Bessborough Trophy for the production of Saint Joan. *This was the highest award at the DDF each year. The award ceremony took place in Ottawa, where the 1948 DDF took place. (Courtesy of LRAHM, London, ON)*

DUBLIN GATE THEATRE COMPANY

In January of 1948, the Grand Theatre hosted the North American premiere of Dublin Gate Theatre. As a direct result of Gielgud's success at London's theatre in January of 1947, the Dublin Gate Theatre Company had chosen The Grand as its site to launch its tour of North America, The 20-member company moved into The Grand and performed *John Bull's Other Island, Where Stars Walk* and *The Old Lady Says "No."* Theatre manager Ken Baskette could not have been happier at the way things were turning out under his management: "I feel that getting two premieres within a year is pretty wonderful for our city. London was considered a good stop some years ago when theatre companies toured North America. Even then theatre-goers in this town were regarded as a good test for any production. More than a few companies have

said that a good show in London meant success in New York."
(– *London Free Press,* December 4, 1947)

MACBETH

The next big thing was a production of Shakespeare's *Macbeth* starring Michael Redgrave and Flora Robson. This company from England arrived at The Grand early in March 1948. In the March 15 edition of the *London Free Press,* Mr. Redgrave admitted to having had some tough luck in London; Flora Robson had a cold sore in one of her tear ducts, and Redgrave was suffering from a terrific cold. In what surely must rank as one of theatre's greatest understatements, he was quoted as saying: "That cold was rather bad. Macbeth is the sort of role which calls for a good voice." (– March 15, 1948)

Legend has it that the Redgrave/Robson company was not thoroughly prepared for their Grand Theatre debut. The first performance was under-rehearsed and did not go smoothly. Audience members were not gracious during the curtain call. Some were heard to call out: "Author!" to demonstrate their disappointment in the production. Many LLT actors felt that they had given Londoners more polished and professional performances than those given to them by these most recent visiting stars from England.

LLT Season #14:
The Male Animal, by James Thurber and Elliott Hugent, directed by Florence Smith
The Circle, by Somerset Maugham, directed by Robina Richardson
Saint Joan, by G.B. Shaw, directed by Barry Hunt
Dear Ruth, by Norman Krasna, directed by Martin O'Meara
Guest in the House, by Wilde and Eunson, directed by Florence Smith
I Remember Mama, by John Van Druten, directed by Peggy Hutchinson

LLT Studio Club season included:
Hedda Gabler, by Henrik Ibsen
A Marriage Proposal, by Anton Chekhov
The Chameleon, by George A. Palmer

Road Shows:
John Bull's Other Island, by G.B. Shaw, *Where Stars Walk,* by Michael MacLiammoir, *The Old Lady Says "No",* by Denis Johnston, *A Festival of Irish Comedies,* produced by the Dublin Gate Theatre
Much Ado About Nothing, by William Shakespeare, starring Donald Wolfit
Macbeth, by William Shakespeare, starring Michael Redgrave and Flora Robson
The Winslow Boy, by Terrence Rattigan
Martha, by Von Flotow, produced by the Rosselino Opera Company

Music:
Hazel Scott, in a Unique Concert of the Modern and Classics

Local Production:
Purple Patches, produced by UWO

Magician:
Blackstone, the World's Master Magician and His Show of 1001 Wonders

Dance:
Alicia Markova and Anton Dolin with Ballet Ensemble

3rd Annual Summer School of Theatre:
A Woman's Privilege, by Marijane and Joseph Hayes
Murder in the Cathedral, by T.S. Eliot, produced by Day Tuttle
Lord Byron's Love Letter, by Tennessee Williams, produced by Day Tuttle
Through a Glass, Darkly, by Stanley Richards, produced by Day Tuttle

1948/49

LONDON LITTLE THEATRE ERA

A FACELIFT

During this season LLT invested $8,000 in upgrades and repairs to its theatre. "Before, during, and since the August dog-days The Grand submitted to a fairly rigorous course of beauty treatment. Donald Routledge planned the operation which we hope you will agree has been a success. Working from the outside in, here is what has been done. The lobby has been painted in three shades of grey, lighted with dead-white and gun-metal. A rich mahogany stain on the doors leading out of the lobby makes a lively contrast. In the foyer, shades ranging from flesh pink to watermelon have been used with, again, accents of dead-white and gun-metal. The house itself has been dolled up in pastel green, while the seats sport French-grey trim. All this constitutes a far cry from the sombre shades in which the Grand was somewhat dowdily dressed for so long." (– LLT *Call-Boy*, October, 1948)

Repair work had to be done to Challener's mural on the proscenium arch. The canvas was loosening and coming away from the arch. This condition was attributed to dampness and the age of the work. Because of the mural's excessive weight, the canvas, originally applied uncut, was cut into eight sections and then replaced.

GOODBYE, MY FANCY

Goodbye, My Fancy, a new play by Fay Kanin on tour with a professional theatre company starring Madeline Carroll, moved into the Grand Theatre in October. The Grand had been selected as the pre-Broadway site. One of the producers, Mr. Aldrich, had come to London for the North American premiere of Michael Redgrave's *Macbeth*, and had so enjoyed The Grand that he now brought his own production. Besides the star power of film actress Miss Carroll, the cast included Shirley Booth, Conrad Nagel and Sam Wanamaker. Miss Carroll, famous for her screen work and her war work, played to a packed house on October 21. The stage was strewn with tossed roses as the curtain came down. In summarizing the performance, F.B. Taylor wrote: "This is a very competent cast and this was a competent performance with a neat sense of detail, a most attractive set with nice lighting and a good atmosphere. The parts are not entirely consistent in the scenes, Miss Carroll's particularly; you could not be quite sure exactly what sort of a person this Agatha Reed was supposed to be. But as

Blanch Tancock (right) is shown reflected in a dressing room mirror, making suggestions as Mabel Fells applies makeup to William Hitchins. (Courtesy of William Ziegler)

Four young actors from LLT production of Shakespeare's **As You Like It** *were photographed as they relaxed in full costume in The Grand's alley: (l. to r.) Kent Jackson, William Ziegler, William Graham and Gordon Reid. (Courtesy of William Ziegler)*

Madeleine Carroll played her, much was to be forgiven her, so loveable she was." (– *London Free Press*, October 22, 1948)

LLT AND SHAKESPEARE

Shakespeare's *As You Like It* was mounted by LLT and garnered the attention of *Globe & Mail* critic Herbert Whittaker. "It is quite newsworthy – for it is the first Shakespeare production ever staged by LLT. The LLT has been, for the last few years, the envy of all the Little Theatre groups in Canada. Under expert guidance, LLT has been built up to a major theatrical organization. Out of a population of 91,000, it has achieved a membership subscription of 10,000. It has bought its own theatre, The Grand, and in addition to its regular season presents professional touring companies. Its reputation has been enhanced by the opening there of a number of professional productions, both English and American. LLT itself has long been highly regarded for Shaw's *Saint Joan*, but somehow the LLT had not ventured into the production of any Shakespeare play until this year. A membership of 10,000 requires careful selection of plays, and it was felt that until a good presentation of any Shakespearean classic could be assured, it was better to wait. This year, however, it was felt that the LLT was finally ready for the Bard. It picked *As You Like It* and put in Blanch Tancock, who had made a success of *Saint Joan*, as the director. The results proved well worth the trip, being satisfactory in many ways, and LLT can build on this achievement to present more Shakespeare in future. Mind you, LLT's *As You Like It* was not the kind of Shakespeare that made history on its own accord. Mrs. Hogg wisely took a conservative line in production. Her Forest of Arden was decorative, rather than experimental; her actors broke no new ground in Shakespearean interpretation but held to a line which had proved popular in the past. The production, designed by Alice Mackenzie, was simple in its elements. …The crowd's favourite of the evening was easily Roy Irving's Touchstone. This actor, who was with the Dublin Gate Company and remained behind in Canada, knows all the techniques of the professional stage by which a character can shine. …For a first venture into Shakespeare, LLT's *As You Like It* had much to commend it. LLT had discovered that it could tackle the Bard and audiences seemed to like it." (– May 21, 1949)

The National Film Board of Canada, in association with the Federal Department of Labour, filmed the production process of *As You Like It*. The resulting film was entitled *Prelude to Performance*. The silent film was used as an instruction on how to produce a play. It covered such details as Interviewing the

Potential Cast, Methods of Casting, Collecting the Properties, Blocking out the Play, and so on. Director Blanch Tancock and her designer, stage manager and actors can be seen in each frame of the film. Viewing the film today provides a window into the inner workings of LLT at its peak.

THREE LEADING LADIES IN LONDON

The *Canadian Home Journal* profiled LLT directors Mary Ashwell and Doris Isard, along with Blanch Tancock, in a feature article entitled "Three Leading Ladies in London, Ontario's Successful Little Theatre Movement" (April 1949): "If you're a play producer in London, Ontario, you're good. Today, the heady pull of big-time theatre is in the London air. This season, their now-famous Little Theatre has a record membership of 10,000 and a waiting list of 3,000. Each of its six major productions runs for a tough nine-night stand." The article disclosed that as successful as LLT was, "criticizing the LLT is London's best in-door sport. The capacity crowds are probably quicker to pounce on a producer's weak spots than any Broadway long-hair would. They've forgotten about the ghosts of by-gone road shows which used to permeate the old Grand Opera House there. Today's business is big business and only a fighting producer can stand the gaff. For this is no afternoon-tea league. Competition is cutthroat; not always polite. Sex is no discriminant. Producing experts – both men and women – vie to direct the most personally appealing productions; players strain to get roles. Even a junior producer whose work is confined to LLT's Studio Club is out to prove he has the theatrical know-how that one day will make him into a senior producer. These are the champs, these senior producers, whom the Little Theatre's Board of Directors appoints. It take incredible work, patience and some curious extra gimmick to make the grade."

SUMMER STOCK

"For the first time in at least a couple of decades, London is to have summer stock this year. The Shelton-Amos Players will open at the Grand Theatre on August 15, 1949, for an engagement running into early autumn. The company of 10 arrives in London on August 8 to begin rehearsal. Hall Shelton, producer, told me during his brief stay in town this week that the undertaking had a long term view; that he hoped to create a public in London and in Western Ontario that will want summer stock season after season. Mr. Shelton, American stage and film producer, is a stock company expert of long standing and the company which he and his gifted actress wife, Ruth Shelton, head, is considered one of the best on the American continent." (– F.B. Taylor, *London Free Press*, June 25, 1949)

When *Meet the Wife* hit the Grand's stage in August, Londoners liked what they saw: "London said a hearty how-do-you-do to the Shelton-Amos Players, welcoming Summer Stock to this city. This personable American company moved in for a seven week run, and an audience of first nighters gave a roaring stamp of approval to the first show. From the start the play was in the lithe and experienced hands of Ruth Amos, character comedienne of wide experience and, it would seem, limitless resource. First night difficulties, a belated start and a topping of local officials still left Miss Amos shining with the lustre of a real trouper when the final curtain came uproariously down." (– F.B. Taylor, *London Free Press,* August 16, 1949)

Who was Ruth Amos? Her official printed program biography stated: "Miss Amos is considered one of the foremost character comediennes on the American stage." By the time her company came to The Grand that stage experience had been earned during 30 years in stock, on tour and on Broadway. She estimated that she had between 500 and 700 roles under her belt by 1949. "If she is as original and attractive on stage as she is off, Ruth Amos will be a good lead in any company. She claims that she has no beauty that Hollywood should desire, but she has more than the necessary good looks, a clear, young voice with an easy, unaccented diction, and a great zest for the theatre." (– F.B. Taylor, *London Free Press*, August 10, 1949)

Ticket prices were kept to between 75 cents and $1 for the evenings, and even lower for Wednesday and Saturday matinees, to compete with movie prices. LLT was grossing approximately $4,000 a week which represented satisfactory business, and also provided a margin of profit for both LLT and Hall Shelton. This 1949 experiment in summer stock at The Grand was a success. Fortunately for London, the Shelton-Amos Players mounted summer stock seasons for six years in a row.

LLT Season #15:
Dream Girl, by Elmer Rice, directed by Peggy Hutchinson
Years Ago, by Ruth Gordon, directed by Patrick West
The Laughing Woman, by Gordon David, directed by Martin O'Meara
All My Sons, by Arthur Miller, directed by Peggy Hutchinson
As You Like It, by William Shakespeare, directed by Blanch Hogg
The Two Mrs. Carrolls, by Martin Vale, directed by Harding Greenwood

LLT Studio Club season included:
Christ's Comet, by Christopher Hassall
Uncle Vanya, by Anton Chekhov
Sitting Bill, by Martin O'Meara

LLT Children's Theatre included:
Snow White and the Seven Dwarfs, by Jessie Braham White

LLT All Canadian Concert Series:
Toronto Symphony Orchestra
Royal Conservatory Opera School
The Canadian Ballet Company
The New World Orchestra

Local Production:
Purple Patches, University of Western Ontario Revue

Road Shows:
Goodbye, My Fancy, by Fay Kanin, starring Madeline Carroll, Shirley Booth and Sam Wanamaker
The Ivy Green, by Mervyn Nelson
Oklahoma!, by Rodgers and Hammerstein
Gilbert and Sullivan Comic Opera Company
John Loves Mary
The Drunkard
Rosselino Opera Company
Fair Week Vaudeville Show
New Years Eve Vaudeville Show

Dance:
The Winnipeg Ballet

4th Annual Summer School of Theatre:
Quality Street, by J. M. Barrie, directed by Roy Irving
We Are Not Afraid, by Laurence Housman
The Londonderry Air, by Rachel Field

Magician:
Blackstone

Summer Stock:
The Shelton-Amos Players: *Meet the Wife, Kiss and Tell, Strange Bedfellows, Three's a Family, Stepping Sisters, The Whiteoaks of Jalna, It's a Wise Child, Cradle Snatchers*

1949/50

LONDON LITTLE THEATRE ERA

PUMPKIN PIE

LLT's Children's Theatre was going strong by 1949. It was another successful endeavour by the thriving organization that had seen extraordinary grown in activity throughout the 1940s. In reviewing a show for children, F.B. Taylor wrote: "For at least two hours today a couple of thousand London children were not reading crime comics. They were at the Grand Theatre enjoying the sheer classicisim of a play, mounted in the Elizabethan period and spoken in an elegant idiom. They loved it…*Pumpkin Pie* was deft and charming. The children were well drilled; their diction was good and, what is still more important, they had an excellent sense of the style and humor of this fairy tale *a la mode*. The legend of Peter Pumpkin Eater becomes a story of Peter the Gardener, winning the hand of the princess because of his personal charm, and the favour of the king because of his pie-making skills…The children were very nearly line-perfect; their work was lively and they managed commendably the formal speech, which, it was interesting to note, seemed perfectly intelligible to the audience. It was a good audience, providing at least a third of the entertainment, though not when the curtain was up. It overflowed the balcony, slid down the stairs and seated itself with appreciation in the boxes, for which there was no extra charge. It took part with uninhibited fervour in the singing of rounds and what not, during the sing song." (– *London Free Press,* November 26, 1949)

SHELTON-AMOS PLAYERS

The Shelton-Amos Players were back in residence in the summer of 1950. "In honour of Fair Week, the Shelton-Amos Players pranced and capered about on stage at the Grand Theatre last night in a piece called *In the Wrong Bed*. All the versatility of a stock company, plus some new players, some guest dancers and a couple of singers were employed in this noisy show which is called 'a comedy with music' and had a lot of the former and some of the latter. The audience, in a holiday humour, liked it and the company played fast to win this approval. This is one of those plays about mistaken identities, a device which Shakespeare was not above using, though did it rather better than these collaborators." (– F.B. Taylor, *London Free Press*, September 12, 1952)

Paul Eck, administrator of The Grand in the 1970s, related how the stock company's sets didn't change, but the set dressing did. Miss Amos liked to use large swatches of fabric on stage. The dry goods department of Simpson's department store, at the corner of Dundas and Richmond Streets, was only too happy to oblige the star. Someone from The Grand would pick up bolts of fabric each week. The company would then drape them tastefully around the set, but at the end of that play's week-long run the fabric was rolled back onto the bolt, returned uncut to the store, and put back on the shelves for purchasers. New bolts were then delivered, and on with the show.

London-born actor Hume Cronyn (left) directed Now I Lay Me Down To Sleep, *starring Fredric March (second from left) and March's wife Florence Eldridge (centre). They are seen accepting the freedom of the city from Mayor George Wenige (right). Also pictured is the co-producer George Nichols. The Grand Theatre hosted the world premiere of the professional theatre production, before it went on tour. (Courtesy of the* **London Free Press** *Collection of Photographic Negatives, the D.B. Weldon Library, The University of Western Ontario, London, ON)*

Grand Theatre
LONDON - CANADA

LLT Season #16:
It's A Boy, by Austin Helford, directed by Florence Smith
An Inspector Calls, by J. B. Priestley, directed by Harding Greenwood
Thunder Rock, by Robert Ardrey, directed by Doris Isard
The Play's the Thing, by Ferenc Molnar, directed by Margaret Glass
Pygmalion, by G. B. Shaw, directed by Blanch Hogg
Grand National Night, by Dorothy and Campbell Christie, directed by Catharine McCormick Brickenden

LLT Studio Club season included:
Leather Jacket and a Red Dress, by William Digby
Orange Blossoms, by Philip Johnson
Overlaid, written by Robertson Davies

LLT Children's Theatre:
Pumpkin Pie, by Dorothy Wein
The Magic Ring, by Lilian Cornelius
The Forest Ring, by William deMille

Road Shows:
On Approval and *Springtime for Henry*, both starring Edward Everett Horton
Caesar and Cleopatra, by G. B.

Shaw, starring Lili Palmer and Sir Cedric Hardwicke
Brigadoon, by Lerner and Loewe, starring Cheryl Crawford
Now I Lay Me Down to Sleep, by Elaine Ryan, starring Frederic March and Florence Eldridge

Music included:
LLT Concert Series:
The New World Orchestra, The Royal Conservatory Opera Company, The Toronto Symphony Orchestra

Festival:
W.O.D.L., February 16–18, 1950
5th Annual Summer School of Theatre:
The Sea-Shell, by Patricia Chown, directed by Blanch Hogg
Making the Bear, by Theodore Apstein, directed by Blanch Hogg
Tobias the Angel, by James Bridie, directed by Blanch Hogg

Summer Stock:
Shelton-Amos Players: *Private Lives, Born Yesterday, Charley's Aunt, Harvey, See How They Run, When Ladies Meet, In the Wrong Bed*

1950/51

LONDON LITTLE THEATRE ERA

"HINTS TO AN ACTOR"

In February 1949, LLT received an information bulletin from the Federal Department of National Health and Welfare. It was from the department's Physical Fitness Division, and this particular bulletin was entitled: "Hints to an Actor." A few are listed below:

1. Speak with feeling.
2. Speak with force.
3. Take plenty of breath.
4. Stand still.
5. Walk as if you know where you are going, and why.
6. Act with energy.
7. Wait before speaking when the audience laughs.
…and, most important…
8. Keep in view of the audience.

WALTER MASSEY

I felt truly privileged to play in The Hasty Heart *by John Patrick. It was a wartime drama with much humour. It took place in a hospital ward for the wounded. I played 'Yank' with a stutter. The production was directed by Doris Isard, bless her.*
– Walter Massey, actor

ROBERTSON DAVIES

Catharine McCormick Brickenden produced *At My Heart's Core*, by Robertson Davies. "Mr. Davies went backstage. He inspected

The ticket line for **No More Ladies** *extending north on Richmond Street. "With a pleasant fanfare of welcome at the Grand Theatre last night the Shelton-Amos Players opened another season of summer stock in London. The curtain calls were as lively as the show when a full house greeted the inimitable Miss Amos and a company of old friends and new, and showered the ladies of the cast with flowers and generally expressed approval of the repeat engagement." (– F.B. Taylor,* **London Free Press,** *July 3, 1951) (Courtesy of the* **London Free Press** *Collection, D.B. Weldon Library, The University of Western Ontario, London, ON)*

stage lighting, looked into the wings and then congratulated the players. Mr. Davies offered no criticism of LLT's production. 'But the audience. They liked it,' he said, inferring this was the important judgement." (– *London Free Press*, May 7, 1951)

THE GOOD KING CHARLES' GOLDEN DAYS

In May 1951, the Grand Theatre was the site of the DDF for the third time. The LLT did not compete in this festival, but hosted eight other groups from across the country. One group was The University Alumnae Dramatic Club of Toronto. It presented George Bernard Shaw's play *The Good King Charles' Golden Days*. In the cast were three young actors who would enjoy long and noted careers in the professional theatre: John Colicos, Ted Follows and William Needles.

THE FOURPOSTER

Jessica Tandy and Hume Cronyn were on stage in the sentimental comedy *The Fourposter* during July 1951. This two-hander was heartwarming, touching, funny and affirmative. Hume Cronyn had trouble getting it to Broadway. Some producers felt that a two-character play about a marriage would spell death at the box office. Others felt that the play was immoral because the young married couple featured in the play actually crawled into the same bed on their wedding night. Fortunately Cronyn could draw on his Canadian background, and he landed dates in London, Sarnia and Niagara Falls. The play opened on Broadway in October of 1951 and *The Fourposter* repaid its backers in six half weeks. Hume Cronyn and Jessica Tandy performed it over 650 times, in New York City and on the road. What started out somewhat haphazardly in Southwestern Ontario in July became a triumph in New York City only three months later.

1951/52

LONDON LITTLE THEATRE ERA

A 50TH ANNIVERSARY

The Grand Theatre achieved a milestone this season – its 50th anniversary. The theatre's owner, the London Little Theatre organization, was not going to let this important anniversary pass without a celebration.

"Echoes of immortal moments in the theatre whisper across the stage of the Grand Theatre as 1951 marks the 50th anniversary of the building of London's playhouse. During the first half of this century, theatre in London has struggled to assert itself and it hasn't been an easy victory. The new medium of motion pictures struck a temporary blow at the legitimate stage, and road shows weren't as prevalent. Built by local interests and handled by the late Ambrose J. Small of Toronto, the Grand Opera House opened September 9, 1901 with the melodrama *Way Down East*. On the 50th anniversary of the building of the Grand Theatre, despite competition from other mediums, the oldest form of show business, the legitimate stage, still flourishes here in London." (– *London Free Press*, October 20, 1951)

"In its original form *Way Down East* was tentatively billed for a 50th anniversary production at the Grand Theatre on September 10 of this year. The Shelton-Amos Players were in for a summer engagement; the melodrama would be a natural. But no script could be found, though sought; if it were in text at all, it could not be found. On the manager's desk at The Grand a pile of letters indicates the search trail. It looks as if the present generation may never see *East* at all." (– F.B. Taylor, *London Free Press*, October 1, 1951)

Dorothy Westhead (left) and Beryl Ivey are pictured in **The Voice of the Turtle,** *a comedy by John Van Druten. Written during WWII, when many people felt an urgency to experience romance and marriages, this play dealt with premarital sex and the relaxation of peacetime moral codes. The play had been a hit when it premiered on Broadway in 1943. (Courtesy of Dorothy Westhead)*

"The theatre will wear a festival air this evening (October 11, 1951). William H. Hogg, president of LLT; Ken Baskette and the manager of The Grand, will come to the stage before the curtain goes up to welcome the new subscribers. The first 50 women to enter the theatre before tonight's show will be presented with a single golden rose corsage. There will be flowers in the foyer to grace the event, gold-coloured chrysanthemums, the gift of Ruth Amos of the Shelton-Amos Players. The new season is exciting. There will be seven major productions instead of the usual six. Two of them will be by Canadian playwrights. *The Shadow of the*

Tree with which Joseph Schull won the LLT playwriting prize of $1000 goes on the boards in November. Later LLT hopes to do Will Digby's *Up She Goes,* a gay musical for which the young London writer has done both tunes and book. Test music is now being recorded for this, which will be LLT's first musical." (– F.B. Taylor, *London Free Press*, October 11, 1951)

THE SHADOW OF THE TREE

I played the lead role in Joseph Schull's Shadow of the Tree, *directed by marvellous Blanch Hogg – who seemed consistently to win DDF awards for plays she entered, either as actress (she was on Broadway as Blanch Tancock) or as director. I played a disillusioned, blinded World War II returning vet, at odds with the selfish, ungrateful society to which he was subjected. He was a pianist/composer who loved martinis, felt dreadfully sorry for himself and whose every single line Schull wrote for him was preceded with the stage direction 'SARDONIC'! Blanch was a wonderful directress and showed me how to find in myself '150,000 different ways to be sardonic!' She also gave me the role and direction to win the WODL Best Actor Award.*
– Walter Massey, actor

THE NATIONAL BALLET AT THE GRAND

The National Ballet of Canada was booked into The Grand this season. In her 1978 book, Artistic Director Celia Franca writes: "In January of 1952 we had made our first out-of-town tour, to Guelph, Kitchener, Montreal, London and Hamilton, all one-night stands except for four nights at His Majesty's Theatre in Montreal and three nights at the Grand Theatre in London. At least in Montreal and London there were humble but legitimate theatres. …We had no orchestra travelling with us and George Crum had made special musical arrangements for two pianos…In London we had decided that the occasion merited the hiring of an orchestra…When we arrived in London, we found that the orchestra retained for us had a student as concertmaster, a fourteen-year-old flutist, and several members to whom George Crum had to teach the rudimentary qualities and techniques of their instruments. There was very little time or money for rehearsal…In the performance of *Les Sylphides*, where the first solo is danced to a brilliant Chopin waltz in G flat

Celia Franca, artistic director of the newly founded National Ballet of Canada. Miss Franca and her company made annual visits to London's Grand Theatre for many years. (From the collection of Don Fleckser)

major, the melody is carried by the flute: it is fast, exposed, wide-ranging, in a tricky key. The less said about this performance the better. The melody also disappeared in the faster parts of the *Polovtsian Dances* when the violins just failed to come in. This time George had no choice but to sing out 'diddily, diddily, diddily, diddily, diddily, diddily,' etc., in his croaking voice in an attempt to keep everyone together. The audience loved it. They were splitting their sides laughing, particularly when George's hoarse voice broke in upon the frantic pandemonium. The dancers, struggling amid the barely recognizable music, dared not take their eyes off the conductor for fear of losing their bearings and bumping into one another. Many people who came on the first night came again to enjoy these great moments in the history of ballet. But good-natured hilarity prevailed over any professional sense of horror. We made staunch friends in London as a result of these performances; Londoners billeted the dancers and fed them; volunteers brought coffee and homemade goodies and set up a cafeteria under the stage." – Celia Franca, *The National Ballet of Canada: A Celebration with Photographs*. The 1952 tour, undertaken the year after the founding of Canada's National Ballet was the start of a long relationship between The National Ballet of Canada and London's Grand Theatre.

Miss Celia Franca was Artistic Director for the National Ballet for many years (1951–1974). Each year the company would play a full week at the Grand Theatre. I became a member of the local Ballet Guild and headed up the publicity for the London engagements. Miss Franca invited me to speak before the children's performances. I would introduce the children to the theatre and tell them the storyline of the ballet to follow. I remember best the kindness of Miss Franca. Each season when the company would arrive she would immediately walk up and

call you by name. That meant a lot.
– Don Fleckser, director, actor

EDWARD, MY SON

In reviewing *Edward, My Son*, F. Beatrice Taylor said that it could be named The Tragedy of Edward Holt. "This is the story of Arnold Holt, industrialist who became a power in the land, and a power in the life of his son. It is the story of his wife, Evelyn, moving from light-hearted young motherhood towards tragedy. It is the story of Edward, their son, but only as seen through their eyes." In reviewing LLT actress Jean Back, Taylor wrote: "Jean Back's playing of Evelyn Holt was a clearly-defined characterization which rose to heights of grandeur in her final scene. The contrast was achieved here in a performance of deep feeling, of most credible conflict. This, it seems to me, particularly in the later scenes, was one of the best feminine performances we have had in a London Little Theatre production in many seasons." (– *London Free Press*, April 18, 1952) In recalling that production and in remembering the widespread impact LLT plays had on the community, Jean Back reminisced: "During the run of *Edward, My Son*, director John Burton went to the liquor store and placed his selection on the counter. To Burton's everlasting surprise the clerk looked at him and, without missing a beat, quoted directly from the play by saying to his customer: 'What, Lady Holt? No gin?'" Mrs. Back also remembers vividly that during rehearsals for this play she saw "a blob" walking across the balcony. At first she thought it was director John Burton, getting a different perspective on his rehearsal, but she soon learned that the balcony had been closed at the time. She concluded that the walking blob she had seen must have been the ghost of Ambrose J. Small.

FIRST MUSICAL FOR LONDON LITTLE THEATRE

Up She Goes, the first musical in the history of LLT, premiered in May 1952. The story involved the arrival on earth of the fierce witch from hell, sent on a mission to discover what it is that is so frightening on earth, that the nether regions are no longer terrifying. It boasted a cast of 50 people and, despite everyone's best effort, the musical was roundly criticized by reviewer F. Beatrice Taylor: "Neither of the leads had sufficient voice for the part; indeed, the whole musical performance lacked brilliance and verve. A musical, even one which, like this, has a certain serious overtone, demands bright and clever singing. There was a muted quality to the vocalization in most of the solo parts and in all of the choruses, stemming perhaps from the orchestra, which also lacked brightness." Taylor did hand out one compliment: "An efficient back stage crew handled the many changes." (– *London Free Press*, May 23, 1952)

LLT Season #18:
The Voice of the Turtle, by John Van Druten, directed by Harding Greenwood
The Shadow of the Tree, by Joseph Schull, directed by Blanch Hogg
Light up the Skye, by Moss Hart, directed by Martin O'Meara
What Every Woman Knows, by J.M. Barrie, directed by Florence Phelps
The Sole Heir, by Jean Francois Regnard, directed by Henri de Menthon
Edward, My Son, by Robert Morley and Noel Langley, directed by John Burton
Up She Goes, by William Digby, directed by Mary Ashwell and Ken Baskette

LLT Studio Club season included:
Miss Julie, by August Strindberg
Socrates, by Lister Sinclair
Mooney's Kid Don't Cry, by Tennessee Williams

LLT Children's Theatre:
The Light of the Silver Lantern, by Dorothy-Jane Goulding
The Invisible One, by Mona Swann
LLT Christmas Pantomime:
Babes in the Woods, staged by John Maddison (first venture into professional theatre by LLT)

Road Show:
The Hasty Heart, by John Patrick

Local Production:
Purple Patches, UWO revue

Dance:
The National Ballet of Canada

Summer Stock:
Shelton-Amos Players: *Yes, My Darling Daughter, The Philadelphia Story, Skylark, John Loves Mary, Come Back Little Sheba, Spooks, Peg O' My Heart, Tobacco Road, Rain, The Velvet Glove*

1952/53

LONDON LITTLE THEATRE ERA

PETER PAN

LLT's Children's Theatre December production was J. M. Barrie's popular *Peter Pan*. Agnes Nancekivell and Stuart Harvey were co-directors. Gwyn Kelly played Peter and George Simpson was the evil Captain Hook. Harnesses for the flying actors were designed and executed by A.J. Carter Manufacturing Co. Ltd. And LLT's reliable and creative sound man, Harry Ronson, was credited in the program as "in charge of wolves and all the noises of Never Land". The program also acknowledged "all the mothers and fathers whose long-suffering co-operation has made this play possible." After each performance some of the young audience members went backstage to learn the fate of Captain Hook. They had to know if he had been drowned or eaten by the crocodile.

A FRIGHTENING EXPERIENCE

"I once tried to run a cable to enhance sound at The Grand, and the job took me down into the crawl space under the auditorium. I crept on my stomach for at least 20 feet into the space when suddenly my flashlight went out. I was in utter darkness. I groped around and my hand landed on some sort of fabric; I think it was denim. It was very frightening because all I could think about was that Ambrose J. Small's body had never been found, and what had he been wearing when he disappeared anyway? As I was thinking these scary thoughts I managed to crawl out of the dark crawl space. I never did find out what that piece of fabric was, but I remember thinking that it must have been someone's garment." – Harry Ronson, LLT sound man

DARK OF THE MOON

On stage in January 1953, LLT presented a production of *Dark of the Moon*. It was a provocative play, based on an old ballad entitled "Barbara Allen." It was the story of people who live in a North Carolina valley and people who live on in the nearby hills. "It is the ancient legend of the lovely, faithless village girl, Barbara Allen, who loves the witch boy from the hills and who, by faithfulness could, if

Harvest of Harmony *on stage at the Grand Theatre in October 1952. The male chorus is under the direction of Arthur Patterson (centre, back to the audience). A number of the performers were ex-music hall performers from Britain who moved to Canada during the post-war years. The well-lit photograph makes the interior of the orchestra pit visible, and highlights features audience members in the box. (Courtesy of Arthur Patterson, Mississauga, Ontario)*

she would, hold him in human guise. Their stormy marriage, the depth of their suffering are real; there is human agony in their relationship against which the persistent luring of the witch girls from the hills seems theatrical contrivance for a drama, though admirable in ballet." (– *London Free Press*, January 16, 1953). This was LLT's most controversial production of the season. Some subscribers rejected the play, and walked out of performances.

To forewarn their subscribers, LLT published the following in its December 1952 *Call-Boy*: "You've probably noted in the advance publicity material that the next LLT production *Dark of the Moon* comes complete with music and dancing. In case you've made a mental note to bring the children along we'd like to pass along a word of advice – don't. For the youngsters this play will fail to grip." (– December 1952)

Beverly Ellis played Barbara Allen and Joey Harris played John. Making his stage debut was teenager Tommy Hunter. His biography in the program read: "Tom Hunter, who plays Burt Dinwitty and sings the ballad at the opening and closing, is making his first appearance on stage. His spare-time interests, when he isn't going to school, include the guitar and model railroading." (– *Call-Boy*, LLT, January 1953). Tommy Hunter parlayed his interest in the guitar into a long and successful career as Canada's Country Gentleman, a country music star of both stage and television.

Another young person in the cast was Flora MacKenzie. Described as "a display artist by profession," Flora would, in future LLT seasons, have starring roles in some of LLT's big musical productions, and enjoy a career in the professional theatre.

At the WODL in Sarnia in March 1953, *Dark of the Moon* was the winning production. This earned LLT a $100 prize. The next stop for the production was the DDF across the country in Victoria, B.C. LLT kicked in a $600 travelling grant, which left $5,300 to be raised to get all 25 members of the company there and back by train. This was raised by remounting the play at The Grand for two performances, and charging $1 per ticket. LLT was nothing if not innovative in raising funds to travel to the DDF.

DON FLECKSER

The Happy Time, on stage in April 1953, starred, among others, Beryl Ivey, Meyer Epstein and Harding Greenwood. Don Fleckser, at the time a high school student at London South Secondary School, was taken by his parents to see this show. He was so entranced by the experience that he went back to The Grand and approached LLT's business manager, Margaret Glass. Fleckser told her: "I want to act," to which she replied: "Come along." Glass put him to work as a member of the backstage crew for the show he had just seen. Thus began Don Fleckser's long association with LLT and his celebrated theatre career.

A MELODRAMA

I did a summer stock season in 1953 with the Shelton-Amos Players. They always did a melodrama, which was such fun! I played the villain who, unusually, did not sport a moustache or wear a parson's collar. The title of the piece escapes me but I remember its sub-title: The Perils of Our Fanny. *When my character is introduced to the household, Fanny is busy scrubbing floors; precisely so she works her way around so as to have her behind face out to the audience. One hears the line: 'May I introduce you to my daughters, Fanny…and Marg.' It was most enjoyable to start up stage left and, slowly but deliberately, descend down right to the unsuspecting Fanny with the audience's loud hisses and screeches ever increasing, louder and louder the closer to her I came, until the uproar was deafening! The program, in the style of the times, admonished the audience they would have to supply their own fruit. As the run progressed, word got out, and supply their own fruit they did. By the end of the run, especially during matinees when matrons and others would come with their supply, the produce would fly! Tomatoes, eggs, a cabbage once and even a cauliflower! It was bedlam, a madhouse, and such fun. I'd hiss right back, thereby increasing the fever even more. The cleanup after each show was something. By the end of the run the expensive chartreuse front curtain was a mess.*

– Walter Massey, actor

LLT Season #19
Treasure Hunt, by M.J. Farrell and John Perry, directed by Henri de Menthon
Death of a Salesman, by Arthur Miller, directed by Harding Greenwood and Florence Smith
Dark of the Moon, by Howard Richardson and William Berney, directed by Mary Ashwell
Boy Meets Girl, by Bella and Samuel Spewack, directed by Ken Baskette
Dead Sea Apple, by Stephen Grey, directed by Catharine McCormick Brickenden
The Happy Time, by Samuel Taylor, directed by Blanch Hogg

LLT Studio Club season included:
My Heart's in the Highlands, by William Saroyan
And Battles Long Ago, by John Stuart Harvey
Knock, by Jules Romain

LLT Children's Theatre:
Peter Pan, by Sir James M. Barrie

Local Production:
Harvest of Harmony

Dance:
Ballet Theatre
The National Ballet of Canada

Road Shows:
Bell, Book and Candle, by John Van Druten, starring Joan Bennett and Zachary Scott
Anonymous Lover, by Vernon Sylvaine, starring Larry Parks and Betty Garrett

Summer Stock:
The Shelton-Amos Players: *Saintly Hypocrites and Honest Sinners, Your Uncle Dudley, Bridal Night, Why Men Leave Home, Natalie Needs a Nightie, The Whole Town's Talking, Dracula, Ada Beats the Drum*

1953/54

LONDON LITTLE THEATRE ERA

AMATEUR VS PROFESSIONAL

Arms and the Man was directed by Henri de Menthon. When interviewed about the state of theatre in London, he said: "LLT is a wonderful organization. I should say there is nothing quite like it in the world. What it has achieved is truly amazing. But it cannot reach greater heights unless the people connected with it have more time to polish their acting, put in more work on the sets and so forth – and that means becoming a professional company. It is rather like people in everyday jobs who go off on Sundays to paint landscapes. Their work is often very good, but it doesn't compare with that of professional artists. It is the same with amateur and professional actors – there's a deal of difference between being very good and being expert." (– *London Free Press*, February 13, 1954)

Talk of professional theatre was not unexpected, given that in June 1953, in a city just 45 minutes north of London, the Stratford Shakespearean Festival had been established on a fully professional basis, and had met with unqualified success.

THE LONDON THEATRE COMPANY

The London Theatre Company (England) moved into The Grand in May 1954 and staged seven productions. The company was headed by Leslie Yeo and Oliver Gordon. Newfoundland was the home of The London Theatre Company, and their tour of 1954 brought them to London, Ontario.

Elizabeth Murray of LLT (left) is pictured with Ruth Amos, the star of the Shelton-Amos Players. Ruth Amos and her husband, producer Hall Shelton, presented summer stock at The Grand for six consecutive summers and created a strong following among Londoners. (Courtesy of the London Free Press Collection of Photographic Negatives, The D.B. Weldon Library, University of Western Ontario, London, ON)

As recounted in his autobiography, Leslie Yeo made these remarks about that engagement: "After a long, tiring drive from New York we arrived at the Grand Theatre to face a fractious group of union stagehands who'd been waiting an hour to discuss our crew needs for the season. Discuss wasn't quite the word. As I entered the room, the business agent stood up, wagged his finger and said, 'Now here's what you're going to do,' at which point everybody started shouting at once. I tried a few polite 'Excuse

mes' and finally shouted 'Shut up!' at the top of my lungs. They were immediately shocked into utter silence. 'As I will be the one paying your salaries, suppose I tell *you* what we're going to do,' I said with a smile and a glint at the same time. They were stunned. I don't believe anyone had ever spoken to them like that before. It took less time to win the stagehands over than it did the audience. Within days, the crew realized that our company's professionalism was on a par with their own, which was something they weren't accustomed to backstage. Good though they were, London Little Theatre, which owned The Grand, was an amateur group which worked sporadically and in their spare time, not regular theatre hours and every day like we did. By the end of our first week the entire crew was enrolled in our fan club…It took Londoners four weeks to decide that we might be worth seeing. They might never have found out if I hadn't stopped a few of them on the street and discovered that they all thought the London Theatre Company was just a summer name for LLT whose shows were always sold out to subscribers. Next day an extra inch on top of our ads screamed: LIVE FROM LONDON ENGLAND and the box office woke up. The upturn in the last four weeks didn't quite make up for the loss on the first four, but we didn't miss by much. …We finished up our London season with a musical revue, giving the lyrics a local flavour. We called it *London Laughs*, and it easily outperformed all the other productions at the box office." (– Leslie Yeo, *A Thousand and One First Nights*)

SHELTON-AMOS PLAYERS

After the London Theatre Company moved out of The Grand, the Shelton-Amos Players moved in for their sixth and final season of summer stock. Hall Shelton informed Grand Theatre officials that during the summer of 1955, the company would be staying in England. Their 1954 playbill included several intriguing titles including *Sex vs. Sex (or, The Picture That's Turned to the Wall)* and *Lullaby for Newlyweds*.

GRAND THEATRE

LONDON, CANADA

H. K. Baskette - Manager

LLT Season #20:
Travellers Joy, by Arthur MacRae, directed by Florence Smith
The Cocktail Party, by T.S. Eliot, directed by Doris Isard
Arms and the Man, by G.B. Shaw, directed by Henri de Menthon
Black Chiffon, by Lesley Storm, directed by Ken Baskette
Anne of the Thousand Days, by Maxwell Anderson, directed by Blanch Hogg
Bunty Pulls the Strings, by Graham Moffat, directed by Florence Phelps

LLT Studio Club season included:
The Taming of the Shrew, by William Shakespeare
The Invisible Worm, by Elda Cadogan
Garrick and the Ancestors, by Stewart Harvey

LLT Children's Theatre:
Toad of Toad Hall, by A. A. Milne
Robin Hood and the Butcher, by Enid Blyton
Puss in Boots

Dance:
The National Ballet of Canada
The London Civic Ballet Theatre

Road Shows:
Mister Roberts, starring Ray Parker and Peggy Scott
Rigoletto, Royal Conservatory Opera Company, featuring Jan Rubes and Jon Vickers

Summer Stock:
The London Theatre Company:
The School for Scandal, The Perfect Woman, Johnny Belinda, Queen Elizabeth Slept Here, Laura, Present Laughter and the musical revue *London Laughs*

The Shelton-Amos Players: *Sex vs. Sex (or The Picture That's Turned to the Wall), Mostly Murder, It's Late My Love, Bedtime Story, What a Woman Wants, Just Married, Lullaby for Newlyweds*

1954/55

LONDON LITTLE THEATRE ERA

THIS WAS LONDON

To mark the City of London's centennial year, the city commissioned historian Reverend Orlo Miller to write a play. *This Was London* was a capsule history of the city's growth since it became a city in 1855, as seen through the lives of the Parker family and its descendants. The cast of 20 people was directed by Roy Irving. In reviewing the play, *London Free Press* arts reporter J. Burke Martin stated: " While this whole production has been a labour of love for London's best-informed historian Orlo Miller, it has also been an enormous amount of old-fashioned work for its many principals and behind-the-scenes workers. *This Was London* makes a handsome finale for this jubilant Centennial Week. It is entertaining, informative and even, at times, really good theatre. What more could anyone ask of a Centennial play?" (– J. B. Martin, July 7, 1955) The cast included Gordon Kidd, Erma Clewlow, Tom Ashwell, Eddie Escaf, Stanley Lacey, Loretta Dickson, Reg Cooper and Colin Bower.

THE STUDIO CLUB

LLT patrons read about the Studio Club in their *Call-Boy*: "An air of suspense was well maintained throughout the production of *Edwina Black* directed by John Long, the second last of the Studio productions for the year. Typical of all the productions this season, it brought to the audience new talent as well as more experienced performers. The last Studio Club evening brought

The Barretts of Wimpole Street. *Pictured are (l. to r.): Mary Mitchell, Rosemary Martin, Alan Gibson, Bob Ewen, Jean Back, Tony Jones and Don Fleckser. Don Fleckser recalled being in the show, directed by Florence Smith. "Florence's cocker spaniel played 'Flush'. The dog loved being on stage and in the dressing rooms. For weeks after the production was over the dog waited at the door at home, ready to leave for the theatre." (Courtesy of Don Fleckser)*

the audience two plays – George Bernard Shaw's *The Great Catherine* directed by Reverend Orlo Miller, and *Liberation*, a one-act play directed by Grace Chorley. Both of these plays had directors who were new to LLT's list of directors. Both plays were well done, and gave the audience an interesting theatre evening. If the Studio Club gives as many interesting evenings next season as

they have done this one under the chairmanship of Charles Brown, excellent things are then in store for Studio members." (– *Call-Boy*, April, 1955)

SUMMER STOCK

The London Theatre Company came back to The Grand starting on May 5 for its second (and last) summer season in London, Ontario. Evening tickets could be purchased for 75 cents, $1.25 or $1.50 each. As reported in the *London Free Press* of June 17, 1955, Grand Theatre manager Ken Baskette had this to say: "How's the London (England) Theatre Company doing? 'Well, we had more patrons in three performances of *Little Women* than we did all week with the higher class *His Excellency*.' One woman said to the usher: 'See what crowds you get when you put on something decent?' "

Doing summer stock at The Grand in the 1950s the people who were there included Leslie Yeo, Honor Shepherd, Joseph Shaw and Barbara Byrne. We subscribed and one night they were doing different little bits throughout the evening, and they were doing a Casablanca-sort of thing, smoking. The actor threw his cigarette down on the stage and was supposed to put it out. The curtain came down, the cigarette caught in the fringe and it went up with the curtain. The place was crowded. People were sitting, and there was only a low murmur as smoke started coming from the curtain's fringe. Nobody moved, until finally one of the people sitting with us went to the usher and asked about the smoke coming down into the auditorium. No one panicked. Nobody moved. They just seemed to want to see what would happen next. Someone put out the cigarette. And they went on with the play.

– Sheila Walker, theatregoer

"Mae Craven, Mrs. T.H. Coffey in private life, is playing a small part in this week's (London Theatre Company) show. The veteran opera, music hall and stage actress who was well-known in England until she came here said: 'I've never played with such fine people. Never have I had such a small part and had so many people in the company wish me luck. Every member of the company came and wished me luck opening night.'" (– *London Free Press*, June 17, 1955)

1955/56

LONDON LITTLE THEATRE ERA

WARDROBE

Time Out For Ginger, a hit show on Broadway, got the season started on a comedic note. "A man's raccoon coat was a necessary part of *Time Out for Ginger*. There was no raccoon coat in LLT's wardrobe. The best method, short of trapping the raccoons themselves, would be to have CFPL-Radio's Joan Pritchard ask her listeners if they had a coat they could donate. Within a day no fewer than 12 persons had called up to lend a coat to the players." (– *London Free Press*, October 29, 1955) At this time LLT's head of wardrobe was Hazel Phillips. She and her 50 volunteers kept tabs on the 3000 costumes in wardrobe storage.

VICTOR BRAUN

The Children's Theatre was active producing two plays this season: *Alice in Wonderland* and *Jack and the Beanstalk*. Appearing in the latter play was a young man with a strong voice, Victor Braun. He was destined for a professional career in the opera world.

I was able to work with Victor Braun. This was his first appearance on stage, as the Giant. I played the Magic Bean Seller, covered in tights and lots of glitter. The scene on the beanstalk was a highlight, as Victor, Yvonne Norton and I clung for our very lives to a rope ladder suspended from piano wire.

– Don Fleckser, actor/director

LLT Season #21:
My Three Angels, by Samuel and Bella Spewack, directed by Martin O'Meara
The Patriots, by Eric Cross, directed by Blanch Hogg
The Curious Savage, by John Patrick, directed by Ken Baskette
The Barretts of Wimpole Street, by Rudolf Besier, directed by Florence Smith
Affairs of the State, by Louis Verneuil, directed by Olga Landiak
This Happy Breed by Noel Coward, directed by Walter Dixon

LLT Studio Club season included:
The Great Catherine, by G.B. Shaw
The Enchanted, by Jean Giraudoux
The Heiress, by Ruth and Augustus Goetz

LLT Children's Theatre:
Cinderella

Dance:
The National Ballet of Canada

Road Shows:
Sunshine Town, by Mavor Moore, from Stephen Leacock, produced by the New Play Society, with Robert Goulet and Robert Christie among the many cast members
The Vagabond King
Vienna Boys Choir
Oklahoma!, by Richard Rodgers and Oscar Hammerstein II

Local Production:
This Was London, by Reverend Orlo Miller

Summer Stock:
The London Theatre Company: *His Excellency, Little Women, See How They Run, Mountain Air, The Importance of Being Earnest, The Moon is Blue, London Laughs Again*
The New York Players: *The Fourposter, This Thing Called Love, Be Your Age, For Love or Money, Bell, Book and Candle, Charley's Aunt, Meet the Wife, The Anonymous Lover*

The cover of the program for Awake and Sing, *designed by celebrated London cartoonist/ illustrator Merle Tingley, or Ting, December 1955. The cover design was used by LLT throughout this season and 1956/57. (Permission of Merle Tingley; Courtesy of Eddie Escaf)*

"With all the pride that's born of brief command
He calls "Alf hour!'
The tone is unimpassioned, bold, but bland,
'Alf hour! 'alf hour!'
He stands for Time,
His voice the chime:
'Alf hour! 'alf hour!'
– "The Call-Boy," poem by Albert Chevalier, 1903

A CASE OF THE DRIES

Disraeli starred Meyer Epstein in the lead role. The play's plot that dealt the trouble encountered by the British in its Suez Canal dealings. Elizabeth Murray went to see the play, and remembers that on the night she attended, Meyer Epstein suffered a case of the dries: "I had never seen a dry like that!" exclaimed Libby Murray during an interview many years later. Jean Back, a close friend of the play's director, recalled that the dry occurred as Epstein was delivering a speech about the purchase of the Suez Canal. From off stage she attempted to throw him his line, but nothing happened. Time seemed to drag by in slow motion for everyone watching, in the audience and backstage. Finally from the wings stage manager Laurie Smith yelled very loudly: "Oh, for God's sake…buy the bloody canal!". The scene commenced, the scene ended, and the curtain was rung down. The story goes that Meyer Epstein had never before been conscious of an individual audience member, but that night he had caught sight of a friend sitting very close to the stage, and this had turned him rigid with fear.

A DISCOURAGING SITUATION

As this LLT season drew to a close, arts reporter J. Burke Martin wrote about his fears that "London was becoming a cultural backwash." To explain this he wrote: "London has been famous for its amateur theatre groups for nearly a century. If there is anything cultural that goes deep into our roots it is amateur drama. It has become a cliche to boast that we have the largest little theatre membership in North America, if not in the world. Well, where do we stand today? The London Little Theatre has a pretty healthy enrolment of 7,636 subscribers this year. But don't get the notion that those 7,636 came panting up to the box office with checks in their hands. It took a small regiment of canvassers several weeks of work to recruit those of you who belong to LLT and, let's face it, a lot of you had to be talked into taking out a subscription which entitled you to six good shows at one dollar a show. Yes, 7,636 is a lot of members in a town this size. But 10 years ago we had 9,600 in LLT and a waiting list. Here, as elsewhere, support not only has not kept pace with the city's growth, it has fallen behind in about the same proportion. …it's a pretty discouraging situation." (– *London Free Press*, May 4, 1956)

TRANS-CANADA THEATRE COMPANY

"LLT embarks on a new venture this summer as it presents the newly-formed Trans-Canada Theatre Company in a group of 10 plays. This marks the first time LLT has produced a season of summer theatre. Guiding hand throughout the season will be that of director Joan White. A veteran in the fields of both acting and directing, Miss White played with the Bristol Old Vic, and in London's West End, before turning to directing in London and in Wales. Since coming to Canada this spring she has appeared at The Crest Theatre in Toronto…Nearly 180 actors and actresses were interviewed by Miss White and Ken Baskette before 19 players were chosen to shape the company theatre-goers will see in London this summer. …Desire to help further the Canadian theatre led officers of LLT to launch into the summer theatre producing field with a company of Canadian players. Hope runs high that this will mark just the beginning of an annual appearance of Canadian companies in summer stock here. 'We feel that this new venture can be very exciting in the field of modern theatre, just as Stratford has proven exciting in the realm of Shakespearean theatre,' Mr. Baskette said. Accent will be on light-hearted fare. The first presentation *Dear Charles* is a saucy comedy." (– *London Free Press*, June 16, 1956)

Members of the company were drawn from across Canada and included young actors Charmion King (of Toronto) and Eric Donkin (of Montreal). Tickets cost $1 each.

On the opening night of *Lucky Strike*, bad luck struck the company. "First-nighters at the Grand Theatre witnessed a rare example of the old stage tradition 'the show must go on', when the leading lady in the comedy *Lucky Strike* was stricken mute with laryngitis two hours before curtain time and the director went on in her place. Up to 6:30 p.m. it appeared that Cosette Lee might be able to carry on. But a final check by her physician, Dr. Peter Rechnitzer, showed that it would have been impossible for Miss Lee to have carried the heavy role. Director Joan White said she would take the role rather than see the first-night audience disappointed. Miss White carried the script throughout the play and earned, and won, an ovation after the final curtain." (– *London Free Press*, July 29, 1956)

LLT Season #22:
Time Out for Ginger, by Ronald Alexander, directed by Ken Baskette
Awake and Sing, by Clifford Odets, directed by Harding Greenwood
Mrs. McThing, by Mary Chase, directed by Charles Brown
The Women, by Clare Booth, directed by Ken Baskette
Disraeli, by Louis N. Parker, directed by Florence Smith
Peg O' My Heart, by J. Hartley Manners, directed by Martin O'Meara

LLT Studio Club season included:
A Doll's House, by Henrik Ibsen
The Last Temptation, by Reverend Orlo Miller
The Cherry Orchard, by Anton Chekhov

LLT Children's Theatre:
Alice in Wonderland
Jack and the Beanstalk

Road Show:
Aida, Carmen, La Traviata, Cavalleria Rusticana, I Pagliacci, The Empire State Grand Opera

Dance:
The National Ballet of Canada

Summer Stock:
Trans-Canada Theatre Company:
Dear Charles, The Seven Year Itch, Anniversary Waltz, When We Are Married, Sabrina Fair, Lucky Strike, White Sheep of the Family, The Tender Trap, I Found April, The Happiest Days of Your Life, Ten Little Indians

1956/57

LONDON LITTLE THEATRE ERA

This portrait of Ken Baskette, manager of the Grand Theatre, was featured on a Christmas card. The sketch is done by "Flori" who has created a bow tie of two Grand Theatre tickets. "Ken Baskette said the two most important things to remember as an actor were 'know your lines' and 'don't bump into the furniture'." – Harry Ronson, LLT sound man (Courtesy of The Grand Theatre)

ARTISTIC DIRECTOR

This season represented the end of an era for LLT. The board had decided to move the LLT to a higher level of production by hiring its first Artistic Director. The search for this person was well underway by January 1957. The salary was to be adjusted according to the qualifications of the applicant. Notes taken at a January 3, 1957 meeting of a special LLT committee contain the following information regarding this quantum leap forward by the company:

"There was some general discussion with regard to the actual needs of LLT and those present agreed that what LLT needed was an Artistic Director. This post would be in addition to that of theatre manager and would be a completely new position. Generally the Artistic Director would supervise, if not produce, the major proportion of the Little Theatre bill and would generally take charge of all the activities. The Artistic Director would be responsible for conducting a course of training either through the production or otherwise. It was pointed out that this need had been discussed earlier and that next year there would certainly be a shortage of major producers, and that no steps appeared to be being made otherwise to fill this gap. It was also pointed out that this was a radical departure for the organization, as it would logically lead away from the amateur organization to possibly a school and perhaps even to a professional touring organization with headquarters in London. It was felt that this would require some changes in the organization but that some change was definitely necessary and this seemed like the most aggressive approach. Salaries were discussed and assuming $5,000 for a Theatre Manager, we might obtain an Artistic Director at $600 per month, for eight months. Applying these figures to this year's budget, the extra sum needed is not too large and some members present thought this extra sum could be raised."

Subsequently the LLT board looked seriously at five candidates for the newly created position of Artistic Director.

MAPLE LEAF THEATRE

By the summer of 1957 the Trans-Canada Theatre Company, founded at The Grand the summer before, had turned into the Maple Leaf Theatre. As reported by Herbert Whittaker in the *Globe & Mail*: "A nation-wide theatre project will get rolling this summer, when Joan White, Vernon Chapman and Robert Grose move into the second year of their summer theatre operation at The Grand, in London. The decision to have a second season in London triggers a large-scale operation called the Maple Leaf Theatre, with plans to take a company on sponsored dates all across the country. Miss White and Mr. Chapman will alternate direction of the plays, with Mr. Grose in charge of design." (– May 16, 1957)

GHOST OF AMBROSE J. SMALL

The actors included Charmion King, Norman Welsh, Cosette Lee, James Edmond and Muriel Ontkean. James Edmond had a ghost-of-Ambrose J. Small experience that summer. While everyone else was out of the building having a meal, he stayed on stage, on set, and stretched out for a rest. He was awakened from his nap by a blast of cold air coming from The Grand's balcony. When he looked up he saw a door swing open. He called out, thinking a staff person would answer, but he was met with silence. He realized that something cold was standing in the balcony on this very warm summer day looking down. He bolted for the door to the alley, not wanting to be alone in the auditorium with the ghost of Ambrose J. Small.

GRAND THEATRE
LONDON, CANADA

LLT Season #23:
The Constant Wife, by Somerset Maugham, directed by Florence Smith
The Rainmaker, by Richard Nash, directed by Harding Greenwood
Another Part of the Forest, by Lillian Hellman, directed by Ken Baskette
Bonaventure, by Charlotte Hastings, directed by Martin O'Meara
Teach Me How To Cry, by Patricia Joudry, directed by Charles Brown
The Torch-Bearers, by George Kelly, directed by Catharine McCormick Brickenden

LLT Studio season included:
The Importance of Being Earnest, by Oscar Wilde
She Stoops to Conquer, by Oliver Goldsmith
Star Crossed, by C. Patrick Malone

LLT Children's Theatre:
Goldilocks and the Three Bears
The Princess and the Swineherd

Dance:
The National Ballet of Canada

Road Shows:
Spring Thaw
Vienna Boys Choir

Local Productions:
Purple Patches
Dorothy Scruton Dance Recital
Bernice Harper Dance Recital

Summer Stock:
Maple Leaf Theatre: *Tea and Sympathy, The Reluctant Debutante, The Solid Gold Cadillac, Light Up the Sky, The Spider's Web, Picnic, Bus Stop, The Browning Version*

Western Ontario Playwriting Seminar:
conducted by Stanley Richards, initiated by Mrs. Virne Johnston

1957/58

LONDON LITTLE THEATRE ERA / PETER DEARING ERA

PETER DEARING

Londoners were introduced to the newly appointed Artistic Director of LLT in April of 1957 when the *London Free Press* reported: "Mr. Dearing has spent virtually his whole life (he is in his mid-40s) around the smell of greasepaint. He began as a boy actor with the Ben Greet Players in England, graduating from minor roles to Romeo and Horatio in later years. In all, Mr. Dearing has starred in more than 20 Shakespeare plays. His experience embraces every phase of acting and producing – in radio, on television and in films. In a career interrupted by six years in the Royal Navy in World War II, Mr. Dearing has made three coast-to-coast tours of this continent…After the war Mr. Dearing produced scores of plays in London's West End. Before leaving for the United States four years ago he completed his third season as dramatic instructor and Shakespearean coach at London's Royal Academy of Dramatic Arts (RADA). In New York, Mr. Dearing undertook a teaching assignment at the American Academy of Dramatic Art and was one of the academy's three executive directors. He went to teach at Rollins College, Florida, in the autumn of 1954." (– April 27, 1957)

Arts reporter J. Burke Martin kept a keen eye on theatre activity in London and made these remarks upon the appointment of Peter Dearing: "Mr. Dearing takes over the post of Artistic Director at a critical time in the life of LLT. It has been the feeling of many of us connected with the theatre here that we have reached a plateau from which we can either advance or regress. Mr. Dearing faces heavy responsibilities, and we wish him well." (– *London Free Press*, April 27, 1957)

In describing the visual impact Peter Dearing made, Don Fleckser described his appearance thus: "A bushy beard, unkempt hair, an exploding voice, tweed jackets and large horn-rimmed glasses."

Besides a new artistic direction, LLT bid a fond adieu to Ken Baskette who moved on in his career. Len Smithson was hired to replace him as business manager for the Grand Theatre.

SOUTH PACIFIC

The first production of the season was the Emlyn Williams play *Someone Waiting*, directed by Harding Greenwood. Next on the playbill was the musical *South Pacific*, directed by Peter Dearing. It was a lavish production. After several months' preparation with a cast numbering 75 and 12 sets, *South Pacific* roared onto The Grand's stage in December. Musical direction was by Clifford Poole, who led an orchestra of at least 12 people in the pit.

I got a call from Peter Dearing offering me the role of Sergeant Luther Billis in South Pacific. *A professional director, Peter demanded more of his actors and he got it. He made a major impact on people.*
– Eddie Escaf, former LLT Board President, actor

"Theatrical history was made Saturday night when LLT's resplendent production of *South Pacific* won one of the greatest ovations this reviewer can remember. The musical, directed by Peter Dearing, was a personal triumph for him and an almost incredible achievement for a troupe of amateurs. First-nighters applauded long and lustily after every one of the musical number, and it's safe to say that seldom has a LLT audience walked out into the night in a happier glow. …This musical was the test of Mr. Dearing's ability, the chief reason for his appointment as Artistic Director. He rose to the challenge and we can all now consider ourselves fortunate that he is with us. …The show was rowdy, romantic and just plain wonderful." (– *London Free Press*, December 2, 1957)

The first year that Peter Dearing was here we produced South Pacific *which was a great success. Except I can remember that the sound broke down and where you were supposed to hear the aeroplanes go over, there was a deadly silence. Peter was standing at the back, behind the crush-rail, making aeroplane noises.*
– Elizabeth Murray, former LLT Board President, actress

TOURING COSTS

In February 1958, a tour mounted by the Stratford Festival brought *Two Gentlemen of Verona* and *The Broken Jug* (a play adapted by Don Harron) to the Grand Theatre. The troupe was headed by Douglas Campbell, who shared the stage with Powys Thomas, Bruno Gerussi, Douglas Rain, Eric House, Lloyd Bochner, Roberta Maxwell, Amelia Hall and Eric Christmas. J. Burke Martin gives a little insight into the costs of touring a show that year: "Stratford came in with all the prestige in the world behind it and did a gross business of just under $7,000 for five performances. …If you think $7,000 was a good take in London, you should be told something of theatre economics. They had to hire The Grand for a week. In addition to all the administrative personnel, 21 actors and actresses had to be paid, housed, transported and fed. Then there was extensive advertising and

other promotional costs. The expenses of simply putting up the set and taking it down again came to $2,000. The unions did nicely out of the week, too. They had no fewer than 20 men on stage the previous Sunday when the set was moved in. In fact, the unions' take for the week came to about $2,300, or more than twice what the Grand Theatre got for the use of the hall all week." (– *London Free Press*, February 22, 1958)

ROBIN DEARING

Actress Robin Dearing, wife of Artistic Director Peter Dearing, made her LLT debut in *Witness for the Prosecution*. She played an important part throughout the eleven seasons Peter Dearing was with LLT. Born Robin Plaisted in New Hampshire, she was acting by the age of 11. Throughout her teenage years she learned her craft by working with stock companies. After graduation from high school, Robin attended Emerson College in Boston, Massachusetts, where she majored in theatre and took a minor in education. Restless after two years of study, she auditioned for the Royal Academy of Dramatic Art. Conducting the audition of 200 hopefuls was Peter Dearing. Robin Plaisted won a place at RADA and went there in September 1954. She returned to the United States and lived in New York for a time, while Peter Dearing was teaching at Rollins College in Florida. They were married and came to London when Peter Dearing was appointed Artistic Director of LLT.

HAZEL PHILLIPS

Hazel Phillips was a dedicated LLT seamstress. In Antigone *I gave her the part of Yocasta, who just sits and knits. It was great to give her that little thing to do.*
– Charles Brown, former LLT President, director

AN EXCITING AND REWARDING YEAR

At the annual general meeting of LLT in June 1958, the board president Elizabeth Murray pronounced the 1957/58 season "the most exciting and rewarding year in LLT's history." She gave "unstinting praise to Peter Dearing for infusing new life into amateur theatre here, not only by his personal productions of *South Pacific* and *Teahouse of the August Moon* but for his help and inspiration to everyone else in the theatre here." Peter Dearing responded by saying "it had been a great experience to work with a sympathetic board of directors whose help made his work easier." It was his constant endeavour to find and use new talent, as he had done in *South Pacific* where twelve of the play's sixteen principals were new to the stage. More than fifty new players had been recruited during the season, which saw a total of 170 roles portrayed on The Grand stage. (– *London Free Press*, June 27, 1958).

As icing on the cake, board vice-president, Kenneth Lemon, reported that LLT had turned the corner after three years of deficits.

Having board members who worked both on stage and backstage, and who also worked in the board room – we thought that was our strength.
– Elizabeth Murray, former LLT president, actress

LLT Season #24:
Someone Waiting, by Emlyn Williams, directed by Harding Greenwood
South Pacific, by Richard Rodgers and Oscar Hammerstein II, directed by Peter Dearing
Antigone, by Jean Anouilh, directed by Charles Brown
Witness for the Prosecution, by Agatha Christie, directed by Martin O'Meara
The Young Elizabeth, by Jeannette Dowling and Francis Letton, directed by Doris Isard
Teahouse of the August Moon, by John Patrick, directed by Peter Dearing

LLT Studio Club season included:
Pygmalion, by G. B. Shaw
Top of the Ladder, by Tyrone Guthrie
Sorry, Wrong Number, by Lucille Fletcher

The Children's Theatre:
The Sleeping Beauty

Festival
WODL, April 9 – 12, 1958

Local Production
Purple Patches

Dance
The National Ballet of Canada

Music
Heidi Krall, Soprano, Metropolitan Opera Association
Joyce Grenfell bids you a "Good Evening" with George Baur on the Piano

Road Shows:
Hamlet, by William Shakespeare, starring William Hutt and Roland Hewgill, produced by The Canadian Players
Two Gentlemen of Verona, by William Shakespeare, and *The Broken Jug*, adapted by Don Harron, produced by The Stratford Festival Company
Die Fledermaus and *The Merry Widow*, produced by the Opera Festival Company
My Fur Lady, Canada's Own Smash Hit Musical Satire, staged, directed and choreographed by Brian and Olivia Macdonald

Western Ontario Playwriting Seminar:
conducted by Stanley Richards

London Theatre School:
joint venture between the LLT and UWO

1958/59

LONDON LITTLE THEATRE ERA / PETER DEARING ERA

SILVER ANNIVERSARY

This year marked LLT's silver anniversary; 25 seasons of entertaining audiences with a wide variety of productions. Board president Elizabeth Murray was justifiably proud when she wrote in *Call-Boy*, October 1958: "A quarter of a century ago, individual groups of amateur players amalgamated to become LLT. Its objectives were and are threefold: (i) service to the community, (ii) the development of the highest standard of amateur theatre, and (iii) the promotion and encouragement of professional theatre, particularly in Canada. Therein lies the uniqueness of LLT. No other organization has so successfully combined the apparently incompatible fields of amateurism and professionalism. Nowhere else does one find an amateur group owning and operating a legitimate theatre. Nowhere else does the little theatre import, promote, and at times even subsidize, professional companies." – Elizabeth Murray

THE BOY FRIEND

The Boy Friend burst onto The Grand's stage in October 1958 and transported audiences back to the roaring twenties. With flapper costumes designed by Flora MacKenzie, dances directed by Bernice Harper, settings and decor designed by Wilf Pegg and musical direction by Don McKellar, Peter Dearing's production made a huge impact on participants and audience alike. "I felt a

Costume sketches created by Flora MacKenzie for the production of The Boy Friend. *The sketches capture the flare and flavour of the musical and also of LLT's successful production of this fun and flamboyant show. (Courtesy of Flora MacKenzie)*

bit like Dr. Jekyll and Mr. Hyde, practising medicine until dusk and then dancing the Charleston in *The Boy Friend* until midnight. Very exciting," remembered Dr. Peter Richnitzer decades later. Don Fleckser was cast as Marcel and remembered:

"Walter Dixon taught the cast the poses and attitudes of the 1920s. I was at the end of the line for the fall at the end – painful! Bernice Harper and Ben Hillier danced an incredible tango with whips and castanets – hilarious! The beauty of this production was the return of John Burton and Mae Coffey to The Grand's stage. They were glorious – remembering every bit of business from their professional years."

The Boy Friend was the first LLT musical I worked on. Peter Dearing hired me to do the music with him. He took people off the street for his shows. He sought people with voices and whose appearance would be compatible with the shows. I worked on six other musicals with Peter. He always had his feet on the ground. It was fun and invigorating work.
– Don McKellar, LLT music director

THE DEVIL'S DISCIPLE

The Canadian Players played The Grand again this year, and presented George Bernard Shaw's *The Devil's Disciple.* Ted Follows had the title role in the play. Among the supporting plays were Norman Welsh, and "one of Canada's prettiest actresses, Dawn Greenhalgh. Miss Greenhalgh became Mrs. Ted Follows at Stratford a few weeks ago. Jack Hutt, once a busy figure in LLT, may be discerned as a soldier in this play, but his full-time occupation is that of production stage manager, the same role he fills for the Stratford Festival." (– J. B. Martin, *London Free Press*, October 25, 1958).

BEHIND THE SCENES

Speaking years later about the production of *The Sleeping Prince,* Noreen De Shane and Peter Lynch, two LLT members who worked behind the scenes, commented: "Wilf Pegg designed this show. He was always late with his designs. He had painted the floor of the stage in black and white squares. For the dress rehearsal Robin Dearing was wearing a white, floor-length dress. Wilf warned her 'not to walk on the black squares because they were probably still wet.'"

THE PLAY MUST GO ON

"In the best tradition of show business the play went on at the Grand Theatre last night without its leading lady. Brenda May, who plays Emily Pennypacker in the current LLT production *The Remarkable Mr. Pennypacker,* was stricken with a severe cast of influenza and sore throat over the weekend. Her temperature moved past the century mark and by Monday noon it was obvious that she would not be able to go on stage. Director Marjorie Lister called Robin Dearing, the wife of LLT's Artistic Director, and asked her if she would substitute. Mrs. Dearing agreed. Director and actress spent a frantic afternoon with costumes, learning entrances and exits, and the hundred and one bits of 'business' every performer must know. Robin Dearing went on at 8:10 and brought it off in brilliant fashion. Since there was no time to learn her lines, she carried a copy of the script throughout the play and succeeded in appearing to be a housewife who was also an assiduous reader. She won an appreciative hand from the audience who knew nothing of the substitution until it was announced just before curtain time." (– *London Free Press*, March 10, 1959)

VICTORIA REGINA

Some stories about some productions live forever. *Victoria Regina,* on stage in May 1959 is one example. The play was a cavalcade of Victoriana and spanned the Queen's reign, from her girlhood in 1837 to her old age in 1897. Directed by Peter Dearing, it starred Jean Back as Victoria, William Ziegler as Albert and Hew Crooks as John Brown, and a large cast of supporting players. Jean Back remembered: "There was a wonderful scene, set in a tent. A little dog appeared for the dress rehearsal and all went well. On opening night I entered, with the dog trailing, but this time he sat down on the prop 'lawn', and the audience began to titter. I dragged the dog *and* the 'lawn' across the stage and the whole tent nearly came down! At another performance the dog lept for John Brown's sporin. I remember also that Bill Ziegler as Albert had to say the line: 'Hark, I think that is our band playing', but there was no sound."

Peter Dearing really pushed you as an actor. He pushed me!
– William Ziegler, LLT actor

"*Victoria Regina* was the last time I stage managed a play, and I swore I would never do it again. There was a large cast, with too many scene changes. On opening night the sound system broke down, the dog got loose, chimes fell on the floor, the gun would not fire, vases fell off a flying set piece. Nothing was ready. Walter Dixon sat in the front row and wept at a Buckingham Palace which was turquoise, yellow and white. As Queen Victoria entered, her lap rug caught in the wheelchair and prevented it from moving forward, or backward. The next night the wrong set flew in, leaving the queen separated by a wall from her visitor, Mrs. Gladstone, played by Muriel Thomson. I loudly announced that I was finished as a stage manager. Peter Dearing assured me that if I would come back everything would straighten out – but it never did." – Don Fleckser, director/actor

LONDON THEATRE SCHOOL

Eleanor Stuart, a member of the Stratford Festival acting company from 1953 to 1956, was named co-director of the London Theatre School (conducted in the summer jointly by LLT and the University of Western Ontario) with Peter Dearing. The six-week course commenced on June 29, 1959. The school served students who wished to make a career in the professional theatre, as well as those who wished to specialize in community and educational drama.

DOUGLAS CAMPBELL

The Canadian Players were on stage at The Grand with George Bernard Shaw's *The Devil's Discipline* and Shakespeare's *As You Like It*. The Stratford Festival founder Tom Patterson and actor/director Douglas Campbell were the driving forces behind this troop. The Canadian Players toured during the fall/winter/ spring theatre season, and utilized many of the Stratford Festival actors who worked on the famed thrust stage during the summer months. Douglas Campbell had come to Canada from Great Britain when Sir Tyrone Guthrie came to kick-start the Stratford Festival. "When Tony was invited to Canada I sort of begged to be taken along. Guthrie believed that the theatre of the 'created star' was a very bad thing. Stars will emerge in a theatrical company and there will always be leading personalities; personalities like Guthrie to whom you will look for leadership. But they will only emerge if it's a good cooperative system to begin with. I emerged through this process. No one would ever take up this redheaded, bellicose, rather fat, tall man and make him into a glamorous star. I'm just not glamorous and I don't have that kind of personality."
– Douglas Campbell, during a taped interview with Grace Lydiatt Shaw in the 1970s

UPGRADING THE THEATRE

At LLT's annual general meeting in the summer of 1959, subscribers learned that yet again LLT would invest some of its hard-earned money in upgrading the theatre. The Grand would undergo several structural alterations throughout the summer. These included a new switchboard to be installed backstage, new lighting and additional fire safety precautions to protect both the army of volunteers working at the theatre, and the thousands of patrons attracted to the shows.

1959/60

LONDON LITTLE THEATRE ERA / PETER DEARING ERA

THE KING AND I

Casting for the 76 roles for *The King and I* started early in June 1959. Throughout that summer, elaborate sets were built. Rehearsals began in late August, in anticipation of the late October opening.

All the long, hot evenings of summer the stage was very busy with blocking and dialogue rehearsals. From the very first rehearsal bare feet and hoop skirts were the order of the day so that the cast would become very familiar with the conditions they would work under. Each night after rehearsal David More, playing the king, would sit and pick the splinters from his feet.
– Associate Director Don Fleckser (– Call-Boy, October 1959)

David More held onto his head of hair right up until the dress rehearsal, then it was all shaved off. Diana Thompson was cast as Anna, with Christopher Hill as her son. Victor Garber, his brother Nick Garber, and their sister Lisa Garber were just three of the 16 Royal Prince and Princesses in the cast. Their mother, Hope Garber, was also on the stage as one of the four Royal Amazons.

The problem was to take 76 typical Londoners and turn them into residents of the Bangkok Royal Palace. For choreographer Bernice Harper, it meant many hours of study in Oriental dancing and customs. She was faced with the very difficult task

LLT Season #25:
The Boy Friend, by Sandy Wilson, directed by Peter Dearing
The Lark, by Jean Anouilh, directed by Charles Brown
A Christmas Carol, from Charles Dickens, directed by Don Fleckser
The Sleeping Prince, by Terence Rattigan, directed by Harding Greenwood
The Remarkable Mr. Pennypacker, by Liam O'Brien, directed by Marjorie Lister
Macbeth, by William Shakespeare, directed by Peter Dearing
The Mousetrap, by Agatha Christie, directed by Florence Smith
Victoria Regina, by Laurence Housman, directed by Peter Dearing

LLT Studio Club season included:
Puzzles, by Charles Rogers
Zanorin, by Catharine McCormick Brickenden
Two Sides of Darkness, by Edwin R. Procunier

Junior Studio Club:
An Evening With Will Shakespeare featured shortened versions of *The Merchant of Venice* and *A Midsummer Night's Dream*, under the direction of Peter Dearing

Road Shows:
The Devil's Disciple, by G. B. Shaw and *As You Like It*, by Shakespeare, produced by The Canadian Players
Purely for Pleasure, a revue starring Paul Hartman

London Theatre School:
joint venture between LLT and the University of Western Ontario, Peter Dearing and Eleanor Stuart, co-directors

Western Ontario Playwriting Seminar:
conducted by Stanley Richards

Local Production:
Night of Harmony, London Chapter of the Society for the Preservation and Encouragement of Barbershop Quartet Singing in America

of telling the story through the skill of her dancers. The Siamese dance is a completely different art to that of our Western choreography. There are over 10,000 different hand movements which are used by the dancers to tell their very beautiful stories, and you will see the dancers portraying flowers and birds through the movement of their fingers. …Robin Dearing was holding makeup classes teaching the cast and crew how to transform the Occidental into the Oriental. A bun had to be made for the head of each wife and child. Then came the dying and tinting of hair and hair pieces. Body makeup had to be bought by the gallon for this show.
– Associate Director Don Fleckser (– Call-Boy, October 1959)

An article about LLT designer Wilf Pegg and his design team for *The King and I* sheds light on backstage working conditions at the Grand Theatre in 1959: "Scene of most of the crew's operations is a large barn-like structure, added to the theatre a dozen years ago specifically as a work and storage area, and within paint-throwing distance of The Grand's cavernous stage. Cans are piled in ordered disarray; the walls are daubed with blotches of black and orange and red, where colours had their first tryout before appearing on stage. In sweaters, paint-spattered slacks and wool-socked feet, the women go into action one or two months before each production. Usually they continue working right up to the moment the curtain rises. Frequently they are working on two productions at once – making sure that scenery for the current one remains shipshape on stage, while preparing the next one in the workshop. Despite the fact that his crew all have other jobs – studies, housework or professions – Wilf Pegg seldom lacks help. 'If I need them,' he said, 'I pick up the phone and let out a shout: Desperation at LLT! Then a few key people contact some more, and we're all set.'" (– *London Free Press*, June 9, 1960)

At the Crumlin Airport on the outskirts of London, Peter Dearing (in dark glasses) and beside him, Robin Dearing, are surrounded by well-wishers. They had just returned from the DDF in Vancouver, B.C., having won the DDF for the first time since 1948, with the production of Six Characters in Search of an Author. *"Our homecoming with family and friends, the mayor and his wife, fanfare, flash bulbs and cheers" (–* Call-Boy, *May 1960) LLT actors Victoria Mitchell and Paul Soles were both discovered by CBC-TV talent scouts as a result of this production. (Courtesy of* The London Free Press *Collection of Photographic Negatives, The D.B. Weldon Library, The University of Western Ontario, London, ON)*

I'll never forget working on The King and I. *We were sewing gilt pot-cleaners on curtains, they give a rich Oriental effect, you know. Then the curtain started to go up. It was either leap for the wings or get caught on stage. I'm no gazelle, but I leaped!*
(– unidentified LLT backstage worker, quoted in the London Free Press, *June 9, 1960)*

AWARDS AT THE WODL

"Congratulations to the directors, the members of the cast, and all those associated backstage with *Six Characters in Search of an Author* on being selected as the best company at the WODL. It is a particular pleasure to note that Victoria Mitchell as the Daughter, and Paul Soles as the director received the awards for the Best Actress and Best Supporting Actor at the festival. The LLT production has now been invited to the DDF in Vancouver in May. We wish them every success." (– *Call-Boy*, April 1960)

I was the vice-president of the DDF in those days. You did a festival show in the fall, so it could be chosen for WODL in February, and then go on to the DDF in May. You had to keep that wretched thing warm from early October to the end of May!
– Elizabeth Murray, former LLT board president, actress, interviewed by Alice Gibb

SPRING THAW

"The infamous Toronto revue *Spring Thaw '60* is to be seen on our big stage in April. Tickets cost $3.00 for the best seats and $1.50 for merely good seats. Direction will be by Brian Macdonald. Among the stars assembled for this year's show are Toby Robbins, Barbara Hamilton and Peter Mews. Of particular interest to Londoners are the two young stars of the show, Carol Morley and Igors Gavon. These two talented artists come from London." (– LLT flyer, 1960)

CALLING FOR PARTNERS

"Do you know that a musical costs more than $10,000 to produce? that our current production budget for sets, costumes and royalties runs over $17,000? that maintaining a 60-year-old theatre as big as The Grand costs over $18,000 per year? that replacing and rewiring our antiquated switch board and wiring for your safety and better lighting cost $12,000? that you are, or can be a partner in this big business for $1.37 per production?" (– *Call-Boy*, May 1960)

VICTOR GARBER

"As far back as I can remember, performing was what I could do, what I was driven to do and obsessed to do. I played Tom Sawyer. I remember auditioning for it and getting it and I thought: 'That's it. I'm hooked.' We did it on the mainstage. It was a Children's Theatre production so it was fairly spare. (Actress) Kate Nelligan told me later she saw it, she was in the audience, and that she wanted to be an actress when she saw it."– Victor Garber, interviewed for Christopher Doty's documentary film *Vagabonds and Visionaries*

LLT Season #26:
The King and I, by Richard Rodgers and Oscar Hammerstein II, director Don Fleckser (Peter Dearing associate director throughout the season)
Bad Seed, by Maxwell Anderson, director Doris Isard
Six Characters in Search of an Author, by Luigi Pirandello, director Wilf Pegg
The Solid Gold Cadillac, by Howard Teichman and George S. Kaufman, director Marjorie Lister
Inherit the Wind, by Jerome Lawrence and Robert E. Lee, director Barry Hunt
Visit to a Small Planet, by Gore Vidal, director Martin O'Meara

LLT Studio Club season included:
The Madwoman of Chaillot, by Jean Giraudoux
Murder in the Cathedral, by T.S. Eliot

LLT Children's Theatre:
Tom Sawyer, directed by Agnes Nancekivell

Local Production:
Caesar and Cleopatra, by G. B. Shaw, presented by The Huron College Drama Society
Purple Patches

Road Shows:
Spring Thaw '60, 14th Annual Review of the Canadian Scene, presented by New Play Society staged by Brian MacDonald

Dance:
The National Ballet of Canada

Festival:
WODL, March 30 – April 2, 1960

Summer Playwrights Seminar: conducted by Stanley Richards, July 4 – 15, 1960

1960/61

LONDON LITTLE THEATRE ERA/
PETER DEARING ERA

RESEATING THE GRAND

"One half of the theatre's ancient seats will have been replaced before the September opening night. The orchestra section seats will have been removed and a work crew from Toronto, which specializes in theatre reseating, will soon be replacing about five hundred of the old, familiar somewhat lumpy gray chairs with newer and softer seats. LLT made a bargain purchase last spring when the Capitol Theatre was entirely reseated, buying the old ones for a dollar each. While these replacements are not factory-fresh, they are larger and roomier than the ones on which tens of thousands of LLT patrons have been sitting for the past thirty years. That's how long it is since The Grand was reseated. LLT subscribers will notice and appreciate another major improvement at The Grand this season; the boxes are gone. The upper boxes were structurally unsafe. Furthermore, the upper boxes not only afforded the worst sight lines of any seats in the theatre, they obstructed the view from thirty or forty balcony seats behind them. They have been pushed back until they now form only a decorative reminder of their former function." (– *London Free Press*, September 10, 1960)

BEHIND THE SCENES

"Like an iceberg, London Little Theatre shows only part of itself above the surface. There's more activity behind the scenes than most of you realize." (– J. Burke Martin, *London Free Press*, October 8, 1960)

A formal studio portrait of Robin Dearing as Hedda Gabler, taken by Walter Dixon. The Ibsen play was directed by Peter Dearing, who was also on stage as Judge Brack. (Courtesy of Don Fleckser)

THE WORKSHOP

The Studio Club changed into the Workshop. "As LLT President Charles Brown explained to members, Workshop now means the Little Theatre's training and educational branch. It costs only $2.50 and ten evenings to join the fun of Workshop. Classes in stage movement are conducted by Bernice Harper. Robin Dearing will demonstrate makeup. Blanch Hogg will come here from Toronto to instruct in the reading of lines. Acting technique will

The season opened with a bang with a hit production of the comedy **Born Yesterday***. "A red-headed first nighter exploded upon the stage of the Grand Theatre. Eleanor Ender, making her debut in the theatrical world as Billie Dawn, the leading feminine role in* **Born Yesterday***, captured a sympathetic audience and made it hers from the opening scene to the final curtain call."* (– *London Free Press, October 1960) Eleanor Ender is seated on the right. Others (l. to r.) Wally Duffield, David Rottman, Florence Scott and Tom Crerar. Peter Lynch was in the cast: "This was my first show. Co-director Doug McCullough wanted me as a walk-on, but then he gave me a short line to say: 'Thank you.' " – Peter Lynch, Grand Theatre board member, LLT set builder (Courtesy of Ruth Rottman)*

be discussed by Mr. Dearing, and there will be some pointers in stage direction. Designer William Lord will wind up the workshop series." (– J. Burke Martin, *London Free Press*, October 8, 1960)

CAROUSEL

Carousel was the season's big musical. The centrepiece of this musical is the beautiful carousel.

> *For the carousel we used a turntable from Chev-Olds. It was very heavy. It broke through the floor of the stage.*
> – Noreen De Shane and Peter Lynch, LLT set builders

"I can remember the intense feeling I had when I won the audition for *Carousel*, the first big break that would launch me into a musical career. The realization that I would be performing before hundreds of people each night for two weeks was, to say the least, daunting. I was a newcomer to theatre and relied on director Peter Dearing to coach me. He was an excellent mentor and drew from me many emotions needed for the role of Julie Jordan, from great joy to great sadness when Billy Bigelow dies in Julie's arms. I was able to cry real tears and portray to the audience the believability of the character. At one point in the play, there were supposed to be blossoms floating down from above and we would always cross our fingers and hope that they would come down slowly, but the odd time there would be globs of blossoms falling like big, wet snowflakes." – Patricia Leavens, LLT actress, singer

---

ORPHEUS IN THE UNDERWORLD

For one performance only, February 18, 1961, the Grand Theatre hosted the Canadian Opera Company. The company performed Offenbach's *Orpheus in the Underworld*. This performance was a homecoming for former LLT performer Victor Braun who was by this time a professional opera singer. Also in the cast was Londoner Joanne Ivey, as well as Jan Rubes, who enjoyed a long career in opera and in acting on stage and in films.

MARY STUART

In reviewing the LLT production of *Mary Stuart*, J. Burke Martin highlighted the design work of William Lord and Martha Mann: "I don't think I was stretching the truth in my review when I compared this to a Stratford Festival production. It was both lavish and tasteful. Bill Lord's sets were truly regal. This is set designing of a high order, and certainly far above the level of amateur theatre. Mr. Lord has the perfect working partner in Martha Mann, whose magnificent costumes for *Mary Stuart* were not only designed but, for the most part, cut and sewn by her in LLT's wardrobe department. What a talent this girl has and how fortunate we are to have her in London. Miss Mann came here in 1960, winner of the DDF trophy for best stage setting. …I can't think of any two people in amateur theatre more surely destined for greatness than Mr. Lord and Miss Mann." (– *London Free Press*, April 16, 1961)

I was still quite young in years and very young in experience when I went to the Grand Theatre. I learned two of life's most important lessons at The Grand. First, never, never, never open a dressing room door, no matter what time of the day or night, without first making a lot of noise, knocking very loudly and waiting to hear a voice say: 'Come in.' Also allow a full minute of dead silence before assuming the room is empty! Secondly, let someone else climb the A-frame ladder when you are 7 and one-half months pregnant. My son only escaped being born on the stage of the Grand Theatre by a few hours! the Grand Theatre, under the aegis of LLT (90 per cent of its staff amateur volunteers) was one of the most professional theatres I've ever worked in. We took life at The Grand very seriously. But, we had an awful lot of fun.

– Martha Mann, designer

ALTERATIONS TO THE GRAND

During the 1960/61 season $15,000 was invested in upgrading the ageing theatre. The stairway on the south side of the theatre was uncovered. It had been bricked up in 1930 when the upper balcony was ripped out. But LLT directors had long been uneasy about the 550 balcony patrons who had to rely on only two fire escapes leading from the balcony to the street level. Inspection by consulting engineers and architects revealed that, in a few more years, the balcony and theatre's rear wall (facing Richmond Street) might begin to part company. For this reason, extra supporting pillars were propped up under the balcony. The summer of 1961 saw the first new stage flooring. The original 1.5″ fir planking was down to 1/2″ in some places, from constant use. Some 3,000 square feet of the best quality tongue-and-groove fir was laid over the subfloor. The Grand's new stage floor meant that of the four original trap doors, only one remained. Doug McCullough, an architect and an active LLT member, planned and supervised the alterations at no cost to the amateur theatre group, and the Ellis-Don Company made the changes without profit.

PROPS AUTHENTICITY

"I remember Paul Soles and I glueing 'blue' American excise stamps on each and every one of the five packs of Camel cigarettes he opened on stage every night playing the tobacco-addicted Louis Howe in *Sunrise at Campabello*. Props authenticity! We cared to get it right."
– Martha Mann, designer

LLT Season #27:
Born Yesterday, by Garson Kanin, and Ruth Gordon, directed by Doug McCullough and Paul Soles
Dark at the Top of the Stairs, by William Inge, directed by Peter Dearing and Harding Greenwood
Carousel, by Hart Rodgers and Oscar Hammerstein II, directed by Peter Dearing and Don Fleckser
Hedda Gabler, by Henrik Ibsen, directed by Peter Dearing and Mary Brown
The Reluctant Debutante, by William Douglas Home, directed by Martin O'Meara
Mary Stuart, by Schiller, directed by Doris Isard
The Heiress, by Ruth and Augustus Goetz, directed by Marjorie Lister
Sunrise at Campabello, by Dore Schary, directed by Peter Dearing

LLT Junior Theatre School;
Heidi

Dance;
The Royal Winnipeg Ballet
Les Ballets Africans, National Emsemble of the Republic of Guinea
The National Ballet of Canada

Road Shows;
Julius Caesar, by William Shakespeare, *Saint Joan*, by G.B. Shaw, directed by Douglas Campbell, presented by The Canadian Players, which was formed in 1954 by Tom Patterson and Douglas Campbell
Vienna Boys Choir
Orpheus in the Underworld, by Offenbach, Canadian Opera Company

Festival;
The Canadian Inter-Varsity Drama League presented a festival of plays

Local Production;
Purple Patches

1961/62

LONDON LITTLE THEATRE ERA / PETER DEARING ERA

WILLIAM HUTT

"Most of the pleasures and a few of the perils of a premiere performance were present at the Grand Theatre last night on the occasion of The Canadian Players' visit there with Shakespeare's *King Lear*, starring William Hutt. To add some more prestige to the occasion, the Players' founder and honorary president, Lady Eaton, was there to applaud the troupe in which she has taken such a deep and abiding interest. Even with its minor imperfections of speech and timing, the production served to reinforce my conviction that Mr. Hutt is one of the greatest actors on the English-speaking stage. King Lear is a character twice Mr. Hutt's age. Most actors will not essay the role until advancing years have brought maturity, wisdom and depth. But this actor has all three in abundance." (–J. Burke Martin, *London Free Press*, October 25, 1961) In supporting roles were Mervyn Blake, Kenneth Pogue, and, as the sisters, Tobi Weinberg, Maureen Fitzgerald and Judith Coates.

VICTOR GARBER

Victor Garber, long before a Broadway career and Tony Award nominations, turned Life With Father *into life about a kid with dyed red hair, who had the fewest lines in the show, but a star quality that was undeniable, even in a boy of ten.*
– Martha Mann, designer

The season opened with a production of Life With Father. *Pictured above (l. to r.): Victor Garber, Brenda May, Jack Scott (on floor), Martin Kinch, Douglas Blackwell and Michael O'Brien.* "We all had our hair dyed red and we went to the same hair dresser at the same time. We all trooped out with newly-red hair, which caused heads to turn on Richmond Street." *– Brenda May, former LLT actress (Courtesy of Brenda May)*

ALAN LUND

Guys and Dolls was another smash hit for LLT. Dance numbers were staged by Alan Lund. "Alan Lund, probably the country's most experienced choreographer, has agreed to stage all the dance numbers for *Guys and Dolls*. With his wife Blanche, Mr. Lund staged all the choreographic numbers for this year's Canadian National Exhibition grandstand show. Alan and Blanche Lund have staged the dances for virtually all the CBC musicals since the advent of television in Canada. Mr. Lund's recent productions also include the dances for this year's Shakespearean Festival in Stratford. Mr. Dearing said Mr. Lund was delighted to accept the challenge of working on Canada's largest legitimate stage surface, and was pleased that he was the first outside choreographer ever to be engaged by LLT. (– *London Free Press*, October 11, 1961)

Sitting in that somewhat faded theatre the opening night of Guys and Dolls, a fast, slick, funny production by Peter Dearing, watching as 80-odd costumes that I had devised appeared and disappeared, thinking: 'This is not a bad looking show. …Maybe I do know what I'm doing…Maybe I do belong here!'
– Martha Mann, designer

DOMINION DRAMA FESTIVAL AWARDS

Playwright John van Druten based his play *I Am A Camera* on Christopher Isherwood's book *The Berlin Stories*, which was later adapted and became the musical *Cabaret*. LLT's production of *I Am A Camera* starred Julia Watts as Sally Bowles and Paul Harding as Christopher Isherwood. Julia Watts' acting career had started very early in her life, in the West End theatre district of London, England. This was Paul Harding's LLT debut. He later enjoyed a career as a professional actor on stage and on television. As one of sixteen plays at the WODL in March 1962 in Guelph, *I Am A Camera* was selected by the adjudicator as one of the plays to go to the DDF in Winnipeg in May. There it captured three of the five major prizes. Charlotte Ronson took the Best Actress award, while Paul Harding was judged Best Actor. In a report from the DDF, Alec Richmond wrote: "Although she received no formal prize, Julia Watts' brilliant, delightful and moving performance had endeared her to everyone who saw her." (– *Call-Boy*, June 1962)

Doug McCullough asked me to audition. There I saw Paul Harding, and I said to him 'I know you…' and he said 'I know you, too.' We had worked together 20 years earlier in England when he was Brian Harding. It had been about 15 years since I'd done anything really demanding, but I felt those 15 years, when I'd been living as a human being, made me a better actress.
– Julia Watts, actress

London Little Theatre
GRAND THEATRE LONDON
GE 9-6564   GE 9-6262
P. O. BOX 95

LLT Season #28:
Life With Father, by Howard Lindsay and Russel Crouse, directed by Don Fleckser
The Sound of Murder, by William Fairchild, directed by Marjorie Lister
Guys and Dolls, by Jo Swerling and Abe Burrows, directed by Peter Dearing
I Am A Camera, by John Van Druten, directed by Doug McCullough
The Deadly Game, by Fredrich Durrenmatt, directed by Peter Dearing
Thieves' Carnival, by Jean Anouilh, directed by Charles Brown
Caesar and Cleopatra, by G.B. Shaw, directed by Peter Dearing
The Pleasure of His Company, by Samuel Taylor and Cornelia Otis Skinner, directed by Paul Soles

LLT Theatre Workshop:
Introduction to Theatre, eight-week course
LLT Children's Theatre:
Legend, by Hilda Hooke
Road Shows:
King Lear, by William Shakespeare, *The Lady's Not for Burning*, by Christopher Fry, directed by David Gardner, presented by The Canadian Players
The Importance of Being Oscar Bousille and the Just, presented by La Comedie-Canadianne, with Gatien Gelinas
Spring Thaw '62
Dance:
The National Ballet of Canada
Caledonia!, singers and dancers of Scotland
Local Production:
The May Court Mad Caps in An Evening's Fun for Every One
Purple Patches
Down the Hatch, directed by Paul Soles, an original musical presented by UWO's Students' Council

1962/63

LONDON LITTLE THEATRE ERA/ PETER DEARING ERA

NEW

"New is the key word. The physical theatre has a greatly enlarged lobby featuring a soft drink bar and exhaust fan for inter-act refreshment. Gone, we hope, are those jam-packed, smoke-filled intermissions at The Grand. And we now have new access from that lobby directly up to the balcony for the convenience of those who prefer to enjoy their plays from on high." (– *Call-Boy*, October 1962)

BRIGADOON

Brigadoon is set in Scotland, so that called for a Scottish accent and we all strove very hard to achieve it. To create the Scottish mist the crew used dry ice and it was a standing joke each evening whether or not the dry ice would work and creep across the stage the way it was supposed to. Most of the time it did, but if it didn't we were hard-pressed to keep straight faces.
– Patricia Leavens, actress, singer

ONE WAY PENDULUM

After enjoying the huge hit, *Brigadoon* subscribers didn't know what to make of *One Way Pendulum*, billed as "a farce in a new dimension." Audience members used a variety of adjectives to describe it: boring, horrid, extremely funny, ghastly, dreadful, delightful. It sent many LLT members home in dismay. "It is no

Brigadoon *was the big musical production for this season. The Scottish highland village of Brigadoon appears for only one day every century. Two American men stumble into the village, which is still in the 18th century, and they must decide whether to stay in the village or to return to their own century. Music Director Don McKellar was quoted in* **Call-Boy** *as saying: "The most interesting experience in theatre is trying to keep the whole show together, from the pit, when the singers turn their backs." (– November 1962). Besides Flora MacKenzie and Doug McCullough, pictured above, in a cast of 21, the show also boasted of 26 singers, 14 dancers and four children. On opening night, fresh heather was flown in from Scotland for every lady in the audience. (Courtesy of Flora MacKenzie)*

secret that *One Way Pendulum* incurred a great deal of disfavour with a large number of the subscribers. But the fact that a play is not popular does not necessarily mean that it is bad, or that it should not have been produced." (– *Call-Boy*, January 1963) Most patrons did not take to the wacky absurdity of such scenes as a mute young man trying to teach weighing machines to sing, or a card-less card game. The production was, nonetheless, entered into the WODL competition, held at The Grand in March 1963. Herbert Whittaker, drama critic of the *Globe & Mail* was adjudicator. *One Way Pendulum* advanced to the DDF held in Kitchener 1963. There, LLT actor Stanley Lacey was recognized as the Best Supporting Actor. Director Peter Dearing wrote to him: "I think you know how delighted we all were that you should have been singled out by adjudicator Pierre LeFevre for this honour, and it couldn't be more richly deserved. …Well now, at last the pendulum has stopped swinging, and I hope you feel the results achieved in Kitchener were worth all the tremendous amount of hard work and personal sacrifice that you have given to the production since October. …I am sure you realize that all the nice things said about the production reflected great personal credit on everyone connected with it." (– May 22, 1963 Peter Dearing letter)

HARVEY

Young Fred Euringer was given the play *Harvey* to direct. When interviewed he revealed his directorial technique: "It's a comedy that's almost director-proof. If you've got a good cast, and I think I have, it almost plays itself. All I really have to do is get them on and off the stage. And I can at least do that." (– *London Free Press*, February 2, 1963). Doug McCullough starred as Elwood P. Dowd in this production of the popular play.

MORE GHOST OF A.J. SMALL

Pinocchio was the production by LLT's youngest actors this season. Playing one of the townspeople was Shelley Matthews (the future professional actress Shelley Peterson). It was during an onstage rehearsal for this production that Shelley encountered the ghost of Ambrose J. Small. One day her attention was distracted by a dull white light moving slowly down from the top of the balcony. As she watched, ignoring the rehearsal going on around her, this light moved down the balcony aisle, on stage right, before it settled into the second seat from the aisle. When she told her director what she had seen she was told that, indeed, she had just seen the ghost of Ambrose J. Small.

LLT Season #29:
Five Finger Exercise, by Peter Shaffer, directed by Peter Dearing
Brigadoon, by Lerner and Loewe, directed by Don Fleckser
One Way Pendulum, by N.F. Simpson, directed by Peter Dearing
The Miracle Worker, by William Gibson, directed by Martin O'Meara
Harvey, by Mary Chase, directed by Fred Euringer
The Vigil, by Ladislaw Fodor, directed by Peter Dearing
Not In The Book, by Arthur Watkyn, directed by Doris Isard
Auntie Mame, by Jerome Lawrence and Robert E. Lee, directed by

Harding Greenwood and Florence Smith

LLT Junior School:
Pinocchio

Local Production:
Purple Patches

Music:
Sweet Adelines

Dance:
The National Ballet of Canada
Bernice Harper – Dance Demonstration
Dorothy Scruton – Dance Demonstration

Festival:
WODL, March 12–16, 1963

1963/64

LONDON LITTLE THEATRE ERA / PETER DEARING ERA

On its 30th anniversary LLT received these words of congratulations from the former Governor General Vincent Massey: "Your theatre has over these years contributed a great deal to drama in Canada and I send you my warmest good wishes for continued success." And from Governor General Georges P. Vanier came these words: "The citizens of London are indeed fortunate in having what I am told is one of the largest and most versatile non-professional groups in the world." And from Prime Minister John Diefenbaker: "London Little Theatre has gained an enviable distinction among groups which have remained in active operation over the years". Jessica Tandy and Hume Cronyn have the last word: "Congratulations to both you and your audience! Long may you flourish." (– 30th Anniversary Souvenir, LLT 1933 – 1963)

KISS ME KATE

"You can add *Kiss Me Kate* to LLT's unbroken string of musical comedy successes. First-nighters at the Grand Theatre gave salvo after salvo of applause to an altogether first-rate production of the show, very loosely based on Shakespeare's *The Taming of the Shrew*…The show must stand or fall on its two principals and it is handsomely served by Flora MacKenzie who has already established herself in LLT annals as a singer and comedienne, and Mel Capener, a fine baritone whose only previous singing had

William Ziegler as the monstrous Jonathan Brewster in **Arsenic and Old Lace.** *This charming play starred Julia Watts and Brenda May as the sisters Abby and Martha. The Grand's trap door, closed for many years, was pressed into service for this production. Brenda May remembers: "Bill Ziegler clutched my waist and lifted me up. In doing so he unhooked my slip. It fell and hit the floor. So, I stepped out of it, put it behind a chair and continued the scene, to the applause of the audience." (Courtesy of William Ziegler)* been with a barbershop quartet. ...Most of the playgoers probably went away rejoicing in the fine pair of gangsters played by David Rottman and Alex Bakerspiegel. Their riotous 'Brush Up Your Shakespeare' was so funny that many of its best lines were lost. ... Don McKellar did his usual admirable job in the pit with an orchestra of 20-odd musicians." (– J. Burke Martin, *London Free Press*, November 1963)

Peter Dearing choreographed his curtain calls like ballets.
– Robin Dearing, former LLT actress

DAVE BROADFOOT

"Just when we needed it the most *The Best of Spring Thaw* arrived at the Grand Theatre and sent us out into a chilly evening glowing with laugh-induced warmth. ...Dave Broadfoot, intentionally or not, is Canada's Red Skelton in manner, voice and the capacity to enjoy what he's doing. He is a moronic hockey player being interviewed, and, in one of the evening's wittiest numbers, the memorable Member of Parliament from Kicking Horse Pass, speaking for the Apathetic Party. ...There's a host of native talent in this show, writers, composers and the performers. ...It's a beautifully paced revue, brightly dressed and expertly staged and it deserved the storm of laughter it stirred up." (– J. Burke Martin, *London Free Press*, March 27, 1964)

A RESPONSIBILITY

As the only source of continuing live theatre in this city and area, we have a responsibility to include in our bill those productions which are unusual, different and significant, as well as the sure-fire mass appeal plays.
– R.A. (Bob) Reinhart, 1st Vice-President LLT, annual general meeting, June 12, 1964

MICHAEL BRADSHAW

Reporting on the production of *Ross*, J. Burke Martin reported: "From what I hear about town, Michael Bradshaw's performance in *Ross* has impressed everyone else as much as it did me. In fact, several enthusiasts have called to tell me that this production by Harding Greenwood was the best Little Theatre play they've ever seen. Others wished they had a chance to see it again. Mr. Bradshaw is as dedicated a theatre buff as I know. He commuted 700 miles a week from Burlington while he was rehearsing for this portrayal of Lawrence of Arabia, still holding down his job as a commercial traveler." (– *London Free Press*, May 9, 1964) The all-male cast of 29 actors included some LLT stalwards, such as O.B. Watts, Meyer Epstein, Hew Crooks and Stanley Lacey. Listed as Arabs were: Jim Daigle, Al Hall, Thomas Hartmann, Ken Sadler and Gord Sandow.

LLT Season #30:
The Desperate Hours, by Joseph Hayes, directed by Don Carter
Kiss Me Kate, by Cole Porter, Samuel and Bella Spewack, directed by Peter Dearing
Gideon, by Paddy Chayefsky, directed by Martin O'Meara
As You Desire Me, by Luigi Pirandello, directed by Peter Dearing
The Seven Year Itch, by George Axelrod, directed by Florence Smith
Amphitryon '38, from Jean Giraudoux, directed by Wilf Pegg
Ross, by Terence Rattigan, directed by Harding Greenwood
Arsenic and Old Lace, by Joseph Kesselring, directed by Don Fleckser

Road Shows:
The Hollow Crown, performed by members of England's Royal Shakespeare Company
The Best of Spring Thaw
Beyond the Fringe
Die Fledermaus, The Canadian Opera Company

Dance:
Les Grands Ballet Canadiens
Jose Molina Bailes Espanoles

Music:
London Symphony Orchestra
Sweet Adelines

1964/65

LONDON LITTLE THEATRE ERA/ PETER DEARING ERA

MY FAIR LADY

LLT's lavish musicals usually garnered good reviews, but *My Fair Lady* did not receive an uncritical rave: "I am sorry that the director, who brought off such a beautiful production, persisted in having Alfred P. Doolittle frantically chase a bug through his clothing, followed by Higgins also slapping one under his sweater and recoiling from Doolittle's breath, and Eliza picking her nose. They showed better taste in the Broadway production. These were vulgar sight-gags, not only unworthy of this lovely show but completely out of character as Shaw conceived Doolittle and his daughter. It is all too easy to milk an audience this way and one thing *My Fair Lady* emphatically does not need is cheap laughs." (– J. Burke Martin, *London Free Press*, October 31, 1964)

Peter Dearing directed an ambitious production of My Fair Lady. *Our costumes, the original New York costumes as I recall, had just arrived and we were wearing them for our first of only two dress rehearsals before opening. It was the first time with crew, multiple sets, complicated technical cues and an orchestra. I was in the chorus and I had designed a very special hair style to go with my spiffy dove-grey Ascott Gavotte costume. One of 30 in the chorus, I promenaded onto the stage singing: 'Every Duke and Earl and Peer is here. ...' Suddenly the number halted, and the orchestra ground to a halt, as we*

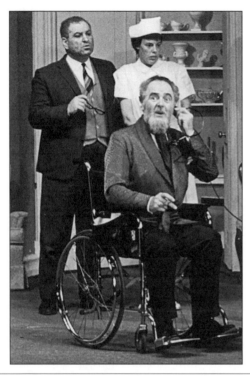

The Man Who Came to Dinner *featured (l. to r.) Eddie Escaf, Joan Brooks and Peter Dearing (in wheelchair).* "When Peter Dearing makes his entrance December 14 to assume his portrayal of Sheridan Whiteside in **The Man Who Came to Dinner**, he will be marking the 40th anniversary of his first appearance on any stage. It was on December 14, 1924, that the 10-year-old Peter Dearing assumed the role of Falstaff's page in Shakespeare's **The Merry Wives of Windsor.** (– **London Free Press**, December 12, 1964) (**Photo: Ron Nelson; Courtesy of Eddie Escaf**)

heard Peter Dearing's inimitable voice roar from the balcony: 'Art Fidler, get rid of that ridiculous spit curl on your forehead IMMEDIATELY!' No detail was ever too small for that remarkable man.

– Art Fidler, director, actor, teacher

TWO YOUNG LONDON ACTORS

The Diary of Anne Frank featured two young London actors. "In the role of Anne Frank is Caroline Dolny, a very talented 17-year-old marking her second appearance on our major bill after graduating from Children's Theatre. Also coming up through the ranks of Children's Theatre is Victor Garber (Peter Van Daan) who last tickled our fancy as the big shaggy dog in *Kiss Me Kate*. Victor's summer was spent at Hart House (University of Toronto theatre) in a summer theatre course under Robert Gill." (– *Call-Boy*, November, 1964). Victor Garber pursued a career as a professional actor, and appeared on stage, on television and in films. He won a Tony Award on Broadway. Caroline Dolny-Guerin also pursued a career in the arts, and is Head of Drama at London South Secondary School.

MOTHER COURAGE AND HER CHILDREN

LLT mounted an ambitious production of the epic play *Mother Courage and Her Children*. Bertholt Brecht's telling of Europe's Thirty Years War (1608 – 1638) underscored the futility of war and was particularly apt programming during the prolonged Vietnam War. Mother Courage, her two sons and a mute daughter travel in the wake of the troops, augmented by a cook, a runaway priest and a camp-following prostitute. Mother Courage's canteen-on-wheels is the focal point for this collection of itinerants. Although not a favourite with LLT audiences this season, it was entered in the WODL and later travelled to the DDF in Victoria, B.C. In May 1966, the 21-person cast, and the wagon, and all the props went to the DDF at a cost of approximately $4,000. There the production scored two trophies: the best presentation in English and Stanley Lacey won the trophy for the Best Supporting Actor, for his role as the Chaplain. Lucille Walker who played the lead character went on stage at the DDF with a temperature of 104 degrees, and a cold that threatened to leave her voiceless at any moment. Robin Dearing played the mute daughter, Kattrin.

I had no lines but dozens of scenes. They were vignettes in sequence. On a plain business envelope which I kept in the pocket of the apron I wore as part of my costume, I had written this sequences of scenes. That envelope was my security blanket throughout the two runs of the show. The second year we took the production to the DDF. But the bandages that were needed were left behind in London. So, someone in wardrobe shredded my apron to use as bandages. Of course they were unaware of the importance to me of that envelope in the apron pocket, and it was simply thrown away. No apron, no envelope, no notes, no security blanket.

– Robin Dearing, former LLT actress

A MAN FOR ALL SEASONS

A Man for All Seasons, starring LLT veteran actor Martin O'Meara in the title role of Sir Thomas More, was cited as "the best Little Theatre production of the season…one of the dramatic landmarks in its annals" by J. Burke Martin. "All non-professional shows have to be labours of love; this one showed it." (– *London Free Press*, May 1, 1965)

I started acting and I acted a long time before I started directing. The acting is more fun, the directing is more rewarding and much more of a challenge. I had a yen for historical plays so I co-directed A Man For All Seasons *with Peter Dearing.*

– Doris Isard, LLT director, interviewed by Alice Gibb

1965/66

LONDON LITTLE THEATRE ERA/
PETER DEARING ERA

LLT Season #31:
My Fair Lady, by Lerner and
Loewe, directed by Peter Dearing
The Dairy of Anne Frank, by
Francis Goodrich and Albert
Hackett, directed by
Charles Brown
The Man Who Came to Dinner, by
George S. Kaufman and Moss Hart,
directed by Harding Greenwood
A Shot in the Dark, from Marcel
Achard, directed by Doug
McCullough
Mother Courage and Her Children,
by Bertolt Brecht, directed by Peter
Dearing
Hay Fever, by Noel Coward,
directed by Barry Hunt and
Florence Smith
A Man For All Seasons, by Robert
Bolt, directed by Doris Isard and
Peter Dearing
One Thousand Clowns, by Herb
Gardner, directed by Don Fleckser

LLT Children's Theatre:
Winnie the Pooh

Road Shows:
Emlyn Williams in his one-man
show celebrating Charles Dickens
Sinbad the Sailor, performed by the
R.O.M. Museum Children's Theatre
Spring Thaw '65

Dance:
The National Ballet of Canada
Jose Molina Spanish Dance Fiesta
Dorothy Scruton – Dance Recital
Caledonia! featuring songs and
dances of Scotland

Music:
London Symphony Orchestra
Concert
Community Concert

Local Production:
Purple Patches

WEST SIDE STORY

Peter Dearing treated people as theatre professionals. He guided us.
– Heather Brandt, LLT actress

LLT invested approximately $10,000 in its production of *West Side Story*, the first non-professional Canadian production of the hit Broadway musical. Alan Lund came from Toronto to stage the exuberant dances. Gordon Sinclair played Tony opposite Jane O'Brien's Maria, while Flora MacKenzie was the spirited Anita, and Leigh Chapman was Bernardo.

We danced, and we danced…and we danced!
– Heather Brandt, LLT actress

Ed Kotanen and I were both working at the Stratford Festival, he as a scene painter/props builder and I as a wardrobe assistant. Ed was asked to design the set for LLT's production of West Side Story, *and he suggested that I design the costumes. It was my very first design job and I was understandably nervous. However, Alan Lund was the choreographer and wonderfully supportive. The show worked well and was full of energy, due to Alan's unflagging enthusiasm.*
– Maxine Graham, designer

SECOND THEATRE

"Another dimension was added to the narrow scope of play going in London last night as Second Theatre opened before about 100 in a warehouse (now 215 Piccadilly Street). Second Theatre sets out to do what used to be done in LLT's Studio Club – to offer avant-garde and intimate works of a type not suitable to either the expanse of the Grand Theatre or the general membership of LLT." (– *London Free Press*, November 27, 1965)

THE CRUCIBLE

Arthur Miller's play *The Crucible* received good reviews, but was not a hit with playgoers. Fraser Boa played John Proctor, and Boa's sister Marion Woodman played his bewildered wife Elizabeth Proctor. Caroline Dolny was the conniving maid-servant Abigail who comes between the Proctors. While 10,000 people came to see *West Side Story* only 5,000 LLT subscribers saw *The Crucible*.

> *When we were rehearsing and performing* The Crucible *I was astonished by the power of suggestion – on stage and off. The adolescent girlfriends of Abigail, for example, would sweep like a flock of birds into my dressing room, crying and giggling, then suddenly sweep out as one body into someone else's – all increasingly propelled by some mysterious power that was great in the play, but alarming off stage. Salem was a smoldering volcano in The Grand.*
>
> – Marion Woodman, writer, LLT actress

SINGLE TICKET BUYERS

At the annual general meeting in June 1966, Peter Dearing broached the subject selling tickets to non-subscribers. Single tickets were not available for LLT shows. Dearing urged board members to open some future LLT productions to single ticket buyers. He suggested that the theatre's directors might have to reconsider their responsibility to London's play-going public. Dearing pointed out that the Grand Theatre was London's only home for live theatre "and LLT directors may have to adopt a more open-house policy in years to come if The Grand is to serve the entire populace, and not just those who want to become full-season subscribers." (– *London Free Press*, June 15, 1966)

A total of 800 subscribers had chosen not to renew for the 1965/66 season, and a deficit of $2,800 was anticipated on the season. Despite Peter Dearing's far-sightedness, it would be several more seasons before LLT adopted an "open box office" policy.

LLT Season #32:
You Can't Take It With You, by Moss Hart and George S. Kaufman, directed by Don Fleckser and Elizabeth Murray
West Side Story, by Leonard Bernstein, Stephen Sondheim and Arthur Laurents, directed by Peter Dearing
Gaslight, by Patrick Hamilton, directed by Georgia Scheel
The Crucible, by Arthur Miller, directed by Kevin Palmer
Chips With Everything, by Arnold Wesker, directed by Charles Brown
Separate Tables, by Terence Rattigan, directed by Harding Greenwood

The Magistrate, by Sir Arthur Wing Pinero, directed by Peter Dearing
Mary Mary, by Jean Kerr, directed by Paul Harding

Second Theatre season included:
The Lesson, by Eugene Ionesco
The Collection, by Harold Pinter
Boxes, by Ron Gobert

Road Show:
Spring Thaw '66

Dance:
The National Ballet of Canada

Music:
London Symphony Orchestra concerts

1966/67

LONDON LITTLE THEATRE ERA/
PETER DEARING ERA

THE MUSIC MAN

With a cast of 50, and with 200 costumes, more than half of them rented from Brooks of New York City, *The Music Man* was LLT's most expensive musical production to date. Ten-year-old Mark Rechnitzer was Winthrop Paroo, and Patricia Leavens starred as Marion the Librarian. In reflecting on this show, director Don Fleckser says: "The dress rehearsal was played for all the Sisters of St. Joseph. It was an historical event because most of them had never been to the theatre."

We had a wonderful cast and some of the cutest children. We had a scene at one point on a foot bridge, and each evening I would slip a note into Harold Hill's hand. Needless to say the note usually said something inane designed to break Fraser Boa's concentration. You learned very quickly to overcome anything and continue as though nothing had happened. I have had my wig fly off in mid-song, one of the cast handed it back, and I put it back on. Usually the audience is unaware of what has happened, and the show goes on. I have worked with some of the best theatre directors and music conductors in London, among them Peter Dearing, Don Fleckser, Don McKellar and Jim White. They gave so much time and help to all of us and were so patient teaching us our craft.
– Patricia Leavens, LLT actress, singer

Fraser Boa was Professor Harold Hill in the delightful musical **The Music Man.** *He is pictured with Dorothy Westhead, who played Mrs. Paroo. (Courtesy of Dorothy Westhead)*

THE THREE DESKS

James Reaney's play *The Three Desks* premiered in February 1967. The central issue was the position of three desks in the English Department of the fictitious Rupertsland University. A young professor (played by Greg Brandt) is newly arrived at the University and is nervous in the new surroundings. He is caught in the power play between the popular professor (played by Fraser Boa) and the aging professor (played by Eric Atkinson). Cast as students were Heather Dennison, Chris Kiteley, Noreen De Shane, Peter Lynch and Paul Eck, among others.

In the January 1967 *Call-Boy*, James Reaney wrote: "Some years ago I was a member of the English Department at the University of Manitoba. It was there that I heard the 'germ' of my plot – about the professors who, sharing the same office, were eventually fired for continually pushing at each other's desks. …This play has been with me a long time. Last spring, with the encouragement of Charles and Mary Brown, Peter Dearing and the Stratford Festival Workshop, I finished the plot and made the necessary last minute adjustments. It wasn't until I'd finished the play that I realized *The Three Desks* was not only about power struggle, but also about the Commonwealth since there are Britishers, Australians, Hong Kongers and Canadians of every stripe involved. Very well – the Commonwealth is also a power struggle too, where Canada's desk stands as good a chance as any at getting to be either pusher or pushee. …I hope that in the years to come LLT will continue to put on one regionally written play each year. James Joyce said that Ireland's culture was like the 'looking glass of a servant girl.' My hope is that, as Canada becomes more developed in its character, we, like Ireland, will one day be able to look, not only in the great and helpful international mirrors, but also in a glass of our own devising."

Peter Dearing had a compelling personality. His directing style was such that once he was set on something, he wasn't about to change it.

– Dr. James Reaney, playwright, poet, writer

LLT ALUMNI

The off-beat musical *The Roar of the Greasepaint – The Smell of the Crowd* featured two young men who were seeking professional careers in the performing arts. Victor Garber had been absent from The Grand's stage for some three years, but he was back in this production. He had been taking theatrical training in Toronto and working with George Luscombe's Toronto Workshop Productions. He was also part of a folk rock group, Sugar Shoppe, and the group had just produced their first record album. Richard Braun, a native of Dorchester, was also onstage at The Grand. He had trained at the Opera School in Toronto, and was a member of Actors' Equity. His brother, Victor Braun, also an opera singer, was another LLT alumnus.

SEEKING A YOUNGER AUDIENCE

At the annual general meeting in July 1967, Peter Dearing suggested that younger, more dynamic audience members should augment the "lavender haired ladies." He went on to say: "We cannot discard their interest and co-operation in making this theatre what it is today, but it's obvious we have to include a younger audience if we want stimulating theatre." (– *London Free Press*, July 17, 1967) The lament for that elusive younger audience is as old as theatre itself.

1967/68

LONDON LITTLE THEATRE ERA / PETER DEARING ERA

LLT Season #33:
The Music Man, by Meredith Willson, directed by Don Fleckser
The Skin of Our Teeth, by Thornton Wilder, directed by Peter Dearing
Never Too Late, by Sumner Arthur Long, directed by Martin O'Meara
The Private Ear, by Peter Shaffer, directed by Harding Greenwood, and *The Public Eye*, by Peter Shaffer, directed by Jean Back
The Three Desks, by Dr. James Reaney, directed by Peter Dearing
Picnic, by William Inge, directed by Barry Hunt
Saint Joan, by G. B. Shaw, directed by Fraser Boa
The Roar of the Greasepaint – The Smell of the Crowd, by Leslie Bricusse and Anthony Newly,
directed by Peter Dearing

Second Theatre season included:
The Bald Soprano, by Eugene Ionesco
The Guardian, by David Garrick
Happy Days, by Samuel Beckett

Dance:
Canadian National Folk Dance Ensemble

Music:
London Symphony Orchestra
Scottish Variety Show

Festival:
WODL, April 4 – 8, 1967, officially opened by Pierre Berton; re-named The Centennial Theatre Festival, featuring works by Canadian writers in Canada's centenary year

A SEASON OF CHANGE

This was a season of change for LLT. Second Theatre became Mini-Theatre. In April, Londoners heard that Peter Dearing had resigned and would leave LLT in June and, at the annual general meeting in June 1968, there was a heated debate about a motion that suggested LLT change its name to Theatre London. The motion was defeated.

MINI-THEATRE

Controversy erupted early in the season when six of the eight members of LLT's executive committee resigned from the board. The dispute which led to these resignations was the John Labatt Limited company's offer to provide facilities for Second Theatre, the experimental branch of LLT. The LLT executive recommended at the September board meeting that LLT reject the offer, claiming the theatre wasn't in a financial position to take advantage of the facilities. When the board voted 8 to 5 to veto the executive's recommendation, it in effect expressed non-confidence in its executive and the mass resignation took place. Less than three weeks after the resignations, this item appeared in the *London Free Press*: "A mini-theatre for experimental plays will be established this year in a 72-year-old Richmond Street church. It will be a joint venture of LLT and John Labatt Limited. The building, near Simcoe Street, will be renovated to seat between 60 and 70

Elizabeth Murray and Doug McCullough starred in Edward Albee's searing drama Who's Afraid of Virginia Woolf? *This production can claim to be the one that introduced profanity to the Grand Theatre's stage. (Courtesy Geoff Farrow)*

persons for small plays. It will house LLT's Second Theatre. Labatt's will loan the building to LLT rent free for five years and is providing $10,000 toward renovation costs. Theatre president R. A. (Bob) Reinhart said the LLT will invest another $2,800." (– *London Free Press*, October 2, 1967) The opening date for Mini-Theatre was November 29. Tickets to shows were $2.00 each.

ELIZABETH MURRAY

The play that introduced the controversial f*** word to the Grand Theatre stage was *Who's Afraid of Virginia Woolf?* It starred Elizabeth Murray as the unhappy Martha and Doug McCullough as her husband George. The other couple was played by Judy Potter (Honey) and Greg Brandt (Nick). "It was a brave step," Elizabeth Murray recalled years later, "I was told at intermission about the number of patrons leaving early." Doug McCullough stated that: "Acting in *Virginia Woolf* was a pleasure."

I clearly remember Libby Murray, at the top of the show making her entrance and uttering the line 'What a dump!' She sounded like screen star Bette Davis in the movie Beyond the Forest. *If I closed my eyes, I could have sworn it was Bette Davis, instead of my mother. Seconds after her entrance, in any role she undertook, I would forget she was my mother – she became the character she was portraying. She was often compared to Katharine Hepburn or Lauren Bacall.*
– Martha Murray, former Grand Theatre employee and former Grand Theatre board member

OLIVER!

Oliver! was a big musical with a cast of 70, a full orchestra of 17 musicians, 200 costumes, and a brand new revolving stage to aid quick scene changes. Seven elaborate sets were designed by Ed Kotanen and Jack King. After auditioning for the role of Fagin, Alec Richmond brought the house down with the musical number "Reviewing the Situation."

MARAT-SADE

Peter Dearing's decision to produce *Marat-Sade* was a daring one. Only too aware that many LLT subscribers would consider this unsuitable entertainment, or too controversial, Dearing forged ahead and directed 35 actors in this difficult play. It was set in 1808, inside an insane asylum. A play-within-a-play, it is a stark commentary on the French Revolution and the madness of society. For therapeutic purposes, the asylum's inmates re-enact the murder of revolutionary Jean-Paul Marat, an historic event which took place during the Reign of Terror following the French Revolution. At the WODL in Sarnia, the adjudicator described LLT's production as "orgiastic, morbid, absurdly funny, but cold, stark and cruel as hydrotherapy in an asylum." In further remarks he said that Robin Dearing as Charlotte Corday was "a commanding theatrical presence with a beautiful voice and carriage. She had aristocratic qualities and the necessary suggestion of sexual and violent overtones." (– *London Free Press*, April 1968). It scored many trophies at the WODL, including the award for best play.

ADVENTURESOME PLAYS

Plays like Mother Courage, *and* Marat-Sade, *and* Six Characters in Search of an Author, *they were all pretty adventuresome, I think, for amateur theatre to be doing. But they were well done, and they may not have been what our audiences were used to, but we always had a feeling, too, that we shouldn't play down to our audiences. And they did come along with us.*

– Elizabeth Murray, former LLT board president, actress

AN UNCERTAIN FUTURE

LLT's future was uncertain. Writing in the *London Free Press*, reporter Helen Wallace discussed three issues facing the amateur company: the theatre's role, its playbill and future plans. "The playbill has long been a target and the theatre admittedly takes audience tastes into consideration when it drafts a season's lineup of plays. However, one segment of the audience is becoming more vocal in demanding more challenging, stimulating, experimental and avant-garde works. The theatre plays it safe, they charge, adhering to a fixed standard – slick entertainment and a respectable box office with little desire to attempt the offbeat. There are also patrons who argue they prefer to be entertained, and claim it as a right after paying a $10 or $14 subscription fee… Is criticism of LLT justified? Should the theatre reassess its position as the city's only flourishing amateur theatre? It must be admitted that LLT has deserved its reputation as one of the best amateur theatres in Canada. It has merited a semi-professional label and has represented the city well in nationwide drama festivals. It offers facilities and productions of a calibre that need make no apologies. Few LLT ventures are ever crushing disasters. They always manage a degree of performance, even when unsuccessful, that rarely sink beneath the mediocre. As a result of its long-standing success, and probably because it is lodged in such an impressive mausoleum, the theatre has acquired an establishment image that makes it a ready target. …The theatre has had to attempt to please all tastes in the bill and at the same time maintain a $100,000 annual operation that doesn't always show a profit. Added to that is the mounting expense of operating a very old theatre and the sad fact that its facilities are unused more than four months of the year. … London could possibly support a professional repertory company. …Transformation from amateur to professional status has worked successfully in Winnipeg and Edmonton. It could happen here." (– *London Free Press*, April 10, 1968)

During this season Peter Dearing tendered his resignation. It took effect at the close of the 1967/68 season. LLT had grown and gained confidence throughout the 11-season tenure of Artistic Director Peter Dearing. Without Dearing, or a replacement for him, what did the immediate future hold for London Little Theatre?

1968/69

LONDON LITTLE THEATRE ERA

NO NEW ARTISTIC DIRECTOR

LLT appointed no new artistic director to succeed Peter Dearing. Instead LLT forged ahead for three seasons, without such an individual at the helm. LLT's board of directors volunteered even more time than usual to oversee the artistic and administrative arms of the organization.

SHOWBOAT

LLT subscribers had come to expect a great big musical and they were not disappointed this season with the production of *Showboat*. The Grand's stage was filled with a cast of 72. Technically it was one of the most complicated productions attempted by LLT. Ten full stage settings were required, designed by Ed Kotanen and Jack King. There was a boat with multiple balconies, paddle wheels and smokestacks. The set revolved and then split in two, to reveal an interior complete with a stage, more balconies, and a top deck where the riverboat customers were entertained. New scrims were purchased in England and were used for the projection of images during the Chicago World's Fair scene. Highlights included images of the ferris wheel and the fireworks display. "The ensemble numbers reached their peak in the play-within-a-play sequence when the actors re-enacted, with proper ham spirit, old-fashioned melodramas to the boos, hisses and cat calls of the audience." (– Helen Wallace, *London Free Press*, October 3, 1968) The season was off to a great start.

LLT Season #34:
Any Wednesday, by Muriel Resnik, directed by Florence Smith
Who's Afraid of Virginia Woolf?, by Edward Albee, directed by Peter Boretski
Oliver!, by Lionel Bart, directed by Peter Dearing
The Persecution and Assassination of Jean-Paul Marat as performed by the inmates of the Asylum of Charenton under the Direction of the Marquis De Sade, by Peter Weiss, directed by Peter Dearing
The Right Honourable Gentleman, by Michael Dyne, directed by Sean Mulcahy
The Knack, by Ann Jellicoe, directed by Bryan Dobbs

Hostile Witness, directed by Peter Dearing
Barefoot in the Park, by Neil Simon, directed by Don Fleckser

Mini-Theatre season included:
The Life and Times of Practically Nobody, by Martin Lager
Balls
The Chairs

Children's Theatre:
Toad of Toad Hall

Road Show:
Stop The World I Want to Get Off!, starring Jackie Warner

Dance:
The National Ballet of Canada

PATRICIA LEAVENS

I would arrive at the theatre an hour before the performance and sit in the dressing room and leave Patricia Leavens at home. Each time I would audition for a role the same feelings would envelop me, that this was a serious undertaking and many times it was up to me to set an example for the rest of the cast, many of whom were very young and needed help. One of the many wonderful things that came from an amateur cast was that we were all ready to help and assist the other members, and a very close-knit association came about between cast members. We would send each other notes on opening night and many times we would take lines out of the production, find a picture in a magazine that would fit, and send it to someone who had that line. There was no jealousy that I could find in the productions I was in, as everyone was doing their best to give the audience the best show they could.

– Patricia Leavens, LLT actress, singer

JACK BEATTIE

"As a student at London South Secondary School, in the mid-sixties, I was encouraged in the theatre by Fraser Boa and his sister Marion Woodman, both wonderful teachers at South. When I graduated and started at the University of Western Ontario, Marion encouraged me to keep up with the acting by auditioning for LLT. My first drama teacher at the University of Western Ontario also pushed me along and soon enough, I was, to my surprise, in the LLT cast of a wonderful parody called *Hamlet, Prince of Quebec*. This was a wacky experimental play which poked fun at Quebec politics using Shakespeare's melancholy Dane as a foil. I was the first grave digger. I was also first on stage, popping out of a trap door built out over the orchestra pit. I was to sit on the front edge of the stage and sing a silly song at the top

Diana Thompson was featured as Julie, the mulatto singer in the LLT production of Showboat. *In his CFPL Radio review, Fraser Boa remarked: "I know of no musical with such great music. Every song is an old standard. And this cast can sell them. Patricia Leavens (Magnolia) has never sung so well on The Grand stage; Diana Thompson certainly has one of the finest voices in London".*
(– CFPL Radio review, October 2, 1968; Courtesy of Diana Stott)

of the show. Things went well enough in rehearsal and soon it was opening night. I was crouched under the trap with my heart pounding at a million miles an hour. My cue light went on; I came out of the trap and sat three feet from the front row of a sold-out house. My chest muscles tightened up so badly that I could not breathe. And of course, I could not sing loud enough to be heard beyond the first row. I was mortified. I stumbled through the rest of opening night, silently confounding my theatre career to the depths of hell. The only problem was, we had 13 more shows to do. It was at this point that my stage partner, the second gravedigger, showed me why community theatre was so wonderful. Alex Bakerspiegel was a former vaudevillian with a wide and varied career in both amateur and professional theatre. He knew what had happened to me on opening night. The next night as I waited nervously to make my entrance, Alex started telling some of the most ribald jokes I had ever heard. Soon I was laughing helplessly. The cue light went on and I vaulted out of the trap and sang to the back of the hall. I have never had a problem with projection (or nerves, for that matter) since." – Jack Beattie, drama teacher

WAIT UNTIL DARK

Wait Until Dark was full of technical gimmicks and trickery. Larry Smith and Brian Brown designed the special effects for this drama that revolves around the efforts of a blind girl to outwit three killers. Heather Brandt, four months pregnant at the time, was cast as the blind girl. Her adversaries were played by Greg Brandt, John Dell and Eddie Escaf. The last 25 minutes of the play were performed in total darkness, except for light thrown from an open refrigerator, or lighted matches or flashlights. This called for a light proof set. The actors were rewarded for their efforts by spontaneous shrieks of terror.

It was very exciting, very suspenseful; the audience screamed!
– Heather Brandt, LLT actress

AN IDENTITY CRISIS

LLT was enduring an identity crisis. Designers Jack King and Ed Kotanen were the subject of a feature story in the newspaper and they took the opportunity to comment that LLT was in the grip of what they called a "creeping professionalism." "The theatre is now trying to decide whether it should turn the whole thing back to the community, or become professional. The theatre is now standing still for lack of an artistic director. A committee doesn't give a place any artistic focus. All it can do is run a theatre and sell tickets." (– *London Free Press*, December 7, 1968)

LLT Season #35:
Showboat, by Jerome Kern and Oscar Hammerstein II, directed by Don Fleckser
Hamlet, Prince of Quebec, by Robert Gurik, directed by Roland Laroche
The Subject was Roses, by Frank D. Gilroy, directed by Doris Isard
Philadelphia Here I Come, by Brian Friel, directed by Harding Greenwood
The Deputy, by Rolf Hochhuth, directed by Roland Laroche
The Hostage, by Brendan Behan, directed by Fraser Boa

Wait Until Dark, by Frederick Knott, directed by Don Fleckser
The Odd Couple, by Neil Simon, directed by Paul Harding

Mini-Theatre season included:
The Royal Gambit, by Hermann Gressieker
Three One Act Farces, by Anton Chekhov
Christmas presentation for children

Dance:
The National Ballet of Canada
Snow White, presented by The Dorothy Scruton Academy of Dance and Fine Arts

1969/70

LONDON LITTLE THEATRE ERA

THEATRE REVIEWS

The Lion in Winter received a scathing review by Helen Wallace in the *London Free Press*. She opened with: "The practice of selecting an over-exposed movie and including it in their annual playbill is one that will have to be reconsidered by LLT if *The Lion in Winter* is any example." Her closing shot read: "Whatever the reason, LLT made a mistake including it on this year's bill and, out of respect for the cast, which no doubt did try hard, it would be a kindness to leave the players unmentioned." (– November 1, 1969)

Fraser Boa, reviewing the production for CFPL-TV, had the opposite view: "Paul Eck's production of *The Lion in Winter* is a delight. It is far and away the best comedy seen at LLT in many a moon not only for its imaginative set but also for the cast who look right in their elaborate costumes and not like actors wandering through some historical mausoleum. To miss *The Lion in Winter* is to miss possibly the best show of the season." (– October 31, 1969)

These opposite points of view resulted in many letters to the newspaper editor discussing that enduring question…just who does the critic think s/he is anyway?! Eva Roche writing from Edmonton commented: "As one who has written drama criticism I know how tempting it is to resort to the cute and clever phrase, but it is less than informative to the public and valueless to the players to write 'it would be a kindness to leave the players unmentioned.' How much more difficult, but rewarding, to comment constructively." (– *London Free Press*, November 6, 1969).

Frank Martin of London wrote: "Helen Wallace's review is an irresponsible piece of immature sarcasm. She has obviously succumbed to the inexperienced critic's temptation to try to display her own wit and try to demonstrate her own superior taste by being almost totally condemning of the play and the performance." (– *London Free Press*, November 6, 1969)

Who were the cast members in *The Lion in Winter*? Elizabeth Murray as Eleanor, Brian Brown as Henry II, Serge Lavoie, Geoffrey Lee and Steven Thomas as their three sons, while Anne Washington, Robert More, Tom Cox, Scott Davidson and Art LaFleur rounded out Paul Eck's cast.

A PUB PARTY REHEARSAL

"*The Anthem Sprinters*, by Ray Bradbury, was set in Ireland. I played the Narrator. Many of the cast members were young Irishmen who had recently arrived to teach in Canada. They had been recruited by the professional director, Hugh Webster, to lend authenticity and local colour to the production. The main set was Heeber Finn's Pub, and it was there that my character, an American, was introduced to the arcane traditions of the Irish. During one rehearsal I finished my monologue downstage and crossed to the bar where the rest of the cast was dressing the set. John Gellard, as Heeber Finn, passed me my prop mug of beer and I discovered that none of the prop beer or whiskey on stage was fake. A real Irish pub party took place on stage during that rehearsal – in fact, it was a breakthrough for the production! I don't think Hugh Webster ever knew what happened." – Art Fidler, director, actor, teacher

EXPERTS

Fraser Boa directed Beyond the Fringe. *During the performance the house lights would go up and two of us would sit*

on the stage and invite questions from the audience, concerning civil defence in the event of an atomic war. This device was used only as a cue for another one of the acting company sitting in a box, in the house. But one evening, directly after the lights went up, someone in the audience asked: 'What makes you think you are experts on civil defence?' My rapid response was: 'Well, I'm civil and he's rather defensive.'

– O.B. Watts, LLT actor, teacher

CURTAIN CALL

Several of my wildest moments on the beloved old stage took place during the curtain call after Ring Around the Moon. *Adorned in a long velvet dress, long white gloves, feather boa and headpiece, I rolled across the stage on roller skates with a royal Queen Mum wave to the audience.*

– Marion Woodman, writer, LLT actress

LLT Season #36:
Miss Julie, by August Strindberg, and *Black Comedy* by Peter Shaffer, directed by Eugene Gallant
The Lion in Winter, by James Goldman, directed by Paul Eck
How to Succeed in Business Without Really Trying, by Abe Burrows, Jack Weinstock, Willie Gilbert and Frank Loesser, directed by Don Fleckser
Loot, by Joe Orton, directed by Ron Hartmann
The Anthem Sprinters and other Antics, by Ray Bradbury, directed by Hugh Webster
Beyond the Fringe, by Peter Cook, Dudley Moore, Alan Bennett and

Jonathan Miller, directed by Fraser Boa
Ring Around the Moon, by Jean Anouilh, directed by Jay Sayer
Cactus Flower, by Abe Burrows, directed by Harding Greenwood

Mini-Theatre season included:
Exit the King, by Ionesco
The Stronger, by August Strindberg
The Lover, by Harold Pinter

Local Production:
Snow White and the Seven Dwarfs and *Anne of Green Gables*, presented by The Audrey Lewis Theatre School

Dance:
Royal Winnipeg Ballet

1970/71

LONDON LITTLE THEATRE ERA

INTERVIEW WITH PETER DEARING

Since leaving LLT, former Artistic Director Peter Dearing had worked with the Hamilton Players Guild. He had also done some work at the Niagara Community College in Welland, and at a fine arts summer camp in northern Ontario. He was back in London to direct two of this season's productions: *Don't Drink the Water* and *The Innocents*. In an interview with reporter Helen Wallace, Dearing reiterated his thoughts of a few seasons earlier: "I do believe in keeping a hard, solid core of subscribers and giving them privileges such as reserved seats because they are subscribers. But then LLT should throw the doors wide open. Until people see what's offered, they're not going to buy…If I were a visitor in the city, staying at a hotel, it's unfortunate that there's no opportunity to see theatre. London is such a subscription city and this is what is killing casual theatre going in the city." (– *London Free Press*, September 26, 1970)

TRAGEDY

Your Own Thing was a modern musical comedy version of Shakespeare's romantic comedy *Twelfth Night*. Director Paul Eck was looking for a cast whose ages ranged from 18 to 25 years. After auditioning 45 hopefuls, he cast 18 young people, including Heather Brandt, Mike Kiteley, Alicia Jeffery and Jim Schaefer. Before the play opened, tragedy struck: "Michael Kiteley, 21, was killed when his car slammed into the CPR overpass on Oxford Street about 1:00 a.m. on December 2 (1970). …Indications are that he was on his way home from a dress rehearsal for LLT's production of *Your Own Thing* when he was killed." (– *London Free Press*, December 3, 1970). Jim Hill took over Mike Kiteley's part in the play.

THE VISIT

Elizabeth Murray, as Claire, and Michael Gibbons, as Anton, played lead roles in the dark drama *The Visit*. The play concerns the visit of the ageing, eccentric billionairess Claire to her impoverished hometown in central Europe. Three decades before this visit, she was forced to leave town in disgrace. She turned to prostitution, but eventually married an oil magnate. She comes back to buy justice and extract ruthless revenge on the man who had ruined her when she was 17 years old. Claire is willing to endow the town with a billion marks, in exchange for the life of Anton. Moral scruples of the villagers begin to give way to avarice and intrigue. After a town meeting, Anton is resigned to his fate. The citizens close around him and when they disperse, Anton lies dead on the ground. The townspeople have their money. Claire has her justice.

> *It was profoundly moving. On opening night you could have heard a pin drop. The next night there were eruptions of laughter. There were inconsistent audience reactions throughout the whole run.*
>
> – Michael Gibbons, LLT actor

Julia Watts as Jean Brodie in **The Prime of Miss Jean Brodie.** *Julia's daughters, Dinah and Caroline, were also cast in the production. Despite some opening night acoustic problems, reviewer Helen Wallace rated this production as "the best I have seen in 10 years of LLT-watching." (–* **London Free Press,** *February 25, 1971; Courtesy Geoffrey Farrow)*

HEINER PILLER AND THEATRE LONDON

In the May 1971 house program, LLT subscribers were introduced to incoming Artistic Director Heinar Piller, aged 32. The announcement of Piller's appointment came at the end of a long season filled with debate about the future of LLT. The board had considered two options: they could sell the Grand Theatre, pay off their debts and give the remainder to charity, or they could struggle on for another three or four years. Piller, then Artistic Director of Halifax's Neptune Theatre, was consulted for advice, and it was he who proposed a third option; LLT could slowly turn professional, over a three-year period, and instead of selling its only asset, the Grand Theatre, LLT could mortgage the building and use the money to pay their professional actors and technical staff, thereby allowing the theatre company to qualify for government grants offered to professional theatres by the Canada Council. LLT's board members liked this idea and decided to proceed with it. The board decided against putting a mortgage on the building. Instead, they went to the community to raise the money.

In his homeland of Austria, Heinar Piller received dramatic training in Vienna. He came to Canada in 1960, planning to stay for two years. During his first months in Toronto, he made contact with amateur groups for whom he acted, directed and did production work. He enrolled at the University of Toronto because, as a student, he could work with Hart House, the campus theatre. Through his work at Hart House, he got his first job with the Canadian Opera Company (COC) as a production assistant, and it was at the COC that he met Leon Major, then Artistic Director at the Neptune Theatre in Halifax. Piller was hired by Leon Major in 1966 as a stage manager for The Neptune. He managed the theatre's Maritime tour and a Festival Canada tour in 1967. After a year as Associate Artistic Director, Heiner Piller was appointed Artistic Director in 1968. Early in 1971, he accepted LLT's offer to oversee the three year process of turning London's theatre company into a professional company.

The *London Free Press* reported that Heinar Piller "plans to explore functions the theatre is not filling, with a special emphasis on youth. He hopes the theatre will become an increasingly important centre for drama appreciation and one which will help high school students bring their dramatic interests and talents into a public situation." (– May 7, 1971)

The June 14, 1971, annual general meeting was pivotal in the history of LLT and the Grand Theatre. At this meeting the decision was made to change the name London Little Theatre to Theatre London. This idea had been voted down when it was tabled at the 1968 annual general meeting, but now board members of LLT felt it was necessary to change the name to "do

away with the dilettante image involved by the 'Little Theatre' " name. (– *London Free Press*, June 15, 1971)

Dr. Brian Brown, second vice-president of the theatre's board stated: "We are not little. We are far from little and it's time we stopped calling ourselves little." (– *London Free Press*, June 15, 1971). London theatre matriarch, Catharine McCormick Brickenden, also supported the name change, saying that the name London Little Theatre was a "misnomer." At the close of this historic meeting, London Little Theatre was retired and Theatre London was born.

The annual general meeting was an opportunity discussion of another grave issue. There was concern that with the new emphasis on professionalism, amateur actors and volunteer production crews would be elbowed aside. There was fear that many outside people would be brought in to play on The Grand's stage and that dedicated local people who loved participating in theatre would be left without a theatre home. While very aware of these feelings, incoming Artistic Director Heinar Piller had a clear mandate from the board: to turn a long-standing, amateur theatre company into a professional theatre company within three years.

LLT Season #37 (final LLT season):
Don't Drink the Water, by Woody Allen, directed by Peter Dearing
The Prime of Miss Jean Brodie, by Jay Presson Allen, directed by Fraser Boa
Your Own Thing, by Hal Hester, Danny Apolinar and Donald Driver, directed by Paul Eck
The Innocents, by William Archibald, directed by Peter Dearing
A Flea in Her Ear, by Georges Feydeau, directed by Roland Laroche
The Visit, by Friedrich Durrenmatt, directed by Fraser Boa
The Star-Spangled Girl, by Neil Simon, directed by Harding Greenwood

Mini-Theatre season included:
Slow Dance on the Killing Ground, by William Hanley
Real Inspector Hound, by Tom Stoppard
Joe Egg, by Peter Nichols

Dance:
The National Ballet of Canada

Play on Tour:
Plaza Suite, by Neil Simon, starring Larry Parks and Betty Garrett

THEATRE LONDON

1972-1982

New Artistic Director Heinar Piller stands on Richmond Street outside the Grand Theatre. London Little Theatre had survived for 37 seasons. With the 1971/72 theatre season, playgoers were introduced to Theatre London. (Courtesy The London Free Press*)*

1971/72

THEATRE LONDON/ HEINAR PILLER ERA

SINGLE TICKETS

1971 was the first year since 1936 that single tickets were available to plays produced at the Grand Theatre. Subscribers would still have first choice of theatre seats. As early as October the decision to "open" the box office was meeting with success. "The season's first show, *Blithe Spirit*, drew 6,017 people. Of these, subscriptions accounted for 5,267 – about normal attendance for a show at the Grand Theatre. The 750 people who bought tickets at the door were a bonus." (– *London Free Press*, October 15, 1971)

ABOUT HEINAR PILLER

I knew Heinar Piller from the early sixties, when he joined me in a Drama Workshop at Toronto's Ryerson Polytechnical Institute. At the time Heinar was just mastering his English, but Toronto media was kind to both of us as actors in Ondine. *The day he arrived in London and was honoured at a reception, he was so nervous that he didn't recognize me. I had the opportunity to exchange several sentences with Heinar in German, and he was so preoccupied that he didn't realize he was running in two languages simultaneously.*

– Ric Wellwood, writer, critic, broadcaster, teacher

THE ECSTASY OF RITA JOE

The Ecstasy of Rita Joe combined local actors, such as Martin O'Meara, Dorothy Westhead, Alicia Jeffery and Jack Beattie, with professional actors like Dennis Thatcher, and young Jerry Franken and Michael Springate. The play was about a young Indian woman, played by professional actress Patricia Ludwick, who leaves the reservation for the city and finds herself unable to adapt. She continually comes into conflict with the laws of the alien society. The design for the production merited these words from reviewer Doug Bale: "The set (designed by Fred Allen) is a free-form, multi-level ramp that covers nearly the whole stage. At different times, different parts of it serve as a mountain meadow, a magistrate's court, a rundown boarding-house room, a prison cell, a rushing river or a city street. The backdrop is a free-form sculptured web of what looks like metal tubing, wire and thread. Depending on the way it is lit (by lighting designer David Wallett) it can look like trees, clouds, lightning flashes, ghosts – the range of effects is extraordinary." (– *London Free Press*, November 6, 1971.)

MEMORIAL SERVICE

In November 1971, a memorial service for Peter Dearing was held by members of London's theatre community. He had died in Toronto on November 6, aged 58. The memorial service consisted of music from the theatre and personal recollections of, and tributes to, Peter Dearing. The service took place before a large audience gathered at The Grand for the sober occasion.

I have a piercing memory of sitting in the audience at Peter Dearing's memorial service. Play after play, detail by brilliant detail! How much we owe to Peter Dearing and Robin Dearing for all they gave to theatre in London.

– Marion Woodman, writer, LLT actress

LOOKING TO THE FUTURE

In the November 1971 house program Artistic Director Heinar Piller wrote: "Dear Audience – Thank you for the warm welcome you extended to Theatre London and to me with your response to the first two productions this season. For many of you it may be difficult to grow accustomed to our new name, as it is often difficult for parents to accept their children as adults. Your theatre has come of age, it has grown into Theatre London, but the heartbeat is still and always will be the same as LLT's. Our LLT is very ambitious – and so it should be; you gave it a first-rate upbringing. It has every reason to look into the future with youthful enthusiasm; – to the day when Theatre London will be among the finest theatre companies in this country."

THEATRE MUST GO BEYOND

To become really successful, the theatre must go beyond the walls of the Grand Theatre and put on plays elsewhere in the community – such as the schools.
– Artistic Director Heinar Piller, December 1971

SOMETHING'S GOT TO BE DONE

Dracula starred Brian Kellow as the vampire, and Heather Brandt as the virtuous Lucy. On opening night the actors had to compete with unwelcome noises from the house. "The theatre's antique heating system clanged and thumped so noisily in the first act that it nearly drowned out the actors. Friday night wasn't the first time that's happened; something's got to be done about those blasted pipes," commented critic Doug Bale. (– *London Free Press*, March 4, 1972)

Something had to be done about the whole building, not just the pipes. The Grand Old Lady of Richmond Street was no longer Grand, just old.

Among the more storied productions during the Heinar Piller era was Dracula, *which drew the attention of a real bat, which hung around somewhere up in the fly tower. During one or two of the shows the bat would hover above the performers and excite the audience, some of whom believed the thing was on a string. Others knew it was alive, but thought it trained to perform.*
– Ric Wellwood, writer, critic, broadcaster, teacher

A SLEEPOVER AND A GHOST

"In July 1972 I directed a Youtheatre Ontario project with a cast of 28 London teenagers, among them Nancy Palk and Tom McCamus. We were creating a collective about Canadian characters and legends, and my cast became interested in Ambrose J. Small. My assistant, Holly Holmes, and I arranged to spend all night in the theatre and to sleep on the darkened stage where my kids held a seance to raise Ambrose J. Small's spirit. This was the night that Tom McCamus saw the ghost of Ambrose J. Small. It was a spookily memorable night. There used to be actual tunnels far beneath the stage, and the old store rooms at the fly floor level were Gothic wonderlands." – Art Fidler, director, actor, teacher

One of my first experiences at the Grand Theatre was a sleepover. I was a teenager and this was before the theatre had been renovated. A group of us who were in a local Youtheatre project spent the night in the theatre to gain publicity for our show. It was late at night. We had spent many hours in the catacombs under the stage and the pathway through the proscenium arch. We were now back on the stage getting our sleeping bags ready for the night. I looked out into the audience and saw a man with a bowler hat sitting in about the third row. I got up and tried to get to the auditorium by the side exit. Every time I looked out through one of the side arches I saw the man, but he had moved several rows back and when I reached the auditorium he was gone. When I got back to the stage I told a friend what I had seen, and she said she thought she had seen someone as well. I worked at The Grand at various times over the next two decades and that was the only time I ever saw Ambrose J. Small.

– Tom McCamus, actor

1972/73

THEATRE LONDON/ HEINAR PILLER ERA

LONDON, A CULTURAL CENTRE

I do believe that London will become the cultural centre of Southwestern Ontario. Theatre London is no longer a private club. The attention of the Canadian theatre world is increasingly focussed on London.
– Heinar Piller, Artistic Director (– London Free Press, April 29, 1972)

ADJUSTING TO CHANGES

London was still adjusting to the changes taking place at the Grand Theatre under Heinar Piller's leadership. Some people who had been active in LLT productions continued to express their feelings of being squeezed out of the theatre. In expressing sympathy and understanding of these feelings Piller was quoted as saying: "It's like the big, bad wolf taking something away. The professionals are doing the same job as you (the amateurs) did and you've been degraded to walk-ons." (– *London Free Press*, November 18, 1972) But the movement toward a fully professional enterprise was underway, and Theatre London was moving very rapidly in that direction.

THE MAN OF LA MANCHA

The Man of La Mancha was on stage in early December 1972. Heinar Piller directed Mike Fletcher as Cervantes/Don Quixote, opposite the statuesque Denise Fergusson as Aldonza. This proved

---

Theatre London season #1:
Blithe Spirit, by Noel Coward, directed by Heinar Piller
The Ecstasy of Rita Joe, by George Rygas, directed by Heinar Piller
Fiddler on the Roof, by Joseph Stein, Jerry Bock and Sheldon Harnick, directed by Fraser Boa
Our Town, by Thornton Wilder, directed by Heinar Piller
Dracula, by Hamilton Deane and John L. Balderston, directed by Paul Eck
Luther, by John Osborne, directed by Heinar Piller
Forty Carats, by Jay Allen, directed by Don Fleckser

Performed by the Young Company:
Noon, by Terrence McNally
The Zoo Story, by Edward Albee
Red Cross, by Sam Shepherd
Rumpelstiltskin, the first full Equity show; it starred Michael Burgess as the Prince

Canadian Puppet Festival:
Pinocchio

Dance:
The National Ballet of Canada
Dorothy Scruton Academy of Dance Recital

The uproarious comedy with the unlikely title of Boeing, Boeing *starred Shelley Matthews (later Peterson) (left), Heather Brandt (above) and Caroline Gordon (lower), and delighted audiences. (Courtesy of Heinar Piller)*

to be the most popular show of the season. The run was extended by four extra shows to accommodate the demand for tickets.

A THEATRE LONDON EXPERIENCE

While the three female leads, playing airline hostesses in *Boeing, Boeing*, ran around the Grand's stage in clad in towels and pyjamas,

the older actress Elsa Pickthorne had fun playing a harassed housekeeper. When she returned to her home in Ottawa, Pickthorne wrote of her Theatre London experience: "Lodged comfortably and luxuriously in an efficiency apartment on Dundas Street, my home for five weeks while I rehearse and then perform in Theatre London's production of *Boeing, Boeing*. Four nights of the two weeks of performances are student previews and what marvellous and enthusiastic audiences they provide, filling the eleven hundred seats to capacity each night. Our play was guest-directed by that fascinating and erudite gentleman of radio and television fame, Andrew Allan. Theatre London is fortunate to have as its Artistic Director a dynamic young man, Heinar Piller. The two great leading men in the show, Jack Medley and David Brown, both live in Toronto but are nomadic as most professional Canadian actors must be. Add to this three lovely and talented London actresses, Heather Brandt, Caroline Gordon and Shelley Matthews, plus yours truly as the housekeeper and peacemaker of the play, and you can imagine the fun we had. Theatre London's genial General Manager, Geoffrey Farrow, provided me with the background story of the ghost of The Grand, after my curiosity had been aroused by several reports, from sane and sober actors and stage technicians, who swear they have seen the ghost of Ambrose J. Small quietly observing rehearsals from a particular seat in the large balcony." (– *What's On In Ottawa*, March 1973)

THE STORY OF BENJAMIN CRONYN

Cronyn was a new play written by London's Reverend Orlo Miller. It was a project initiated by Theatre London and Bishop Cronyn Memorial Church in London. The play had been commissioned by the church to commemorate its 100th anniversary. It was an historical dramatization of the rich and colourful life and times of the Right Reverend Benjamin Cronyn, first Anglican Bishop of

Huron. The Reverend had been a strong-willed, outspoken and firey man, and had played a key role in shaping religious and secular events in Southwestern Ontario from the time of his arrival in 1832 until his death in 1871. The playwright was quoted as saying: "A bishop per se is a rather dull subject, but when I write about an historical figure I'm interested in the historical setting; I'm interested in the background; I'm interested in the larger canvas on which he did his work. This is the story of Benjamin Cronyn, his life and his times. The times were pretty bloody rough. In 1832, London was a raw frontier town." (– *London Free Press*, December 13, 1972) Critic Doug Bale pronounced it: "Not dull at all. It is bright. It is colourful. It combines low comedy, high wit, cynicism and idealism, a great deal of painstaking research and a generous historical imagination." (– *London Free Press*, April 7, 1973)

Antonin Dimitrov and Olga Dimitrov provided a set that called for a minimum of scenery-shifting. John Horton played Cronyn, and Joyce Campion starred as the bishop's first wife Margaret. Joyce Campion commented: "I like Margaret because she wasn't an aggressive person. Her husband called her a loving and humble Christian. You know, playing a good person is much more challenging than playing a bad person – making them interesting. If Margaret had been called an evil, sinful harlot, I'd be away." (– *London Free Press*, April 10, 1973)

ADMINISTRATIVE CHANGE

As Theatre London changed from amateur status to professional status, the administration of the theatre changed. In April 1973 Paul Eck was appointed administrative director. He had been associated with LLT as an actor, director and producer and, in Heinar Piller's first season, he had directed *Dracula*. A few months after this appointment, the theatre's general manager Geoffrey Farrow resigned from his position. Board president Eddie Escaf

commented in the newspaper: "Geoffrey Farrow came into the theatre when we were really sick, and then worked his guts out for six years. We work from one money crisis to another. After awhile it would get to anybody. Geoff has been working under pressure for six years." (– *London Free Press*, August 17, 1973)

Eddie Escaf commented at Theatre London's annual general meeting in June, 1973: "We got by the hard year. This was the make-or-break year. Not that we're not going to have a hard year next year, but at least I can see a little light ahead at the end of it. Last year (1972/73) there were times when I wasn't sure I could see any light at all."

THEATRE LONDON

Theatre London season #2:
The Talisman, by Johann Nestroy, directed by Heinar Piller
Eccentricities of a Nightingale, by Tennessee Williams, directed by Keith Turnbull
The Man of La Mancha, by Dale Wasserman and Mitch Leigh, directed by Heinar Piller
Boeing, Boeing, by Marc Camoletti, directed by Andrew Allan
The Good Woman of Setzuan, by Bertholt Brecht, directed by Joseph Shaw
Cronyn, by Reverend Orlo Miller, directed by Heinar Piller
Charley's Aunt, by Brandon Thomas, directed by Joseph Shaw, starring Robert Joy

Theatre London Young Company:
Creeps, by David Freeman
Krapp's Last Tape, by Samuel Beckett
The Ascension, by William Cameron

Don't Shoot the Piano Player, a revue conceived and directed by Wayne Burnett
The Twain Meets at Midnight, excerpts from Mark Twain
Loki, by Paddy Fletcher
Waiting for Godot, by Samuel Beckett
The Tinderbox
Brussels Sprouts, by Larry Kardish
Fortune and Men's Eyes
Puss In Boots and *The Dandy Lion*, by Dodi Robb and Pat Patterson
plus a secondary school theatre tour

Road Show:
Ballade, a musical starring Dennis Thatcher,
presented by The Charlottetown Festival of Prince Edward Island

Ontario Youtheatre Summer School:
Dark of the Moon, by Howard Richardson and William Berney

1973/74

THEATRE LONDON/ HEINAR PILLER ERA

A SLIPPERY FLOOR

The set for Ondine *was designed by Antonin Dimitrov and had a rake that was at quite a steep angle. It came down to the lip of the stage. The floor was smooth and slippery. All the actors had to learn to stand and move on the raked stage without appearing like idiots. This was fun. One actor, Claude Tessier played a courtier and in one scene he had to run madly on stage from right, cross on the lip, stop at centre, speak to the king and then exit quickly stage left. So, we're all in place in the court scene, holding ourselves upright on the rake, in character, and Claude enters, crosses madly to centre, puts on the brakes and suddenly realizes he cannot stop. So, still sliding on the slippery floor, he speaks his line, gives a little bow and glides off stage left. We went on with the scene desperately holding onto our demeanor, our characters and our positions on the rake, knowing full well that Claude had a second entrance, quick line and exit coming up. This time he used the slippery floor to execute a little turn and flourish, still saying the line and not stopping from entrance to exit. We were biting lips, choking on hands, looking upstage, trying to keep going on with the scene and wondering whether he would be back. He didn't appear again. After that they roughed up the soles of his shoes to give him some grip.*

– Jim Shaefer, actor, director, teacher

FOOTSTEPS IN THE NIGHT

When they were rehearsing for Anne of Green Gables, *the entire company of actors was on the stage. It was about 10:30 p.m. and they started hearing footsteps walking over their heads and across the balcony whenever there was a moment of silence. In those days the theatre floor was painted board, except for carpet on the aisles, but even then the floor did creak a lot, as did the old heating pipes. They kept glancing at the balcony because that is where, it is said, Ambrose J. Small walks. But they didn't see anything. Everyone did their best to ignore the footsteps going back and forth until sand started drifting down on them from the flys. Everyone on stage froze. Of course, the director cleared the stage immediately as he was fearful that one of the sandbags might drop at any moment. He discontinued rehearsing that night. First thing next morning he had the technical crew go up to the fly floor and check every sandbag. Each bag was in perfect condition. No one could figure out where the sand had come from. The company, however, said they not only felt the sand, they had to brush it out of their hair.*

– Rob Wellan, Theatre London Public Relations Director

A SIX-MONTH STUDY

In the fall of 1973, the firm of Lett/Smith Architects started studying the state of the Grand Theatre. The building was in need of repair, and the theatre's equipment sorely needed upgrading. "Toronto theatre architect, Peter Smith, is in the midst of a six-month study, trying to find ways to create that vital extra space and of bringing the old theatre into the 1970s. He'll come up with alternative proposals, in various price ranges, for the theatre and the public funding agencies to consider. 'It's a beautiful, stately old place. The stage layout and the main seating area, the things that would be difficult to change, all seem to function very well. The things that tend not to work are the bits and pieces tacked on around them.'"– architect Peter Smith (– *London Free Press*, December 14, 1974)

THE YOUNG COMPANY

We were everywhere.
– Artistic Director Heinar Piller

In January 1974 Theatre London announced that six apprentice actors had been hired to be active as the Young Company. The actors were Tim Grantham, Karna Ivey, Alicia Jeffery, Tom McCamus, Rick Prevett and Jim Shaefer. All of them had had previous stage experiences. They would present *Ahtushmit*, a dramatization of an Indian legend at the Central Library auditorium, and then tour it to London high schools. Alec Stockwell directed the young actors.

Heinar wanted the Young Company to feed the mainstage. He brought me in to teach movement to the Young Company.
– Kip Longstaff, director, teacher

A PROFESSIONAL COMPANY

Elizabeth Murray was cast in *Butterflies are Free*, along with Tom Stebing, Heather Brandt and Wayne Burnett. The hit comedy was about a blind man's struggle for independence. Cast as the young man's domineering mother, this was Elizabeth Murray's first stage role since LLT turned into a professional company. "Heinar has been terribly generous about offering me things to do, but it's a little different on a professional schedule – you've pretty well got to have six weeks clear, and I have a few other interests and I could never clear six weeks in a package until this time. On the other hand when they suggested I might do this, I thought 'If I don't get my feet wet soon, I will lose my nerve.' I hadn't done anything since *The Visit* three years ago, so I thought, 'It's now or never time; do it!' It's great. I was a little bit nervous about working in a professional context, but once I got into it, it wasn't bad at all. There's more perfectionism in it now, better organization especially on the backstage side. Technical rehearsals went just like a dream. I couldn't believe it. I'm used to technical rehearsals where nothing goes right." (– *London Free Press*, January 18, 1974)

THE JOY OF THEATRE

I first started going to The Grand when I was in high school. My English teacher arranged for preview subscriptions to be available for her classes. I lived in a little town, approximately 40 miles southeast of London, so it was a big deal to borrow my parents' car and drive to London on a school night to see a play. But it was worth it. I saw plays that fed my mind and enriched my soul. Going to the theatre was a necessary part of my life from that point forward. I remember the first time I saw Patricia Collins on stage. She played Toinette in The Imaginary Invalid. *I had seen Miss Collins on television and I thought she was a great actress. But it was a thrill to see her in person – and it was my introduction to Molière. Over the years I have seen other productions but I still remember the joy I felt watching that play, six rows, back centre orchestra. I have watched some of the greatest actors and actresses in Canada perform on The Grand's stage, in world-class theatre. The list includes Jessica Tandy and Hume Cronyn, Seana McKenna, William Hutt, Martha Henry, Goldie Semple, Brent Carver and Frances Hyland.*

– M. Lucille (Sam) Grant, subscriber

THE DONNELLYS

Our production of The Donnellys *represents a milestone in the development of Theatre London. It is a documentary-drama based on events which took place in this area less than a hundred years ago. It was written and researched by one of Theatre London's actors (Peter Colley); original music composed by Theatre London's musical director Berthold Carriere; performed by our combined Resident and Young Company; augmented by community actors; designed by our resident designers Antonin Dimitrov, sets, Olga Dimitrov, costumes, David Wallett, lighting, and directed by myself. It is community theatre in the truest sense.*
– Heinar Piller, house program, April, 1974

I had written and was performing in The Donnellys. *One of the tricky things about acting in your own play is that you don't always get a chance to see how every scene plays in front of an audience, since you are stuck backstage. There was one particular scene I had never viewed from the front, so one night I snuck down by the proscenium arch and found a little alcove from where I could watch the scene in progress. It went very well and the audience seemed completely engrossed, as was I, until there was a sudden pause and everything came grinding to a halt. I realized from the exchanged glances of terror among the actors that some bone-headed thespian had forgotten his cue. I cursed the ill-fortune of all playwrights who have to deal with damn-fool actors. I was sure the culprit was backstage drowning in gin or listening to a hockey game on the radio, when I realized that it was MY cue, for MY entrance. I leapt up from my hiding place, raced around the back of the set, bounded onto the stage quite out of breath, blew my opening line, and scarcely managed to retrieve the scene from total disaster. The rest of the cast found the whole incident completely hysterical, and on my exit I found myself greeted by a sea of grinning faces and handshakes. As one wag put it: how often do you get a chance to see a playwright blow his own lines?*
– Peter Colley, playwright

One highlight of the production was the use of projected slides and moving pictures. Tom Celli played Jim Donnelly and Jim Shaefer played Pat Farrell. When Donnelly killed Farrell the murder was depicted by the use of huge images of Farrell's bloody and agonized face. The barn burnings were given realism when the actors played out the drama before a projected backdrop of leaping flames. Eighteen of Heinar Piller's 24 actors played multiple roles, presenting a challenge to both actors and director. For example actor Tom McCamus was listed as: Settler/Patrick Donnelly/Wedding Party/Johnny O'Connor. Other members of the acting company included Patricia Collins, Art Fidler and David Wasse.

The company of The Donnellys *got the sense that we were perhaps invoking the spirits of the Scottish play, the one by Shakespeare. Sometime during the afternoon of the opening night, the head of Tom Donnelly disappeared. The head was crafted by Vera Hrdlicka, and she based it on the actor playing Tom, Tom Stebing. It really looked like him, very lifelike. Well, the head went missing and this drove the actor to distraction. A second head was used during the performances. It was the rough model Vera had used before making the finished prop, which was never recovered. Also, during one of the performances David Wallett, who played James Carrol the constable, had to fire a pistol on stage. We had lots of practice*

with the gun, an old Webley revolver loaded with blanks. One night, early in the performance run, David held the gun too close to his head when he fired it and the concussion from the blank permanently ruptured his ear drum. For the rest of the performances someone else fired the gun, and David would go to the farthest corner offstage and plug his ears for the shot and then have to rush on stage and into the scene. Descendants of the vigilantes showed up at one performance. I played John Purtell who was killed by old Jim Donnelly early in the story. The box office had told us that there were Purtells in the front row, and I could feel their eyes on me in the murder scene. A shotgun with specially-made blanks was also used in one scene, in which three of us, myself, Tom McCamus and Rick Prevett, were fired upon and had to flee. Before one performance, the actor who used the shotgun and was into some intense method-acting stuff, came up to us and showed us some real shells he said he was going to use on stage that night. We didn't believe him, but there was no doubting the alacrity of our exits from the stage during that scene that night.
– Jim Shaefer, actor, director and teacher

The Donnelleys was a huge success for Theatre London. The National Arts Centre (NAC) in Ottawa asked Theatre London to restage its hit for the 1975/76 season in the nation's capital. The NAC booked the show unseen; word-of-mouth about the show in Canada's theatre community alone led to the invitation. Theatre London gladly accepted the invitation. Actor/playwright Peter Colley tightened the script, smoothed the transitions between scenes and strengthened the characterizations before the remount of The Donnellys in Ottawa.

Peter Colley's The Donnellys, directed by Heinar Piller was a

major local event, selling out well in advance, and raising controversy in Biddulph Township where ancestors of many of the characters we were playing still lived. We heard that many were coming to the show. I've never felt audiences as electric as during that production. On opening night we were approaching the climax of Act I, and Berholdt Carriere's brilliantly discordant music was crashing. I strode onstage as one of the conspirators and bellowed: 'We need a leader. One who does not fear the Donnellys!' And then we heard a frantic voice from the balcony: 'Is there a doctor here? My father has just collapsed!' And then, David Wallett ended the act with the curtain line: 'I'll drive them out of Lucan, or see them buried here!'
– Art Fidler, director, actor, teacher

ALMOST A REPETORY COMPANY

We developed almost a repetory company, a very good rep company. The community developed a certain curiosity. What's Piller going to do? There was so much goodwill. There was so much talent.
– Artistic Director Heinar Piller

SOME RESTRUCTURING

During the 1973/74 season some restructuring took place, dealing with the legal entity of the theatre and the theatre company. The Theatre London Corporation was created. It is a non-shareholder company operating the business of live theatre. An elected board of directors culled from the community by nomination, serves one, two or three year terms. In addition to the corporation, the theatre building and all its assets is owned by a second company, the Theatre London Foundation. This, too, is governed by the theatre's board of directors.

1974/75

THEATRE LONDON/
HEINAR PILLER ERA

Theatre London season #3:
Ondine, by Jean Giradoux, directed by Heinar Piller
Anne of Green Gables, from Lucy Maud Montgomery, adapted by Don Harron and Norman Campbell, directed by Heinar Piller
Butterflies are Free, by Leonard Gershe, directed by Alec Stockwell
The Imaginary Invalid, by Molière, directed by Albert Millaire
Leaving Home, by David French, directed by David Wallett
The Donnellys, by Peter Colley, directed by Heinar Piller

The Boy Friend, by Sandy Wilson, directed by Heinar Piller

Theatre London Young Company:
One for All, by Ric Wellwood
Antigone, by Sophocles
Here's a Queer Thing, a reading on gay literature
Jack and the Beanstalk
Ahtusmit

Ontario Youtheatre Summer Training:
culminated in the production of a full length play

SAINTE MARIE AMONG THE HURONS

Playwright James W. Nichol's epic *Sainte Marie Among the Hurons* had 42 characters. The play dealt with the Indians' reaction to the first white settlement west of the Ottawa Valley. Established by the Jesuits in 1638, Sainte Marie is situated near what is now Midland, Ontario. The settlement was destroyed when the Iroquois overran the Hurons in 1649. The story about the clash of two cultures was told in terms of the clash among three men: the Jesuit missionary Blackrobe (played by Colin Fox), the Huron convert Sleeping Water (played by Wayne Burnett) and Only Broken Rock (played by August Schellenberg) who advocated the murder of the priest. Director Heinar Piller infused the play with tension. This was bold and daring programming.

I was a busy mother with a baby when Heinar called to tell me that one of the actresses in Sainte Marie Among the Hurons *had suffered a ski accident and asked if I would step in, immediately? I said I would. The role was a mime and mask role. I created my own makeup and it was a great experience. I remember a huge staircase was part of the set, and there was a revolve. The second story of the set was high enough to be parallel to The Grand's balcony.*

– Kip Longstaff, director, teacher

FULL PROFESSIONALISM

When we hired Heinar, we didn't imagine that full profes-
sionalism would happen so fast. I think we felt that maybe in
five years' time we'd be closer to it, but now we've arrived there
in three years. He came in here and outlined a plan that scared
the living hell out of us. We just didn't believe it. We're still sort
of taken aback, because everything he said was going to
happen, has happened. For instance, he took us from a budget
of $140,000 to a budget of half a million dollars in three years.
We just told ourselves, 'There's no way' ... and yet look what's
happened. ...When he said we'd go from 3,000 ticket sales at
the open box office to 8,500 in three years, we all thought, 'How
can we?' But we did.

– Eddie Escaf, former Theatre London president (– *London*
Free Press, November 16, 1974)

REPORT FROM LETT/SMITH ARCHITECTS

The study of the Grand Theatre conducted by Lett/Smith
Architects of Toronto, resulted in a report outlining the feasibility
of refurbishing The Grand. The architects presented the report in
March 1975. The purpose of the refurbishing was threefold: (i) to
provide a complete arts facility which would meet 1970s professional theatre standards for production, performance and
audience, (ii) to meet 1970s standards of construction and fire
safety, and (iii) to retain and renovate the historic auditorium. As
stated in the report: "The City of London has recognised both the
elegance and history of The Grand by designating the auditorium
interior as architecturally and historically worthy of retention.
However, as a professional regional theatre the facilities are
inadequate and the condition of the building is questionable."
(– Lett/Smith Architects, 1975)

In April, 1975 the Grand Theatre became an historic site. Artistic
Director Heinar Piller is pictured with the plaque. Catharine
McCormick Brickenden and Mrs. Alan Skinner unveiled the plaque.
Both women had been active and influential LLT members. Sponsor
of the plaque was the Historic Sites Advisory Committee of the
London Public Library. The plaque is affixed to a wall backstage at
The Grand. (Courtesy London Free Press)

GOURMET DINNER AND AUCTION

As Theatre London grew, so did the need for funds to cover the operating costs of the theatre. For this reason Theatre London's past president, Eddie Escaf, and Art Ender, a future board president, created and organized a fundraising event entitled the Gourmet Dinner and Auction. Nearly 500 people purchased tickets at $50 each for the event which was held at Centennial Hall. London auctioneers, Jason C. Gardner and his auctioneer son Paul Gardner, were assisted in their task of taking bids on donated items, by radio and television personality Bill Brady. It was a successful event and started a tradition of an annual auction to raise funds for Theatre London.

THE COLLECTED WORKS OF BILLY THE KID

The Collected Works of Billy the Kid by Michael Ondaatje was a risk, to put it mildly. In programming it, Artistic Director Heinar Piller predicted that the production would cost the theatre one-third of Theatre London's subscribers. He put it in the hands of guest director Ken Livingstone. On opening night approximately 60 people left the theatre at intermission. Why did Piller program it? He explained in the March 1975 Theatre London house program: "To present the play in London is a daring step into unexplored territory. I expect that audience reaction will range from praise and enthusiasm, to shock and repulsion. It is a play that demands attention and reaction. One will either reject the violence and blood-spattered world of Billy, or penetrate this facade to discover the agony and joy, the humour and hatred and deep love for life which has spurred the human race to go on living throughout the ages. As artists, it is our duty to stimulate thought and discussion, even controversy. I am certain that our production will create a great deal of controversy, but it will prove that we are alive and that our audience is alive."

Controversy did erupt. The *London Free Press* printed a variety of letters to the editor. One writer from Toronto, who had seen the Theatre London production, wrote: "It was a joy to hear language coming from the stage as rich and beautiful as Michael Ondaatje's poetry." A London letter-writer had this to say: "The show was a direct affront to the intelligence and sensibilities of the majority of Theatre London goers. The play was well acted … the biggest problem was the total lack of a plot. It was a big blank." Someone in Lambeth wrote: "Horray for Theatre London! The play is a masterpiece. I heartily congratulate the board for giving us such a superb play. It is provocative and totally absorbing." The final word goes to another playgoer: "The play (one might describe it as a non-play) is obsessed with violence, sex, insanity and vulgarity. It is a presentation completely lacking in dramatic and poetry merit – an orchestrated exercise in total debauchery – degrading, demeaning and contaminating the players, the audience and ultimately the history of theatre."

The lead roles in the production were taken by Wayne Burnett as Billy the Kid, Michael Kirby as Pat Garrett, and Patricia Collins as Angela Dickinson.

THE WAR SHOW

I was performing in The War Show, *a play I had written about Canada's involvement in World War II. There was one powerful sequence in the play in which I attempted to recreate the experience of the infamous Dieppe raid, during which so many Canadians lost their lives. After the play one night, the stage manager said there were some people who wished to see me. They turned out to be an older couple – she was a kindly lady, but he was a tough old coot with a set jaw and a very unsettling scowl on his face. I could tell from his Legion blazer and beret, he was a Veteran. Age had made him a bit unsteady on his feet, but he looked like he could still make mincemeat out of a skinny kid like me. The old lady helped him towards me, and he fixed me with the most unnerving stare I have ever been subjected to. 'You the writer?' he barked. I toyed with the idea of saying I was the janitor, but I realized that since I was still taking off my stage makeup I was pretty well cornered. 'Yes,' I replied expecting his big grizzled hand to grab me by the throat. Instead, he just kept staring at me with those terrifying beady eyes. 'I was at Dieppe,' he rasped, putting his face even closer to mine. 'You got it right in that scene, kid, that's exactly how it was! I was a tank driver. Saw the whole thing through the driver's slot at the front of my tank – until a big shell hit us.' Then he pointed to his steel-blue piercing eyes: 'I lost both my eyes at Dieppe!' It was only then I realized that those eyes that had filled me with such terror were made of glass.*

– Peter Colley, playwright

COMMENTS FROM PATRONS

Theatre London collected comments from its patrons throughout the season. A sampling of these, reprinted in the May 1975, house program, reinforce the saying you can't please all of the people all of the time:

"May we have more Canadian plays?"

"I don't want to see any more Canadian plays."

"The theatre needs refurbishing."

"I wish you had a bar."

"We are delighted with the direction the theatre is taking."

"Cut down on religious themes."

"We do not appreciate the bad language."

"The sets and costumes are magnificent."

"Please, no more of those dreary sets."

"Why don't you hire professional actors?

… and …

"The old amateur actors were better."

AGENDA OF HEINAR PILLAR

Heinar Piller's agenda during his time at Theatre London was (i) to build a theatre company, and (ii) make professional theatre viable in London. When he planned a season's playbill he did so as a writer writes a play or a story. He paced the season with a rousing beginning, a middle and a climactic ending. He constructed each season in that way. And he was successful.

– Rob Wellan, Theatre London Public Relations Director

Theatre London season #4:
The Fantasticks, by Tom Jones, directed by Heinar Piller
Sainte Marie Among the Hurons, by James W. Nichol, directed by Heinar Piller
Sleuth, by Anthony Shaffer, directed by Timothy Bond
Godspell, by John-Michael Tebelak, directed by Dean Regan
The Collected Works of Billy the Kid, by Michael Ondaatje, directed by Ken Livingstone

The War Show, by Peter Colley, directed by Heinar Piller
How the Other Half Loves, by Alan Ayckbourn, directed by David Wallett

Theatre London's Young Company: improvisational drama for children aged 6 through 13
play reading group
Shortshrift
Snow White
The History Show

1975/76

THEATRE LONDON/ HEINAR PILLER ERA

INTERNATIONAL HISTORIC ENTERPRISES

On a Sunday night in July 1975, seven psychics assembled on stage at the Grand Theatre. An organization called International Historic Enterprises brought in four men and three women psychics from London. Their mission was to try to contact the spirit of Ambrose J. Small. Unfortunately for those involved, Ambrose J. Small's spirit did not show up. However, one of the psychics did go into a trance and a voice spoke through him saying that Mr. Small would not be coming that Sunday night; Small needed more time.

THEATRE LONDON ASSOCIATION

I was a very active member of the Theatre London Association (TLA), along with other members like Barbara Ivey and Nonie Jeffrey. There was a Feydeau farce opening at The Grand and to launch it in style, members of the TLA. met at a member's home for crepes prior to the opening. Some of us dressed up French style – myself in a can-can outfit. We had borrowed an antique convertible, in which we rode down Richmond Street. When we arrived in front of The Grand, where all the opening nighters were gathering, I danced the can-can on the seat of the car, accompanied by another TLA member who was playing the accordion. Oh LA LA!

– Patricia Black, critic, writer

SHELLY PETERSON

"Theatre London's most glamorous gift to show business, Shelley Peterson, returns to the company for its first production of the new season, the comedy *Chemin De Fer*. Shelley, perhaps better known to London audiences by her maiden name, Shelley Matthews, joins a cast of leading performers from Canadian stage, film and television. As Shelley Matthews she was a member of Theatre London's first Young Company, playing in Mini-Theatre hits. On the main stage she did supporting roles in shows and graduated to major parts in productions like the title role of *Ondine*." (– *London Free Press*, October 11, 1975)

GETTING CHILDREN INVOLVED

Heinar wanted children to be involved with Theatre London more than just Saturday drama lessons. So we started to teach other things using people like Jim Shaeffer, Mary Dow, and Brian Longstaff, besides myself. I thought we could take this thing and make it fly, so I went to Paul Eck. He was amazing. Everything Paul touched turned to gold.

– Kip Longstaff, teacher, director

CO-PRODUCTION AGREEMENTS

Co-production agreements between professional theatre companies were common in the 1980s and 1990, but in October 1975, when Theatre London entered into its first "co-pro" they were still a novelty in the theatre business. The partner theatre was Toronto Arts Productions (TAP), which performed at the St. Lawrence Centre for the Arts. A double bill was mounted by both companies, consisting of *Surprise! Surprise!* by Michel Tremblay, and *Shelter* by Carol Bolt. The plays moved from Toronto to London, bringing their cast of Jayne Eastwood, Brenda Donohue, Wendy Thatcher, Kay Hawtrey and Marilyn Lightstone. In commenting on the advantages of a co-pro with the Toronto-based company, Heinar Piller said: "Most of the advantages of the arrangement are on our side. With inflation's effect on material and labour costs, there's no way we could put on these plays on our own. The arrangement also gives us a breather this season, since we won't have to spend more than a week mounting and rehearsing the plays for the London engagement." For his part, TAP's artistic director, Leon Major, said: "Theatre groups are going to have to work together, just to get by financially. Collaboration helps to save more than money. It allows us to use the efforts of our people better. Their energies aren't duplicated, they're multiplied." (– *London Free Press*, October 28, 1975)

WILLIAM HUTT, ARTISTIC DIRECTOR

In November 1975, Heinar Piller's resignation was announced. His future plans included forming an independent production company that would devise and produce shows in the performing arts field on a commercial/contractual basis. He planned to work with his wife, Clare Piller, his designers Antonin and Olga Dimitrov, David Wallett and musicial director Berthold Carriere on the new enterprise.

In January 1976, Theatre London's board of directors announced that actor William Hutt, the Stratford Festival Theatre's leading actor, would replace outgoing Artistic Director Heinar Piller. The changeover would take place at the end of the 1975/76 season. While the appointment of Heinar Piller had raised fears in some Londoners that professionals would swamp amateur endeavours at the Grand Theatre, the appointment of William Hutt raised fears in some people that Theatre London would be gobbled up by the Stratford Festival, and become nothing but a "branch plant" of that successful enterprise. Some Londoners were concerned that an influx of Stratford actors, directors and designers would change the face of Theatre London. Mere months after his appointment was announced, incoming Artistic Director William Hutt was quoted in the newspaper denying that people should have such fears: "It just simply is not true. The suggestion is ludicrous. The Stratford Festival has quite enough to do in Stratford and has absolutely no interest in taking over Theatre London." (– *London Free Press*, May 6, 1976)

HANSEL AND GRETEL

For the production of the musical *Hansel and Gretel,* Heinar Piller brought together the London Symphony Orchestra's Synfonia, St. Michael's Church Choir, and students from various London ballet schools to work with Theatre London on the show. The first two performances went well, but on the third night water pipes in the theatre's basement burst. Water reached the electrical circuitry, short-circuiting the lighting board. Fuses blew, and the theatre was plunged into soggy darkness. The building was so cold that Theatre London staff wore heavy coats for five days. The antiquated toilets in the ladies' washroom finally gave up and had to be replaced. A major leak in the roof, over centre balcony, had to be hastily patched. Plumbers worked around the clock for over two days to keep the building safe for performers and audience members. In addition to all the backstage drama, one performance of *Hansel and Gretel* suffered a technical glitch on stage. In the third act, in a scene in front of the gingerbread house, the witch sings of flying through the air on her broom. She then disappears behind the house, only to be depicted flying high above the stage. "All went well until the third pass across the front of the stage. Somehow the dummy witch didn't quite swing all the way and became stranded, dangling in the centre of the stage. Meanwhile, the music called for the real witch to reappear in front of the house and continue to sing, which she did. But to add insult to injury, the dangling dummy was dragged back into the wings unceremoniously backwards – as though the broom had gone into reverse." (– *London Free Press*, December 20, 1975)

Joanne Ivey played the witch, while the role of Hansel was shared by Olwyn Chipman and Diane Loeb, and the role of Gretel was shared by Penny Speedie and Janet Field.

Joanne Ivey is statuesque, elegant and graceful, with that wonderful glint of mischief in her eyes. As I remember, she wanted to fly all over the house, but we couldn't afford the mechanical equipment required. She would have done it. She was fabulous in the role of the witch.

– Rob Wellan, Theatre London Public Relations Director

DAVID FERRY

My first show at The Grand was in a production of Death of a Salesman, *with Sean Sullivan, Joy Coghill and Wayne Burnett, directed by Heinar Piller. This was pre-renovation, and in those days there was a dressing room in the proscenium, approximately where the stage right box is. It had a window overlooking the lane, and a very old comfy armchair, and I couldn't believe that no one wanted it. They all wanted to stay together downstairs. I spent many an hour sitting in that dressing room contemplating its old-fashioned ambience. It was my first solo dressing room as an actor, and to this day my favourite. The stairs came right down to the stage and I swear, if Ambrose J. Small was anywhere, he was in the peeling paint of that dressing room's walls. That was my first IATSE (International Alliance of Theatrical Stage Employees) show, and my mother, who had worked backstage in theatre herself, sent me $20 and said: "Buy the crew a bottle of rye," and I did, learning one of the more important lessons in my career!*

– David Ferry, actor, director

STORIES OF A.J. SMALL

Ambrose J. Small stories abound in this particular season. Perhaps it was because the theatre seemed to be on its last legs. Walt Drennan, a long-time stage hand at The Grand told this story in Theatre London's newsletter *Small Talk*, February 1976: "One night, very late after a show, I was alone in the theatre making a phone call. Suddenly I got the feeling I was being watched, the room got ice-cold. I said good-bye, hung up, and walked darn fast out of that theatre. I've never actually run into Ambrose, but I believe in him, and some day he'll show himself, but just to a group of real theatre people, when they're least expecting him."

HEINAR PILLER

Another season draws to its close. … Five years we have wandered along the same road, building Theatre London upon the solid foundations of London Little Theatre. Sometimes it was a pleasant walk, and often it was a steep climb. Many of our friends fell behind and many more joined us along the way. Today we are a very large group, from all walks of life, coming together regularly to experience and share another evening of theatre. Theatre London is known and respected across the country. We are envied for our huge audiences, and admired for our versatile programming, high standards of production and deep roots in the community… I am grateful and proud that I was allowed to contribute my share and be part of these five years of struggle and achievement. I would like to thank you and all my friends and colleagues, on either side of the footlights, for their contributions and support.

– Artistic Director Heinar Piller, house program, May 1976

1976/77

THEATRE LONDON/ WILLIAM HUTT ERA

Theatre London season #5:
Chemin de Fer, by Georges Feydeau, directed by John Horton
Surprise! Surprise!, by Michel Tremblay, and *Shelter*, by Carol Bolt, directed by Eric Steiner
Hansel and Gretel, libretto by Adelheid Wette, music by Engelbert Humperdinck, directed by Heinar Piller
Death of a Salesman, by Arthur Miller, directed by Heinar Piller
Frankenstein (The Man Who Became God), by Alden Nowlan and Walter Learning,

directed by Timothy Bond
Hedda Gabler, by Henrik Ibsen, directed by Ken Livingstone
Jubalay, by Patrick Rose and Merv Campone, directed by Dean Regan

Theatre London's Young Company:
Too Many Kings, by Paddy Campbell
Cinderella
History Show 2
Snow White

Music:
Theatre London/Symphony Orchestra Series

A TREASURED ASSET

This was actor/director William Hutt's first year as Artistic Director of Theatre London. As he noted in the 1976/77 season brochure: "That the citizenry of London has cared so deeply about one of its most treasured assets, the Grand Theatre, to keep it open for three-quarters of a century is a record all but unmatched in the theatrical lore of this country." The Grand Old Lady of Richmond Street just kept on sailing. She was unsinkable.

"AMBROSE IS OUT"

The ghost of Ambrose J. Small just would not rest. In July 1976, another attempt was made to communicate with the spirit of the theatre impresario. "Eight persons participated in a seance at the Grand Theatre and heard a voice, speaking through one of the group, telling them Ambrose couldn't make it, but would at a later date. According to one participant, a very loud and very old voice told of Ambrose's life following his disappearance." (– *London Free Press*, July 24, 1976)

During one of the seances, when the person made actual contact with the other world we asked the question: 'Where is Ambrose J. Small?' The voice answered: 'Ambrose is out.'... And

Artistic Director William Hutt. This was his first of four years at the helm of the Grand Theatre.
"I am acutely aware and appreciative of the contribution Theatre London has already made to the cultural image of Canada, and especially to London theatre-goers, and the City of London itself. It is therefore a source of both pleasure and price to become associated with such a distinguished enterprise." – Incoming Artistic Director William Hutt (brochure copy, 1976)

that sort of tickled me because I didn't know quite where out was, from wherever he was.
– Rob Wellan, Theatre London Public Relations Director

In August in a feature story about the Grand Theatre, Theatre London public relations director Rob Wellan mentioned to the reporter that "sometimes when I am working late in my office the drawers of my filing cabinets slowly open by themselves. I don't believe in ghosts, but when that happens, I put down whatever I'm working on, put on my coat, tiptoe down the stairs and go straight home." (– *London Free Press*, August 14, 1976)

THE GRAND'S 75TH BIRTHDAY

This was the Grand Theatre's 75th birthday and it was celebrated in style on the opening night of *The Many Faces of Love*. Board president Art Ender escorted special guest Lieutenant-Governor Pauline McGibbon up the red carpet and into the theatre. After the performance, McGibbon officiated at a cutting of a gigantic cake shaped like the Grand Theatre.

HUME CRONYN AND JESSICA TANDY

Not a play, but a reading concert, *The Many Faces of Love* enchanted the audience with dramatized excerpts from literature. Featured writers included Edward Albee, Dostoevsky, Edna St. Vincent Millay, Shakespeare, Dorothy Parker, Ogden Nash and Tennessee Williams. "Here were two people, alone on a 42-foot stage except for a couple of lecterns and a couple of chairs, keeping 1,000 people spellbound for two-and-one-half hours with a grab bag of recitations. With only their voices, their faces and a minimum of movement, they conjured up imaginary worlds for the audience, spun them, flashed them, dropped them, and created new ones." (– Doug Bale, *London Free Press*, October 29, 1976).

Londoners hadn't seen Hume Cronyn and Jessica Tandy on stage at The Grand since 1951, when they appeared in *The Fourposter*. Cronyn was born in London in 1911 to Major and Mrs. Hume Cronyn. The young Hume attended Lord Roberts Public School. He then left the city to attend Ottawa's Elmwood School, then progressed to Ridley College. Cronyn went to Montreal's McGill University, where he studied law. At the end of his second year, however, he announced to his family that he intended to pursue a career as a professional actor, because while at university he had acted at the Montreal Repertory Theatre. He enrolled at the American Academy of Dramatic Art. During the Depression he worked in New York City theatres, and his first big break came in 1938 in *Three Men on a Horse*. By the early 1940s, Cronyn was in Hollywood acting in movies. He was nominated for an Academy Award in 1944 for *The Seventh Cross*. In 1942 he married actress Jessica Tandy, who along with her young daughter, had emigrated to the United States from their native England. Cronyn and Tandy established themselves as principal players on stage and in films. Jessica Tandy predeceased her

Hume Cronyn and Jessica Tandy on stage at the Grand Theatre in The Many Faces of Love *in 1976. This was a return engagement for the celebrated acting team of Cronyn-and-Tandy. Both London-born actor Hume Cronyn, and his wife Jessica Tandy, had been on The Grand's stage in* The Fourposter *in 1951. (Courtesy of The Grand Theatre)*

husband in 1994. The Grand Theatre's large rehearsal hall is named the Jessica Tandy Rehearsal Hall.

REBUILDING THE GRAND

Playgoers were informed by board president Art Ender about the upcoming changes to the Grand Theatre in their *Candida* house program of November 1976: "The classical arch will remain, restored to its original beauty; lobbies will become people places, and new seats will provide comfortable legroom; and there will be year-round climate control. The Grand Theatre will be a practical, modern working theatre for today's artists and audiences. Indeed, it will be a people's theatre, dedicated to maintaining the fine traditions of The Grand. When completed, London will have a theatre unique among theatres in North America, to fully serve its public and give the community and the region the theatre it deserves."

The words of John Ruskin (b. 1819 – d. 1900), the British essayist and art critic, are appropriate to the Grand Theatre's situation as it prepared for its year of rebuilding:

Watch an old building with an anxious care;
guard it as best you may, and at any cost,
from every influence or dilapidation.
Count its stones as you would jewels of a crown;
set watches about it as if at the gates of a besieged city;
bind it together with iron where it loosens;
stay it with timber where it declines;
and do this tenderly, and be firm.

LES BELLES SOEURS

An all-female cast was on stage in Michel Tremblay's *Les Belles Soeurs*. The 15 characters are unhappy, angry, lonely, bitter and desperate women. The cast included London actresses Peggy Watson, Julia Watts, Caroline Guerin and Alicia Jeffery, and actresses from out of town, Marylu Moyer, Maureen Fitzgerald, Mary Dow, Irene Hogan, Laura Press, Doris Petrie, Jan Kudelka, Pam Rogers, Claire Crawford, Carol Forte and Diana Leblanc. Directing these wonderful actresses in this tragi-comedy was Bernard Hopkins.

The play is about housewife Germaine Lauzon (played by Maureen Fitzgerald) who wins one million trading stamps. She invites her friends and relations over to help her paste the stamps into the required booklets, all the while dreaming of what she plans to buy with her windfall. Her good fortune inspires jealousy in her guests. The women begin to steal the stamp booklets they have filled on Germaine's behalf. Gossip, fights, unexpected visitors and personal revelations ensue. The language was salty and strong. Some Theatre London audience members objected to the use of such language, especially spoken by women.

I was playing Lisette, who is very proper and is the only one who does not use bad language. The stage blacks out – a single bright spot shone on me for a soliloquy, which begins: 'It's like living in a barnyard!' a voice from the back of the stalls bellowed. 'Right on. You're all a pack of whores.' He seemed to go on all through my speech. I wish I could have come out of character and told him where to go!
– Julia Watts, actress

CLOSED FOR RECONSTRUCTION

As this 75th Anniversary Season drew to a close, Theatre London produced the Molière classic *School for Wives*. The play was to run until May 14, when the curtain would come down, not just on the production, not just on the season, but also on the Grand Theatre building, as playgoers had known it. Renovations were to start in the summer of 1977. As reporter Doug Bale noted in his review of this show: "Even the ancient theatre itself seemed to be playing tricks, as if she knew this would be her last opening night. First her sound system developed a buzz that threatened to drown out the actors, then one of her lighting units dropped a filter frame that fell clattering into the orchestra pit. Finally, her planked stage, worn smooth by 76 years of actors' pacing, betrayed the young hero of the play (played by Jan Muszynski) into an unexpected pratfall." (– *London Free Press*, April 28, 1977)

During opening night I was in the lobby area during intermission and one of the ushers ran up to me and said there was an emergency in the men's washroom. When I went to investigate I found that two of our theatre-goers, who moments before had been standing facing the urinals, had suddenly dropped through the floor and were now standing knee-deep in rotted wood and linoleum. Fortunately the bare sand which was the sub-basement floor under the urinals was only a foot or so below the washroom floor. The old floor at the foot of the urinals had simply, and inconveniently, given way, due to 75 years of unintentional splashing or termites, if we have any in this part of Canada.
– Rob Wellan, Theatre London Public Relations Director

For the curtain call on closing night of *School for Wives,* the play's cast and crew, as well as Theatre London's entire staff, donned hard hats and assembled on stage. They asked that evening's audience to join them in singing 'Auld Lang Syne.' When the curtain finally came down, everyone on stage, cast, crew and staff, rushed around to the lobby and made sure that they shook the hands of each departing patron. Thus began 18 months of rebuilding the Grand Theatre.

Theatre London season #6:
The Many Faces of Love, conceived and compiled by Eleanor Wolquitt, production supervised by Robert Walter, performed by Hume Cronyn and Jessica Tandy
Candida, by G.B. Shaw, directed by William Hutt
Alice Through the Looking Glass, adapted and directed by Keith Turnbull
Long Days Journey Into Night, by Eugene O'Neill, directed by Robin Phillips
Les Belles Soeurs, by Michel Tremblay, directed by Bernard Hopkins
Private Lives, by Noel Coward, directed by Donald Davis
School for Wives, by Molière, directed by Jean Gascon

Children's Theatre:
The Four Musicians of Bremen
The Bunyip of Berkeley's Creek, by Jenny Wagner
Aesop's Fables
Beware the Quickly Who, by Eric Nicol
Cinderella

Music:
Theatre London/Symphony Orchestra Series
National Arts Centre Orchestra
The Irish Rovers
Moe Koffman and his Quintet

Dance:
The National Ballet of Canada
The Royal Winnipeg Ballet

1977/78

THEATRE LONDON/
WILLIAM HUTT ERA

FUNDRAISING AND RECONSTRUCTION

With the Grand Theatre under reconstruction, Theatre London's season went up at the Aeolian Hall. There were only 240 seats at Aeolian Hall (795 Dundas Street), meaning Theatre London could accommodate only the first 5,000 subscribers on a first come first served basis.

Theatre London's Mini-Theatre (at 214 Richmond Street) re-opened its doors, where a new Young Company performed. The Mini-Theatre season included productions for young audiences in London libraries and a tour of public schools in the region. William Hutt created an "intrepid band of vitality." He had auditioned approximately 250 young actors, and in the end chose Michael Caruana, Robert LaChance, Tom McCamus (of London), Donna Killoran, Philippa King, Jacquie Presly, Mark Bolton, Abraham Guenther, Stephen Hill and Ralph Small.

Meanwhile, over at the Grand Theatre, two teams were in place to realize the ambitious plans to rebuild. The fundraising campaign was in the hands of: Honorary Co-Chairmen, Joseph Jeffery and John H. Moore; Chairman, Clarence M. Peterson; Steering Committee: John F. McGarry (chairman), Barbara Ivey (co-chair), William Baldwin, Bruce C. Foster, P.B. Eck, and J.H. Porter; Building Committee: Clarence M. Peterson (chairman), G.E. Humphries, P.J. Ivey, D.D.C. McGeachy, P.F. Tillmann and Gerald E. Wilson

As an actor the art of gentle persuasion is not entirely beyond my comprehension, but the art of fundraising, that craft of diplomatic pressure and persuasion which can extract reluctant dollars from hidden purses, remains a process as magical and mystic as the emergence of Santa Claus from all those chimney tops at Christmas. I speak in tribute to one man who virtually gave up two years of an already crowded life to chair both the building committee and the building fund, whose optimism never waned, whose precision of judgement never wavered, and whose ebullience kept even the most flagging spirits afloat. And more than anything, I pay tribute to the wizardry of his magic wand, and the inventiveness of his own unique brand of gentle persuasion which opened so many purses to release a fine and fulsome spread of goodwill – I speak in special tribute to Clarence Peterson.
– William Hutt, Artistic Director, grand opening address, January 1979

The design and construction work was in the hands of: Lett/Smith Architects; Hastings & Aziz Ltd. (structural engineers); Chorley & Bisset Ltd. (mechanical engineers); the ECE Group (electrical engineers); Ellis-Don (General contractors); and Valcoustics Ltd.

The many changes that took place included: the last eight rows of orchestra seats were removed to enlarge the lobby; the pillars under the balcony were taken away, never again to obscure theatre-goers' sight lines; new dressing rooms were built beneath the mainstage to accommodate a maximum of 38 artists, while other new dressing rooms off the new McManus Studio were built to accommodate up to 12 artists; the level of the stage was lowered; a new lounge, the Poster Lounge, took advantage of space under the balcony; and the orchestra pit was covered with a retractable ceiling.

Rob Wellan, Theatre London's Public Relations Director, is pictured in the new Poster Lounge, still under construction, two stories above Richmond Street. Rob Wellan served the Grand Theatre during the tenures of Artistic Directors Heinar Piller, William Hutt and Bernard Hopkins (in the 1970s and '80s) and Michael Shamata and Kelly Handerek and Susan Ferley. His love for the Grand Theatre is profound. (Courtesy London Free Press, and the Grand Theatre)

The Grand Theatre reminded me of a big old ship. Where cinema is passive, theatre is interactive. Our job was to take this huge building and make it intimate. But we wanted to keep the spirit of the Edwardian house. Along the way we discovered some things about the theatre. The old Grand wasn't insulated, which meant that the snow on the roof melted immediately. This was a good thing because the original roof was not sturdy enough to hold the weight. Also, we found that the balcony was pulling away from the east wall by a good two to three inches. The original building had been badly constructed around the boxes and the arch. In general, it wasn't built well – the original builders had bought off-the-shelf fixtures. During the work we looked carefully but nothing showed up about the mystery surrounding the disappearance of Ambrose J. Small. We did, however, find old posters in the fly gallery, stage left.
– Peter Smith, architect

Londoners were shocked by the extent of the renovation. The west wall of the stage remained intact, as did the north and south walls as far as they wrapped around the stage. But beyond that everything else was stripped away, until the theatre's interior was exposed to the sky and to the elements. People going by on Richmond Street passed a great gaping hole where the facade, the lobby and the auditorium used to be. The arch remained standing, high above the street.

Rob Wellan tells the story of the day members of the construction crew were assiduously removing the boxes, and clearing debris from around the north and south bases of the arch when the workers came within a hairbreadth of toppling the entire proscenium arch. A heavy equipment operator, intent on his work, was annoyed when the machine stopped short. As he and co-workers examined the machine, they discovered that their work was so thorough that only two small bricks were holding up the whole north side of the arch. Had the machine not broken down, the next dig would have loosened the two bricks and then nothing could have saved the arch from toppling over and crumbling on impact.

Another story concerns the lighting fixtures attached along the walls of the theatre. The plaster insert in the centre of the fixtures was to be copied. The architects wished to find someone to re-make them. In the Toronto area there were three suppliers of such plaster inserts. One supplier, Balmer Company, was on Pape Avenue. When asked about the work, Balmer Company said they still had a mould from 1901. It turned out that Balmer Company was the original supplier for London's Grand Opera House interior. They used their original mould for the recast.

The work halted for a time as trade agreements and contracts were negotiated in the spring of 1978. A carpenters' strike delayed the reconstruction, but the reopening was scheduled for November 22 and Theatre London officials were determined that the show would go on, on schedule. So crews worked all-out to complete public areas of the theatre such as the auditorium, lobbies and washrooms. The official opening was postponed to January 1979.

Five-and-a-half million dollars, raised through grants from three levels of government and from corporations, foundations and donations from the general public, covered the costs of the extensive work. Architect Peter Smith estimates that had the job been undertaken in 1988, the total cost would have been $12.5 million; had it been delayed until 1994 the cost would have been a minimum of $17 million.

Theatre London season #7 (at Aeolian Hall):
An Intimate Evening With Tony Van Bridge as G. K. Chesterton – a program of comedy and light verse from the writings of British humorist G.K. Chesterton
An Evening With Tom Kneebone and Dinah Christie – a potpourri of lesser-known songs by well-known songwriters; a potpourri of songs
The Victorians, with Eric Donkin, Pat Armstrong and Alan Laing – an illumination of the humour, the music, the morals and the manners of the Victorian age

Mini-Theatre:
Twelfth Night, by William Shakespeare
The Land of Magic Spells, by Larry Zacharko
The Strolling Players, by Darwin Reid Payne and Christian Moe

1978/79

THEATRE LONDON/ WILLIAM HUTT ERA

KISS ME KATE

Imagine! An incredibly beautiful, newly renovated theatre with such a rich history. Working with Bill Hutt and an absolutely wonderfully talented cast. What more could you ask for?
– A. Frank Ruffo, dancer, choreographer Kiss Me Kate, *1978*

In October of 1978, rehearsals for *Kiss Me Kate* were held at the London Armouries on Dundas Street, as workmen continued to prepare the Grand Theatre for its November opening night. The 33-member cast included Wanda Cannon as Kate and Edward Evanko as Petruchio. Rick Whelan and Jack Roberts played the hilarious pair of gangsters who sing the show-stopper "Brush Up Your Shakespeare," while A. Frank Ruffo led the chorus line of exuberant dancers. An extra week of performances was added, to accommodate playgoers who wished to see the show, and who couldn't wait to see the reconstructed theatre.

The original idea for the musical grew from an idea of Arnold Saint Subber, a stage manager who had worked on a production of Shakespeare's *The Taming of the Shrew*. The show had starred leading American theatre couple, Alfred Lunt and Lynn Fontaine. The young stage manager had been amused to hear the couple bickering onstage and off. Subber's idea for a backstage musical based on *The Shrew*, and starring two bickering actors, grew into the acclaimed and popular Cole Porter/Samuel and Bella Spewack musical.

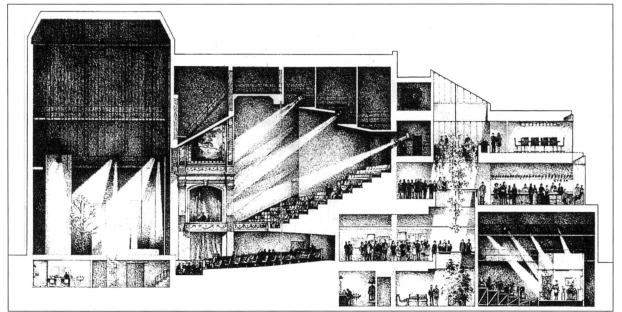

Lett/Smith Architect's rendering of the newly reconstructed Grand Theatre. (Courtesy of Peter Smith)

One night, during a dress rehearsal for Kiss Me Kate, *a group of actors went out for a few beers to celebrate what we felt had been a very successful run-through. After a couple of hours at The Marienbad Restaurant, we departed, full of good cheer. It had been raining and the streets were awash with puddles. A car went by and splashed us. Emboldened by the promise of a wonderful performance and, no doubt, a few pints, we turned and shouted menacing threats at the offending vehicle. Much to our surprise, it stopped, backed up and six of the biggest young men I have ever seen got out and started coming for us. You never saw a group of singers, actors and dancers move faster in your life! Those who act and run away, live to act another day!*

– Rick Whelan, writer and former actor

ALL GUSSIED UP

"If you want to know what's been done to The Grand, just imagine that your mom has gone and got herself all gussied up. She looks as gorgeous as in her wedding pictures or when she gets dressed up for a special occasion, but underneath it all, it's still mom." (– Joe Matyas, *London Free press*, November 23, 1978)

GRAND OPENING

For the opening night of *Kiss Me Kate*, the Grand Theatre re-opened in all its new splendour. The facade was completely redone, but the auditorium was recognizable as the original. Many people paid the architects, engineers and contractors the highest compliment: "Many people expressed how pleased they were to see that the spirit of the Grand Theatre had been maintained." – Peter Smith, architect

The official reopening took place on the last Sunday in January 1979, completing a 21-month reconstruction. Mayor Al Gleeson officially declared the 78-year-old theatre open, speaking before 800 people gathered at the theatre for the special occasion. Board president John F. McGarry introduced Rabbi Israel Kestenbaum, Dean Kenneth B. Keefe and the Reverend Monsignor J.A. Rooney, who dedicated the "new" playhouse. The 90-piece London Youth Symphony, conducted by James White, was on stage to provide music for the occasion.

I speak in tribute to the miracle worker himself, Architect Peter Smith. One tries very hard to scour the language for adjectives which can, even remotely, do justice to the singular achievement of this superb artist who restored to the dowager such grace, dressed her with such taste, used her strengths with such ingenuity and rebuilt her weaknesses with such firm tact, who melded the old grandeur with a new magnificence that can only be described as a triumph of beauty, artistry and technical perfection.

– William Hutt, Artistic Director, Grand opening address, January 28, 1979

OTHERWISE ENGAGED

"If bare breasts and a few four-letter words offend you, then perhaps you'd better stay home and watch murder on TV," William Hutt was quoted as saying in the *London Free Press*, March 15, 1978, in issuing an early warning about *Otherwise Engaged*. The play, directed by Donald Davis, and starring Douglas Rain, Domini Blythe, Eric Donkin, Barry MacGregor and Diana Leblanc. It was about a busy publisher trying to spend a quiet Sunday at home listening to a recording of Wagner's *Parsifal*, but he is interrupted constantly by people bringing him their troubles. It outraged many theatre-goers, because in one scene Domini Blythe appeared nude from the waist up.

The Theatre London Association was responsible for a bar in the main lobby after opening night performances. That was a lot of fun. I used to pour the mixes and I still remember serving both William Hutt and Donald Davis. I had worked for Donald's brother, Murray, at the Crest Theatre in Toronto in the early 1960s, and I also know their sister, Barbara Chilcott, who acted at the Crest. I was able to renew my acquaintance with her when she played in The Killing of Sister George *in the McManus Studio, at The Grand, during the 1980/81 season.*
– Patricia Black, critic, writer

JOHN A. HIMSELF!

Writer and former actor Timothy Findley wrote *John A. – Himself!*, a celebration of Canada's first prime minister. Starring William Hutt as Sir John, the piece was conceived as a Victorian music-hall entertainment. The events of Macdonald's life were re-enacted as if they were part of a rousing show. Director Peter Moss explained: "It is virtually a one-man show, in the sense that William Hutt is on stage maybe one hour and 45 minutes out of two, and he is clearly the focus. But as well, there is a cast of 17 others who do everything from magic tricks to flying trapeze acts…The premise is that he sees his career as The John A. Macdonald Show – Twenty-four Years in Her Majesty's Theatre, Ottawa! and that the events of his life are re-enacted in his memory with little emotional involvement from him, while he keeps contact with us, the audience, and lets us in on his little secret, which is: 'The only way I stayed alive for 24 years in this horrible place is by being an actor.' " (– *London Free Press*, January 24, 1979) Berthold Carrier composed and played all the music himself, positioned out front, in one of the theatre's boxes

Just before a Saturday matinee of John A. – Himself! *a very bad snowstorm hit. There was a subsequent power failure. The show was cancelled, but for some reason none of the actors left the theatre. Instead, we all sat around in the darkened Grand, illuminated only by candlelight and flashlights, singing songs and telling stories. I remember it now as one of the most enchanting times I have ever spent inside a theatre.*
– Rick Whelan, writer and former actor

"My first experience in the Grand Theatre was attending a performance of Timothy Findlay's play *John A. – Himself!* starring William Hutt as Himself. Hutt's portrayal of Sir John in the television series, *The National Dream,* had been, as far as I was concerned, nearly perfect, and the play, I thought, would be more of the same. Hutt was again Sir John personified, but this certainly wasn't historical writer Pierre Berton's version of Canada. The most memorable scene involved 19th century members of parliament in top hats, singing, dancing and swinging from trapezes in Canada's House of Commons. I had met Findley the day before the performance, in a bookstore on Richmond Street. He was doing a book-signing, and though knowing nothing about him, I had taken home his new book *The Wars.* That book made me a loyal reader. And, so, thanks to Sir John, and Mr. Hutt, I had been introduced to a great writer and a great theatre. I have been with them ever since."
– Mike Baker, historian, theatre-goer

MCCMANUS STUDIO

A studio space for smaller productions had been part of the Lett/Smith vision for the rebuilt Grand Theatre. Located one floor below street level, it quickly became a favourite place for performers and audience members. A donation from the McManus family of London established the new studio's name.

RHYTHM AND BLUES AND ALL THAT JAZZ

Young composer/musician, Christopher Mounteer, teamed up with Theatre London Publicity Director Rob Wellan to create a hit show entitled *Rhythm and Blues and All That Jazz*.

For a long time my mother was dead against me going into theatre. She wanted me to get a real job – something secure, and so on. Understandable. The money for Rhythm and Blues and All That Jazz *was just an honorarium, certainly it was nothing to put away in the bank. But it was important for me to do it. Mom and I fought about it quite regularly. She was upset that I was doing so much work for next-to-nothing. Well, after much twisting of her arm she did come to see the show. She said to me afterwards: 'Well, I guess you really should be in theatre.' From that moment on she gave me her full support. She even snuck her cassette recorder into the theatre. Staff saw her leave at intermission but when they found out she was my mother they let her get away with it. She went into the ladies' room and started to play back the first act for anyone who would listen, saying: 'That's my son!'*

– Christopher Mounteer, composer, musician, pianist

Louise Pitre is an incredible talent. Mesmerizing. A lyricist's dream. A very special lady. I worked with Louise in Rhythm and Blues and All That Jazz *– it was her second show; she had just finished university. At our first rehearsal she sang 'Maybe This Time' and she did it full out with all the heart and drama that makes her so dynamic. When she finished, the rest of the cast cheered. She looked at me with that look of 'I'm not sure I like what I did.' I asked her to do it again, and to stand perfectly still, no sweeping gesture with the arms, and hold back...hold it back, hold it back, hold it back until you feel*

everyone in the room ready to scream to let go...then let go. She did it, she smiled and winked at me when she finished. She stopped the show every night. I still feel that if Christopher Mounteer ever wrote music to the proverbial telephone book, Louise could sing it and stop the show every night.

– Rob Wellan, Theatre London Public Relations Director

HUTT RESIGNS

In May 1979, William Hutt announced that he would be resigning from the position of Grand Theatre Artistic Director and moving on after completing the 1979/80 season. The theatre's board of directors began its search for Hutt's successor.

Theatre London season #8:
Kiss Me Kate, by Cole Porter and Bella and Samuel Spewack, directed by William Hutt
Otherwise Engaged, by Simon Gray, directed by Donald Davis
John A. – Himself!, by Timothy Findley, directed by Peter Moss
Rope, by Patrick Hamilton, directed by William Hutt
Same Time, Next Year, by Bernard Slade, directed by Keith Batten
Little Mary Sunshine, by Rick Besoyan, directed by William Hutt

McManus Studio:
The Marvellous, Magical Circus of Paddington Bear, by Blaine Parker

Oscar Remembered, by and starring Maxim Mazumdar
Theatre Beyond Words
Rogues and Vagabonds, adapted by Michael Meyer, with Marti Maraden and Nicholas Pennell
Androcles and the Lion, based on the Italian fable
Rhythm and Blues and All That Jazz, a revue by Rob Wellan and Chris Mounteer

Dance:
The National Ballet of Canada

Local Production:
Jesus Christ, Superstar, produced by London Sanctuary Theatre

1979/80

THEATRE LONDON/
WILLIAM HUTT ERA

BERNARD HOPKINS

This was William Hutt's fourth and final season as artistic director. By October 1979, the board was able to announce that Bernard Hopkins would be the Grand Theatre's next artistic director. Described as a 42-year-old British-born graduate of the Royal Academy of Dramatic Art, Hopkins would direct *Equus* during this season.

EQUUS

Bernard Hopkins' production of Peter Shaffer's startling play *Equus* was received well by critics and audience members, despite the play containing one scene of total nudity. Critic Rick Whelan captured the essence of this stunning production when he wrote that it would "leave you breathless, elated and wondering how they kept all of it going at once." Calling it a *tour de force*, he commented: "Its players, all solid practitioners of the stage art, slowly, quietly begin to tell their story. It's a fascinating story, a story of sexual fixation and lost innocence and passion in a passionless landscape. The story proceeds and before you know it, without anyone seeming to pop a vein or raise the roof with frenzied elocution, the theatrical magic begins to cast a spell over the audience." (– *London Free Press*, January 21, 1980). Heading the cast was William Hutt, as psychiatrist Martin Dysart, and Stephen Ouimette as the boy patient, Alan Strang. The boy has been taken

Signs promoting the 1979/80 plays are suspended over the sidewalk on Richmond Street. (Courtesy of The Grand Theatre)

to a psychiatric hospital after committing the cruel and senseless crime of violently blinding horses. The psychiatrist probes the boy's inner life in an attempt to learn something about him besides the gruesome headlines Alan has provoked. This was strong stuff. Five actors were cast as the horses: Christopher Blake, Marshall Button, Robert LaChance, Colin Legge and Tom McCamus. They moved on stage on elevated horses' hooves, created for them in the prop shop by Edward Elsbury, Gerald Smuin and John Van Lieshout. Anyone lucky enough to see this production found it unforgettable.

ROB WELLAN

The McManus Studio featured plays for young people. Compared to the large number of excellent companies today, theatre for young audiences in the late 1970s was at the toddler stage. Although there was that rare exception, the majority of shows that came to the McManus seemed to be a variation on the theme of : Look kids, this is an 'A'. There was very little theatricality, more a classroom with actors working as teachers-in-costume. William Hutt, The Grand's artistic director, was becoming increasingly worried about sales dropping and the low attendance of our matinees. Bill made it a point to have a visit every day and over coffee we would discuss a number of things, most of it related to The Grand and some not (the some not was my favourite as Bill knew my sense of humour and he is a master at telling anecdotes). We talked about the decreasing attendance at the McManus and he asked me if I had any thoughts as to why. I voiced my thoughts – cautiously. In those days publicists were rarely asked for their opinions, input or suggestions. I was very fortunate, both with Heinar and with Bill. Bill took a thoughtful sip of coffee and turned to me with his thoughtful artistic director look – the one you know you cannot say anything to: "If you can do better then do it, and we'll do it." So I adapted the folk story of 'Ichabod Crane and the Headless Horseman.' Robert LaChance was cast as The Headless Horseman, and Tom McCamus was Ichabod. It was done in-the-round, and Jack King designed a beautiful set complete with bullrushes, a bridge crossing a creek and a great, huge, full moon. Victor Elliott brilliantly designed and built two horses, a white stallion for the horseman and a nag for Ichabod. The white stallion was complete with flaring nostrils that sprayed talcum powder on the kids, and the nag's tail and mane shot straight up when it saw the Headless Horseman. I'm happy to say the play was received very well. As artistic director, Bill was totally a joy to work with, and as an actor he

still is. He taught me a great deal about the artistic side of theatre – about diplomacy, and laughter.

– Rob Wellan, Theatre London Public Relations Director

DEPARTURE OF WILLIAM HUTT

As William Hutt prepared to leave the Grand Theatre, he imparted these thoughts to Doug Bale of the *London Free Press*: "One thought that was very prominent in my mind was that I am in pretty high profile around Stratford during the season, and that quite a number of people come from London to see the Festival. I didn't want to inundate them with William Hutt so that every time they went to the Grand Theatre they'd see that grey-haired old fart on stage and be bored to tears. Enough is enough. The experience at Theatre London has been an extremely enjoyable one for me, not to mention just the challenge of having a theatre under my own fingertips for a while, and seeing it through such an expansion. I have quite regretful feelings about leaving, of course, but I felt the theatre had to have an artistic director who was younger and was able to spend more time than I could spend over there. I probably would have stayed on at Theatre London, the board was really very generous in saying that I could virtually stay on as long as I liked, had I not known that over the next couple of years I will have some pretty interesting challenges at Stratford." (– April 29, 1980)

1980/81

THEATRE LONDON/ BERNARD HOPKINS ERA

Theatre London season #9:
Absurd Person Singular, by Alan Ayckbourn, directed by Jack Roberts
The Lady of the Camellias, adapted by Suzanne Grossman, directed by Robin Phillips
Equus, by Peter Shaffer, directed by Bernard Hopkins
Irma La Douce, by Alexandre Breffort, directed by Jack Roberts
The Glass Menagerie, by Tennessee Williams, directed by Keith Batten
The Relapse, by Sir John Vanbrugh, directed by Graham Harley

McManus Studio:
Creeps, by David Freeman
The Hollow Crown, devised by John Barton

Ichabod Crane, by Rob Wellan
Ready, Steady, Go, by Sandra Jones, directed by Kip Edinburgh Longstaff, produced by Minico Theatre Company
The Wonderful World of Sarah Binks, with Eric Donkin
Boiler Room Suite, by Rex Deverell
Rhythm and Blues and All That Jazz, a remount of the revue by Rob Wellan and Chris Mounteer
Workshop of two one-act plays:
The Questioning of Nick, by Arthur Kopit, and
The Indian Wants The Bronx, by Israel Horovitz

Music:
London Symphony Orchestra

Dance:
Les Grands Ballets Canadiens
Dance London

Local Production:
Fiddler on the Roof, produced by London Sanctuary Theatre

Road Shows:
Anne of Green Gables
Blue Champagne
Spring Thaw

ANTLER RIVER

Before Theatre London's season got underway, *Antler River* by James Reaney, was on stage at The Grand. The Urban League of London had asked Reaney to write a play in honour of the City of London's 125th birthday. The play's title was inspired by the area's Native People, who had given the name Antler River to the forks of the Thames River. Work on the production had begun months before. Over five hours of material was accumulated by the writer. Everyone involved, from actors with lines, to extras with no lines, to people working backstage, did their own research into the region's past and also contributed ideas to the playwright about how they saw the production. Finally, after all the collaboration, *Antler River* was shaped into a two-and-a-half hour play. Patsy Lang designed 21 interchangeable, rolling set pieces, and 57 actors came on board. It was a mammoth production. On the final night of the production's run, a smouldering cigarette in a dressing room burst into flames. The automatic sprinkler system turned on and sent gallons of water onto the floor and onto stored costumes. The fire was discovered at approximately 11:00 p.m. Authorities decided that the night's audience, about to leave the theatre anyway, would disperse more quickly and safely if no alarm was sounded. The theatre emptied without incident. The damage was estimated at $3,000.

Artistic Director Bernard Hopkins. As incoming Artistic Director, Hopkins expressed a desire to build upon Theatre London's already strong involvement with the community, and to put emphasis on the importance of work being done in the McManus Studio. (Courtesy Bernard Hopkins)

THE KILLING OF SISTER GEORGE

I want to see people coming to the McManus though I'm not sure how I'm going to do it. I hope we attract people by opening with The Killing of Sister George, *which is a solid piece of work on human relationships. And then I'm bringing in two plays that might offend. And by offend I do not mean ... well, let's just not have a conversation about nudity or the word f***, because it bores the s*** out of me. The word f*** doesn't appear in either play and nobody gets undressed. They are plays about ideas, about relationships, and they may confuse people.*
– Artistic Director Bernard Hopkins (– University of Western Ontario's *Gazette*, October 28, 1980)

BEAUTY AND THE BEAST

When the classic story *Beauty and the Beast* was staged in the McManus Studio in March 1981, critic Dennis Kucherawy praised the work of designer Jack King: "King's set is a visually effective enchanted castle. The illuminated trees, two mirrors which swing back and forth allowing characters to enter and exit through them, vases which magically break, and candles which easily split in two when sliced by the Beast's sword, all contribute to the magical ambience. King's 18th century silk and lace costumes give an aura of refined elegance and civilization to mask the Beast's dark secret." (– *London Free Press*, March 12, 1981) The design concept occurred to both designer and to director Bernard Hopkins: "I was lying in the bath one day, thinking about it, and I finally made up my mind that the only way to do it was in the 18th century. I thought to myself, 'Jack's not going to like this,' because 18th century costumes are horribly expensive to do, compared to just about anything else. But a couple of days later, before I could break it to him, he called me up and said, 'You're going to hate this, but you know, don't you, that there's no way to do it except 18th century?'" (– *London Free Press*, February 20, 1981)

PAUL ECK

In May 1981, after eight years on the job, Theatre London administrator, Paul Eck, resigned from his position and stated his plans to move to Toronto. He had been a key figure in the London theatre scene for years. He started acting in and directing amateur productions, and finally left a career in the insurance business to become a professional theatre administrator. In a newspaper article Paul Eck said: "I like the involvement. I like the challenge. I like the chance to meet hundreds of interesting, fascinating, different people. You're not stuck to a desk in this kind of a job – although I sometimes feel that I'm stuck to a phone. You're continually on the go. There are continually new problems. Nothing's ever the same twice and there is no routine, because you're constantly immersed in the creative process as well as in the business aspect. I've done a fair amount of acting, but I don't have the commitment required by an actor. And when you're six feet, six inches tall there are only so many roles you can play. You can be the butler forever, I suppose, but I never found a challenge in those roles. I find the greatest challenge in the overall management and organization of the whole thing. I think there are so many other people who can do the acting part so much better. I'm more interested in providing the milieu in which they can do it." (– *London Free Press,* February 1979)

Theatre London season #10:
Deathtrap, by Ira Levin, directed by Bernard Hopkins
The Browning Version, by Terence Rattigan, and *Black Comedy*, by Peter Shaffer, directed by Bernard Hopkins
She Loves Me, by Joe Masteroff, Jerry Bock and Sheldon Harnick, directed by Bernard Hopkins
The Incredible Murder of Cardinal Tosca, by Alden Nowlan and Walter Learning, directed by Richard Whelan
The Rainmaker, by Richard Nash, directed by Brian Rintoul
The Misanthrope, by Molière, directed by Bernard Hopkins

McManus Studio:
The Killing of Sister George, by Frank Marcus
The Gymnasium and *Lunchtime Concert*, by Olwen Wymark
Eight to the Bar, by Stephen Witken and Joey Miller
Inside Out, by Rob Wellan
Leacock at Leisure, by and starring Ric Wellwood

Children's Theatre:
Beauty and the Beast
Mr. Cappledooper's Dilemma

Local Productions:
Jacob Two-Two Meets the Hooded Fang, from Mordecai Richler
Antler River, by Dr. James Reaney
It's Better in Barbershop, Sweet Adelines
The Man of La Mancha, produced by London Sanctuary Theatre

Film Production:
The Last Great Vaudeville Show, Global Television production, starring Donald O'Connor as George M. Cohan and Debbie Reynolds as Sophie Tucker

Dance:
The National Tap Dance Company of Canada
Les Ballets Jazz de Montreal

Road Show:
Vincent: The Story of A Hero, adapted by and starring Leonard Nimoy in the story about the life of artist Vincent Van Gogh

---

1981/82

THEATRE LONDON/
BERNARD HOPKINS ERA

A COMPELLING THEATRICAL EXPERIENCE

Ibsen's A Doll's House *is not a play dealing only with women's rights, else it would have been forgotten years ago. Not because women's rights are no longer an issue (they are) but because 'issue' dramas become quaint almost as quickly as newspapers.* A Doll's House *has continued to be produced as frequently as* Hamlet *ever since its first presentation in 1879 because, like* Hamlet, *it is a compelling theatrical experience. The Helmers' youth is vital to the play. Torvald's (played by Sten Hornborg) pomposity, his priggishness, his delight in his masculine superiority become intolerable – not to say incredible – in an older man; but they are not so surprising in a younger one. And Nora's (played by Sharry Flett) flightiness, her sense of mischief, her naivete, her delight in Torvald and her fear of him, her little vanities, her pathetic faith – all of these traits are only lovable and engaging if the role is played by a young woman. Usually the age level of the entire cast is too high.*
– director Bernard Hopkins, house program, January 1982

MATURE NATURE OF THE DIALOGUE

In 1982 my mother and my 11-year-old brother went to see Automatic Pilot *at The Grand. My mother hadn't realized the mature nature of the dialogue and was alarmed as a torrent of four-letter-words spilled from the stage. During the intermission*

---

she apologized to my brother for taking him to such an adult production. 'Oh, don't worry, Mom,' he said. 'I've heard worse things at school.
– Christopher Doty, subscriber

GOVERNOR GENERAL'S MEDALS FOR ARCHITECTURE

On June 1, 1982, His Excellency The Honourable Edward Schreyer presented the first ever Governor General's Medals for Architecture. One of the 20 medal winners, chosen by a jury of architects, was the firm of Lett/Smith Architects of Toronto, for their work redesigning and rebuilding London's Grand Theatre.

BELATED THANKS

I attended the opening night of A Visit to Cal's Mother *and one other evening during the run. I had planned also to go on the closing night – a last chance to thank the cast and crew for an excellent production of a play I'd written. That Sunday afternoon I took the London Opera Guild bus to a matinee in Toronto. On the way home, on an icy ramp to Highway 401, the bus skidded into the ditch, near Ingersoll, where we remained for the next two hours. I never saw the final performance of my play. This note will, I hope, convey my belated thanks to The Grand.*
– Edwin R. Procunier, playwright, teacher

Top right: *An interior shot of the Grand Theatre taken after the 1978 rebuild.* Bottom right: *Compare this to the interior shot taken in 1975/76. (Courtesy of The Grand Theatre)*

1982/83

THEATRE LONDON/ BERNARD HOPKINS ERA

Theatre London season #11:
Blithe Spirit, by Noel Coward, directed by Bernard Hopkins
Bells are Ringing, by Betty Comden, Adolph Green and Jule Styne, directed by Joel Greenberg
A Doll's House, by Henrik Ibsen, directed by Bernard Hopkins
Gwendoline, by James W. Nichol, directed by Bernard Hopkins
Automatic Pilot, by Erika Ritter, directed by Jack Blum

Who's Afraid of Virginia Woolf?, by Edward Albee, directed by Brian Rintoul

McManus Studio:
The Wonderful World of Sarah Binks, with Eric Donkin,
Exile, by Ric Wellwood
A Visit to Cal's Mother, by Edwin R. Procunier
Vanities, by Jack Heifner

Children's Theatre:
Beauty and the Beast
Kid Show Madness, a magic show for children

Local Productions:
Tommy Hunter and Gordie Tapp
Cinderella, The Happy Prince

Road Show:
Maggie and Pierre, by Linda Griffiths

Dance:
The National Ballet of Canada

ROBIN PHILLIPS

Early in September 1982, it became public knowledge that Artistic Director Bernard Hopkins' third season at the helm of Theatre London would be his final one. He was going to resume his freelance career as a director and actor at the end of the 1982/83 season.

And on September 21 of 1982, it was announced in the London media that Robin Phillips had been hired as incoming artistic director. Phillips' plans for the next three seasons, beginning with the 1983/84 season, included dropping the subscription plan; developing a permanent acting company of 40 members; producing an extended season; and developing film and television productions. It was anticipated that this new activity would create 100 new jobs within the theatre. John Porter, vice-president of the Theatre London board, and head of the search committee that hired Robin Phillips, said at the time that the extended season planned by Phillips for 1983/84, plus the film and television production projects he had in mind, were expected to pay the increased costs of having a permanent acting company on site at the Grand Theatre. Also, Porter expressed hopes that granting organizations, such as the Canada Council, would come forward with financial assistance.

BARRY MORSE

Barry Morse starred as Scrooge in the December 1982 production of Dickens' beloved story, *A Christmas Carol*. Tom McCamus was Bob

Janelle Hutchison played Tessie Tura, the Texas Twirler in Gypsy. *The production was Bernard Hopkins' swan song as artistic director of The Grand, and was a smash hit. (Courtesy of* **London** Free Press*)*

Cratchit. The show was scheduled to close on December 24, but the demand for tickets was so great that it was extended first to December 31, and then until January 7, 1983. After that date, it was forced to close because the next production had to be mounted on The Grand's stage. On January 6, when Morse had a free evening, he performed his own popular one-man show, *Merely Players*, a charming piece celebrating theatre and theatre people.

THE GRAND THEATRE COMPANY

In January 1983, the theatre sent out a press release stating the following: "The Grand Theatre proudly announces the participation of leading Canadian theatre artists in its inaugural season as a repertory theatre performing the classics, together with contemporary plays and musicals. The premiere season of eight productions opens September 19, 1983. Incoming Artistic Director Robin Phillips will direct *The Doctor's Dilemma, Timon of Athens* and *The Club*."

In March 1983, Theatre London sent its subscribers ticket information about the upcoming 1983/84 season. Subscribers were informed that there would no longer be subscriptions. Instead, there would be a membership fee, and single tickets could be purchased on a play-by-play basis. Subscribers also learned that Robin Phillips' company of actors included Martha Henry, William Hutt, John Neville, Rod Beattie, Carole Shelley and others.

Why did Phillips choose to work at London's Grand Theatre when he could have worked in theatre or film anywhere in Canada, England or the United States? Phillips believed that all he wanted to work with was at London's Grand Theatre: technology, opportunity, talent and board support. His new repertory company was named The Grand Theatre Company. As of 1983/84, and after twelve seasons, Theatre London was no more.

GYPSY

As his three years as artistic director of Theatre London at the Grand Theatre drew to a close, and as announcements about the next season continued to flow from the theatre, Bernard Hopkins prepared to go out with a bang, not a whimper. Hopkins directed a big, glitzy, joyful show that dealt with making it in the world of show business. *Gypsy* went onstage on April 20 and was originally scheduled to run for four weeks. With lineups of hopeful ticket buyers at the box office, the show was extended for a full week, and then for a full week more. In all, it ran for six weeks, closing on May 28.

The musical was based on the memoirs of the legendary stripper, Gypsy Rose Lee. Julie Amato starred as Gypsy's fiercely ambitious stage mother. Her daughters were played by Charlotte Moore and Colleen Winton. Set designer Philip Silver devised 17 major set pieces and 11 smaller ones for the show's 28 scenes.

FROM HOPKINS TO PHILLIPS

"As artistic director of Theatre London for the last three seasons, Bernard Hopkins has been responsible for 23 productions and has been instrumental in this theatre's coming of age. It's fair to say that Hopkins' spadework has provided a solid base for the new Artistic Director Robin Phillips to carry out his formidable plans. Don Grant, administrative director of the theatre, emphasizes that without that base, built by Hopkins, Phillips' planned projects would be extremely difficult, if not impossible, to carry out." (– *London Free Press*, April 15, 1983)

In fact, Robin Phillips' plans were extremely difficult to carry out, as the impending season demonstrated. The 1983/84 season is known as the "repertory season," and is also known as the "Phillips' Season." However it is referred to, the 1983/84 season was a pivotal one in the history of London's Grand Theatre. It has given rise to debate and conjecture for the last seventeen years.

Theatre London season #12:
Tally's Folly, by Langford Wilson, directed by George Bloomfield
A Christmas Carol, from Charles Dickens, directed by Bernard Hopkins
Murder Game!, by Dan Ross, directed by Brian Rintoul
Antigone, by Jean Anouilh, directed by Bernard Hopkins
Nurse Jane Goes to Hawaii, by Allan Stratton, directed by Brian Rintoul
Gypsy, by Stephen Sondheim, Jule Styne and Arthur Laurents, directed by Bernard Hopkins

Other:
Merely Players, by Barry Morse

McManus Studio:
Proudfoot Papers, by Reverend Orlo Miller
Relative Strangers, by James W. Nichol
Sting Like a Butterfly, by Ric Wellwood
The Princess and the Handmaiden, by Leslie Arden

THE GRAND THEATRE COMPANY

1983-1986

Tony Van Bridge in the mystery An Inspector Calls.
Years after seeing this production, actor Rod Beattie
remembered that during the scene where all the loose
ends are revealed and tied up, Tony Van Bridge faced
upstage, with his back to the audience, something only a
great actor could do effectively. (Photo: Robert Ragsdale;
Courtesy of The Grand Theatre)

1983/84

THE GRAND THEATRE COMPANY/ ROBIN PHILLIPS ERA

AN AMBITIOUS SEASON

This season is best described by the word "ambitious." A star-studded company of actors and other artists had been hired. Fifteen dazzling productions were programmed to run in repertory on the mainstage, with another six productions set for the McManus Studio. A three-show deal was signed with independent television producers Prime Media in Toronto. Three productions were to be filmed for the cultural pay TV C-Chanel. A budget of $4.4 million was set. A box office gross of 80 per cent for each mainstage play was calculated. And finally a name change: Theatre London became The Grand Theatre Company. Ambitous? Yes. Doable? It remained to be seen.

The arrival of Robin Phillips at The Grand was the most heralded and most misunderstood moment in the history of the Grand Old Lady. Phillips was considered a 'genius' by many who worked with him, and he was certainly very gifted. He scrapped the subscription series, which had been years and years in the building, and literally thousands of annoyed Londoners decided to boycott the season, regardless of its quality. Contrary to popular belief, Robin Phillips never ran over budget, and his financial downfall came through the failure of additional funding to materialize.
– Ric Wellwood, writer, reviewer, broadcaster, teacher

REPERTORY THEATRE

Robin Phillips' lofty plans for London's Grand Theatre were matched by the theatre board's equally lofty plans. The board had approved a $4.4 million budget, more than double that of the previous season. A deficit of $105,000 was projected. Phillips' vision, and the board's enthusiasm to achieve that vision changed London's professional theatre company from a subscription-based endeavour to a repertory theatre company. This would help move the Grand Theatre to the number three spot on the national Canadian theatre scene, behind the Stratford and Shaw Festivals.

Going into the season, it seemed feasible that the theatre could achieve the high box office projections for two reasons: because Phillips had surpassed 80 per cent attendance, per play, during his seven seasons as artistic director at the Stratford Festival, and

A candid photo taking in the theatre's lobby of two dedicated Grand Theatre volunteers, Wally Duffield (left) and Peter Lynch. Both men had been involved with LLT in various capacities for many years, and continued their close affiliation with the Grand Theatre after LLT became Theatre London. (Courtesy of The Grand Theatre)

because in recent seasons, Theatre London had been achieving 85 per cent capacity overall.

For the 1983/84 season, the theatre was still counting on the Ontario Arts Council to provide four per cent of its revenue, and the Canada Council to provide five per cent. It also expected that people would purchase a $25 membership, in lieu of a subscription, and purchase single tickets as well. In September 1983, $400,000 was granted to the theatre from the Province of Ontario, to help pay for a $1.2 million upgrade. Projects included additional lighting, stage rigging, and bringing the theatre into the computer age, a box office computer system. One wonders what Ambrose J. Small and his manager John R. Minhinnick would make of the advance of technology.

As it turned out, the season started without a big advance sale of tickets or memberships, and cash flow was a concern by October 1983.

ROBIN PHILLIPS

I was working in the publicity department when Robin Phillips was there with his amazing and wonderful season. We all adored and worshipped him, and worked long hours. This was all very exciting, fun and rewarding. He had such taste, class, sophistication in every detail of the productions, and of his personality. Robin had a great sense of humour and sense of fun. One of my duties was to go each day or so with my special box marked Chips Ahoy to Talbot Street and Queen's Avenue, to the then-famous blue-and-white chip wagon. I am sure that many of Robin's gorgeous effects – the striking creams, greys and sands against the shiny reflective back-sets – were planned as he ate his favourite lunch – a plate of chips.

– Min (Marilyn) Fidler, former employee (during the tenures of William Hutt, Bernard Hopkins and Robin Phillips)

A BUDGET SQUEEZE

A rosy announcement was made in October: box office revenue was standing at $1 million, just ten weeks into the season. But by January 1984, announcements were not so positive. General Manager Lucille Wagner resigned, and eight staff members were laid off. There was a budget squeeze. And by the time a February 8 press conference was held, The Grand Theatre Company was in a fight to save its life. Basic objectives were outlined: (i) take all actions necessary to operate within a balanced budget for the forthcoming 1984/85 season and (ii) start to reduce the deficit created in the current 1983/84 season. That deficit was, in February, estimated at $1.4 million, much above the $105,000 projected. It was announced that the repertory format was being abandoned in time for the next season, and that the theatre would return to subscription sales.

On February 24, 984, Robin Phillips resigned. In March, Don Shipley was appointed as the new Artistic Director. In May, the 1983/84 season, the repertory season, the Phillips season, came to an end.

What went wrong? Ticket sales fell short of the necessary 80 per cent. In fact, the most popular show of the season, *Godspell*, achieved 77 per cent capacity, while the least-attended show of the season, *Timon of Athens*, sold at just 36 per cent capacity. Fundraising targets set by the Board were not achieved. Prime Media declared bankruptcy, eliminating revenue for the contracted film and television tie-ins. And, something as mundane, yet as important, as the foul winter weather in Southwestern Ontario, was a deterrent to theatre lovers who may well have travelled to London, had the repertory company performed in the summer, rather than in the depths of winter.

ARRIVAL AND DEPARTURE

"This was my first year on air at CFPL TV and I was plunged into covering the most exciting time the Grand Theatre had witnessed since The Grand was built. I was a young, neophyte television reporter with a love for the theatre and a passion for covering it for the news department. Little did I know at the beginning of the season that within six months I would co-produce and host a documentary called *Grand Expectations*, as the season would fail with a huge financial loss. There was a lot of media hype surrounding the new Artistic Director, Robin Phillips, who was renowned for his work at The Stratford Festival. Phillips arrived with great national coverage. He was bringing with him top actors, like William Hutt, Brent Carver, Sheila McCarthy and Carole Shelley, to do repertory theatre and abolish the usual subscription season. He also announced movie deals with the company and touring shows. It was groundbreaking. Robin Phillips had a great reputation among actors, all of whom sang his praises. As I discovered, he was able to breed fierce loyalty from anybody who worked with him. Robin Phillips also ran a closed operation; no cameras were allowed to capture the rehearsal or behind-the-scenes process. That blanket rule from Robin Phillips was like waving a carrot in front of a horse; I could not stand to be a television reporter in The Grand's backyard with no access to the story! So, I wrote to Robin Phillips; I pleaded my case, telling him I wanted to represent him and his theatre the way he envisioned it and it would be a huge loss to theatre everywhere if more people could not sample his vision. To my surprise, I received a telephone call from Robin, which led to a subsequent meeting and the opportunity to shoot clips from every production as long as Robin set up the shot through the viewfinder. In retrospect, it is something I would not do now as a reporter, although sometimes you have to compromise to get the story. Robin fancied himself a movie director, but he knew nothing about news or how it should be shot. However, he was happy and I was happy and it was the beginning of a great relationship.

Six months later there was a rising deficit of over $1 million dollars. There's no doubt it was great theatre. The productions were all memorable but they were far from sell-outs. Robin Phillips resigned, the theatre went back to subscriptions and I wrote the documentary with interviews from actors, Ontario Arts Council members, national reporters, board members and Robin Phillips. The Grand learned that its audience counted on subscriptions." – Janice Zolf, arts and entertainment reporter CFPL TV

HAZEL DESBARATS

The notorious Phillips' season, while fuelling discussion for the next two decades, also left some lasting impressions on those people who were part of Phillips' company, and on playgoers who attended that season.

After completing my studies in my home city of London, England, I spent about 25 years working in, first British television, and then in Canadian television. My final position was senior news producer for Global Television in Ottawa. I then made a career switch, in the early 1980s, after moving with my husband to this London. My first professional involvement was in Dear Antoine, *by Jean Anouilh. It was the last play in Robin Phillips' magical season at The Grand. The cast was made up of major theatre heavyweights – Martha Henry, Susan Wright, William Hutt and John Neville, to name a few. I was extremely nervous and had nightmares for several weeks before rehearsals started. The first time I rehearsed I had to do a two-handed scene with Martha Henry, and I was so nervous my hands were shaking very noticeably. When I mentioned to someone in the cast how scared I was, they simply said they had thought it very good character work. They* were all very supportive and gentle with me.

– Hazel Desbarats, actress

SURPRISE AND DELIGHT

The Christmas show that season included a carol sing-along in the Poster Lounge, to which the audience was invited. Ever an enthusiastic singer of hymns, I was joining in with gusto and was reaching all the high Cs. Imagine my surprise and delight when actor Brent Carver came over to share my song sheet and duet with me! I was the envy of everybody, including a friend who lamented, 'I have worked in this theatre all the time he has been here, and he has never even noticed me, much less offered to sing with me!'

– Sheila Martindale, critic, poet, writer and theatre-goer

AN INCREDIBLE YEAR

In 1983/84, I was incredibly fortunate to be asked to be a member of what was supposed to be a three-year-plan, a repertory company headed by Robin Phillips. Unfortunately, it lasted but one year, yet it was the most incredible year. A fabulous selection of incredible acting and wondrous theatre. Many moments remain vividly in my mind's eye, after all these years. In Timon of Athens *there was a banquet scene at which many of Timon's so-called friends were dining. During the scene there was a troop of dancers who wove their way across the dining table. One of them was the delightful Kay Tremblay. All the dancers were clothed in scanty but layered materials that flowed behind them. Somehow Kay's train caught a candle and began to flame. Kay could not see it and had no sense of the danger. She was in imminent danger of combusting before our eyes, but Rod Beattie acted quickly. He wrapped her in his arms and carried her off stage. Kay was bewildered and wondered why she had been swept away. Thereafter, she was affectionately referred to as 'Kay Flambe.'*

Later that season Robin Phillips directed Arsenic and Old Lace, *with William Hutt and John Neville as the sweet (or sweet-and-sour?) ladies. I was assigned the role of Mr. Hoskins who had very few lines. In fact, I was a dead body hidden in the window box. It truly required no acting ability and all I had to do was crawl into the window box from behind, be discovered and then be carried across the stage. A brief ten-second appearance. But just before being carried, I would be discovered when one of the actors would lift the window-box seat, see me, shriek and slam the lid shut. One night I climbed in a little earlier than usual. Being a very small, dark space, with not much air, and being slightly tired I quickly fell asleep, which was fine for the discovery of the 'dead body' but not so good when the actor who discovered me slammed the lid down (as usual) and from within the window box the 'dead body' (me) came suddenly awake and screamed!*

– David Kirby, actor

LAST NIGHT

"It was the last night of Robin Phillips' superb tenure at The Grand. Brent Carver who was not on stage that night, was in the audience. He walked up the aisle toward me after the final curtain. Everyone on stage and in the audience was feeling terribly emotional – losing Robin was a terrible blow. I looked at Brent Carver and said, with a great deal of feeling: 'Thank you.' And he looked right back, touched my arm, and replied: 'Thank you', with just as much feeling."

– Patricia Black, critic, writer and theatre-goer

1984/85

THE GRAND THEATRE COMPANY/ DON SHIPLEY ERA

The Grand Theatre Company season:

Godspell, by John-Michael Tebelak, directed by Gregory Peterson

The Doctor's Dilemma, by G.B. Shaw, directed by Robin Phillips and Don Shipley

Waiting for the Parade, by John Murrell, directed by Robin Phillips

Timon of Athens, by William Shakespeare, directed by Robin Phillips

The Club, by Eve Merriam, directed by Robin Phillips

Arsenic and Old Lace, by Joseph Kesselring, directed by Robin Phillips

The Prisoner of Zenda, directed by Robin Phillips and Gregory Peterson

Hamlet, by William Shakespeare, directed by John Neville

Dear Antoine, by Jean Anouilh, directed by Robin Phillips

McManus Studio:

The Snow Goose, by Paul Gallico

Ludmila, by Paul Gallico

The Small Miracle, by Paul Gallico

Thomasina, by Paul Gallico

Miracle in the Wilderness, by Paul Gallico

Plus, a special Christmas concert

DEMONSTRATION OF SUPPORT

A minimum of 10,000 subscribers was needed for the Grand Theatre to break even for this season. Fortunately, by November 1984 the theatre had sold 12,653 subscriptions. Londoners who had not supported the 1983/84 repertory season, demonstrated their support for the Grand, as a subscription-based theatre company

MOVIE SHOOT

The Grand Theatre was a location for a movie shoot early in September 1984. ABC-TV was shooting a movie about media mogul William Randolph Hearst, starring Robert Mitchum. The movie star was at The Grand, along with a 60-member film crew, for two days. Actress Virginia Madsen was on hand to play actress Marion Davies, Heart's mistress. The scenes at the Grand Theatre evoked a New York City theatre, circa 1917. Almost 600 Londoners went to a casting call, and approximately 200 lucky people were picked as extras for the shoot.

A GALA DINNER

The Grand Theatre announced a special week in October to mend broken bridges within the community. As director of communications Ann Tanner said, "to reassure people that The Grand knows where its roots are." October 12 was "A Grand Day at the Holiday Inn," an attempt to boost the theatre's profile among

Londoners, in the wake of the financially disastrous 1983/84 repertory season. A gala dinner was followed by a 75-minute Grand Theatre Alumni Cabaret. This featured Charlotte Ann Eamon and Eddie Escaf doing the "Honeybun" number from *South Pacific*. Heather Brandt sang Eliza Doolittle's song "Wouldn't it be Lovely" from *My Fair Lady*. Judy Potter sang "Hello Young Lovers" from *The King and I*. Patricia Leavens sang "If I Loved You" from *Carousel*, and Alec Richmond sang "Reviewing the Situation" with gusto, as he had done in the 1967/68 London Little Theatre production of *Oliver!*

'NIGHT MOTHER

I think that of all the years I have been going to The Grand and of all the plays that I have seen, both on the mainstage and in the McManus Studio, the play that most affected me was 'Night, Mother, *directed by Martha Henry and starring Diana Leblanc and Rita Howell. I knew nothing about the play when I sat down, but within moments I was totally involved. It was the most amazing piece of theatre. I sat and watched a meticulously directed production of two women revealing their dreams, their losses and their solutions to their lives. I laughed with them. I shared their disappointments. And, at that final moment, when the mother sat waiting for her son to come, the lights slowly fading, the tears streamed down my face. That was a moment that I will carry with me for the rest of my life.*
– M. Lucille (Sam) Grant, subscriber

THE GRAND THEATRE COMPANY

Grand Theatre season:
You Can't Take It With You, by George S. Kaufman and Moss Hart, directed by Derek Goldby
Celimare, by Eugene Labiche, directed by Wendy Toye
Captivatin' Cole, conceived and compiled by Don Shipley, directed by Don Shipley and Judith Marcuse
A Day in the Death of Joe Egg, by Peter Nichols, directed by Don Shipley

Painting Churches, by Tina Howe, directed by Hutchison Shandro
An Inspector Calls, by J.B. Priestley, directed by Derek Goldby

McManus Studio:
The Music Cure, by G.B. Shaw
Piaf Encore, by Pauline LeBel and Don Shipley
'Night, Mother, by Marsha Norman
Letter from Wingfield Farm, by Dan Needles

1985/86

THE GRAND THEATRE COMPANY/
DON SHIPLEY ERA

LARRY LILLO

As the new season got underway, the board of directors was again searching for a new artistic director. In July 1985, Don Shipley had tendered his resignation, and was due to bow out of the job in January 1986. In November, Londoners learned that Larry Lillo would be stepping into the job of artistic director as of June 1, 1986. Lillo, aged 39, had spent ten years as a founding member, actor, writer and director of Tamahnous Theatre, Vancouver. He had also been a freelance director at theatres across Canada.

I'm excited about running a theatre. It presents lots of challenges but this is the right time for me to take on this task. I've freelanced for the past four years. That's been a great experience but what I've missed most is the sense of being in a community. I like the feeling of belonging, of doing shows for and about the group of people living in the area. It's very important for a theatre to make connections with its community.
— Larry Lillo (– *London Free Press*, November 19, 1985)

SIGN LANGUAGE

When I did Children of a Lesser God *I had to learn American Sign Language for the role. Three actors in the company were deaf, and my leading lady was also vocally silent. The*

Rod Beattie in **Letter from Wingfield Farm***, written by Dan Needles and directed by Douglas Beattie. It told the story of a jaded stockbroker who traded in his business suit and briefcase for a pair of rubber boots, overalls and a 100-acre farm. Walt Wingfield's rural neighbours were thoroughly amused at the city slicker's attempts to farm. The play was embraced by audiences everywhere it played. The trio of writer, director and actor went on to produce four more Walt Wingfield plays, truly a phenomenon in the history of Canadian theatre. (Photo: Elisabeth Feryn; Courtesy of The Grand Theatre)*

production had a translator for rehearsals, but once we opened the translator was gone. So I ended up translating backstage for the stage manager and the hearing cast. I'll never forget being on stage with a house of hearing-impaired students and having enough skill to answer questions myself, with sign language.
– David Ferry, actor/director

AN ADLIB HIGHLIGHT

Barnum, a musical extravaganza, was a co-production between the Grand Theatre and Winnipeg's Manitoba Theatre Centre. It was a huge show, featuring a cast of 23 on stage, and a full orchestra in the pit. The orchestra, belted out melodies, marches, ragtime and burlesque numbers. The show followed the 50-year career of Phineas T. Barnum, king of the big top, who made millions with his circus enterprise through sheer razzle and dazzle. "At one point in the opening night performance a snag interrupted the trapeze scene. Staying within character as the flamboyant flim-flam man, Rick Scott (starring as Barnum) stepped forward, nodded toward the troublesome aerial bar, quipped 'theatre humbug!' and offered the spectators their money back if the problem wasn't quickly remedied. The good-natured ad lib turned a potentially embarrassing moment into one of the evening's highlights." (– *London Free Press*, November 26, 1985)

THANKS A MILLION CAMPAIGN

Still staggering under the weight of a huge deficit held over from the 1983/84 season, and increased by a deficit incurred during the 1984/85 season, the Grand Theatre launched a seat endowment program, called the Thanks a Million campaign, in December 1985. Its goal was to raise $1 million to help retire the accumulated debt of $1.9 million. The campaign's honorary chairs were Hume Cronyn and Jessica Tandy; chairman was Peter White. It was hoped that this campaign, plus the theatre's endowment from the Wintario Challenge Fund, would end the theatre's debt.

LETTER FROM WINGFIELD FARM

The wildly popular *Letter from Wingfield Farm*, starring Rod Beattie as Walt Wingfield, and a variety of other characters, played the McManus Studio for one week in April 1985. The show was brought back for three weeks in September. Dan Needles based his play on his award-winning series of newspaper columns. Rod's brother, Douglas Beattie, directed the play.

Grand Theatre season:
Ring Round the Moon, by Jean Anouilh, directed by Derek Goldby
Children of a Lesser God, by Mark Medoff, directed by Michele George
Barnum, by Cy Coleman, Michael Stewart and Mark Bramble, directed by Don Shipley
Passion, by Peter Nichols, directed by Brian Rintoul
Noises Off, by Michael Frayn, directed by Derek Goldby

Pack of Lies, by Hugh Whitemore, directed by Stephen Katz

McManus Studio:
Letter from Wingfield Farm, by Dan Needles
Bob Berky – a clown, a juggler, a musician for children

Dance:
The National Ballet of Canada

Children:
Children's Film Series

THE GRAND THEATRE

1987-2001

Susan Wright in Shirley Valentine. *This was Susan Wright's last time on stage, for in December 1991, she, and her parents, died of smoke inhalation during a fire at a house in Stratford. The Grand Theatre named its Green Room the Susan Wright Lounge in her honour after the tragic event. (Photo: Robert Ragsdale; Courtesy of The Grand Theatre)*

1986/87

THE GRAND THEATRE/ LARRY LILLO ERA

"GETTING TO KNOW YOU"

It'll be a 'getting to know you' season. Not a season to strengthen me or the audience but a time for us to get acquainted with each other. The priority, financially speaking, is to break even. This theatre has to start making some money. I see incredible potential for this theatre despite the financial difficulties. If I didn't feel The Grand's future was going to be exciting and fun I wouldn't be here. There are lots of things easier to do.
– Artistic Director Larry Lillo (– *London Free Press*, February 1, 1986)

ERIC WOOLFE

Brighton Beach Memoirs was directed by Martha Henry who was quoted in the newspaper as saying: "It's American and I'm American-born. It also takes place in the year I was born (1937)." (– *London Free Press*, November 29, 1986) Henry worked with a solid cast: James Blendick, Paulina Gillis, Deborah Kipp, Mark Krause, Jennifer Link, Nicola Lipman and 15-year-old London actor Eric Woolfe. Woolfe appeared as Eugene, the youngest member of the family playwright Neil Simon invented, a family facing the trials of the great Depression that gripped North America in the 1930s. In Grade 10 at Oakridge Secondary School at the time he appeared in *Brighton Beach Memoirs*, Woolfe had previously appeared at The Grand in *A Christmas Carol*.

Artistic Director Larry Lillo in a candid photograph snapped in the lobby of the Grand Theatre. "Larry taught me that you can proceed with generosity." – John Cooper, director (Courtesy of the Grand Theatre)

YOUNG PLAYWRIGHT'S COMPETITION

Public readings of three winning scripts in the Young Playwrights' Competition took place in the McManus Studio in May 1987. Students between 12 and 19 years of age were eligible. There were cash prizes, as well as the workshopping of each winner's play by professional actors and directors, and a public reading.

I love this theatre! It has been a large part of my life since I was nine years old, taking drama lessons at LLT. Then I had my first part on The Grand stage, one line in The Sleeping Beauty. *I returned to The Grand when Larry arrived, and held a series of acting workshops which led to the Young Playwrights' Competition.*
– Caroline Dolny-Guerin, actress, educator, April 1988

Grand Theatre season:
Billy Bishop Goes to War, by John Gray and Eric Peterson, directed by Larry Lillo
Brighton Beach Memoirs, by Neil Simon, directed by Martha Henry
Gaslight, by Patrick Hamilton, directed by Larry Lillo
Master Harold and the Boys, by Athol Fugard, directed by Larry Lillo
Educating Rita, by Willy Russell, directed by Charles McFarland
Pump Boys and Dinettes, by John Foley, Mark Hardwick, Debra Monk, Cass Morgan, John Schimmel and Jim Wann, directed by Patrick Rose

McManus Studio:
The Komagata Maru Incident, by Sharon Pollock
The Occupation of Heather Rose, by Wendy Lill
Talking With, by Jane Martin

Local Production:
Wassail!, produced by Tom Siess, an old-fashioned Christmas celebration with traditional carols, Morris and Sword Dances, English Country Dances, and a Mummer's play

Other:
Young Playwrights' Competition

1987/88

THE GRAND THEATRE/LARRY LILLO ERA

RETIREMENT OF THE DEFICIT

"Grand wipes out deficit, starts season in the black," read the *London Free Press* headline on September 18, 1987. The deficit, which had grown to a staggering $2.2 million, was finally wrestled to the ground by the theatre's endowment fund, special grants, fundraising drives and a successful 1986/87 theatre season. The Ontario Citizenship and Culture Ministry helped with a $500,000 financial-stabilization grant, and with its Investment in the Arts program. Special contributions came from the Canada Council and from the Theatre's Grand Gesture campaign. The City of London assisted by extending the theatre's tax-exempt status permanently. As well, Artistic Director Larry Lillo's first season produced a $445,000 surplus. Expenses were cut and box office revenues increased. All this added up to the retirement of the deficit that had plagued the Grand Theatre since 1984.

MARTHA HENRY

In December 1987, Larry Lillo announced his decision to resign from his position as artistic director of the Grand Theatre, to become artistic director of the Vancouver Playhouse. Lillo's immediate plans included seeing the 1987/88 season through to the end, and planning the 1988/89 season. Early in January 1988, Martha Henry was announced as Larry Lillo's successor. At the time of the announcement she was busy directing George F. Walker's play, *Filthy Rich*.

What we've talked about, the board and I, is my being involved in three shows, whether that's acting or directing. But it seems to me that I might be useful here as an actor. There are things that I could play. I would like to keep the acting to a minimum. I might do one thing a year, but it's tricky, because then I have to hire my own director. It's kind of an odd position to be in.
– Incoming Artistic Director Martha Henry (– *London Free Press*, January 13, 1988)

RUSS DUFTON

The program for *Mass Appeal* featured The Grand's master electrician Russ Dufton: "I'm the guy who can put a complete stop to proceedings. You see, nothing can happen on stage without lights, and I control the lights. People tell me where to hang them. People tell me what colours they should be. People tell me how bright or dark each scene should look. People always seem to be telling me to do things. And I do them too (with the help of my computer lighting board). I'm a humble person. I can take orders."

It was during this show, with Russ at the lighting controls, that The Grand's lighting board fried during a Tuesday evening performance. The result was no stage lighting. Larry Lillo went on stage to appeal to the patrons, who upon hearing of the problem, clapped when told that the show would go on under the overhead work lights.

ROCK AND ROLL

In 1988 one of my fantasies came true. I got to play in a real rock and roll band. I had just left the acting business when from out of the blue I was asked to audition for John Gray's musical Rock and Roll. *I was, at that time, a real estate agent, and only went to the audition for a laugh. I played a song that*

Maurice Godin starred as Screamin' John in the production of **Rock and Roll.** *The opening night audience gave the cast a standing ovation. General manager Elaine Calder, called playwright John Gray and director Larry Lillo up on stage. "It was the opening night of* **Rock and Roll,"** *Calder remembered years later when speaking to a reporter about one of her favourite Grand Theatre moments. "It was Larry's last production. The audience was on its feet screaming. Everyone was so happy."(Courtesy of The Grand Theatre)*

I had been playing for years, one I knew well. I was asked to read a bit of the role and much to my surprise I was offered the role of Brent, the insurance salesman and straight-shooter of the group. I took a sabbatical from my real estate career, a sabbatical that has lasted ever since. In a clever casting move, Larry Lillo convinced Doug Bennett, of the band Doug and the Slugs, to play the lead singer of The Monarchs in the play – a band that soared from bad garage band to the toast of the

Maritimes. At this time Doug and the Slugs were enormously popular and Doug Bennett was used to life on the road, so eight weeks in one place was a shock to him, albeit a pleasant one. On the first day of rehearsal, he showed up just a little late and our stage manager, Dawn Brennan, shrugged it off, knowing she was in for the ride of her life. Doug then wondered out loud: 'Where are all the people who get you stuff?' We all laughed, and wondered what we were in for. What we were in for was a great show!! It was wildly popular and sold out practically every night. The band jelled and we became a very tight unit. Alec Willows on drums, Randy Kempf on bass, Doug Balfour our musical director on piano, Peter Brennan on backstage guitar, Louise Pitre as Shirley and myself on rhythm guitar.

The show also featured Maurice Godin as our ghostly inspiration Screamin' John. The show was a blast and remains to this day one of the highlights of my career on stage. During Act I, in the course of the medley, each night Doug Bennett would go out into the audience. Not in the conventional way through the aisles. No, he would just step off the stage and into the front row. He would find a very attractive female anywhere between the first and fifth rows and crawl over everyone to get to her. He would then lounge on, sit on, cajole and otherwise flaunt himself onto this victim, with the usual aside of: 'Mind yer own business,' to people in the immediate vicinity. He had incredible charm, charisma and chutzpah and always got away with it. The band, frequently in fits of laughter at his antics, would vamp away onstage until he returned. The audience ate it up and loved him. The saying on my now worn-out sweatshirt from that show sums it up: 'When the situation's out of control, You'd better ROCK, You'd better ROLL.'
– David Kirby, actor

MAURICE GODIN

The Grand Theatre means a great deal to me. It is a place that, for me, embodies all the beauty and magic that drew me to acting in the first place. I think that if you are lucky as an artist, you are provided with moments of challenge that give your work a lucidity and truth that move you up a level in your creative development. If you are very lucky, you recognize those moments when they happen. They may have been subtle, but I consider some of my most profound challenges happening on the stage at The Grand.

– Maurice Godin, Screamin' John in *Rock and Roll*

LARRY LILLO

I've had a wonderful time here in London, and I will keep a place in my heart for The Grand. May her seats always be warm!
– Larry Lillo, Artistic Director (– *Stage Write* newsletter, March 1988)

Grand Theatre season:
Born Yesterday, by Garson Kanin and Ruth Gordon, directed by Larry Lillo
Papers, by Allan Stratton, directed by James Roy
Filthy Rich, by George F. Walker, directed by Martha Henry
Top Girls, by Caryl Churchill, directed by Larry Lillo
Mass Appeal, by Bill C. Davis, directed by Miles Potter
Rock and Roll, by John Gray, directed by Larry Lillo

Plus:
Merely Players, with Barry Morse

McManus Studio:
Theatre Beyond Words
One Thousand Cranes, by Colin Thomas
New Canadian Kid, by Dennis Foon

Local Production:
Suffering Fools, by Herman Goodden
Wassail! produced by Tom Seiss

Dance:
Desrosiers Dance Theatre

Music:
Orchestra London, Beethoven Festival No. 2

Other:
Young Playwrights' Competition

1988/89

THE GRAND THEATRE/MARTHA HENRY ERA

Artistic Director Martha Henry. "I am honoured that my long association with the Grand Theatre has evolved into my first season as Artistic Director." – Martha Henry (– Season Brochure, 1988/89; Photo by V. Tony Hauser)

ELVIS IMPERSONATOR

In Toronto, Mississippi *I played an Elvis impersonator. Martha Henry was directing. I was terrified because I had to sing Elvis songs, and I have a low opinion of my singing ability. To boost my confidence, every time I rehearsed the songs, Martha would make all the women in the room, herself included, sit in front of me and scream like teenage groupies. It was a wonderful elixir.*

– David Ferry, actor/director

PAL JOEY

Pal Joey was a hugely popular musical hit that enjoyed three separate lives. It went on stage at the Grand Theatre in April 1989. Maurice Godin starred as the enjoyable cad Joey Evans, Martha

Henry as Mrs. Simpson, and Cynthia Dale as Linda English. The musical went to the National Arts Centre in Ottawa for three weeks. After that it returned to the Grand Theatre for performances in May.

I remember during rehearsals for Pal Joey, *when Shawn Austin-Olsen, playing the nightclub owner, had wanted to try some little bit of business with his cigar. He felt it would illuminate the character's pretension. It didn't work the first time in rehearsal. It didn't work the second time, either. It was getting in the way of Shawn's dialogue, and he was dropping the cigar half the time. Shawn was ready to forget about the bit, and he was sure that Martha Henry wasn't crazy about it. But, every time we came up to that point in the show, Martha insisted that he try the bit again. It got to the point where Shawn thought he was being punished. I soon learned that this was one of the hallmarks of Martha Henry's directing. She has faith in the instinct of the actor that verges on the implacable. Often times we come up with moments that expose the character in ways we had not intended, and Martha realizes the value in honouring those moments, as well as the ones which just show how clever we are. By the time we got to performance, Shawn's awkward attempt at facility with the cigar said more about his character's pathos and pretension than had he been adept.*

MORE WALT WINGFIELD
Rod Beattie was back at the Grand Theatre as Walt Wingfield, but this time he was on the mainstage, not in the McManus Studio. Dan Needles had written a second installment, *Wingfields's Progress.* It was such a success that it was held over for four extra performances.

Diana Leblanc as Lizzie Borden and Frances Hyland as The Actress in **Blood Relations.** *Set in 1902, the play's action took place ten years after the double murder of Lizzie's father and stepmother. Astrid Janson designed a breathtaking set that not only represented the home Lizzie shared with her family, but also exposed stage machinery, cables, curtains, catwalks and lights, thereby making it highly theatrical. The dominant colour on the set was blood red. Unforgettable. (Photo: Robert Ragsdale; Courtesy of The Grand Theatre)*

Rod Beattie is masterful in portraying multiple characters. Audiences couldn't get enough of Beattie as Walt, and as his neighbours. In speaking about the challenges of performing more than one character, Rod Beattie stated in an interview: "They (the cast of characters) are so distinct for me in my mind that I don't think I could confuse them. I don't always remember right away what they should say, but I always know who they are. …I've got to the point with this where I do see the guys. I've got to the point where I don't feel alone on stage. …And the other thing about that is that they surprise me sometimes. They change their attitudes to things and they'll show up some nights with something completely different. …One of the characters, the Squire, has always had arthritis, and at one point in the first scene that he had in *Letter from Wingfield Farm,* he looked at Walt and he was looking at *me* this time, not at Walt, and I could see on the Squire's face as clear as anything the thought, 'There. You thought it was funny, didn't you? That's what it feels like.' I expect to be hospitalized quite soon." (– *London Free Press,* April 14, 1989)

Grand Theatre season:
Biloxi Blues, by Neil Simon, directed by Martha Henry
The Man Who Came to Dinner, by Moss Hart and George S. Kaufman, directed by Larry Lillo
Blood Relations, by Sharon Pollock, directed by Martha Henry
Toronto, Mississippi, by Joan MacLeod, directed by Martha Henry
Pal Joey, by Richard Rodgers, Lorenz Hart and John O'Hara, directed by Larry Lillo and Martha Henry
Wingfield's Progress, by Dan Needles, directed by Douglas Beattie

McManus Studio:
A Midsummer Night's Dream, by William Shakespeare
Alligator Pie, by Dennis Lee
Two Weeks, Twice a Year, by Colin Thomas
The Crackwalker, by Judith Thompson
Hosanna, by Michel Tremblay

Local Production:
Wassail! produced by Tom Siess

Music:
Orchestra London, Beethoven Festival

Other:
Young Playwrights' Competition

1989/90

THE GRAND THEATRE/MARTHA HENRY ERA

SUBSCRIBERS

14,575 people subscribed to this season. In future seasons the theatre company would try to match the 1989/90 subscription total, without success. This was the season that became a benchmark of success, in terms of number of subscribers, for later seasons.

THE ROAD TO MECCA

The Road to Mecca by Athol Fugard, was about Miss Helen, a remarkable and artistic woman who was about to be moved into an old folks' home unless she could stand up for herself. The ageing artist was memorably played by Frances Hyland. Playing opposite her was William Hutt, so effective as a man of the cloth who had harboured loving feelings toward this woman for so long. Lit candles were everywhere on stage, and a propane stove was also part of the set design. Scenic artist, Lynne Millman, had to fireproof all the wood used on the set.

GLENGARRY GLEN ROSS

Glengarry Glen Ross was, in the words of Artistic Director Martha Henry, "hard-hitting, foul, fast and funny" (– *London Free Press,* October 14, 1980). The play investigated the world of the no-holds-barred American salesman. It was about obsession, making it, getting to the top, becoming a somebody, and grasping power. Playwright David Mamet used strong language in telling his story,

language too strong for many theatre-goers' tastes. Thirty patrons walked out during Act I of the first preview; 32 people went home during the second preview; and 45 patrons walked out into the night during the third preview. Actor Ron White was quoted in the paper as saying: "Some people just don't care to listen to language like that, and that's their right. You don't take it personally (when people leave the theatre). What might tend to break your concentration is if you know there's nothing overtly offensive about the piece and you've still got people walking out. Then you know they're walking out because they think you're a terrible actor, or something like that. Then you take it personally."
(– *London Free Press*, February 20, 1990)

It is an anti-establishment play. It's like taking Arthur Miller's character Willie Loman in Death of a Salesman *and putting him in the office, seeing him operate at work, not at home. The office is an environment that can breed man's inhumanity to man. Mamet's play is a heartfelt 'ouch' for salesmen who are victims of their own system. The idea that working men can behave the way these business cats do in this play is unsettling. The play makes people feel uncomfortable, and we were doing this unsettling, uncomfortable play in London, Ontario – the home of many salesmen, the home of a large insurance company. People do not like being made to feel uncomfortable.*
– John Cooper, director of *Glengarry Glen Ross*

Of nineteen letters received by Artistic Director Martha Henry, only one was supportive of the play. Henry addressed the controversy in the April 1990 edition of the theatre's newsletter, *Stage Write*: "I am at the moment replying to the letters I and the board have personally received about this production, most of them objecting to the language that the men in Mamet's play use. …I

Starring in the controversial play **Glengarry Glen Ross**, *by David Mamet, were: (front l. to r.)* **Garrison Chrisjohn and Ron White.** *(rear l. to r.)* **Jay Brazeau, Walter Massey, Ric Reid and Robert King.** *The rivetting play by David Mamet, directed by John Cooper, chronicled two days in the lives of a group of obsessed real estate salesmen. (Photo: Robert Ragsdale; Courtesy of The Grand Theatre)*

have tried to think how I feel when I see something in the theatre that upsets me. I certainly feel resentment and anger. The theatre is a powerful tool. The presence of living, breathing human beings in front of us, talking *to* us, overrides our common sense. We imagine that this experience is directly pointed at us, that the actors somehow knew we were going to be there, sitting in just that seat, and that they prepared a full onslaught for our benefit, to degrade us. ...Logically, of course, we know this isn't true. We know it's a play. ...I am responsible for the sensibilities of all my subscribers, all the time. The only way I can honour this responsibility is by bringing you work that I believe in. ...A bad play with the cleanest language in the world (or a good play, carelessly done), makes me angry and resentful and hurts us all, artists and audience." – Martha Henry

I was in a downtown gym and a fellow recognized me from the show Glengarry Glen Ross. *I was a little gun-shy of the public, since a very harmless looking older woman had slapped my face for 'bringing racism to London'. So it was with care that I started a conversation with this fellow. He was of Japanese heritage, although the Japanese homeland was a few generations ago. He mentioned that he liked the show, which was a relief to me. The show had struck a chord with him and he found it a good account of what he had to face in the city. Not to the extreme that Mamet's play had portrayed, but the intent of being 'not one of us.' He also mentioned that the friends with whom he had attended the performance, had found his reaction to the show very unacceptable, and he felt at that time that he may have lost four good friends because of it. When I asked why they didn't like his response, he said that it was their opinion that he only found it funny because the Japanese were not specifically singled out, and therefore he was a racist for*

laughing at the plight of other races. They continued that, had he had to face such attitudes he would not find it so amusing. When he explained that he faced these attitudes often in London, they would not believe him, and slammed him for overreacting to their comments. It was upsetting to him that these friends would not believe him and would not accept that, in this city of London, racism really was present in very subtle and overt ways, and that he was a target of it. He concluded that friends who would walk away from his point of view as unacceptable, without a dialogue of what the show and what London had to say, were not really friends at all.

– Ric Reid, actor

Grand Theatre season:
Bordertown Cafe, by Kelly Rebar, directed by Martha Henry
The Philadelphia Story, by Philip Barry, directed by Robin Phillips
The Road to Mecca, by Athol Fugard, directed by Diana Leblanc
Glengarry Glen Ross, by David Mamet, directed by John Cooper
Wingfield's Folly, by Dan Needles, directed by Douglas Beattie
Girls in the Gang, by John Roby and Raymond Storey, directed by Martha Henry

McManus Studio:
Schoolyard Games, by John Lazarus
Not So Dumb, by John Lazarus
Night Light, by John Lazarus
Warm Wind in China, by Kent Stetson
La Sagouine, by Antonine Maillet
Cecil and Cleopaytra, by Daniel Libman

Music:
Orchestra London, Mozart Festival

1990/91

THE GRAND THEATRE/MARTHA HENRY ERA

FARTHER WEST

The season opened with *Farther West*. Set in the 1880s, it tells the story of May Buchanan (played by Lorena Gale), a prostitute attempting to come to terms with her identity. Her desire for freedom and her search for a place where she can live without being judged, forces her to travel farther and farther west.

"We have nudity. We have rape. We have profanity, violence, death and a whole catalogue of unpleasantries," wrote critic Ian Gillespie in his review (– *London Free Press*, October 13, 1990) Director John Cooper had directed last season's controversy-magnet, *Glengarry Glen Ross*, and he was the director for *Farther West* as well. "Part of the gas of doing what we do is that you get to challenge people's ideas. Art is to challenge. Art is to invite you to look at something from an alternative perspective." – John Cooper (– *London Free Press*, October 6, 1990) Ten years later, during an interview, John Cooper gave credit to former Artistic Director Martha Henry for suggesting that he cast Lorena Gale in the lead role. "It was unusual for a black actor to be offered a lead role in a play at a regional theatre," Cooper said. "And it presented some pressure to the actor, who then had to claim her territory as the lead. But she had stellar moments in that production. *Farther West* is a very difficult play. It is operatic in size. The audience must buy into that scope, and it must also accept that the lead character, a prostitute, is a tragic figure. You cannot let this play get down to naturalism. Perhaps this production never quite flew. But bless Martha Henry for her courage."

During a preview performance of John Murrell's Farther West *I was part of a very unusual audience. It was one of those performances when nothing mechanical worked on stage and the audience wasn't into willing suspension of disbelief. It started with a nude scene of the lead actress. When she revealed herself in a voluptuous manner the audience got a little giddy. Then came the gun that wouldn't work. It was one of those moments when, after pulling the gun and aiming it at the intended victim and saying a long speech, the killer pulls the trigger and the victim dies. Well, not this time. Or the next five times that the actor pulled the trigger. Then he tried to strangle the intended victim. This did not look promising. So the killer and the intended victim just gave up and the victim fell over, dead. Some audience members started tittering, while others mumbled to one another. A boat was docked in real water on stage left. The actor was supposed to put the body of his beloved in the boat, untie it, and let it float out to sea. Well, he couldn't get it untied and when he had run out of lines trying to cover the time he was taking, he finally succeeded in getting it untied but he couldn't launch it. The boat would not budge. The audience got on him, snickering and guffawing. He lay draped over the bow of the boat sobbing. Was it the actor? or the actor-in-character? There was, by now, a restless energy in the audience and they waited to pounce on the next gaff. In the writing, there were a lot of repeats of the title,* Farther West. *And it seemed that pauses took place before the line, so the audience got to know when it was coming up and they actually jumped the cue at least twice, shouting "Farther West!" before the actor could say it. Later, in a long scene about one character's decision about life, an audience member didn't wait and shouted, "Why don't you go Farther West?" This brought the house down. The actors missed cues, sped through scenes*

Martha Henry and William Hutt co-starred in The Cocktail Hour. *"I finally had a chance to work with Peter Moss, a director I had long admired. He asked me to design the set and costumes for* The Cocktail Hour. *The Grand, under Artistic Director Martha Henry, was a superb machine, with the highest standards of any regional theatre in the country. The cast of William Hutt, Martha Henry, Peter Hutt and Kate Trotter was excellent. Working with Peter Moss was wonderful. That production will always have a rosy glow in my memory."*
– Maxine Graham, designer
(Photo: Robert Ragsdale: Courtesy of The Grand Theatre)

and just tried to get to the end. At the curtain call, the actors glared at us and we at them. It was the strangest feeling, and although I did not join in during the outbursts, I felt caught up in the energy of that audience. Is this what audiences were like in Shakespeare's time?

– Jim Shaefer, actor, director, teacher

FIRE

The opening scene in the hit show *Fire* was set in a church.

Members of the cast acted as church ushers and passed collection baskets among The Grand's audience members. The money that was raised was donated to the London Food Bank, Mission Services, and the Daily Bread foundation. Michael McManus starred as piano-thumping Cale, opposite Maurice Godin who played gospel-shouting Herchel. "I'm really playing. There is no piano roll. It's a lot of work, but I expect I'll make enough mistakes that it will be perfectly clear that I'm doing it myself."
– actor Michael McManus (– *London Free Press*, April 12, 1991)

The power of Martha Henry's faith in the actor was apparent when we did Fire *together. I was playing Hershel Blackwell, a young zealot who becomes a skilled practitioner in the exploitation of faith. In Act II, I led a revival meeting, which, on some nights, transcended a night in the theatre. Encouraged by Martha and the playwrights, Paul Ledoux and David Young, I sometimes stray from the script. I swear, there were nights where the spirit moved through the audience and those of us on stage, and it inspired people to testify. Yes, I am saying that people yelled 'Halleluiah!' and 'Amen!' in the house!*
– Maurice Godin

1991/92

THE GRAND THEATRE/MARTHA HENRY ERA

A REAL EYE-OPENER

One of the reasons that I felt good about taking over in London was that I assumed that I was very like the London population. I'm not a political activist. I haven't come from running a small left-wing theatre in Toronto. I'm pretty conservative and middle-class and all those things. Initially, I felt that as long as I thought a play was good and whole and written with integrity and a skilled pen, that it could stand on a stage anywhere. I thought if I liked a play, then my subscribers would too. It's been a real eye-opener. I'm beginning to realize that I have to be very careful how I put some plays in front of my audience. What I found was that if a subscriber didn't like one show, they'd complain. If they didn't like two, they would think seriously about resubscribing. And if they didn't like three, forget it.
– Artistic Director Martha Henry

ENTERTAINMENT

The 1990/91 season showed a deficit of $92,825. In order to rebuild attendance after producing challenging-yet-controversial productions like *Glengarry Glen Ross* and *Farther West* in recent seasons, the 1991/92 playbill emphasized entertainment. The more popular playbill prompted the Canada Council to encourage The Grand to return to more challenging material in the 1992/93 season. Artistic Director Martha Henry and administrative director

Grand Theatre season:
Farther West, by John Murrell, directed by John Cooper
The Cocktail Hour, by A.R. Gurney, directed by Peter Moss
Jacques Brel is Alive and Well and Living in Paris, by Valerie Moore
Woman in Mind, by Alan Ayckbourn, directed by Martha Henry
My Children! My Africa!, by Athol Fugard, directed by Maurice Podbrey
Fire, by Paul Ledoux and David Young, directed by Martha Henry

McManus Studio:
White Biting Dog, by Judith Thompson
Under the Skin, by Betty Lambert
My Boyfriend's Back and There's Gonna Be Laundry, written by and starring Sandra Shamas
Square Eyes, by Joanne James
Liars, by Dennis Foon
I Ain't Dead Yet, by Chris Heide
Land of Trash, by Ian Tamblyn

And:
Young Playwrights' Competition

Lascelle Wingate tried as best they could to please everyone. Fortunately, this "lite" season turned in a surplus of over $76,000.

SUSAN WRIGHT

A real crowd-pleaser was popular actress Susan Wright in *Shirley Valentine*. The one-woman comedy celebrated a middle-aged housewife who had an unappreciative husband and selfish children. She escapes her home in England by travelling to the Greek islands where she revels in life.

The show was a huge hit. Susan Wright, at the age of 44, was at the height of her career as one of Canada's hardest working, and most beloved actresses. As the show came to an end in London, there were plans to remount it at the Stratford Festival in the summer of 1992. Unfortunately, on December 29, 1991, Susan Wright, along with her parents Major John Wright and Ruth Wright, died of smoke inhalation when the home they were in, in Stratford, caught fire. The blaze destroyed the house. It was a devastating loss for Susan's three siblings, Anne, Janet and John, for her family of friends, and for Canada's theatre community. "She was at the peak of her powers. She gave a remarkable performance," Richard Monette, who had directed her in *Shirley Valentine*, was quoted as saying in the *Stratford Beacon Herald* (– January 30, 1992). A memorial service for Susan Wright and her parents was held at the Stratford Festival Theatre on January 2, 1992.

I've always loved the support that The Grand has offered its young audiences. My favourite memory is of Katherine. She was a new student at Catholic Central Secondary School, had never been in a theatre before and couldn't afford the low ticket price. I have a belief that everyone needs to experience the joy of live theatre, and my school backed me on that principle, so she got a free ticket. My one condition was that someday Katherine had to introduce someone else to theatre's magic by giving that person a free ticket. She got to see Shirley Valentine, *starring Susan Wright. It was perfect for Katherine, a play of dreams unrealized and new opportunities. The final wonderful moment of the captivating production had Shirley Valentine throwing her sun hat into the audience. It was inscribed: 'All my love, Shirley Valentine' and then signed 'Susan Wright.' Of course, Katherine was the one to catch it. The perfect ending to a perfect play. Unfortunately, only a few weeks later Susan Wright died in a house fire in Stratford. On the first day back in school in January, Katherine appeared at my office door with the hat, and with tears in her eyes . We talked about what a special thing had happened to her during her visit to the Grand Theatre. A few years later I was taking students to Stratford to see* Cyrano de Bergerac. *Many of the students were first-time theatre-goers, having been convinced to attend because I had told them the story of Katherine. We were leaving the theatre to board our bus when I heard my name called from a distance. There was Katherine, pulling her boyfriend who had the awed look of someone dazzled by incredible theatre. 'Sir,' she said, 'I've kept my promise!'*

– Mark Mooney, teacher, actor, director

DRESSING A SET

Former Grand Theatre props builder Irene Fretz remembers the set for *A Walk in the Woods* as the most magnificent she had ever seen on The Grand's stage, and Irene had helped dress many a Grand set. Designed by Leslie Frankish, this set contained no less than 500 square feet of chicken wire (the size of a football field) to create trees and branches, 19 gallons of glue, 1 kilometre of aircraft cable (plus the theatre's permanent 15 kilometres in the fly system), 15,000 individual squares of paper towels (to create tree bark), 20,000 handmade leaves, 72 feet of bicycle brake cable, 36 cubic feet of Spanish moss, 480 cubic feet of Styrofoam and 800 feet of steel tubing. These raw materials created a wood in the Swiss mountains, outside Geneva near the French border, all on The Grand's stage. Actor Peter Hutt portrayed an idealistic young American arms-control negotiator and James Blendick portrayed a cynical old Soviet official who has seen idealists come and go.

Grand Theatre season:
The Odd Couple, by Neil Simon, directed by Martha Henry
Shirley Valentine, by Willy Russell, directed by Richard Monette
A Walk in the Woods, by Lee Blessing, directed by Martha Henry
The Affections of May, by Norm Foster, directed by John Cooper
The Woman in Black, by Susan Hill, directed by Derek Goldby
The Perils of Persephone, by Dan Needles, directed by Douglas Beattie

McManus Studio:
My Boyfriend's Back and There's Gonna Be Laundry II...The Cycle Continues, by and starring Sandra Shamas
The Two-Headed Roommate, by Bruce McCullouch
If Betty Should Rise, by David Demchuk

Warriors, by Michel Garneau
Snowsuits, Birthdays and Giants, by Robert Munsch

And:
Young Playwrights' Competition
Twelve Angry Jurors, (on the mainstage) based on the play by Sherman L. Sergel, directed by Charlie Tomlinson a fundraising event for the theatre, starring members of the local legeal community: Geoff Beasley, Charles W. Brown, Gord Cudmore, Doug Dawson, Jane Ferguson, David Hamer, Mark Lerner, Anthony Little, Dave Little, Peter Mercer, Brian Phillips, Judy Potter, Paul Siskind and The Honourable Justice B. Thomas Granger

1992/93

THE GRAND THEATRE/MARTHA HENRY ERA

SOME STRONG RESPONSES

Live theatre, when it is done well, can evoke some strong responses from its audience. I remember such a moment at The Grand. We were enjoying a performance of Wrong for Each Other *when, in one touching scene, the play's comic back-and-forth gave way, for a moment, to a stab of pain. The two characters on stage, formerly a married couple, spoke angrily about their grief over her miscarriage – grief that eventually destroyed their marriage. A young woman sitting in front of me burst into tears and rushed out of the theatre, followed a moment later by her husband, who was also in tears. I overheard that same young woman in the lobby, later that evening, telling a friend that she had never been able to cry about her own miscarriage until that moment in the theatre. When Art imitates Life, it reaches out and pulls us in and makes us feel things we thought we had buried long ago. What a wonderful tonic!*

– Michele Ebel, theatre-goer

THE STILLBORN LOVER

Martha Henry first heard that playwright/novelist Timothy Findley was writing *The Stillborn Lover* when she and William Hutt were asked to act some lines from it for a television broadcast featuring Findley's work. At that time Henry thought the scenes were from a new novel by the prolific author, but she soon learned

Peter Donaldson and Sheila McCarthy starred in Norm Foster's charming romantic comedy Wrong for Each Other. *"Opening night. Nerves. I hadn't been on stage for ages and I had a two-month-old baby in the wings. The revolver got stuck and just…stopped. The audience laughed, we laughed and finally we got back on track. It was the best thing that could have happened that night. We had a blast after that! The show must go on, and around and around and around…" – Sheila McCarthy, actress (Photo: Robert Ragsdale; Courtesy of The Grand Theatre)*

that it was a play, which Findley had hoped would star Martha Henry and William Hutt. Set in the 1970s, William Hutt's character was a Canadian ambassador. A married man with a family, the ambassador has been having a discreet affair with a young Russian man. The KGB discovers this, kills the young man, and threatens to expose the ambassador's secret, unless he agrees to work for them. William Hutt's character reports the threat to his superiors. His loyalty is repaid by being thrown to the wolves, along with his ailing wife (played by Martha Henry) and his daughter (played by Kate Trotter). "Here is a man in terrible trouble, with a wife whose memory is in trouble. So, how do you recall what really happened? That was what was intriguing to me because there were so many possibilities to develop from the situation." – Timothy Findley (– *Stage Write* newsletter, spring 1993)

A TRIBUTE

On June 28, 1993, a Tribute in Celebration of Larry Lillo was held on the stage of the Grand Theatre. The former artistic director had died on June 2, from complications from AIDS. Martha Henry hosted the event.

Grand Theatre season:
The Dining Room, by A.R. Gurney, directed by Martha Henry
A Christmas Carol, from Charles Dickens, directed by Charlie Tomlinson
Wrong for Each Other, by Norm Foster, directed by Janet Wright
A Moon for the Misbegotten, by Eugene O'Neill, directed by Martha Henry
The Stillborn Lover, by Timothy Findley, directed by Peter Moss
Italian American Reconciliation, by

John Patrick Shanley, directed by Michael Shamata
The Wingfield Trilogy, by Dan Needles, directed by Douglas Beattie

McManus Studio:
The Paper Bag Princess and More Stories, by Robert Munsch
Slippery – You Can't Get There from Here, by Hermann Goodden;
Miss Julie, by August Strindberg,
Democracy, by John Murrell

Other:
Young Playwrights' Competition

1993/94

THE GRAND THEATRE/MARTHA HENRY ERA

ROOM FOR RISK

You have to have some room in there for risk or you can't call yourself a theatre.
– Artistic Director Martha Henry, *London Free Press*, October 23, 1993

"A GREAT PRIVILEGE"

London actor Aiden de Salaiz was cast as Tiny Tim in the production of Dickens' tale *A Chrsitmas Carol*. This was not the only time Grand Theatre audiences had the opportunity to watch this talented local actor on stage. He went on to act in *The Secret Garden*, *West Side Story* and *Guys and Dolls*.

I think it is a great privilege to be able to appear on a stage in a theatre that possesses so much beauty, magic and history, as does London's Grand Theatre. I have been extremely fortunate to be able to work with artists like William Hutt, Martha Henry and Miles Potter. The multitude of things I have learned are infinite! I worked quite closely with Mr. Hutt and I remember having a great time joking around with him during rehearsals, and offstage. He is one of the most hilarious and kindest men ever (not to mention a brilliant actor!). He is also a great piano player. I recall walking into the Jessica Tandy Rehearsal Hall and finding him at the piano, playing jazz. It has always been an honour to appear on The Grand's stage, as I think of the

Award-winning artist/designer Andrew Lewis cleverly and dramatically incorporated both Challener's proscenium arch mural and the ghost of Ambrose J. Small in his design for the season poster. The alleged ghost of The Grand, Ambrose J. Small, had captured the imagination of Grand Theatre audiences long ago, and would not loosen its grip. (Courtesy Andrew Lewis)

legends who have appeared there before me. In this aspect it is almost a place of reverence for me. I have a great deal of respect for the dedicated and hard-working people who help the theatre run every day. The legendary ghost story has always thrilled me. I would sometimes investigate the less occupied areas of The Grand hoping to see some evidence of Ambrose J. Small!
– Aiden de Salaiz, actor

DANCING AT LUGHNASA

Dancing at Lughnasa was an unforgettable and precious experience. It is one I will always be grateful for. There was a remarkable company, full of intensely talented people. It was, also, the last time I would share the stage with the gentle and so, so kind Roland (Roly) Hewgill, who passed away in 1998. The play was magical and we, as a company, felt surrounded by all the ghosts that playwright Brian Friel's Ireland and the Grand Theatre's history had to offer us. Janet Wright was our fearless director. Before we opened, she gathered us together and said: 'This is an amazing play about five amazing women who are fighting for their very survival – and we have to do it for Susan – we have to do it in her memory!' Susan was Janet's sister, actress Susan Wright, who had died with her parents in a house fire in 1991. Susan Wright was a beacon to us all – an actress who set standards few of us would ever even come close to matching in our careers. Every night we five Irish women danced that dance in her name and to her memory. For that period of time she danced with us.
– Kate Trotter, actress

MARTHA HENRY

Martha Henry has a magical, mysterious and eloquent way of speaking to an actor when she is directing, and it is more often

than not without the use of actual words. During the rehearsals of The Miracle Worker, *she would glide up on stage gently parting the energy without disturbing anyone's focus or concentration. Sometimes Martha would touch your arm, sometimes stroke your hair, sometimes, every so gently, squeeze your hand. She would make a sound, breathe in a certain way, give you a hug or a smile. You just knew what she wanted and how deeply you wanted to respond to that vision. She would glide back to her place at the director's table – touching someone else on her way – and the world of Helen Keller would grow richer. The production was finally full of those moments or unspoken truths and hopes and dreams and needs; an appropriate energy in which that play was cradled. We were a family. With Martha as the director nothing less is conceivable.*
– Kate Trotter, actress

Grand Theatre season:
Love Letters, by A. R. Gurney, directed by Martha Henry
A Christmas Carol, from Charles Dickens, directed by Miles Potter
Dial M for Murder, by Frederick Knott, directed by Derek Goldby
Dancing at Lughnasa, by Brian

Friel, directed by Janet Wright
I Ought To Be in Pictures, by Neil Simon, directed by Marti Maraden
The Miracle Worker, by William Gibson, directed by Martha Henry
Ned Durango Comes to Big Oak, by and directed by Norm Foster

McManus Studio:
Flowers, by Deborah Porter
Moonlodge, by Margo Kane
A Fertile Imagination, by Susan G. Cole
Murmel, Murmel, Mortimer, Munsch, by Robert Munsch

Other:
Young Playwrights' Competition

1994/95

THE GRAND THEATRE/MARTHA HENRY ERA

MARTHA HENRY'S LAST SEASON

Martha Henry's last season as artistic director was met with enthusiasm from theatre-goers. Not only was it an artistic success, but it was also a financial success. By season's end, the Grand Theatre had realized a surplus of $144,731. Commenting on the season, one former staff member said:

One of the great pleasures of working in theatre is getting to read the scripts. I remember the chills and excitement I felt when I finished Oleanna *by David Mamet. The final scene was just as powerful on the page as it was later portrayed on the stage. The conclusion was shocking, disturbing and violent. The play was a far cry from the typical crowd-pleasers most audiences prefer. I worried that the theatre's board of directors might not approve this particular play and instead insist upon a 'safer' play offering, that London theatre-goers might object, and thereby hamper ticket sales. It's a familiar dilemma – the need to satisfy subscribers, the theatre's bread and butter, versus an artistic director's responsibility to present great works; not only those that entertain, but also those that enlighten and expand the audience's horizons. It's along this fine line that the final playbill is chosen. Fortunately, the management team of Martha Henry and administrative director Lascelle Wingate presented two different playbills to the board; one dynamic, including* Oleanna *and* The Rez

Sisters; *the other a safer bill. The board backed the dynamic, adventurous playbill, after carefully discussing options and possible outcomes. And so began one of the Grand Theatre's most exciting seasons. Martha Henry left the theatre on an artistic and financial high note. The plays that had first been debated in the boardroom became the talk of the town. The theatre was buzzing all year. It was a magical time when everything came together; the marvellous scripts to work from, the casts, the crew, production and design teams, staff, board and community, all making it happen. Many familiar artists came back while new ones were welcomed into the fold. There are so many memorable stage moments, including Seana McKenna's* Search for Signs of Intelligent Life *in a universe full of stars, to John Thompson's amazing set design for* Whale Riding Weather *where water came crashing through the walls of the McManus Studio. On top of a full regular season there was a benefit performance of* The Caine Mutiny, *with a cast of local lawyers and Mr. Justice John F. McGarry in the starring role as Lt. Commander Queeg. Under Martha Henry's and Lascelle Wingate's wings, we were all one big happy family.*

– Christine Overvelde, former assistant to the Administrative Director, *de facto* producer of the McManus Theatre 1993 – 1996, co-producer of *The Caine Mutiny*, 1995

SPECIAL EFFECTS

For *The Secret Garden*, The Grand's carpenters built a revolve, which turned throughout the performance to expose three separate sets. The play ended in the garden, where roses had to magically bloom spontaneously. This effect was achieved by using 500 plastic roses, gently placed inside 500 condoms, arranged along compressed air wires. The effect was magical.

OLEANNA

David Mamet's *Oleanna* was about a male college professor (played by Rod Beattie) who is charged with sexual harassment by a female student (played by Sandra Oh). When he attempts a reconciliation, the encounter ends in violence. Audiences were warned in the season brochure that the play contained "adult situations and strong language." It was performed without an intermission. For ninety minutes audience members witnessed two characters trying to come to grips with a situation that spiralled downward. After each performance there was a talk-back session. With a moderator on hand in the Poster Lounge, over 100 people per performance gathered to discuss what they had seen. The play evoked strong emotions, strong comments and rivetting debate.

While actress Sandra Oh was preparing for her role as Carol in the controversial David Mamet play Oleanna, *she was billeted with me and my husband Stephen at our London home. At the time Sandra was reading Susan Faludi's book* Backlash: The Undeclared War Against American Women. *I also happened to be reading the same book at the same time. I remember, on one of Sandra's days off, that she and I were lounging on my bed, both reading our separate copies of* Backlash. *Stephen rushed into the room, jumped on the bed between us and said, "Hello ladies!" Then he gave both Sandra and me a huge kiss on our foreheads.*

–Young In Turner, former theatre employee

THE REZ SISTERS

Doing a play like The Rez Sisters *in stately London was a real risk. Although Martha Henry had not seen a production, after she met playwright Tomson Highway the year before when he was receiving an honorary degree from the University of*

Western Ontario, she became interested in his work. She and I had gone to the luncheon prior to the ceremony, and afterwards we brought him back to The Grand where we showed him the building. When his play showed up on Martha's playbill for 1994/95, I was very excited, and had great confidence that we could pull it off. We were very careful in letting our subscribers know what the play was all about, and particularly informing them about the strong language used in the play. Then we got in touch with artists and artisans from the Native community and asked them to set up their booths in the lobbies. I had never seen The Grand's sterile lobbies look so lively. I knew it was important to create an atmosphere for the audience, from the moment they entered the theatre's doors. It sort of prepared them for what they were about to see.

– Lascelle Wingate, former Grand Theatre administrative director

This trio of talent lit up the stage when, for the Christmas holiday season, Maggie Blake, Aiden de Salaiz (centre) and Eric Woolfe starred in **The Secret Garden.** *Former Artistic Director Bernard Hopkins was also in the cast.(Photo: Robert Ragsdale; Courtesy of The Grand Theatre)*

REKINDLE A PASSION

In May 1995, the Grand Theatre launched a major capital renewal appeal, entitled Rekindle a Grand Passion. Nancy F. McNee was the chair of the campaign. The campaign raised over $1.4 million and helped pay for such improvements to the theatre as upgrades to the electrical and lighting systems, repairs to the roof and skylights, upgrades to the stage, and replacement of the air exchange and control system. The campaign came not a moment too soon; during the run of *Hay Fever*, the auditorium's temperature soared to an uncomfortable 35 degrees celsius. The lighting console crashed during a preview performance of *The Secret Garden*, leaving the actors in the dark. And when the National Ballet toured to The Grand in March 1995, propane heaters had to be pressed into service to warm the stage.

RAIN INSIDE

Forever Plaid was a huge success, a real crowd-pleaser, when it played The Grand. I clearly remember the May 10 matinee. I was in the lobby and glanced at the monitor that carried a black and white broadcast of the performance-in-progress. There, on the surface of the stage, were huge rectangular swatches of grey things. I knew that the stage design did not include huge swatches of grey things so I asked the front-of-house manager what was going on. Jennifer Duncan said that the torrential rain falling outside was also falling inside. The roof over the stage was leaking. Despite the unexpected shower, the four actors and pianist Christopher Mounteer weren't missing a beat. Towels began to appear from offstage. It was the towels that were showing up as huge swatches of grey on the monitor.

I distinctly remember the moment I first became aware of our extra 'special effect.' The actor playing Sparky was singing 'Catch a Falling Star' from a chair downstage right, and the rest of us were singing backup, upstage left. We backup guys were standing posed together in a group and my two partners were busy playing the spoons as percussive accompaniment to the song. But I was blocked to just stand and gaze up towards the heavens. Seconds after I looked up I became aware of a dripping sound, and as my eyes became adjusted to the lighting effect which had just taken place, I was able to see that there was a steady stream of rain falling a few feet in front of our little group! The audience must have thought we were paying homage to a production of Singing in the Rain. *None of us were getting wet, and the 'shower' could have not been more strategically placed! Though the rain did continue for a little while, it started to taper off after its spectacular entrance. Not knowing what else to do, and since there didn't seem to be any danger, we simply went offstage and got towels from the assistant stage manager to try and soak up the excess water while continuing with the show. A bit of choreography had to be steered around the worst of it, and our audience volunteer had to be alerted as she came on stage to help us with a song. The only downside was when John Devorski slipped on the wet stage and fell to his knee. Luckily he was not seriously injured and the show continued. The incident even got written up in the newspaper a few days later.*

– Jim Soper, director, actor

MICHAEL SHAMATA

After an extended nationwide search for Martha Henry's successor, Michael Shamata was appointed artistic director. Shamata came to the Grand Theatre from Theatre New Brunswick where he had been working as artistic director.

Grand Theatre season:
Hay Fever, by Noel Coward, directed by Marti Maraden
Search for Signs of Intelligent Life in the Universe, by Jane Wagner, directed by Miles Potter
The Secret Garden, from Frances Hodgson Burnett, directed by William Hutt
Oleanna, by David Mamet, directed by Martha Henry
The Rez Sister, by Tomson Highway, directed by Larry Lewis
Broadway Bound, by Neil Simon, directed by Martha Henry
Forever Plaid, written and directed by Stuart Ross
McManus Studio:
Murmel, Murmel, Mortimer, Munsch, from Robert Munsch
Close to the Bone, by Sensible Footwear (Alex Dallas, Alison Field, Wendy Vousden)
All Fall Down, by Wendy Lill

Whale Riding Weather, by Bryden MacDonald

And:
The Caine Mutiny Court-Martial (on the mainstage), by Herman Wouk, directed by Charlie Tomlinson, produced by Christine Overvelde and Jim Dunlop; a fundraising event starring members of the local legal community: Serge Anissimof, Malcolm Bennett, Paul M. Bundgard, James Caskey, Ian Dantzer, Jim Dunlop, David Hamer, Stephen Jarrett, John Judson, Ian Leach, Dan Mailer, Marko Pasic, Alan Patton, Mary F. Portis, Peter H. Schwartz, Andy Wright, with Mr. Justice John F. McGarry

Local Production:
The Dark Ages, by Herman Goodden

Other:
Young Playwrights' Competition

1995/96

THE GRAND THEATRE/MICHAEL SHAMATA ERA

CAT ON A HOT TIN ROOF

Tennessee Williams' classic drama *Cat on a Hot Tin Roof* starred Seana McKenna as Maggie the Cat and Stuart Hughes as Brick. These two actors brought sizzle and spark to the production, which was directed by Miles Potter. Douglas Campbell was a delight as Big Daddy and anyone who saw this wonderful production could not forget the late Marion Gilsenan as Big Mama explaining over the telephone that her husband's suffering was just a "SPASTIC CO-LON!" The line reached the back wall of the balcony each time it was uttered.

This play is full of surprising classical allusions. It struck me when I first read it that it was more like a great Greek drama than a soap opera. Tennessee Williams follows a classical line: his character of Big Daddy is like the king who is suffering a great sickness and has to pass on his kingdom. In this instance the kingdom is a sprawling plantation on the banks of the Mississippi River. He has two sons: Brick who fulfills the role of the good prince, but who has a spiritual illness, and Gooper (played by Ric Reid) the bad prince, who is only interested in the material world. Who will gain the kingdom? It is Maggie who represents the life force in this scenario - she is the only one who strives to preserve the kingdom, to help her husband Brick and herself to fulfill their destiny. It is a titanic story.' – Miles Potter, director (– *Stage Write* newsletter, September, 1995)

A PREDICTION?

In September 1995 I attended a lecture delivered by Artistic Director Michael Shamata on his upcoming maiden season at The Grand. One of the plays on the bill was Dracula, *which had been slated as the 1927 stage version by John Balderston and Hamilton Deane. Shamata, however, announced he was abandoning this stiff warhorse in favour of his own adaptation which would, he stated, be more faithful to novelist Bram Stoker. I had always enjoyed the novel and I asked him how he was going to capture the sweep of the original in the confines of The Grand's stage. 'Well, you'll just have to buy a ticket and find out, won't you?' he shot back. I remember thinking, at that time, that The Grand was in trouble.*
– Christopher Doty, subscriber

A VISIT FROM BATS

Word had travelled fast about the December production of Dracula. *This became apparent on August 14 when a bat disturbed an audition in the fifth floor rehearsal hall. No sooner had Michael Shamata, assisted by Young In Turner, settled in for a day of general auditions, than the bat appeared apparently out of nowhere and temporarily halted the proceedings. It fell to John Stephenson, technical director, to pursue the bat and make sure it found its way, somewhat dazed, to the outside world. Mission accomplished. Until Bat #2 began careening around the hallway outside the fly gallery. John donned gloves and went to work. This bat was safely dispatched into the wild blue yonder. Bat #3 appeared within minutes in the design room, but this one did not go so quietly. He was wide awake, unlike his two bat accomplices. Eventually he was coaxed into a big black bag, and John flung him from the theatre. It was unclear why they chose audition day for*

The comedy **Goodnight Desdemona, Good Morning Juliet** *romped across the stage and featured (l. to r.) Stephanie Morgenstern, Nancy Palk and Jonathan Crombie. It was like watching Shakespeare being turned upside down and inside out. (Photo: Elisabeth Feryn; Courtesy of The Grand Theatre)*

their visit, but perhaps it had something to do with Junior McInnis, who had that morning applied spit and polish to the stage door sign. Could he have stirred up a bat's nest? Or did the trio of bats plan to crash the auditions? Hmmm. Only Ambrose J. Small knows for sure.

– Sheila Johnston (– *Stage Write* newsletter, September 1995)

STAGE FANGS

I remember accompanying actor Stephen Russell to the dentist.

My dentist, Chris Storey, is a prosthodontist. He makes crowns and bridges. So, when Stephen was cast as Dracula, *he went to Chris for a fitting. I called Chris, and The Grand, and asked for permission to shoot film. So, there we were, in Chris's office, as he tried out Stephen Russell's stage fangs. It was a first for everybody!*

– Janice Zolf, arts and entertainment reporter, CFPL TV, London

A DEFICIT

This season posted a deficit of $274,201. Unfortunately, this deficit grew throughout the next four seasons. The deficit that started in 1995/96 at over $200,000 grew, unabated, to $1,100,000 by the spring of 1999.

Some of the magic that had returned to the Grand Theatre, first under the leadership of the late Larry Lillo, and then sustained throughout the tenure of former Artistic Director Martha Henry, seemed to gradually slip away between 1995 and 1999, and with it slipped the financial health of the Grand Theatre.

Grand Theatre season:
Later Life, by A. R. Gurney, directed by Michael Shamata
Cat On A Hot Tin Roof, by Tennessee Williams, directed by Miles Potter
Dracula, from Bram Stoker, directed by Michael Shamata
If We Are Women, by Joanna McClelland Glass, directed by Joseph Ziegler
Goodnight Desdemona, Good Morning Juliet, by Ann-Marie MacDonald, directed by Jackie Maxwell

A Little Night Music, by Stephen Sondheim, directed by Michael Shamata

McManus Studio:
Poking Fun, by Sensible Footwear (Alex Dallas, Alison Field and Wendy Vousden)
Not Spain, by Richard Sanger
Frida K, by Gloria Montero
A Promise is a Promise, from Robert Munsch
Toronto at Dreamer's Rock, by Drew Hayden Taylor

Local Production:
I Hate Hamlet, by Paul Rudick
Nature Abhors a Vacuum, by Herman Goodden
Joseph and the Amazing Technicolour Dreamcoat, by Andrew Lloyd Webber, directed by Don Fleckser
(on the mainstage)
Baltimore Waltz, by Paula Vogel, produced by Louise Fagan

1996/97

THE GRAND THEATRE/MICHAEL SHAMATA ERA

UNUSUAL EFFECTS

For the production of *Atlantis*, the Grand Theatre's stage was literally flooded. Seven inches of water covered the entire surface of the stage. Tanja Jacobs and Benedict Campbell spent the entire play ankle-deep in water. In order for the actors to keep as warm as possible, the water was kept at a little above room temperature. As a result the theatre's auditorium turned into something resembling a sauna. Humidity made some audience members very uncomfortable. As Rick Whelan wrote in his review, "And then there's the water. For reasons which really escape me, the entire evening is swamped in 4,000 gallons of water. In a recent interview, the actors said they thought the addition of authentic H2O somehow made the play more dangerous. I wonder. I found myself asking myself a bunch of questions not directly related to the play's happenings; like 'How brave these actors must be to be cavorting in water in the midst of all this high-voltage electrical lighting' and 'How much did this mini-reservoir cost, anyway?!' One gets the sense that the water made irrelevant demands on the creative process. 'Gee, we've got all this water to play with. Let's really make the most of it!' If the play had gone on much longer, jet-skis and pontoon shoes would have been a distinct possibility. For me, the chief pleasure of the evening was watching the different luminescent patterns that lighting designer Robert Thomson has managed to coax out of the water's many reflections. Unlike the play itself, this bit of stage

Patricia Gage (left) and Liisa Repo-Martell as mother and daughter in The Glass Menagerie. *This Tennessee Williams classic, which premiered in 1944, never failed to deeply move the emotions of audience members. the Grand Theatre's audience was hushed each night as Liisa Repo-Martell and James Gallanders, playing her Gentleman Caller, sat centre stage, lit by a candelabra, and opened their hearts to one another. (Photo: Elisabeth Feryn; Courtesy of The Grand Theatre)*

artistry was truly inspired." (– Rick Whelan, *Stratford Beacon Herald*, November 11, 1996)

The November 7 show report mentioned something strange: "In Act II the actors noticed a light on the house right side of the orchestra section – some kind of mysterious gold band." This light was not part of the lighting design. Could it have been another manifestation of the alleged "Ghost of The Grand"? Was Ambrose J. Small acting up again?

"ALIVE AND WELL"

Michael Shamata directed Great Expectations *with his usual attention to detail and focus on the integrity of the story. He staged a spectacular scene for poor, sad Miss Havisham during which she (well…I) spun in a circle of flames. Pieces of gossamer-like costume parts appeared to catch fire as I screamed out her last anguished cries of repentance and sorrow. Lighting effects, staging and sound all conspired to create a theatrical moment of stage truth. One night, Rob Wellan, publicity director, came back stage. He was holding the hand of a young boy from the audience. Rob requested that I speak with the young lad, because the boy refused to leave the theatre until he could see for himself that Miss Havisham was, in fact, alive and well and removing her make up!*
– Kate Trotter, actress

THE GRAND THEATRE

Grand Theatre season:
Private Lives, by Noel Coward, directed by Glynis Leyshon
Atlantis, by Maureen Hunter, directed by Peter Hinton
Great Expectations, from Charles Dickens, directed by Michael Shamata
The Glass Menagerie, by Tennessee Williams, directed by Miles Potter
Three Tall Women, by Edward Albee, directed by Joseph Ziegler
Money and Friends, by David Williamson, directed by Michael Shamata
Wingfield Unbound, by Dan Needles, directed by Douglas Beattie
A Closer Walk with Patsy Cline, by Dean Regan, directed by Max Reimer

McManus Studio:
Mad Ballades, by Kate Hennig and Alan Laing
Big Face, by Marion De Vries
Beo's Bedroom, by Ned Dickens
Little Sister, by Joan MacLeod

Other Productions:
The Zoo Story, and *The Shadow of the Glen*, Stagecraft projects, produced by Douglas Beattie Productions

Dance:
The National Ballet of Canada
Danny Grossman Dance Company
Margie Gillis

Music:
An Evening with Michael Burgess

1997/98

THE GRAND THEATRE/MICHAEL SHAMATA ERA

MOLLY SWEENEY

Brian Friel's haunting play *Molly Sweeney* was directed by Miles Potter. Molly, played by Nancy Palk, is blind and lives in a world she has constructed and understands. Her husband, played by R.H. Thomson, wants her to change her life, and encourages Molly to undergo an operation that may restore her sight. It was a poignant story, played beautifully by three extraordinary actors. John Neville, last seen at The Grand during the 1983/84 repertory season, was especially moving as the doctor who saw Molly's operation as an opportunity to restore his broken reputation in the medical field.

Neville received the Order of the British Empire for his distinguished career on the British stage. After moving to Canada he was artistic director of the Citadel Theatre (Edmonton), the Neptune Theatre (Halifax) and the Stratford Festival. In the late 1990s, he was often seen in films and in television series.

TWO GREAT ARTISTS

How does an art historian meet two great artists of the twentieth century long after they've died? She attends the Grand Theatre's 1996 production of Gloria Montero's Frida K, *and the 1998 production of Steve Martin's* Picasso at the Lapin Agile. *Frida Kahlo and Pablo Picasso came to life for me as I watched actors Allegra Fulton and Alex Ferguson capture the essence of these innovative painters. When I delivered slide-illustrated lectures for The Grand in conjunction with each of*

In the hit comedy **Picasso at the Lapin Agile**, *by Steve Martin, Daryl Shuttleworth (left) played café owner Freddy and David Storch made a perfect Albert Einstein. This play was a zany romp. Set in Paris, France, in an alcohol-soaked café, the nineteenth century had just ended and the twentieth century was just beginning. Picasso played by Alex Ferguson, and Einstein and an assortment of supporting players, engaged in witty banter and repartee. At the final curtain, when the set literally fell silently away, revealing a deep blue, night sky dotted with a million tiny stars, there was an audible intake of breath by each audience, each performance. Magical. (Photo: Elisabeth Feryn; Courtesy of The Grand Theatre)*

these productions, I was elated that the stars themselves were there. How many art historians can say: 'Here is a self-portrait of Picasso from 1901 – would you mind standing beside it, Pablo?'

– Sonia Halpern, theatre-goer, art historian

John Douglas, drama teacher at London's Westminster Secondary School, brought his idea of a show to be performed by local high school students at The Grand, to Artistic Director Michael Shamata. Douglas' idea was greeted with enthusiasm by the artistic director. After the two discussed some ideas for an appropriate play, Shamata suggested *West Side Story*, an idea that John Douglas fully supported. Thus was born The Grand's High School Project.

Grand Theatre season:
Sleuth, by Anthony Shafer, directed by Michael Shamata
Vigil, by Morris Panych, directed by Patrick McDonald
A Christmas Carol, from Charles Dickens, directed by Michael Shamata
Molly Sweeney, by Brian Friel, directed by Miles Potter
Picasso at the Lapin Agile, by Steve Martin, directed by Peter Hinton
Who's Afraid of Virginia Woolf?, by Edward Albee, directed by Michael Shamata
Mom's the Word, written and performed by Linda A. Carson, Jill Daum, Alison Kelly, Robin Nichol, Barbara Pollard and Deborah Williams
Red Rock Diner, written and directed by Dean Regan

High School Project:
West Side Story, by Leonard Bernstein and Stephen Sondheim, directed by Michael Shamata

McManus Studio:
Mid-Life Crisis, by Sensible Footwear (Alex Dallas and Alison Field)
Miss Chatelaine, written and performed by Damien Atkins
End of Season, by Noel Greig
The Nightingale
One Thousand Cranes, by Colin Thomas

Other:
Ghosts, by Henrik Ibsen, a Stagecraft project, produced by Douglas Beattie

Local Production:
Gathering of the Arts, event co-ordinated by Rick Verrette, Sheila Johnston and Sue Perkins

Dance:
Toronto Dance Theatre
Ballet British Columbia
Ballet Jorgen

1998/99

THE GRAND THEATRE/MICHAEL SHAMATA ERA

THE STONE ANGEL

Because I was invited to give a talk on Margaret Laurence and her book The Stone Angel, *as part of the Grand Theatre's lecture series, I had the opportunity to sit in on the first reading of the script of* The Stone Angel *by the newly assembled cast. I keenly observed the uncertain actors tentatively reading their lines (in the presence of the painfully expressionless playwright). Sure, staging a play is a process, I thought, but will this complex production actually be ready for its much-anticipated run? Several weeks later when I attended a per-*

On the season's opening night for Cabaret, Grand Theatre volunteer Al Green, dressed to the nines, warmly welcomed theatre-goers. "After the curtain came down on opening night of Cabaret, my grandson, Michael Suitor, went around to the stage door to get autographs from the acting company. He was hoping to get Jeff Hyslop's autograph, especially, and Jeff's sister kindly escorted him backstage to get it."
– Al Green, Grand Theatre volunteer (Courtesy London Free Press)

Michelle Lundgren, Diana Coatesworth, Andrew Petrasiunas and Eric James in the sassy production of **Side by Side by Sondheim,** *directed by John Gerry. This cabaret show was staged in the McManus Studio and raised the roof each night. (Courtesy* **London Free Press***)*

formance, it was a highly polished, perfectly orchestrated, expertly acted, intensely emotional play. I was utterly amazed by the evolution. The magic of theatre? I'd call it a lot of dedication and hard work.

– Dr. Monda Halpern, theatre-goer, historian

A MIDSUMMER NIGHT'S DREAM

In February 1999, Artistic Director Michael Shamata announced his resignation from the Grand Theatre. Before his departure, he directed the Grand Theatre High School Project production of Shakespeare's *A Midsummer Night's Dream*, which was on stage in May.

THE KEY TO SUCCESS

In reviewing *I Love You, You're Perfect, Now Change*, Noel Gallagher said: "The key to the show's success is the casting of four very talented actors, Milo Shandel, Blythe Wilson, Charlotte Moore, and Londoner Edward Glen, who make a formidable stage team. The fast-paced program, directed and choreographed by Timothy French, connected with its audience. Anyone who's ever dated, mated or coupled with another human being will be all too familiar with its themes." (– *London Free Press*, June 6, 1999)

Grand Theatre season:
Cabaret, by Joe Masteroff, John Kander and Fred Ebb, directed by Michael Shamata
Ethan Claymore, by Norm Foster, directed by Miles Potter
The Wind in the Willows, from Kenneth Grahame, directed by Michael Shamata
The Stone Angel, from Margaret Laurence, adapted by James W. Nichol, directed by Janet Wright
Homeward Bound, by Elliott Hayes, directed by Joseph Ziegler
The Importance of Being Earnest, by Oscar Wilde, directed by Michael Shamata
Billy Bishop Goes To War, by John Gray and Eric Peterson, directed by John Gray and Eric Peterson
I Love You, You're Perfect, Now Change, by Joe DiPietro and Jimmy Roberts directed by Timothy French

High School Project:
A Midsummer Night's Dream, by William Shakespeare, directed by Michael Shamata

McManus Studio:
Kicked, by Michael Healey
Bang, Boy, Bang, by Edward Roy
Peacemaker, by David Holman
New Canadian Kid, by Dennis Foon

Dance:
Toronto Dance Theatre
Montreal Dance
The National Ballet of Canada
Local Production:
Side by Side by Sondheim, directed by John Gerry, produced by Fountainhead Theatreworks
Wassail! Produced by Tom Siess

1999/2000

THE GRAND THEATRE/KELLY HANDERK ERA

THE ANGELS AND HEROES CAMPAIGN

In October 1999, the Grand Theatre's financial crisis, which had remained out of the public eye since the deficit began to accumulate in 1995, burst into the spotlight when the October annual general meeting was cancelled at, literally, the last moment. To raise much needed funds The Angels and Heroes Campaign was initiated. The goal was to raise $500,000 in three months. Cash donations, pledges and gifts-in-kind were accepted, as the Grand Theatre tried to achieve the goal. Don Smith came on board as the campaign's chair at the rescheduled annual general meeting, held on November 23, 1999. The remainder of 1999 and early 2000 was a tense time for the Grand Theatre. But miracles had happened at the "Grand Old Lady of Richmond Street," and once again the theatre was hoping for a miracle.

SHE STOOPS TO CONQUER

Oliver Goldsmith's classic comedy *She Stoops To Conquer* hit the stage under the direction of Christopher Newton. His assistant director noted: "*She Stoops to Conquer* contains all the best bits of plays we love. It's a fairy tale, with real underpinnings. There's an odd – not evil, but odd – stepmother, two sets of lovers, classic bits we recognize from Shakespeare…it's familiar, it's been done before and since. Sex is dealt with quite frankly. Everyone is quite eager to get on with it." – Nicholas MacMartin (– *Scene Magazine*, January 13, 2000)

SUBSCRIBERS SPEAK

Jason Sherman's play *Patience* enjoyed many productions across Canada. One of these was at the Grand Theatre. "I saw *Patience* and was struck with the power of the play. The star, Jim Mezon, was quite wonderful and the staging was very creative. The plot development was a little mystifying, as to how it all worked out and who paired off with whom at the end."– D. Jones, subscriber

Over the years I have been delighted to host actors and other theatre professionals in my home. I have been given so many backstage tips about how to audition, perform and stage productions. Ten years ago actor Victor Ertmanis was performing at The Grand in a production of The Odd Couple. *He was going through his performances with a bad back he had injured while bowling. He was seeing a chiropractor as often as he could work it in. This season, Victor returned in* Patience, *and I watched him wait for a malfunctioning set piece to move into place, without losing the moment. I am in awe of what people do on stage to tell the story in spite of personal or mechanical problems.*

– Ann MacMillan, drama teacher, subscriber

ALAN ACKBOURN

As theatre reviewers for Scene Magazine, *Patricia Black and I were invited by The Grand to deliver the two lectures for the comedy* Communicating Doors *by Alan Ackbourn. I once had a small connection with Sir Alan. When I was living in Scarborough, a seaside resort town on the east coast of Yorkshire, England, he came to join the Stephen Joseph Theatre. I attended most of the performances, being very keen on all types of theatre in those days, too. A few years later he returned as artistic director and the theatre became a year-*

round performance space. I left Scarborough at the end of the 1950s, but retained my memories. When I began the research for the lectures at The Grand I found my way to the web site for the Stephen Joseph Theatre. From there it was a small step to send an e-mail to the famous playwright/director, so, I asked him to provide a capsule comment on the play. Back came the answer: "Take a generous sprinkling of the movie Back to the Future, add a pinch of Hitchcock's movie Psycho, and stir well." So that is how I began my part of the lecture, which I felt was much enhanced by Sir Alan's personal contribution.
– Sheila Martindale, critic, writer

STUDENT AUDIENCES

In the early 1990s as a teacher at London South Secondary School, I was moved by my love of theatre to try to get as many students as possible to attend The Grand's wonderful student subscription series. With the help of the wonderful Grand staff, and a sympathetic school administration, I developed a plan. In the summer, a play list and a permission form was mailed to all students. Parents were encouraged to fill out the permission forms and send in their cheques during the first week of school. Before developing this play, I had been bringing up to 90 students to the student matinees, and so was astounded that first year to sell over 150 subscriptions. The number has never dipped below that, and during the 1999/2000 season I brought 172 South students to each of the mainstage plays. The students I bring pay attention, and enhance the theatre experience for both themselves and the actors. The Grand Theatre's attention to student audiences has made all this possible, no doubt encouraging new generations of theatre goers.
– Jack Beattie, former LLT actor, drama teacher, subscriber

London actors Hazel Desbarates and Dave Semple appeared in Driving Miss Daisy, *playing mother and son in the poignant drama. "I played the title role in* Driving Miss Daisy *for the new theatre company, Fountainhead Theatreworks. Before we opened, many Londoners told me how much they had liked Jessica Tandy in the role in the movie version, so it was very rewarding to have an extremely positive reaction to the show. I think I incorporated a great deal of my late mother's character into the role of Miss Daisy. I felt that the two women were kindred spirits. During the past few years I have spent a great deal of time visiting my mother in a local nursing home before she died, and I had first-hand awareness of the very old. In fact, I think that my work in this role was done in memory of my mother. I was so happy when it was such a success." – Hazel Desbarats, actress (Photo: Ken Wightman; Courtesy of* The London Free Press*)*

2000/01

THE GRAND THEATRE/KELLY HANDERK ERA

GESTURE OF SUPPORT

After the financial crisis endured by the Grand Theatre in 1999/2000, it came as a relief that the City of London boosted its aid to the theatre. On July 4, 2000, the City announced that financial stability, in the form of a $1.1 million loan guarantee from the City, would be enjoyed by the theatre. "The city also pledged to boost to as much as $450,000 its annual operating grant to The Grand, provided the theatre meets stringent financial and operating benchmarks." (– *London Free Press*, July 5, 2000)

London City Council had agreed to help the theatre refinance its $500,000 operating debt and allow for $600,000 worth of building improvements. The City was not offering to loan money to The Grand, but the City would guarantee any loan the theatre could get from a financial institution.

Artistic Director Kelly Handerek was quoted in the *London Free Press* as saying: "What this will offer is a strong endorsement for the theatre. It's a gesture of support." (– July 5, 2000)

LONDON ARTISTS

Artistic Director Kelly Handerek made a concerted effort to include London artists in this season. Actors, directors, playwrights, musicians, composers and set and lighting designers were offered work on The Grand's mainstage and in the McManus Studio.

Edward Glen was cast as Charlie Brown in *You're a Good Man, Charlie Brown*, the show produced to please Christmas crowds.

The Grand Theatre. London's architectural touchstone, anchoring the heart of the city. (Photo: Sheila Johnston)

Denise Pelley, a London-based singer, was cast as the star of *Ain't Misbehavin'*. London-raised playwright, Greg Nelson, had his play *North* produced, and London-raised Allan Stratton had his play *The Phoenix Lottery* produced as well.

London actors Ray Bowen, John Schram and Hayley Gratto were cast in shows, as was former Artistic Director Bernard Hopkins, and Strathroy-based actor Dave Semple.

These artists were but some of the 30 local people whom Handerek sought out to include in the season. "We don't want them leaving here and saying later that they never played here," he was quoted as saying in the *London Free Press*. (– September 23, 2000)

A READING

The Annual General Meeting, held on October 12, 2000, offered more than just the typical audited financial statement and various other reports. Rick Kish directed a reading of *Born Yesterday*. When the play was presented in October 1960 by London Little Theatre, the cast included Eleanor Ender, Eddie Escaf, Alec Richmond, Wally Duffield and Mary Porter. These five actors were on hand in October 2000 to reprise their roles. The reading was staged as entertainment following the business of the Annual General Meeting. A good time was had by all, actors and audience members alike.

REMINISCENCES

As the Grand Theatre's 100 anniversary approached actress/educator Caroline Dolny-Guerin reminisced about various directors she had worked with at the Grand Theatre:

From my first step on that beloved stage with Don Fleckser's Children's Theatre production of The Sleeping Beauty, *to playing Aunt Polly opposite Victor Garber's Tom Sawyer and his Peter to my Anne in* The Diary of Anne Frank, *I fell in love with "The Grand Old Lady." All the years of performing there in amateur productions culminated in Heinar Piller's formation of the Young and Resident companies – a time filled with so many memories, so many experiences! I remember director Andrew Allan taking me out to dinner, while I was in his production of* Boeing, Boeing *and talking about Jorge Luis Borges. I remember playwright Peter Colley's* The Donnellys *performance the day my grandmother died, and performing* How The Other Half Loves *while pregnant with our first child. Then, playing the floosie in red satin in* Death of a Salesman, *I would rush downstairs at intermission to breastfeed – Bernard Hopkins' production of* Les Belles Soeurs *as that baby got bigger. And then coming back to those boards again in Larry Lillo's* Born Yesterday, *when the number of children born had reached four! Beloved Larry invited me, for the first time, to the other side of the footlights to be the theatre's education coordinator, a role which I had the privilege of continuing for Martha Henry. And now, the third of those children, Natasha, continues the tradition, joyfully playing in The Grand's special High School Projects –* A Midsummer Night's Dream, *directed by Michael Shamata, and* Guys and Dolls *directed by Kelly Handerek. Many artistic directors, many joyful memories. For her 100th anniversary this old lady would love to mount those boards one more time…at least!*
– Caroline Dolny-Guerin, actress, drama teacher

Caroline Dolny-Guerin got her heart's desire when she was cast as Joanne in *Come Back to the Five and Dime, Jimmy Dean, Jimmy Dean*, the 2000/2001 season opener, directed by Kelly Handerek.

HANDEREK DEPARTS

In March 2001, the resignation of Artistic Director Kelly Handerek was announced. In July of 2001, after a two-year stint at The Grand, Handerek returned to Saskatchewan, to his job as associate professsor in the University of Regina's theatre department.

Grand Theatre season:
Come Back to the Five and Dime, Jimmy Dean, Jimmy Dean, by Ed Gradczyk, directed by Kelly Handerek
North, by Greg Nelson
You're A Good Man, Charlie Brown, by Charles Schultz, book, music and lyrics by Clark Gesner
The Phoenix Lottery, by Allan Stratton
On Golden Pond, by Ernest Thompson

Ain't Misbehavin', by Murray Horwitz, Richard Maltby Jr., music by Fats Waller

McManus Studio:
Good Bones, by Margaret Atwood
Peter Pan and *The Princess and the Pea*, by Duffelbag Theatre, with Marcus Lundgren and Michelle Lundgren
The Beauty Machine, presented by Green Thumb Players

2001/02

100TH ANNIVERSARY SEASON OF THE GRAND THEATRE!

THE GRAND THEATRE/ SUSAN FERLEY ERA

FINALE

The history of London's Grand Theatre, or of any theatre, is the accumulation of moments; moments that remain in the hearts and the minds of the actors and the audience. Actors strive to achieve perfect moments on stage; moments that register honestly and emotionally with the audience. The accumulation of those moments is the history of a theatre.

The Grand Theatre is a building, but a building is just a structure, unless it is enriched and infused with culture. The Grand has been enriched in this way. It has been infused for one hundred years with culture, with dance, music, scenic art, and performances enacted by artists. It is this uninterrupted enrichment of culture that has renewed The Grand's spirit, time and again, that has recharged its energy despite challenges and crises.

What makes a building come to be loved? The simple answer is – age. This answer applies to all old buildings, including buildings much older than The Grand. But in speaking of London's Grand Theatre the answer is more complicated.

In August of 2001, Susan Ferley started her tenure as Artistic Director of the Grand Theatre. She had previously worked as Artistic Director at the Globe Theatre in Regina, Saskatchewan.

Age is but one component; magic, glamour, applause, ovations, and bravos are all elements that exist within the beautiful and dignified Grand Theatre. These elements make us love it. The Grand Theatre is London's architectural touchstone; it is the proud building anchoring the heart of London, Ontario; it is a loved building. The Grand Theatre is a living building; one with a bright future ahead.

Grand Theatre 100th Anniversary Season:
A Funny Thing Happened on the Way to the Forum, by Burt Shevelove and Larry Gelbart, directed by Bob Ainslie
The Gin Game, by D.L. Coburn, directed by Susan Ferley
Miracle on 34th Street, by Mountain Community Theatre, from Valentine Davies, directed by Bernard Hopkins

Nurse Jane Goes to Hawaii, by Allan Stratton, directed by David Oiye
Macbeth, by William Shakespeare
Wingfield on Ice, by Dan Needles, directed by Douglas Beattie, starring Rod Beattie

McManus Studio:
J.R.R. Tolkien's The Hobbit, adapted by Kim Selody
Seven Potato More!, Theatre Beyond Words

APPENDIX I:
Just the Facts (1934 - 2002)

Dorothy Saunders (later Westhead) as she appeared in costume ready for a dance number in the **Kiwanis Follies** *at the Grand Theatre, early 1930s. (Courtesy of Dorothy Westhead)*

1934/35 1st London Little Theatre (LLT) season
    Board President John Stevens
        Subscriptions: $3 for 5 plays
    LLT rented the Grand Theatre for a fee of $2,400/year
    End of season surplus: $150
    Subscribers = 784

1935/36 2nd LLT season
    Board President Charles R. Hunt
    Subscriptions: $3 for 5 plays
    LLT income: $3,808; LLT
        expenses: $3,808

1936/37 3rd LLT season
    Board President Charles R. Hunt
    Subscriptions: $3 for 5 plays

1937/38 4th LLT season
    Board President Dr. Alan Skinner
    Subscriptions: $3 for 5 plays
    Productions cost approximately
        $650/each to mount

1938/39 5th LLT season
    Board President Dr. Alan Skinner
    Subscriptions: $3 for 5 plays

1939/40 6th LLT season
    Board President Dr. Alan Skinner
    Subscriptions: $3 for 5 plays
    LLT expenses: $3,474
    Subscribers = 1,600

1940/41 7th LLT season
    Board President Dr. Alan Skinner
    Subscriptions: $3 for 5 plays.
    LLT expenses: $5,013
    End of season surplus: $730
    Subscribers = 1,650

1941/42 8th LLT season
    Board President E.S. Detwiler
    Subscriptions: $3 for 5 plays
    Subscribers = 1,696

1942/43 9th LLT season
    Subscriptions: $3 for 5 plays
    Subscribers = 1,950

An exterior shot of the Grand Theatre as it appeared during the 1945/46 season, featured on a souvenir flyer in recognition of LLT's purchase of the theatre. (Courtesy of The Grand Theatre)

1943/44 10th LLT season
    Board President Ted Margrett
    Subscriptions: $3 for 5 plays
    Subscribers = 3,000

1944/45 11th LLT season
    Board President Dr. Alan Skinner
    Subscriptions: $3 for 5 plays
    Subscribers = 4,850

1945/46 12th LLT season
    Board President Fred Phelps
    Subscriptions: $4 for 6 plays
    $35,000 spent by LLT to purchase
        the Grand Theatre
    Subscribers = 6,769

1946/47 13th LLT season
    Board President F.N. Phelps

A tense moment in the play **Papa Is All**, *1943/44. Pictured l. to r. are: Jerry Campbell, Janet Kippen, Marvin Kenyon with gun drawn, Christine Thomas, Tex Thorne and Erie Ross. (Courtesy of Dorinda Greenway)*

Subscriptions: $4 for 6 plays
    LLT expenses: $36,550
    LLT's annual budget to operate
        and maintain the building:
        $1,000/month
    End of season surplus: $4,033
    Subscriptions = 6,969

1947/48 14th LLT season
    Board President F.N. Phelps
    Subscriptions: $4 for 6 plays
    Subscribers = 9,495

1948/49 15th LLT season
    Board President W.K.V. Smith
    Subscriptions: $4 for 6 plays
    Retirement of the $17,000 mortgage
    $8,000 invested by LLT in ren
        ovations and repairs to The
        Grand Theatre
    End of season deficit: $17,000
    Subscribers = 10,500

1949/50 16th LLT season
    Board President W.K.V. Smith
    Subscriptions: $5 for 6 plays
    LLT expenses: $55,177; LLT income
        $64,478
    Subscribers = 10,636

1950/51 17th LLT season
    Board President W.K.V. Smith

This photograph shows LLT dancer/choreographer Bernice Harper doing what she loved to do - teach young people to dance. This chorus line is composed of nursing students from the University of Western Ontario (1947), including Elizabeth Lawson. In no particular order the novice dancers are: Marilyn Casy, Mickey McLaughlin, Pearl Putney, Bev McQueen, Betty Lou Quickey, Isobel Hersher, Ruth Clemens, Mary Nichols, and Pauline (surname unknown). Blake (surname unknown) looks on from above. (Courtesy of Elizabeth Lawson)

Subscriptions: $5 for 6 plays
LLT expenses: $51,045; LLT income: $66,889
Subscribers = 10,143

1951/52 18th LLT season
Board President William Hogg
Subscriptions: $6 for 7 plays
End of season surplus: $9,160
Subscribers = 9,917

1952/53 19th LLT season
Board President William Hogg
Subscriptions: $6 for 6 plays
LLT expenses: $61,594; LLT income: $72,168
LLT spent $5,578 on improvement

and upkeep of the Grand Theatre
Subscribers = 9,707

1953/54 20th LLT season
Board President R.J. Churchill
Subscriptions: $6 for 6 plays
End of season surplus: $7,147
Subscribers = 9,603

1954/55 21st LLT season
Board President W.E. McIlroy
Subscriptions: $6 for 6 plays
End of season deficit: $3,500
Subscribers = 7,958

1955/56 22nd LLT season
Board President W.E. McIlroy

An Inspector Calls was LLT's second production of the 1949/50 season. Pictured is Pat Harrington and young London lawyer, Alec Richmond who became a familiar actor in future LLT productions. In reviewing the play Muriel G. Pope said: "Mr. Richmond plays his part with easy assurance which is delightful" and "Miss Harrington gives nice shading to the role." (Courtesy of Alec Richmond)

The Studio Club was in full swing, presenting opportunities for aspiring directors and actors to flex their theatrical muscles. A rehearsal is underway in this shot, featuring actors (l. to r.): Alan Gibson, Ruth Rottman (behind screen door, centre) and Saul Hallif. The play All Summer Long was directed by Barry Hunt, March, 1956. (Photo by Barry Montgomery; Courtesy of Ruth Rottman)

Subscriptions: $6 for 6 plays
LLT expenses: $46,500; LLT income: $57,534
Subscribers = 7,636

1956/57 23rd LLT season
Board President W.E. McIlroy
End of season surplus: $66

1957/58 24th LLT season
Artistic Director Peter Dearing (1st season)
Board President Elizabeth Murray
Subscriptions: $8 for 6 plays
End of season surplus: $4,000
Subscribers = 6,700

1958/59 25th LLT season
Artistic Director Peter Dearing
Board President Elizabeth Murray
Subscriptions: $8 for 6 plays
End of season surplus: $16,000
Subscribers = 9,200

1959/60 26th LLT season
Artistic Director Peter Dearing
Board President Charles Brown
Subscriptions: $8 for 6 plays
LLT spent approximately $18,000/year improving and maintaining the theatre
Subscriptions = 8,200

Eddie Escaf (seated right) is surrounded by players from the 1957 production of South Pacific. The photograph was taken backstage at The Grand. On the reverse side Eddie Escaf has written: "French girls flirting with Luther Billis". (Courtesy of Eddie Escaf)

1960/61 27th LLT season
Artistic Director Peter Dearing
Board President Charles Brown
Subscriptions: $11 for 8 plays
Subscribers = 8,200

1961/62 28th LLT season
  Artistic Director Peter Dearing
  Board President Ken Lemon
  Subscriptions: $11 for 8 plays
  LLT income: $95,000
  Budget for producing a big LLT
    musical: $12,000
  Subscribers = 8,700

Auntie Mame brought the 1962/63 season to a close. It starred Elizabeth Murray (above) as the non-conformist Mame, and as her wide-eyed nephew, Richard Ivey (above) shared the role with James Ready, for alternating performances. The flu went through the cast and a doctor was in attendance at performances. Pails were conveniently placed in the wings. (Courtesy of Peter Lynch)

1962/63 29th LLT season
  Artistic Director Peter Dearing
  Board President Ken Lemon
  Subscriptions: $12 for 8 plays
  LLT expenses: $101,200; LLT
    income: $101,400

End of season surplus: $200
Subscribers = 9,208

1963/64 30th LLT season
  Artistic Director Peter Dearing
  Board President Doug McCullough
  Subscriptions: $12 for 8 plays
  LLT expenses: $105,700; LLT
    income: $105,700
  Subscribers = 8,868

1964/65 31st LLT season
  Artistic Director Peter Dearing
  Board President Doug McCullough;
    succeeded mid-season by
    R.A. Reinhart
  Subscriptions: $12 for 8 plays
  LLT income: $114,603
  $5,000 spent by LLT for a major

Taken in the LLT scene shop, this photograph features (l. to r.) Roger Smith, Noreen De Shane, Ron Gobert and Edna Whyte. They are working on the set and props for the season's first show You Can't Take It With You. (Courtesy of The London Free Press Collection of Photographic Negatives, The D.B. Weldon Library, The University of Western Ontario, London, Ontario)

A portrait of actor O. B. Watts as he appeared in the production of The Hostage. Teacher by day – actor by night. (Courtesy of Geoffrey Farrow)

  repair job to the Grand Theatre
End of season surplus: $56
Subscribers = 9,440

1965/66 32nd LLT season
  Artistic Director Peter Dearing
  Board President R.A. Reinhart
  Subscriptions: $12 for 8 plays
  End of season deficit: $1,000
  Subscribers = 8,600

1966/67 33rd LLT season
  Artistic Director Peter Dearing
  Board President E.J.R. Wright
  End of season deficit: $6,400
  Subscribers = 8,703

1967/68 34th LLT season
  Artistic Director Peter Dearing
    (11th and last season)
  Board President R.A. Reinhart
  Subscriptions: $14.50 for 8 plays
  End of season surplus: $21,298
  Subscribers = 7,700

1968/69 35th LLT season
  (No Artistic Director)
  Board President Barbara Ivey
  Subscriptions: $14.50 for 8 plays

1969/70 36th LLT season
  (No Artistic Director)
  Board President Barbara Ivey
  Subscriptions: $16.50 for 8 plays
  End of season deficit: $4,966

1970/71 37th LLT season
  (final LLT season)
  (No Artistic Director)
  Board President Florence Smith
  Subscriptions: $15 for 7 plays
  Subscribers = 6,300

1971/72 1st Theatre London season
  Artistic Director Heinar Piller
    (1st season)
  Board President Florence Smith
  Subscriptions: $16 for 7 plays*

Geoffrey Farrow, general manager of the Grand Theatre. During the three seasons when the LLT did not have an artistic director, Geoffrey Farrow ran the business of LLT and ran The Grand. (Courtesy Geoffrey Farrow)

End of season deficit: $46,843
Subscribers = 6,199
* hereafter the subscription price quoted is for the most expense subscription "package"

1972/73 2nd Theatre London season
Artistic Director Heinar Piller
Board President Eddie Escaf
Subscriptions: $25 for 7 plays
Operating Budget: $350,000
End of season deficit: $120,000
Subscribers = 6,920

1973/74 3rd Theatre London season
Artistic Director Heinar Piller
Board President Eddie Escaf
Subscriptions: $25 for 7 plays
Operating Budget $400,000
Subscribers = 11,400

1974/75 4th Theatre London season
Artistic Director Heinar Piller
Board President John F. McGarry
Subscriptions: $32 for 7 plays
Operating Budget $521,000
Subscribers = 12,361

1975/76 5th Theatre London season
Artistic Director Heinar Piller
(5th and last season)

Board President Arthur Ender
Subscriptions: $40 for 7 plays
End of season surplus: $1,000

1976/77 6th Theatre London season
Artistic Director William Hutt
(1st season)
Board President Arthur Ender
Subscriptions: $40 for 7 plays
Subscribers = 12,742

1977/78 7th Theatre London season -
at Aeolian Hall
Artistic Director William Hutt
Board President Arthur Ender
Subscriptions: $21 for 3 productions
240 seats available at Aeolian Hall while the Grand Theatre under reconstruction

1978/79 8th Theatre London season
Artistic Director William Hutt
Board President Arthur Ender; succeeded in mid-season by John F. McGarry
Subscriptions: $42.50 for 6 plays
Operating budget: $1,086,700
Subscribers = 11,852

1979/80 9th Theatre London season
Artistic Director William Hutt

Art Ender, Theatre London board president, and Ontario's Lieutenant Governor, Pauline McGibbon, are pictured cutting a cake, shaped like the Grand Theatre, in celebration of the theatre's 75th anniversary, the 1976/77 season. (Courtesy of **The London Free Press***)*

(4th and last season)
Board President William Baldwin
Subscriptions: $47.50 for 6 plays
Subscribers = 11,882

1980/81 10th Theatre London season
Artistic Director Bernard Hopkins
(1st season)
Board President William Baldwin
Subscriptions: $51.00 for 6 plays
Subscribers = 11,603

1981/82 11th Theatre London season
Artistic Director Bernard Hopkins
Board President Noreen De Shane
Subscriptions: $55.00 for 6 plays
Subscribers = 11,970

1982/83 12th Theatre London season
(final Theatre London season)
Artistic Director Bernard Hopkins
(3rd and last season)
Board President Noreen De Shane
Subscriptions: $55.00 for 6 plays
Operating budget: $1,900,000
Subscribers = 12,695

1983/84 1st Grand Theatre Company season
Artistic Director Robin Phillips
(1st and last season)
Board President: John Porter
Subscriptions: dropped in favour of a repertory system with single tickets
Operating Budget: $4,400,000
End of season deficit: $1,820,000

1984/85 2nd Grand Theatre Company season
Artistic Director Don Shipley
(1st season)
Board President Robert Mepham
Subscriptions: $90 for 6 plays
Operating budget: $2,400,000

Arsenic and Old Lace *featured John Neville (left) as Martha Brewster, and William Hutt as Abigail Brewster. The two actors played the eccentric spinster sisters in this crowd-pleasing play. "My husband and I are a match made in heaven, if in fact opposites do attract. the Grand Theatre's 1983/84 season gave us a wonderful common denominator. The first performance that we attended together featured two great actors in drag, as two old dames. John Neville and William Hutt provided the bait. We've come back to The Grand ever since." – Michele Ebel, theatre-goer. (Photo: Robert Ragsdale; Courtesy of the Grand Theatre)*

End of season deficit: $146,000
(excluding accumulated deficit)
Subscribers = 12,653

1985/86 3rd Grand Theatre Company season
Artistic Director Don Shipley
(2nd and last season)

Board President Robert Mepham
Subscriptions: $90 for 5 plays
Operating budget: $1,400,000
End of season deficit: $192,733
Accumulated deficit since the
    1983/84 repertory season:
    $2,161,442
Subscribers = 12,048

1986/87 1st Grand Theatre season
("Company" dropped from name)
    Artistic Director Larry Lillo
      (1st season)
    Board President Robert Mepham
    Subscriptions: $105.00 for 6 plays
    Accumulated deficit paid off.
    End of season surplus: $445,000
    Subscribers = 11,867

Kate Trotter and Tom McCamus in **The Affections of May.** **"The Affections of May...***can you imagine anything more thrilling than playing a game of sexual chess opposite gorgeous Tom McCamus?... Can you imagine anything funnier than Benedict Campbell in a bunny suit? Both experiences are what dreams are made of!"*
– Kate Trotter, actor (Photo: Robert Ragsdale; Courtesy of the Grand Theatre)

1987/88 2nd Grand Theatre season
    Artistic Director Larry Lillo
      (2nd and last season)
    Board President Tom Siess
    Subscriptions: $112.50 for 6 plays
    Operating budget: $2,600,000
    End of season surplus: $220,511

1988/89 3rd Grand Theatre season
    Artistic Director Martha Henry
      (1st season)
    Board President Tom Siess
    Operating budget: $3,800,000
    End of season surplus: $54,379
    Subscribers = 13,650

1989/90 4th Grand Theatre season
    Artistic Director Martha Henry
    Board President Gerald Wheaton
    Subscriptions: $126.00 for 6 plays
    Operating budget: $3,340,000
    End of season surplus: $78,775
    Subscribers = 14,575

1990/91 5th Grand Theatre season
    Artistic Director Martha Henry
    Board President Gerald Wheaton
    Operating budget: $3,400,000
    End of season deficit: $92,825
    Subscribers = 11,375

1991/92 6th Grand Theatre season
    Artistic Director Martha Henry
    Board President Anne Hubbell
    Operating budget: $3,300,000
    End of season surplus: $76,789
    Subscribers = 10,524

1992/93 7th Grand Theatre season
    Artistic Director Martha Henry
    Board President Anne Hubbell
    Subscriptions: $180 for 6 plays
    End of season surplus: $67,211
    Subscribers = 11,110

1993/94 8th Grand Theatre season
    Artistic Director Martha Henry
    Board President Roger Lillyman
    Subscriptions: $185.00 for 6 plays
    End of season deficit: $322,673
    Subscribers = 11,021

1994/95 9th Grand Theatre season
    Artistic Director Martha Henry
      (7th and last season)
    Board President Roger Lillyman
    Subscriptions: $195.00 for 6 plays
    End of season surplus: $144,731
    Subscribers = 10,293

1995/96 10th Grand Theatre season
    Artistic Director Michael Shamata
      (1st season)
    Board President Keith Bowman
    Subscriptions: $270.00 for 6 plays
    End of season deficit: $274,201
    Subscribers = 9,936

1996/97 11th Grand Theatre season
    Artistic Director Michael Shamata
    Board President Keith Bowman
    Subscriptions: $219.00 for 6 plays
    End of season deficit: $70,442
    Subscribers = 8,274

1997/98 12th Grand Theatre season
    Artistic Director Michael Shamata
    Board President Jim Dunlop
    End of season deficit: $365,531
    Subscribers = 7,930

1998/99 13th Grand Theatre season
    Artistic Director Michael Shamata
      (4th and last season)
    Board President Douglas B. Weldon
    Operating budget: $3,400,000
    End of season deficit: $447,284
    Accumulated deficit since the
      1995/96 season: $1,100,000

Subscribes = 7,794

1999/2000 14th Grand Theatre season
    Artistic Director Kelly Handerek
      (1st season)
    Board President John Judson
    Subscriptions: $220.00 for 6 plays
    Operating budget: $3,400,000
    End of season surplus: $228,673
    Subscriptions: 7,553
(Publication deadlines preclude the presentation of further details.)

2000/2001 15th Grand Theatre season
    Artistic Director: Kelly Handerek
    Board President: John Judson

20001/2002 100th anniversary season
(1901 - 2001)
    16th Grand Theatre season
    Artistic Director: Susan Ferley
    Board President: John Judson

APPENDIX II:

1 FREDERICK CHALLENER

a) Biography

The painted mural on the proscenium arch of London, Ontario's Grand Theatre was created by Canadian artist Frederick Sproston Challener (1869-1959). Challener, originally from Whetstone, England, studied in Toronto, where he attended the Ontario School of Art (c. 1884-1886), the Toronto Art Students League (1885-1889), and where he privately studied in the 1890s under the tutelage of famous Canadian academic painter George A. Reid. Challener was also a member of various arts organizations, including the Ontario Society of Artists and the Royal Canadian Academy, to which he was elected as the youngest member in 1900. In 1908, he also became a founding member of the Arts and Letters Club, a meeting place for the arts community in Toronto. In the 1920s, Challener was a teacher at Toronto's Central Technical School and the Ontario College of Art. His easel paintings were primarily exhibited in Canada, the United States, and England, and are found in many major Canadian art galleries and private collections.[1]

b) Interest in Mural Decoration

Challener defined decorative painting as "the appropriate filling with graceful lines, subtle or strong, light or dark, masses and harmonious colours, of spaces of various shapes and sizes which are made by the architectural lines of a building."[2] His particular interest in mural decoration was evident at the turn-of-the-century. Soon after returning from the Middle East in 1898, where he was drawn to its light and colour, he began creating murals for a variety of building interiors. Murals not only allowed him to express elements of design on a vast

A close-up of the centre roundel of Challener's mural on the proscenium arch of London's Grand Theatre. (Photographer unknown; Courtesy of the Grand Theatre)

scale, but to underscore his view that mural decoration was not an inferior medium, as was commonly thought by those who valued easel works.[3] Furthermore, mural decoration, Challener maintained, could be economically advantageous to the Canadian city – people are attracted to beauty "displayed on the walls of its most important buildings," he wrote, and will assuredly spend money to see it. One need only look to Michelangelo's fresco decorations at the Sistine Chapel in Rome, asserted Challener, to realize the potential profits of beautiful painted interiors.[4] By the early twentieth century, Frederick Challener became synonymous with mural painting in Canada.[5]

c) Proscenium Arch Murals

Structures which Challener decorated include the proscenium arches at three major Canadian theatres: the Russell Opera House in Ottawa (1898-1901); the New Grand Opera House in London (1901); and the Royal Alexandra Theatre in Toronto (1906-07).[6] He contended that theatre decoration, in particular, is beneficial because "between acts, when the curtain is down, people get tired of looking at each other…and long for something to rest their eyes on that will have a nice restful feeling in contrast to the movements on the stage."[7]

II THE GRAND'S PROSCENIUM ARCH MURAL

a) Materials

The London mural of 1901 consists of three sections, a centre roundel with two flanking panels. The work resembles the fresco technique of paint directly applied onto a wall/ceiling surface; however, it is specifically for The Grand's interior, and adhered to the structure. This technique was popularized in European building decoration in the mid eighteenth century.

b) Subject Matter

The subject matter of the Ottawa and Toronto theatres have been identified as the "Triumph of the Drama" and "Venus and Adonis," respectively; however, the title and subject of the London work has, to my knowledge, never been identified. Indeed, in a 1932 *Globe & Mail* newspaper article entitled *Meet Frederick S. Challener, R.C.A.*, the writer vaguely described the painting as having "characters from mythology."[8] In a 1976 doctoral dissertation on the Royal Alexandra Theatre, the author cites the subjects of virtually all of Challener's mural decorations with the notable exception of London's Grand,[9] and in a 1976 *London Free Press* article on The Grand's mural, trivially entitled *Now…about those half-naked women…*, the writer reports on the mystery surrounding the work's origin and subject.[10]

The painting appears to be a loose representation of the Muses, the mythological goddesses of creative inspiration in dance, song, poetry, and other arts. I assert the term "loose" because neither all of the identified Muses nor all of their attributes are present in this work; however, some are, and the overwhelming theme of the painting points to the Muses' general artistic activities as a group in a Classical setting. This subject is indeed suitable in the context of theatre, where virtually all of these forms of artistic expression can be found. Challener himself espoused the importance of appropriate subjects in public building murals: "the decoration …should be significant, either symbolical or commemorative…." [11] Interestingly, Challener flanks the entire scene with a depiction of tied-back drapery; this no doubt parallels open theatrical curtains that reveal action on a stage.

The centre roundel consists of two women in an idealized pastoral setting containing Neoclassical architectural features. The women are dressed in Classical-style garb, each engaged in her own activity: the standing figure holds a stringed musical instrument resembling a harp, and the seated figure paints a pot. A stringed instrument, particularly a harp, is a common Muse attribute, although the depiction of a female figure painting pottery is relatively unusual in Muse imagery. The figure paints a reclining nude woman, perhaps referring to Venus, the Goddess of Love, who, since the Italian Renaissance period, has been rendered in this standardized way. This artistic reference to the Goddess of Love could point to the passion that the Muses have for their various artistic pursuits (indeed, allusions to Venus appear in all three canvases). This being the case, Challener takes artistic license here, as Muse and Venus narratives are not typically connected in Classical mythology. The standing figure wears a garland on her head, another common attribute associated with certain Muses.

The left canvas depicts four groupings of female figures in a similar Classically-inspired landscape setting. At the left, three women appear to be holding various offerings: a generous serving of food, a lamb, and a tray of fruit. Beside them is a bird, likely a swan. Classical writers professed that the swan loved music, and it is perhaps for this reason that it became associated with particular Muses. The swan, however, is also an attribute of Venus, whose presence is also suggested in the foreground by the four doves, and the back of the half-draped, seated female figure. The dove is a chief attribute of Venus because of its symbolic reference to love, and the figure, if not Venus herself, is at the very least, a Venus type. In the background, are two more groups of female figures: three girls who carry garlands; and three women who also bring offerings of food. At the right of the scene, three women, connected by floral garlands, all dance, a common artistic expression of the Muses.

The right canvas features four female musicians, and numerous symbols of love all within a comparable Classically-inspired landscape. From left to right, women play a double flute, a tambourine, a violin, and another a double flute. These instruments are strongly connected to various Muses of dance, song, and poetry, and may also refer to the Goddess Venus because of their symbolic meaning of love. Another allusion to Venus may be present in the background, which depicts a goat surrounded by four young boys, the only male figures in the mural. As three boys push, ride and pull the animal, another is playing the drum, suggesting a pseudo-ceremonial procession. Indeed, in mythological triumphs that celebrated the Gods and Goddesses, the goat was the animal typically used to draw the chariot of Love, ridden by Venus or her son Cupid. In the right foreground of the scene, a parapet, illustrated in the grisaille method, shows five nude female figures "carved" in conventional Venus poses. Two additional women appear to the left of the structure, offering trays of what appear to be flowers.

The three panels, then, while each conveying their own motifs, all share a larger theme. All are loosely based on the creative arts of the Muses, with each panel featuring the women engaged in artistic activities. The allusions to Venus, the Goddess of Love, appear to reference the Muses' passion for these creative pursuits, and are present in all three canvases. This consistency should not be surprising considering Challener's belief that "a mural decoration…should tell as a whole from one corner of the subject to the other." [12]

c) Style

The mural is painted in the spirit of the Rococo painting style, an eighteenth-century French style that emphasized the sensual use of soft pastel colours, and that commonly set figures in a luxurious pastoral landscape ripe with Neoclassical references. Challener's attraction to this style is understandable given that it was popular, not only in eighteenth-century easel painting, but also in mural decorations of French Rococo building interiors.

Footnotes:

(1) Challener, Frederick Sproston, in *Who's Who in Ontario Art*, File: Challener, F.S. - Canadian Artists, London Public Library

(2) F.S. Challener, "Mural Decoration," *The Canadian Architect and Builder*, Vol. 17, (April 1904): 90.

(3) Ibid., 92.

(4) Ibid., 91

(5) J.W. Beaty, RCA, in Newton MacTavish, *The Fine Arts in Canada* (Toronto, 1925), 128.

(6) Mora Dianne Guthrie O'Neill, *A Partial History of the Royal Alexandra Theatre, Toronto, Canada, 1907 - 1939*, Ph.D. diss., Louisiana State University and Agricultural and Mechanical College, 1976, fn. 49, 65 - 66.

(7) Challener, 96.

(8) *Meet Frederick S. Challener, R.C.A.*, *The Globe & Mail*, September 10, 1932, L-Drama- Theatre Groups - Grand Theatre.

(9) O'Neill, fn. 49, 55-66.

(10) Doug Bale, *Now … about those half-naked women …*, *The London Free Press*, January 3, 1976, np.

(11) Challener, 90.

(12) Ibid.

SELECTED BIBLIOGRAPHY

Atkinson, Brooks: *Broadway*. New York, NY: The MacMillan Company, 1970.

Baily, Leslie: *The Gilbert & Sullivan Book*. London: Cassel and Company Ltd., 1952.

Baral, Robert: *Revue: A Nostalgic Reprise of the Great Broadway Period*. New York, NY: Fleet Publishing Corporation, 1962.

Barnes, Philip: *A Companion to Post-War British Theatre*. London, England: Croom Helm, 1986.

Barrymore, Ethel. *Memories: An Autobiography*. New York, NY: Harper and Brothers, 1955.

Bernhardt, Sarah. *My Double Life*. London, England: Hutchinson Publishing Group, 1907.

Benson, Eugene and L.W. Conolly. *The Oxford Companion to Canadian Theatre*. Toronto, ON: Oxford University Press, 1989.

Beyer, Edvard. *Ibsen: The Man and His Work*. New York, NY: Taplinger Publishing Co., Inc., 1980.

Blackstone, Harry Jr.. *The Blackstone Book of Magic and Illusions*. New York, NY: Newmarket Press, 1985.

Bordman, Gerald: *American Musical Comedy: From 'Adonis' to 'Dreamgirls'*. New York, NY: Oxford University Press, 1982.

Bowen, Croswell. *The Curse of the Misbegotten: A Tale of the House of O'Neill*. New York, NY: Rupert Hart-Davis, 1960.

Brownlow, Kevin. *Hollywood: The Pioneers*. London, G.B.: Collins, Sons & Co. Ltd, 1979.

Busby, Roy. *British Music Hall; An Illustrated Who's Who from 1850 to the Present Day*. London, England. Paul Elek Limited, 1976.

Charlesworth, Hector. *Candid Chronicles - Leaves from the Note Book of a Canadian Journalist*. Toronto, ON: The MacMillan Co. of Canada, 1925.

Courtney, Marguerite. *Laurette: The Intimate Biography of Laurette Taylor*. New York, NY: Limelight Editions, 1955.

Cronyn, Hume. *A Terrible Liar: A Memoir*. New York, NY: William Morrow and Co., 1991.

Csida, Joseph and June Bundy Csida. *American Entertainment*. New York, NY: Watson-Guptill Publications, 1978.

Davis, Peter G.. *The American Opera Singer*. New York, NY: Doubleday, 1997.

Deschner, Donald. *The Films of W.C. Fields*. Secaucus, NJ: The Citadel Press, 1966.

Disher, M. Willson. *The Last Romantic: The Authorised Biography of Sir John Martin-Harvey*. London, England: Hutchinson and Co., Ltd., YEAR?

Disher, M. Willson. *Melodrama: Plots That Thrilled*. London, England: Rockliff Pub. Co., 1954.

Donaldson, Frances. *The Actor-Managers*. London, England: Weidenfeld and Nicolson, 1970.

Dunbar, Janet. *J.M. Barrie - The Man Behind the Image*. London, England: Collins, 1970.

Edwards, Murray D.. *A Stage in Our Past: English-Language Theatre in Eastern Canada from the 1790s to 1914*. Toronto, ON: University of Toronto Press, 1968.

Field, Jonathan and Moira. *The Methuen Book of Theatre Verse*. London, England: Methuen Drama, 1991.

Franca, Celia. *The National Ballet of Canada: A Celebration, With Photographs by Ken Bell*. Toronto, Ontario: University of Toronto Press, 1978.

Franklin, Joe. *Classics of the Silent Screen: A Pictorial Treasure*. Secaucus, New York: The Citadel Press, 1959.

Garebian, Keith. *William Hutt: A Theatre Portrait*. Oakville, ON: Mosaic Press, 1988.

Goodden, Herman (author) & Mike Baker (researcher). *Curtain Rising: The History of Theatre in London*. London, ON: London Regional Art & Historical Museums, 1993.

Graham, Martha. *Blood Memory - An Autobiography*. New York: Doubleday, 1991.

Hay, Peter. *Broadway Anecdotes*. New York, NY: Oxford University Press, 1989.

Harwood, Ronald. *Sir Donald Wolfit: His Life and Work in the Unfashionable Theatre*. London, G.B.: Secker & Warburg, 1971.

Holledge, Julie. *Innocent Flowers: Women in Edwardian Theatre*. London, G.B.: Virago Press Limited, 1981.

Hooke, Hilda Mary. *One-Act Plays from Canadian History*. Toronto, Ontario: Longman's Canada, 1942.

Hughes, Langston and Milton Meltzer. *Black Magic: A Pictorial History of the Negro in American Entertainment*. Englewood Cliffs, NJ: Prentice-Hall, Inc., 1967.

Johns, Eric. *Dames of the Theatre*. London, England: W.H. Allen, 1974.

Kerensky, Oleg. *Anna Pavlova*. New York, New York: E.P. Dutton and Co., Inc., 1973.

Lee, Betty. *Marie Dressler: The Unlikeliest Star*. The University Press of Kentucky, 1997.

Lee, Betty. *Love and Whiskey: The Story of the Dominion Drama Festival*. Toronto, ON: McClelland & Stewart Limited, 1973.

Lerner, Alan Jay. *The Musical Theatre: A Celebration*. New York, NY: McGraw-Hill Book Company, 1986.

LeVay, John. *Margaret Anglin - A Stage Life*. Toronto, ON: Simon & Pierre, 1989.

Lewis, Philip C./ *Trouping - How the Show Came to Town*. New York, NY: Harper & Row Publishers, 1973.

Lindsay, John. *Palaces of the Night - Canada's Grand Theatres*. Toronto, ON: Lynx Images Inc, 1999.

Lydiatt Shaw, Grace. *Stratford Under Cover*. Toronto, ON: N.C. Press Limited, 1977.

Mason Green, Lynda and Tedde Moore. *Standing Naked in the Wings*. Toronto, ON: Oxford University Press, 1997.

McCabe, John. *George M. Cohan - The Man Who Owned Broadway*. Garden City, NY: Doubleday, 1973.

McClement. *The Strange Case of Ambrose Small*. Toronto, ON: McClelland & Stewart Limited, 1974.

McDonald, Cheryl. *Emma Albani, Victorian Diva*. Toronto, ON: Dundurn Press Limited, 1984.

McRaye, Walter. *Town Hall Tonight*. Toronto, ON: The Ryerson Press, 1929.

Mews, Diane (editor): *Life Before Stratford: The Memoirs of Amelia Hall*. Toronto, ON: Dundurn Press, 1989.

Mitchenson, Joe and Raymond Monder. *Victorian and Edwardian Entertainment; From Old Photographs*. London, England: B.T. Batsford Ltd., 1978.

Mitchenson, Joe and Raymond Monder. *Theatrical Companion to Shaw*. New York, NY: Pitman Publishing Co. 1955.

Money, Keith. *Anna Pavlova; Her Life and Art*. New York, NY: Alfred A. Knopf, 1982.

Morley, Sheridan. *Punch at The Theatre*. London, G.B.: Robson Books Ltd., 1980.

Musser, Charles (in collaboration with Carol Nelson): *High-Class Moving Pictures: Lyman H. Howe and the Forgotten Era of Travelling Exhibition*. Princeton, New Jersey: Princeton University Press, 1991.

Nagler, A.M.. *A Source Book in Theatrical History*. New York, NY: Dover Publications, Inc., 1952

Peters, Margot. *The House of Barrymore*. New York, New York: Simon and Schuster, 1990.

Randi, James. *Conjuring*. New York, NY: St. Martin's Press, 1992.

Richardson, Joanna. *Sarah Bernhardt and Her World*. New York, NY: G.P. Putname's Sons, 1977.

Robbins, Phyllis. *Maude Adams: An Intimate Portrait*. New York, NY: G.P. Putnam's Sons, 1956.

Rose, Frank. *The Agency: William Morris and the Hidden History of Show Business*. New York, NY: Harper Business, A Division of Harper Collins Publishers. 19ºº

Rubin, Don. *Canadian Theatre History - selected readings*. Toronto, ON: Copp Clark Ltd. 1996.

Saddlemyer, Ann. *Early Stages: Theatre in Ontario 1800-1914*. Toronto, ON: University of Toronto Press, 1990.

Saddlemyer, Ann. *Later Stages: Essays in Ontario Theatre from the First World War to the 1970s*. Toronto, ON: University of Toronto Press, 1997.

Smiley, Sam. *Theatre: The Human Act*. New York, New York: Harper & Row, 1987

Smith, Gene. *American Gothic: The Story of America's Legendary Theatrical Family - Junius, Edwin, and John Wilkes Booth*. New York, New York: Simon and Schuster, 1992.

Sperdakos, Paula. *Dora Mavor Moore - Pioneer of the Canadian Theatre*. Toronto, ON: ECW Press, 1955.

Stagg, Jerry. *A Half-Century of Show Business and the Fabulous Empire of The Brothers Shubert*. New York, NY: Random House, 1968.

Stein, Charles W. *American Vaudeville As Seen By Its Contemporaries*. New York, NY: Alfred A. Knopf, 1984.

Tarbox, Charles H. *The Five Ages of the Cinema*. Smithtown, NY: Exposition Press, 1980.

Thorndike, Russell. *Sybil Thorndike*. London, England: Salisbury Square, 1950.

Van Bridge, Tony. *Also in the Cast: The Memoirs of Tony Van Bridge*. Oakville, ON: Mosaic Press, 1995.

Wallace, William. *Harry Lauder in the Limelight*. Sussex, G.B.: The Book Guild Ltd., 1988.

Wilson, G.B.. *Three Hundred Years of American Drama and Theatre*. New Jersey: Prentice-Hall Inc., 1973.

Yeo, Leslie. *A Thousand and One First Nights*. Mosiac Press: Oakville, Ontario, 1998

Ziegfeld, Richard and Paulette. *The Ziegfeld Touch: The Life & Times of Florenz Ziegfeld, Jr.* New York, NY: Richard N. Abrams, 1993.

MAGAZINES/PAPERS/ARTICLES/SOUVENIR PROGRAM:

Brickenden, Catharine McCormick. *Catharine Keziah...Her Story*. Personal manuscript. London, ON, 1978.

Brown, Mary. *Ambrose Small: A Ghost in Spite of Himself*. Theatrical Touring & Founding in North America, ed. by L.W. Conolly. Greenwood Press: Westport, CN, 1982.

Fleckser, Don. *Stages in my Past: A Book of Memories, Plays, People and Events*. Unpublished manuscript, London, ON.

Fraser, Dr. Kathleen. *London's Grand: An Opera House on the Michigan-Ohio-Canadian Circuit, 1881 - 1914*. Theatre History in Canada, Vol. 9, No. 2, 1988

Gibb, Alice. *Sewers & Sidewalks: A Look at the Development of Theatre London*. 1975

King, Karla N.. "Amateur to Professional: A Difficult Transformation For the Grand Theatre". University of Guelph, Guelph, ON, December, 1992.

Manning, Edward B.. "The London Little Theatre and The Grand: A Brief History". London Little Theatre Seasons 36, LLT Souvenir Programme, 1970

Miller, Orlo. *Old Opera Houses of Western Ontario*. London, ON, 1962.

Penistan, V. M. (Jane). *The Canadian Players*. Vancouver, BC, 1994

Spicer. *Our Past Made Present, Part II*. London, ON: London Public Libraries and Museums, 1978

Theatre Arts magazine, published in New York, NY; October, 1952, August 1954, December 1956, August 1958.

Wellan, Rob. *Grand Theatre Special Souvenir Edition 1978/79*. London, ON: Theatre London.

DIRECTORIES:

Canadian Theatre Review Yearbook, 1974 (1975, 1976, 1977, 1979, 1981/82, 1982/83, 1983/84, 1984/85, 1985/86, 1986/87, 1987/88).

CTR Publications, Faculty of Fine Arts, York University, Toronto, Ontario.

London South Secondary School, 124, 154, 163, 249
London Symphony Orchestra, 152, 155, 156, 159, 185, 187, 191, 201
London Theatre Company, The (England), 125, 128, 129
London Theatre School, 136, 139, 140, 146, 148
London Youth Symphony, 196
Londonderry Air, The (see Rachel Field)
Long, John, 127
Long, Sumner Arthur, 159
   Never Too Late, 159
Long Days Journey Into Night (see Eugene O'Neill)
Longstaff, Brian, 184
Longstaff, Kip, 177, 180, 184
Loot (see Joe Orton)
Lord, William, 144, 145
Lord and Lady Algy, 45
Lord Byron's Love Letter (see Tennessee Williams)
Lord Chumley (see David Belasco and Henry C. deMille)
Love, Mary, 18
Love, Police Magistrate, 1
Love for Love (see William Congreve)
Love Letters (see A. R. Gurney)
Lover, The (see Harold Pinter)
Lover's Lane (see Clyde Fitch)
Lowland Wolf, The, 71
Luck of the Navy, The, 33
Lucky 7 (see the Dumbells)
Lucky Strike, 131
Ludmila (see Paul Gallico)
Ludwig, Patricia, 171
Lullaby for Newlyweds, 127
Lunchtime Concert (see Olwen Wymark)
Lund, Alan, 147, 148, 155
Lund, Blanche, 147
Lundgren, Marcus, 252
Lundgren, Michelle, 247, 252

Lunt, Alfred, 195
Luscombe, George, 158
Lusitania, the, 28
Luther (see John Osborne)
Lydiatt, Grace (see Grace Shaw)
Lydiatt, R. Jeffery, 44
Lynbrook, Lillian, 21
Lynch, Peter, 138, 144, 158, 211, 256

Macbeth (see William Shakespeare)
MacDonald, Anne-Marie, 243
   Goodnight Desdemona, Good Morning Juliet, 242, 243
MacDonald, Brian, 136, 142
MacDonald, Bryden, 240
   Whale Riding Weather, 238, 240
MacDonald, Ian, 102
MacDonald, Olivia, 136
MacGregor, Barry, 196
MacKenzie, Alice, 112
MacKenzie, Flora, 96, 114, 137, 149, 151, 155
Maclean's Magazine, 103
MacLiammoir, Michael, 109, 110
   Where Stars Walk, 109, 110
MacLeod, Joan, 224, 226, 244
   Little Sister, 244
   Toronto, Mississippi, 224, 226
MacMartin, Nicholas, 248
MacMillan, Ann, 248
MacRae, Arthur, 127
   Travellers Joy, 127
Mad Ballades (see Kate Hennig/Alan Laing)
Mad Hopes, The (see Romney Brent)
Madwoman of Chaillot, The (see Jean Giraudoux)
Madame Butterfly (see Puccini)
Madame X (see Alexandr Bisson)
Maddison, John, 122
Madonnas and Men, 49
Madsen, Virginia, 215
Magic Ring, The (see Lilian Cornelius)
Magistrate, The (see Arthur Wing

Pinero)
Maggie and Pierre (see Linda Griffiths)
Maid and the Mummy, The, 11
Mailer, Dan, 240
Maillet, Antonine, 228
   La Sagouine, 228
Major, Leon, 168, 185
Majorlaine (see Louis N. Parker)
Making the Bear (see Theodore Apstein)
Malcolm, Cara, 89
Malcuzynski, Witold, 103, 107
Male Animal, The (see James Thurber/Elliott Hugent)
Malloch, Douglas, 39
Malone, C. Patrick, 133
   Star Crossed, 133
Maltby, Richard Jr., 251, 252
   Ain't Misbehavin', 251, 252
Mamet, David, 226-228, 237, 238, 240
   Glengarry Glen Ross, 226-229, 231
   Oleanna, 237, 238, 240
Man For All Seasons, A (see Robert Bolt)
Man From the West, The, 15
Man of La Mancha, The (see Dale Wasserman/Mitch Leigh)
Man of the Hour, The, 22
Man Who Came to Dinner, The (see Moss Hart/George S. Kaufman)
Manitoba Theatre Centre, 217
Mann, Martha, 145, 146, 148
Manners, J. Hartley, 28, 30, 122, 131
   Peg O' My Heart, 28, 30, 122, 131
Mantell, Robert B., 23
Many Faces of Love, The (see Eleanor Wolquitt)
Maple Leaf Theatre, 133
Maraden, Marti, 198, 237, 240, 250
   The Persecution and Assasination of Jean-Paul Marat... (see Peter Weiss)
March, Frederic, 116, 117

Marcin, Max, 65, 66, 67, 96
   Silence, 66, 67
   Three Live Ghosts, 65, 96
Marcus, Frank, 203
   The Killing of Sister George, 197, 202, 203
Marcuse, Judith, 216
Margrett, Ted C., 102, 254
Marionettes, The (see Pierre Wolff)
Markova, Alicia, 110
Marks Bros. (No. 1) Company, 2, 3, 11, 25, 30, 31
Marks Bros. Dramatic and Vaudeville Co., 25
Marks, Ernie (Ernest), 25, 35, 43
Marks, Gracie, 25
Marks, Joe (Joseph), 25
Marks, Kitty (Katherine), 25, 30, 31, 35, 43
Marks, May A. Bell, 30, 31
Marks, Tom (Thomas Henry), 2, 3
Marks, Robert William (R.W.), 25, 30
Marleau, Louise, viii
Marriage Proposal, A (see Anton Chekhov)
Marsh, Marian, 75
Martha (see Von Flotow)
Martha by Day, 31
Martha of the Lowlands, 31
Martin, Frank, 165
Martin, J. Burke, 127, 130, 134, 135, 138, 143-146, 152, 153
Martin, Jane, 221
   Talking With, 221
Martin, Rosemary, 128
Martin, Steve, 245, 246
   Picasso at the Lapin Agile, 245, 246
Martindale, Sheila, 214, 249
Martinez Sierra, Gregorio, 98
   The Cradle Song, 98
Martin-Harvey, John (Sir), 57, 75, 85
Marvellous, Magical Circus of Paddington Bear, The (see Blaine Parker)

LET'S GO TO THE GRAND!

ABOUT THE AUTHOR

Sheila Johnston was raised in Stratford, Ontario. She earned a B.A. in English in 1980 from the University of Western Ontario, London. During a 20-year career in arts marketing, Sheila worked at The Stratford Festival, The Globe Theatre (Regina, Saskatchewan), The Nuffield Theatre (Southampton, England), The Lighthouse Festival Theatre (Port Dover, Ontario), the Grand Theatre (London, Ontario) and the Gateway Theatre (Richmond, B.C.).

Sheila is the author of *Buckskin & Broadcloth: A Celebration of E. Pauline Johnson-Tekahionwake, 1861-1913*, also published by Natural Heritage (1997). Both of Sheila's books celebrate the love she has for Canada's theatre history. She feels privileged to have been associated with Canadian theatre and Canadian theatre artists throughout her career in the arts.

She lives in Richmond, B.C., with her husband playwright, director/producer Simon Johnston.